MORE PRAISE FOR *CRAZY RICH*

"It would seem that having enough money to do every stupid thing that strikes your fancy is no blessing. . . . [*Crazy Rich*] is gossipy and fast moving, with surprising emotional resonance." —*The Star-Ledger*

"Wealthy as they are, the heirs of the Johnson & Johnson company have seen so many tragedies that one must wonder if there's been a hex. . . . The Johnson dynasty, along with the families Kennedy and Onassis, has for decades provided the most vivid illustrations that money not only can't buy happiness, it also ushers in tragedy." —*The Daily Beast*

"A breathless tell-all . . . Oppenheimer trains his gaze on the Johnsons, the cursed Kennedies of pharmaceuticals. . . . An impressive example of journalistic synthesis, bringing together bits of tabloid journalism not usually connected around a strong narrative core [about] a family whose money can buy influence and power, but comes with costly personal consequences." —*Publishers Weekly*

"Oppenheimer follows the clan of dysfunctional Band-Aid and baby-powder millionaires through the adulterous affairs, ugly divorces, drug and alcohol addictions, tragic accidents, suicide attempts, paternity disputes, will contests, and other turmoil as the family reaps the rewards of inheritance through privilege, opulence, and excess, for better and for worse." —*Booklist* (starred review)

"A prolific biographer of the rich and infamous, Oppenheimer digs into five generations of the Johnson family . . . A gossipy, character-driven saga suggesting that the spoiled rich are their own worst enemies." —*Kirkus Reviews*

PRAISE FOR *MARTHA STEWART: JUST DESSERTS*

"A juicy biography . . . A wicked debunking of Stewart's carefully crafted persona." —*People* magazine

"A sharp-clawed biography . . . if Oppenheimer has done dirty work, he has done his homework too. He presents Ms. Stewart as a tireless, unscrupulous self-promoter who, in creating the corporate omelet that is now Martha Stewart Living Omnimedia, has broken many an egg."

—*The New York Times*

PRAISE FOR *THE OTHER MRS. KENNEDY*

"Shocking . . . Relentlessly chips away at the veneer of the Kennedy mystique."

—*Publishers Weekly*

"Provides all the dish about Ethel Kennedy."

—*The Washington Post*

PRAISE FOR *HOUSE OF HILTON*

"After reading what Mr. Oppenheimer has dug up, you'll wonder why anyone wouldn't have begged to be dropped from the speed dial of a family that makes the Osbournes look like the Brady Bunch."

—*The New York Times*

"The reader will gasp to learn of the Hilton men's sexual athletics—and shudder to hear that such a privileged family could be so shockingly uneducated and uncouth."

—*Publishers Weekly*

PRAISE FOR *TOY MONSTER*

"This juicy exposé shows that life inside the sixty-four-year-old company was hardly always fun and games."

—*People* magazine (four stars)

"Jerry Oppenheimer, best known for mordant biographies like *Just Desserts* (about Martha Stewart) or *State of a Union* (on Bill and Hillary Clinton's marriage), has now trained his sights on the world's biggest toy company— its egos, scandals, and flawed products. In his toyland, nothing is cute. Mr. Oppenheimer unpacks a trove of colorful details."

—*The Wall Street Journal*

"No one thinks a lot about the prepubescent Barbie, but she was young once too, and she's got a doozy of a nativity narrative. . . . Oppenheimer has found a great [story]."   —*Newsweek*

"Oppenheimer takes a tour of Mattel's seamier side, highlighting its dubious corporate practices and kooky cast in this scathing portrait. . . . Fast paced and engaging, this exposé will absorb readers until the last page and will forever change the way they think about the company."   —*Publishers Weekly*

"'Behind every great fortune is a great crime.' So wrote Balzac, which gave *The Godfather* its opening epigram. But a great crime behind the sweet House of Barbie? Yikes! Terrors in toyland! The scandal. The skullduggery! This book is enough to scare Santa Claus."

—Kitty Kelley, author of *Oprah: A Biography*

PRAISE FOR *MADOFF WITH THE MONEY*

"A titillating read, based on dozens of interviews with people who knew Madoff intimately. These range from disgruntled relatives to Hollywood victims, such as Zsa Zsa Gabor, now in her nineties, and her ninth husband, Prince Frederic Von Anhalt, sixty-five, to those who lost life savings through feeder funds."   —*USA Today*

PRAISE FOR *FRONT ROW*

"The revealing unauthorized biography unveils the Anna Wintour even those closest to her don't know. . . . If you liked *The Devil Wears Prada*, get your gossip fill with *Front Row* . . . we couldn't put it down." —*Complete Woman*

"For inquiring minds, it's a juicy, tabloidesque read."   —*Houston Chronicle*

"Filled with gossip and scandals and peppered with celebrity names and tales . . . [A] fascinating read about one of the great queen-bee bosses and her mission to determine and define fashion."   —*Booklist*

"Schadenfreude enthusiasts will enjoy Oppenheimer's latest, *Front Row*, which offers Anna Wintour in extreme close-up."   —*Los Angeles Times*

"To Oppenheimer's credit, the book charts a series of seismic shifts that Wintour—for good and ill—helped navigate: the shift from written to visual culture; the triumph of style over content; the transfer of power from the mature to the young . . . how Wintour, the single-minded diva, schemed and screamed her way to the top of the fashion-magazine world."
                                        —*New York* magazine

"A fast-paced biographical romp . . . Mr. Oppenheimer uses *Front Row* to ladle out dish—just as he did in *Just Desserts,* his 1997 biography of Martha Stewart. What he serves up is pretty juicy . . . *Front Row* is an entertaining chronicle of Ms. Wintour's life . . . A study in power."
                                        —*New York Observer*

"A blistering new biography. The most eagerly awaited unauthorized biography. . . . Better than fiction."   —*New York Post*

"Whether you love fashion or dissections of the sort of cold-blooded creatures who inhabit it, Jerry Oppenheimer's *Front Row* is for you: an equally cold-blooded portrayal of the reigning queen of a world defined by frivolity . . . and abject fear."   —Michael Gross, author of *Model* and
                    Genuine Authentic: The Real Life of Ralph Lauren

PRAISE FOR *STATE OF A UNION*

"Having taken on such politically significant figures as Martha Stewart and Rock Hudson, Oppenheimer aims to lay bare the real Bill and Hillary."
                                        —*Library Journal*

PRAISE FOR *SEINFELD*

"Oppenheimer who has indeed become a master of his own domain delivers a rollicking, sensational account of this 'one-time poor boy from blue-collar

Long Island who [became] very wealthy from being very funny.' . . . Anyone looking for a juicy summer read will be all over Oppenheimer's book like white on rice."
—*Publishers Weekly*

"Oppenheimer has taken on tough cookies like Barbara Walters and Martha Stewart, so he probably won't have too much trouble with the king of irony."
—*Library Journal*

ALSO BY JERRY OPPENHEIMER

The Other Mrs. Kennedy: Ethel Skakel Kennedy

*State of a Union: Inside the Complex
Marriage of Bill and Hillary Clinton*

Just Desserts: Martha Stewart

*Front Row: Anna Wintour—The Cool Life and Hot
Times of Vogue's Editor in Chief*

House of Hilton: From Conrad to Paris

Toy Monster: The Big, Bad World of Mattel

Madoff with the Money

Seinfeld: The Making of an American Icon

Barbara Walters

*Idol: Rock Hudson—The True Story of
an American Film Hero* (with Jack Vitek)

CRAZY RICH

Power, Scandal, and Tragedy Inside the
Johnson & Johnson Dynasty

Jerry Oppenheimer

St. Martin's Griffin

New York

CRAZY RICH. Copyright © 2013 by Jerry Oppenheimer. All rights reserved. For information, address St. Martin's Press, 175 Fifth Avenue, New York, N.Y. 10010.

www.stmartins.com

The Library of Congress has cataloged the hardcover edition as follows:

Oppenheimer, Jerry.
    Crazy rich : power, scandal, and tragedy inside the Johnson & Johnson dynasty / by Jerry Oppenheimer.—First edition.
        p.   cm.
    Includes bibliographical references and index.
    ISBN 978-0-312-66211-0 (hardcover)
    ISBN 978-1-250-01093-3 (e-book)
    1. Johnson, Robert Wood, 1893–1968—Family.   2. Johnson & Johnson—History.   3. Pharmaceutical industry—United States.   4. Rich people—United States—Biography.   5. Children of the rich—United States—Biography.   I. Title.
    HD9666.9.J6O67 2013
    338.7′6151092273—dc23

                                                                    2013009878

ISBN 978-1-250-04908-7 (trade paperback)

St. Martin's Griffin books may be purchased for educational, business, or promotional use. For information on bulk purchases, please contact Macmillan Corporate and Premium Sales Department at 1-800-221-7945, extension 5442, or write specialmarkets@macmillan.com.

First St. Martin's Griffin Edition: August 2014

P1

For Caroline, Trix, Mr. R, Toby and Jesse, Louise, Julien, and Max,
and in memory of Cukes

CONTENTS

LEADING CAST OF CHARACTERS

Robert Wood "Woody" Johnson IV—The great-grandson of one of the three founding brothers of Johnson & Johnson, he was the de facto patriarch of the contemporary Johnson dynasty, a Republican power broker, and the billionaire owner of the New York Jets.

Nancy Sale Frey Johnson Rashad—Woody Johnson's first wife, the mother of his three daughters, was from a prominent Jewish family in St. Louis. She met the Johnson heir while she was helping to market his Florida condo development. Divorced, she married ex-footballer Ahmad Rashad.

Sale Trotter Case "Casey" Johnson—Woody and Sale Johnson's troubled firstborn who was struck as a child with diabetes, and in the midst of very public scandals years later was secretly diagnosed with a debilitating mental illness before her 2010 death at age thirty.

Robert Wood "Bobby" Johnson III—Father of Woody Johnson, he was the namesake of his father, the "General"—fiery ruler of Johnson & Johnson who humiliatingly fired him as president of the family business after years of battling. They died two years apart, both from cancer.

Betty May Wold Johnson Gillespie Bushnell—Mother of Woody Johnson and his four siblings, she was the daughter of a St. Paul physician, became de facto matriarch of the contemporary Johnson dynasty, and married twice after her husband, Bobby Johnson, died at fifty, in 1970.

Keith Wold Johnson—Woody Johnson's troubled brother, the second of his parents' brood, he began using drugs in his teens, and was considered effeminate as well as extravagant with his inherited wealth. He wrecked many exotic cars and overdosed while shooting up cocaine in 1975 in his midtwenties.

Willard Trotter Case "Billy" Johnson—Born after his brothers Woody and Keith, he was considered the brightest and most creative of the siblings, but was also a recreational drug user and often reckless. He died just weeks after Keith in a high-speed motorcycle accident.

Elizabeth Ross "Libet" Johnson—The only daughter among unruly brothers, Woody Johnson's sister blossomed into a beautiful, eccentric heiress with a ravenous appetite for boyfriends and husbands—five of them, with whom she had four children, and adopted another.

Guy Vicino—A gay interior decorator and boutique owner, he was Woody Johnson's best friend from childhood, and was his *GQ*-like advisor and tastemaker. When he was diagnosed with AIDS in the Rock Hudson era, Woody did everything he could to save him, and make his final days easier.

Michael Richard Spielvogel—An aggressive entrepreneur in his twenties from Long Island, he became Woody Johnson's first business partner because the Band-Aid heir's father advised him to team up with a successful Jew who wasn't born with a silver spoon. They had a rocky partnership.

J. Seward Johnson Jr.—The once-troubled namesake of J. Seward Johnson, the second in command of the family's business, his first marriage included *attempted* suicide, *claims of* live-in lovers, a bizarre shootout, *and* a decades-long paternity battle. But he came into his own as an internationally noted sculptor.

Robert Wood "The General" Johnson Jr.—Until his death in 1968, Woody Johnson's grandfather controlled Johnson & Johnson with an iron hand, brilliantly marketing and obsessively overseeing virtually each and every product. A martinet and a roué, he had three wives and many lovers.

Evangeline Brewster Johnson—The heiress sister of Seward Johnson Sr. and the General, she was cheated out of company stock and Johnson & Johnson control by her greedy, domineering, misogynist brothers. Bisexual, she had two daughters and three husbands, one of whom was gay.

J. Seward Johnson Sr.—Second in command of Johnson & Johnson under his brother, the General, he was a playboy who divorced his second wife to marry his household's sexy Polish chambermaid, leaving her his fortune, sparking a scandalous will battle by his six children who wanted their share.

Mary Lea Johnson Ryan D'Arc Richards—The first infant face to grace the Johnson & Johnson Baby Powder container, she was the firstborn of playboy Seward Johnson Sr.'s four children with the first of his three wives. After his death, she questionably claimed that he molested her into her teens.

JOHNSON FAMILY TREE

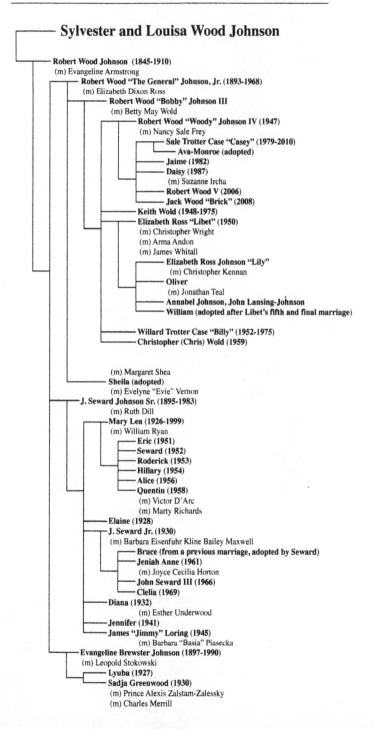

Sylvester and Louisa Wood Johnson

Robert Wood Johnson (1845-1910)
(m) Evangeline Armstrong
Robert Wood "The General" Johnson, Jr. (1893-1968)
(m) Elizabeth Dixon Ross
Robert Wood "Bobby" Johnson III
(m) Betty May Wold
Robert Wood "Woody" Johnson IV (1947)
(m) Nancy Sale Frey
Sale Trotter Case "Casey" (1979-2010)
Ava-Monroe (adopted)
Jaime (1982)
Daisy (1987)
(m) Suzanne Ircha
Robert Wood V (2006)
Jack Wood "Brick" (2008)
Keith Wold (1948-1975)
Elizabeth Ross "Libet" (1950)
(m) Christopher Wright
(m) Arma Andon
(m) James Whitall
Elizabeth Ross Johnson "Lily"
(m) Christopher Kennan
Oliver
(m) Jonathan Teal
Annabel Johnson, John Lansing-Johnson
William (adopted after Libet's fifth and final marriage)

Willard Trotter Case "Billy" (1952-1975)
Christopher (Chris) Wold (1959)

(m) Margaret Shea
Sheila (adopted)
(m) Evelyne "Evie" Vernon
J. Seward Johnson Sr. (1895-1983)
(m) Ruth Dill
Mary Lea (1926-1999)
(m) William Ryan
Eric (1951)
Seward (1952)
Roderick (1953)
Hillary (1954)
Alice (1956)
Quentin (1958)
(m) Victor D'Arc
(m) Marty Richards
Elaine (1928)
J. Seward Jr. (1930)
(m) Barbara Eisenfuhr Kline Bailey Maxwell
Bruce (from a previous marriage, adopted by Seward)
Jeniah Anne (1961)
(m) Joyce Cecilia Horton
John Seward III (1966)
Clelia (1969)
Diana (1932)
(m) Esther Underwood
Jennifer (1941)
James "Jimmy" Loring (1945)
(m) Barbara "Basia" Piasecka
Evangeline Brewster Johnson (1897-1990)
(m) Leopold Stokowski
Lyuba (1927)
Sadja Greenwood (1930)
(m) Prince Alexis Zalstam-Zalessky
(m) Charles Merrill

CRAZY
RICH

PROLOGUE

They have been called perhaps the most dysfunctional family in the Fortune 500.

From the founders of the Johnson & Johnson health-care behemoth near the close of the nineteenth century up through the fourth and fifth generations of the twenty-first century, which included billionaire New York Jets owner Robert Wood "Woody" Johnson IV, the Johnson dynasty has been beset by scandals, tragedies, and misfortune. To be clear, these were not wicked people. Most if not all of the horrors they faced were attributable to the vast fortunes they had inherited, and the psychological impact on them of all that unearned wealth.

Money was always both a blessing and a curse for members of the very private, insular, and Byzantine dynasty. Many of the family members, like Woody, had grown up wondering whether people liked them for who they were, or because of their wealth. Sadly, it was usually the latter rather than the former, a fact of life that a number of them would often comprehend when it was too late. Women and men who married into the dynasty were routinely suspected of being gold diggers, and based on the number of bitter, sometimes violent divorces through the generations, some might have been.

Over the years money and the attendant greed had pitted Johnsons against Johnsons over trust funds, wills, divorce settlements, paternity, and other familial issues. What was internationally known as Johnson *and*

Johnson for health-care products began showing up more frequently through the generations as Johnson *versus* Johnson on court dockets.

Drug addiction, alcoholism, overdoses, adultery, homosexuality, child abuse in the form of molestation, suspected kidnapping, a murder plot, a shooting, tragic accidents, suicide, attempted suicides, and other mayhem—all were part of the ongoing drama and soiled fabric of one of the richest and most powerful families in the world. For a number of the family members, their fortune—all of that inherited wealth—was intoxicating and toxic at the same time.

"We used to make a comparison between the Kennedys and the Johnsons," states Neil Vicino, a veteran broadcast journalist and close Johnson family friend, "that there was kind of a Kennedy curse *and* a Johnson curse."

The Johnson dynasty drama began with the brash, entrepreneurial spirit of three relatively uneducated but ambitious brothers—Robert, who was Woody Johnson's great-grandfather, James, and Edward Mead Johnson—who, in 1886, founded what became the world's largest health-care business.

The brothers operated fast and loose, sometimes using cutthroat tactics, even going up against an early business partner who had helped give one of them, the very ambitious and shrewd first Robert Wood Johnson, his start in the business that made him extremely wealthy. The tough-talking Johnson once promised to "stick the knife right into the bowels" of his mentor's medical supply business and others. The brothers audaciously appropriated from others without authorization, such as when they brazenly emblazoned legendary nurse Clara Barton's iconic Red Cross symbol on their early products—Johnson & Johnson Absorbent Cotton Rolls and Johnson & Johnson Red Cross Bandage. She eventually was sweet-talked into accepting a dollar bill in exchange for exclusive use of the bloodred symbol as the company's internationally recognizable logo.

At the same time, it was those same Johnson siblings, sons of a poor farmer and his baby-making machine of a wife (mother of eleven), who saw the dire need and marketed the world's first sanitary, packaged, ready-to-use antiseptic surgical dressings at a time when doctors were still using rags to dress wounds and incisions. Their marketing inspiration came from the landmark work of the British surgeon and pioneer of antiseptic surgery Dr.

Joseph Lister, and their eponymous surgical dressings and plasters saved lives in wars and disasters and epidemics.

After an apparent feud—the first of many vicious familial battles in the Johnson dynasty through the generations—one of the founding brothers, Edward Mead Johnson, split off and started his own eminent and very prosperous business. But there was a synergy between Johnson & Johnson of New Brunswick, New Jersey, and Mead Johnson & Company of Evansville, Indiana. While some of the Johnson & Johnson products powdered and oiled the dimpled bottoms of America's babies, many of Mead Johnson's helped to settle and feed their little tummies with Pablum and cod liver oil.

Before long it became practically impossible to get well without products made by the New Jersey-headquartered Johnson & Johnson that eventually became a publicly traded, global juggernaut with more than 250 companies located in some sixty countries. Generations have grown from bassinet to adulthood using Johnson & Johnson products—from baby powder and Band-Aids, to the female sanitary pad Modess, to the schizophrenia drug Risperdal, to the pimple medication Remicade, the lubricant K-Y Jelly, the over-the-counter cold and headache pill Tylenol, and scores more drugs and sundries.

The red "Johnson & Johnson" script on the company's products actually was the handwriting of James Johnson, the second head of the family business following the passing of his ruling brother, Robert.

While the corporate side is one amazing international success story, the family members behind the household brand are even more astonishing. The Johnsons through the generations are to everyday health-care products what the Kennedys have been to politics and public service—a genuine royal dynasty, and an all-American Greek tragedy.

The immense wealth accumulated by the first, second, and third generations of Johnson men (not women) who ran Johnson & Johnson—chauvinism reigned—made for regal lifestyles of their descendants through family trusts and inheritances. And the result was often vicious court battles over the money involved.

One such mindboggling case was ignited by the adult progeny of a Johnson senior over the $400 million he left his much younger wife, the family's former chambermaid, after divorcing his second wife, a suspected lesbian. In another of the many cases, a twelve-year-long court battle ensued over the definition of just a single word—"spouse"—because tens of millions of inherited dollars were at stake. New Jersey's highest court once took a subtle shot at the very litigious Johnson family, noting that a case it was hearing "is one of the many such disputes involving trusts or trust property that have arisen within the Johnson family over the past three decades."

Johnson inherited wealth was immense. When Robert Wood Johnson Jr., known as the General—Woody Johnson's grandfather—took the family owned, privately held Johnson & Johnson company public on the New York Stock Exchange on September 24, 1944, a block of one hundred shares sold for $3,750. By the end of the twentieth century those same shares reportedly were worth a whopping $12 million (not including dividends), and with splits had ballooned to 125,000 shares. Every Johnson dynasty member—past, present, and future—became wealthy beyond anyone's imagination as the value soared in the open market.

Many Johnsons never had to do much except clip coupons and live large. Woody Johnson, for one, never worked a day in his life in the Johnson dynasty's health-care monster. He never had a chance. When he was still in prep school his martinet of a grandfather, who ran the company with an iron hand, humiliatingly fired Woody's driven father from his position as company president. Like a scene in a Greek tragedy, the two, who hadn't spoken in years and were both critically ill, had a virtual deathbed rapprochement. Both succumbed to cancer a couple of years apart.

Woody had to find his own way in life. It didn't hurt that he received his first trust fund check of ten million dollars when he turned twenty-one and then millions more every five years until his midforties. His first business partner was a young entrepreneur, Michael Richard Spielvogel, who says Woody chose him because he was "a Jew" who wasn't a silver spoon—a choice based on curious advice from Woody's dad. They went into the condo construction business in South Florida and lived the good life with Woody's trust fund millions. He finally acquired an identity by buying the Jets for a record $635 million of his own money in 2000 when he was in his fifties—thanks to the sales of Band-Aids and baby powder, Tylenol and Modess.

As his first wife, Nancy Sale Frey Johnson Rashad, observes, "He didn't have to do a damn thing. He could have been a total ne'er-do-well, sailing around on a boat and smoking pot, but he didn't. He just went right to work."

His life, though, was littered with tragedy. But as the de facto patriarch of the dynasty in the twenty-first century, he was a rarity in that he had actually pursued a calling. Many others didn't, resulting in a sometimes bizarre and often eccentric cast of characters who populated the ongoing Johnson dynasty drama.

As one who became involved intimately with them and their soap opera–like lives observes: "They are a mixed-up, weird bunch. You couldn't make them up in fiction. The whole family is like a great big spiderweb that innocent people drop into—normal people who get caught in the Johnson web of craziness. It's almost like European royalty."

From the entrepreneurial wheeler-dealer founders to those Johnsons of later generations—the fascinating, complex, and enigmatic lucky sperm club members who have lived royally on their trust fund inheritances—this, then, is their story.

PART I

POWER BROKER

1

When Woody Johnson was vigorously and aggressively raising funds for what would become the failed 2008 Republican presidential campaign of the Vietnam war hero and conservative senior U.S. Senator from Arizona, John McCain, and his controversial vice-presidential running mate, Sarah Palin, he began hitting up as many masters of the universe and captains of industry as he knew—and, in his American Express Black Card milieu, he knew many.

Woody, sixty-one at the time, had actually turned the notoriously secretive fifteenth-floor Rockefeller Center offices of his privately held investment firm, the bland-sounding Johnson Company, of which he was chairman and CEO—no relation to the Johnson & Johnson empire of his forebears—into McCain campaign central. It became a war room from which he was making dozens of calls every day, soliciting money for his candidate.

Woody was working the phones like a maestro conducting a symphony orchestra, much like the legendary baton-wielding Leopold Stokowski, who was the first of the three husbands of Woody's eccentric great-aunt, Evangeline Brewster Johnson.

The walls of Woody's office had once been covered with splendid family photographs. His favorite showed Woody's father, Robert Wood "Bobby" Johnson III, looking down at his father, Robert Wood Johnson Jr., known as the "General," holding baby Woody. Looming behind was an oil portrait of

Woody's great-grandfather, Robert Wood Johnson. There was also much Johnson & Johnson memorabilia on the wall, including a framed copy of the corporate Credo penned in 1943 by the General.

All of it, though, seemed a bit misplaced and a trifle hollow since Woody's father, Bobby, had been harshly treated throughout his life by Woody's grandfather, the General, who ultimately punished him by firing him from the presidency of Johnson & Johnson. Woody would never be a part of the family business, and would have to find his own way. The dynastic ephemera on his office wall made for fascinating decoration, however, and impressed visitors.

Now that wall of memories had been stripped bare, replaced with slips of paper imprinted with the names of superrich potential McCain-Palin contributors from whom he hoped to extract six-figure amounts.

Among those Woody hit up were some prominent classmates from his prep school days at Millbrook School, an elite British-style academy in the Hudson Valley of New York State where the caustic conservative author and commentator William F. Buckley Jr. first learned to write an essay. One of those from Woody's class of 1965 who took his call was the Wall Street legend Steve Kroll, managing director at Monness, Crespi, Hardt & Company, where Martha Stewart was once a broker.

For a number of years Kroll and another classmate, Robert Anthony, who became Millbrook's director of alumni relations—and who along with Kroll had played Millbrook varsity football with Woody—had been trying to get the billionaire scion to contribute to the school fund, but without much great success. If Woody gave some, Kroll believed, the billionaire certainly had the wherewithal to give much more.

So Kroll was a bit taken aback when Woody turned the tables and was asking *him* for money, big money, to support the McCain-Palin ticket.

"Bobby Anthony and I would call Woody once a year and try to take him out to lunch, or dinner at '21,' and try to hit him up for donations to his alma mater," says Kroll. "But now Woody calls me up and says, 'You've got to come to my benefit.' I said, 'Great, send me the paperwork.' Now to go to the benefit for drinks and to rub shoulders with McCain was going to cost me one hundred and fifty grand! I don't know about anybody else, but I didn't like McCain *that* much."

It wasn't the first time the baby oil and baby powder scion had hit up Kroll for money. It had initially happened almost a half century earlier when they were preppy sophomores.

At the time, Kroll didn't have a clue about the pudgy, blond-haired, blue-eyed kid's family background because he was "nondescript. So I gave him the money and then somebody asked me, 'Why the fuck is Johnson borrowing twenty dollars from *you?*'"

Kroll, who was far less wealthy, might have known more about the Johnson boy's heritage before he gave him the double sawbuck, but he had missed that Kodak Moment at Millbrook, the morning when a huge, twin-rotor Sikorsky helicopter hovered over the prep school's bucolic grounds, and then landed on the football field, and Robert Wood Johnson IV—known as Bob back then, not the hip-sounding Woody—was spotted running down the sweeping lawn toward the chopper. Another student from Woody's class, Tom Doelger, who, like Kroll, didn't know anything about the Johnson youngster's family, because "no one knew how wealthy anyone else was at Millbrook," had witnessed the scene, was impressed, and thought, "My goodness, *that* must be something special."

Immediately afterward the inquisitive Doelger, who would be named the editor in chief of Woody's class of 1965 yearbook *The Tamarack,* and publish a cutting profile of him, asked the assistant headmaster, "'What was *that* all about?' And I was told that Johnson was being flown to New York City for a dental appointment—*a dental appointment and by helicopter*—and I thought, *wow!*"

While Steve Kroll didn't write the big check for the McCain fundraiser, a star-studded event that Woody and the Republican National Committee hosted jointly at the Sheraton Hotel on May 7, 2008—McCain's first major New York money-raising affair—many other leaders in the city's hierarchy of financiers, media moguls, and industrialists contributed a whopping seven million dollars in just one razzle-dazzle, *ka-ching,* win-one-for-the-Gipper-style evening.

It was clear from the flowing money and masters of the (Republican) universe turnout that Woody was of weight. Everyone in attendance that evening had dreams of another four years of Republican rule in the White House after two terms of Woody's political idol George Bush, for whom he was a major supporter, financially, politically, and philosophically. Even more, Woody and his compatriots surely had nightmares about what would happen to the country if the liberal Democratic hopeful, the black guy with the funny-sounding name, won.

Immediately after the hotel shindig, Woody personally hosted a dinner party at his spectacular apartment high above Fifth Avenue. Those invited included a group described as McCain's "biggest bundlers," who had *each* pledged to raise $100,000 or more, with the sky being the limit.

Bundlers in both political parties have been defined by groups such as OpenSecrets.org, which billed itself as the Center for Responsive Politics, as, "People with friends in high places who, after bumping against personal contribution limits, turn to those friends, associates, and, well, anyone who's willing to give, and deliver the checks to the candidate in one big 'bundle.' "

One of the successful McCain bundlers working in Woody's high-powered operation who could deliver a big bundle was his cousin Keith Clinton Wold Jr., a multimillionaire self-employed New York City attorney, also a Johnson & Johnson trust-funder, who had personally contributed $57,700 in a half-dozen separate donations to the McCain Victory Committee, and was listed as a bundler in the $100,000 to $250,000 category.

The Wold name was important in Woody's branch of the Johnson dynasty because two of the four Wold siblings—Woody's mother, Betty, and her brother Keith Sr.—had won what is wryly whispered about within the dynasty as "the Megamillions Jackpot" by marrying into the super-wealthy Johnson family back in the 1940s.

Betty Wold had wed Bobby Johnson, grandson of one of the company founders, and Keith Wold had followed his sister to the altar by tying the knot with Elaine Johnson, one of the three heiress daughters from the first marriage of playboy J. Seward Johnson Sr., then second in command at the family business.

Not everyone in the Johnson dynasty agreed with Woody's staunch Republican beliefs—he wasn't considered by them to be the brightest bulb in the chandelier—and his politics had even caused fissures within the dynasty. While the Johnsons were once a GOP stronghold dating back more than a century to the Johnson & Johnson company founders, more contemporary Johnsons had turned to liberal Democratic politics. Among them was John

Seward Johnson III, son of the controversial sculptor, J. Seward Johnson Jr. John had worked as hard in the successful 2008 Barack Obama presidential campaign as Woody had labored in the failed McCain run.

"John [III] certainly contributed intellectual capital as well as physical capital, particularly in terms of Obama's use of social networks like Facebook, which was a big part of Obama's campaign," says his cousin Eric Ryan, also a liberal Democrat. "John was out on the dais with Obama during the inauguration with the president's closest friends and supporters."

Ryan's own liberalism ran the gamut to include the legalization of marijuana.

John Johnson's father, Seward Jr., had himself turned from the Grand Old Party to become a liberal as he aged.

In his eighties in the second decade of the twenty-first century, he was one of the remaining elders of the third generation of Johnsons, and he was aghast when he learned that Woody had invited Sarah Palin to be his very special guest in the owner's booth at a Jets game during the 2010 season. "I don't know that we could have a relationship, we're so different. He's a Republican through and through." He recalls attending the wedding of one of Woody's nieces—a daughter from one of the five marriages of Woody's sister, Elizabeth Ross "Libet" Johnson—where Woody was treated as a virtual pariah because of his conservative politics, crazy as it sounds. "Everybody kept moving their place away from Woody," Seward Jr. says. "It was because he had just been the biggest giver to George Bush."

Even Woody's first wife, Nancy Sale Frey Johnson Rashad, mother of his three daughters, and a born and bred Missouri Republican, turned against him when it came to his rabid support of McCain-Palin. "Woody and I always had the same views on politics *until* he backed that ticket, and then my views changed. I said to Woody, 'I just canceled out your vote—all that work you've done and now your vote doesn't count.'"

The 2008 Republican National Convention was held in Saint Paul, Minnesota, in early September. Three other cities, including New York, had vied for the honor, but the Republican National Committee decided on the Twin City, causing some political insiders to wonder whether Woody, so powerful as a moneyman in the party, had influenced the decision because Saint Paul just happened to be the hometown of his mother, Betty, and her brother Keith. Their father, Dr. Karl Christian Wold—Woody's maternal grandfather—had been a prominent local opthalmologist, and a staunch Republican who had once written an exposé about President Franklin Delano Roosevelt, the New Deal Democrat.

Because of the longstanding Johnson-Wold family ties to Saint Paul, and the fact that the convention's host committee was facing a budget deficit of some ten million dollars, Woody, his mother, and their wealthy and powerful friends were believed to have generated some sizeable checks to help out for what became the first ever national political convention held there.

While federal law had some limits on actual campaign contributions, no such limits are imposed on the big money spent by billionaire high rollers like Woody Johnson for such hoopla as costly political conventions.

But as Woody brashly boasted when Saint Paul was chosen, "I'm not a real believer in limits."

The long and storied saga of the Johnson dynasty well supports that philosophy of no limits, absolutely none. Members of the very secretive family have always played by their own set of rules—it's often been about *them vs. us,* for better or for worse—and Woody Johnson, of the fourth generation of Johnsons, was no exception.

2

The Saint Paul convention was a very special, well-deserved honor for Betty Wold Johnson Gillespie Bushnell, Woody's spry, shrewd, eighty-something, thrice-married philanthropist-dowager mother—thought to be *the* largest holder of Johnson & Johnson stock in the dynasty, and its de facto matriarch in the first decade of the twenty-first century.

People who knew the Johnsons intimately often compared them to America's royal family, the Kennedy clan, not because of politics, or public service, but rather because of the many scandals and tragedies faced over generations by both of the wealthy and powerful dynasties.

And Woody's mother was often compared to Ethel Skakel Kennedy, that clan's eighty-something de facto matriarch, because of what both had gone through during their lifetimes.

Both women had had eerily similar lives, both glorious and sorrowful. They both had very wealthy, charismatic husbands named Bobby who had died in their prime. Betty's husband—Woody's father—died at fifty of cancer in 1970 a few years after being shot down from his high post at Johnson & Johnson by his own father.

Ethel's husband, the popular former U.S. Attorney General, U.S. Senator from New York, and the 1968 Democratic presidential candidate, died at forty-two when he was shot down by an assassin's bullet like his brother Jack.

And both Bobby Johnson and Bobby Kennedy were known to have been womanizers like their fathers before them.

Moreover, without their husbands at the helm, both Betty Johnson and Ethel Kennedy suffered deteriorating relationships with their eldest sons. Worse still, after becoming widows, both matriarchs lost sons to tragic drug overdoses and horrific accidents.

Two of Betty Johnson's four beloved boys shockingly died just six weeks apart in 1975. The troubled and self-destructive twenty-seven-year-old Keith Wold Johnson, the second of Betty's brood of five, overdosed while shooting up cocaine in a Fort Lauderdale, Florida, apartment.

Ethel Kennedy's fourth-born, twenty-nine-year-old David Anthony Kennedy, also long troubled with drugs, died shooting up heroin in 1984 in a Palm Beach, Florida, motel room.

Just a few weeks after Keith Johnson died, Betty's fourth child, twenty-three-year-old Willard "Billy" Trotter Case Johnson, thought to be the brightest and most creative of her sons, but also a recreational drug user and often reckless, was killed driving at high speed on a motorcycle at a time when Billy was struggling to break into the movie business as a producer.

Ethel Kennedy's thirty-nine-year-old son Michael Lemoyne Kennedy died in 1987 when he skied at high speed into a tree, at a time when he was struggling with allegations that he had had an affair with his family's teenage babysitter.

For Betty, there would be a couple of points in her firstborn Woody's life where she almost lost him, too.

The tragedies and their similarities seemed so endless and unendurable to Johnson friends and family that they had begun living with the wrenching questions: Who's next? What's next?

"In our family we said, 'Oh, my God, these people are cursed just like the Kennedys,'" says longtime Johnson family friend Neil Vicino, who along with his brothers, Guy and John, had grown up with the Johnson boys, and continued to be close as they grew into manhood.

While Ethel Kennedy went to Catholic mass every day, it was Betty Johnson who had earned the sobriquet "Mother Superior" behind her back among other members of the Johnson family because, according to the sculptor Seward Johnson Jr., "She always would talk down to everyone as though her word was law, and it would almost make you laugh as though you were actually going to do what she said. She tried to straighten everybody out. She tried to straighten me out. If you had anything that was different, well, she'd try to straighten that kink out."

If she had tried more with her sons Keith and Billy—and especially with Keith—she was sadly unsuccessful.

Betty Johnson and Ethel Kennedy were lifelong loyalists to their families, the only difference being that Ethel had never remarried after her Bobby's death, while Betty had two marriages after her Bobby died. But like Ethel, who never let go of the Kennedy name, Betty always kept the iconic Johnson surname through her subsequent marriages to two husbands, one of whom she divorced, both of whom she had outlived.

3

Next to John McCain and Sarah Palin, who were formally nominated by the delegates at the Saint Paul convention, Woody seemed the most visible as a major player and power broker in the Grand Old Party of the early twenty-first century.

Of all the top donors, only Woody and the manager of McCain's campaign partnered in a skybox overlooking the convention floor at the Xcel Energy Center. Of all the top donors, only Woody had a hospitality suite that had his name conspicuously inscribed on the door: WOODY JOHNSON MINNEAPOLIS-ST. PAUL 2008 HOST COMMITTEE PRIVATE LOUNGE.

Woody, whose public persona was low-key and mild-mannered—Clark Kent to his inner Superman—certainly must have savored seeing his name emblazoned on the door like the gilded initials that had been inscribed on the wall behind his place at the dining table in his Fifth Avenue palace of an apartment. When a cousin, Quentin Ryan, was there to dine and first saw RWJ on the wall he thought, "What an out-of-touch asshole."

Around his neck at the convention, Woody sported a thicket of credentials that gave him access to the highest levels of meeting rooms and command centers, which were off-limits to most others. He was photographed wearing a headset over his virtually bald pate, smiling nervously, and dressed in a conservative *Men in Black* suit festooned with a MCCAIN FOR PRESIDENT lapel pin, sporting a New York Jets green tie, and looking more like plain-clothes convention security than the power behind the podium.

The photo was taken for a *New York Times* story that was headlined "Convention Limelight Shines on a Big Donor."

The Times observed that Woody was "the party's most coveted donor," and further pronounced that "Mr. Johnson's exalted status here shows that for all of Mr. McCain's efforts to purge the influence of money in politics, the big donors can still get singular access to the campaign . . ."

The next day the tabloid New York *Daily News* made reference to the *Times* piece and noted much less diplomatically that Woody "is richer than a sheikh, and his party needs him more than ever . . . because in Barack Obama they are up against the greatest grassroots fundraiser in political history."

Written by columnist Mike Lupica, the piece noted with far more candor that the *Times* story "illustrates how Johnson has spent a fair amount of time over the past several years accumulating (or just buying) political muscle. And even though it didn't help him or the Jets scam their way . . . into a new stadium on the West Side of Manhattan"—Lupica pointed out that Johnson's Jets and the New York Giants would soon move into a new stadium in the New Jersey Meadowlands—"one that has Jersey taking on $100 million in debt as part of the contract."

Lupica characterized the popular line that new stadium deals are good for the taxpayer as "the biggest lie of modern sports," and added, "They benefit the taxpayer who owns the team, usually one of the richest men around . . ."

He was referring, of course, to Woody Johnson.

$ $ $

Fast forward to 2011.

Woody's presidential choice, John McCain, had lost the election—the second largest youth (and black and Hispanic) voter turnout in history had made Barack Obama the nation's forty-fourth president.

With the next presidential election scheduled for 2012, Woody had now put his big money and clout behind another conservative Republican presidential wannabe, Willard Mitt Romney, the Mormon multimillionaire businessman—who had assets of his own of between $85 million and $264 million, according to his late summer 2011 financial disclosure statement—and former one-term Massachusetts governor who had lost the 2008 Republican nomination to Woody's then choice, McCain.

Woody shared with Romney the same political philosophies, a similar kind of private equity business, the same CEO status at one point, and both were born a month apart in 1947. Moreover, his candidate shared the same given first name, Willard, as Woody's late brother, who was nicknamed Billy. Like Woody, Romney was a low-key sort of fellow, and was considered a head-down campaigner, thought by Democrats to be out of touch with the concerns of average Americans.

As early as November 2010, Woody had overseen a conference call with wealthy supporters of Romney and informed them that a large chunk of McCain supporters were up for a Romney presidency.

In January 2011, Woody had accompanied Romney to Israel on what was described as "an education trip and two days of meetings" with officials there. A couple of weeks later, Woody also was at Romney's side at a private dinner with Woody's friend, and another talked-about presidential contender, the notoriously hard-line conservative Republican New Jersey governor Chris Christie, at Drumthwacket, the tongue-twister-named palatial official mansion of the governor, located in Princeton, near the impressive estate where Woody himself had grown up.

Early in the summer Woody tossed two $2,500-a-plate VIP breakfasts for Romney at the fashionable Cipriani restaurant in New York, and at the exclusive University Club where he told the gathering of about three dozen Republican high rollers, "Mitt's the right guy to get the country back on track."

As with McCain, Romney's big money-man was the Band-Aid heir who would later boast to a reporter that he touched base with "every Republican in New York . . . several thousand," spending some two dozen hours of the week dialing for campaign dollars and support.

"As Woody sees it, we have a world championship, Super Bowl country with very, very poor management," one of his hedge fund pals, using a football analogy, told the *New York Observer*.

$ $ $

Then came a big surprise.

In 2011 Woody himself was being talked up for political office—as a potential candidate to run for the U.S. Senate from New Jersey, the home state of his forebears who had founded Johnson & Johnson in the gritty industrial city of New Brunswick in the late nineteenth century, and where it was still headquartered in the twenty-first century. New Jersey also was the home and headquarters of Woody's controversial Jets football team.

And New Jersey was the Johnson dynasty's home for generations, where their mansions, estates, and farms were located, all of which were big pluses, and had made Woody a contender in the hearts and minds of some GOP strategists—if he ever chose to run.

The big question was: Could Woody Johnson pass the smell test? Was there anything in his background that would surface and hurt him if he decided to run, or at the minimum raise issues about his character? At the same time he was an unknown quantity as a campaigner, and as a public speaker. As one high-ranking New Jersey Republican operative who liked Woody for the Senate observed, "We know him, and we don't know him. He's an enigma."

Until Woody joined the exclusive club of National Football League owners when he bought the Jets for $635 million in 2000—the third highest price ever paid for a an NFL team—and later dove into the political arena as a behind-the-scenes power broker, his private life had been shrouded in secrecy, one of the hallmarks of the Johnson dynasty except for when they wound up in the gossip columns, or tabloid headlines, or court dockets.

With the Jets in his portfolio, Woody had become a very public figure—perhaps the best known and celebrated of the contemporary Johnsons.

Yet many secrets about his life still remained.

By early 2011, stories about Woody's political prospects had begun appearing in the media.

The *Time* magazine Web site Real Clear Politics headlined a story, "Republicans Raise Prospect of Johnson Senate Bid in N.J.," and quoted "several politically involved Republican sources" as saying that Woody was "toying" with the idea of a Senate run.

Clearly, some thought, Woody could be a candidate and a contender if he wanted it.

To some, he even had rock-star qualities.

"There's a certain Springsteen-esque nature of being Woody Johnson," was the feeling of former New Jersey state GOP chairman and influential political strategist and lobbyist Tom Wilson, one of those who by mid-2011 foresaw a political future for the Johnson heir. "Springsteen's a folk hero to New Jerseyans, but so's a local guy gone good by the name of Woody Johnson, a very visible and public figure operating a very visible and public business, the Jets, that puts him in front-line contact with a whole group of people which might not typically be thought of as possible Republican voters."

Besides the Jets fans there was an even bigger constituency, according to Wilson, and that was "the number of people who live in New Jersey who are connected in some way to Johnson & Johnson, which is is a household name, a dynasty."

Woody's biggest plus for political office, his supporters all felt, was his fortune, because he could finance his own campaign. If the billionaire trust-funder ever decided to take the challenge and run, he could easily pay for his campaign out of pocket, at least fifty million dollars, the political experts computed, which was a drop in the proverbial bucket for him.

$ $ $

A measure of the kind of money that Woody Johnson had, and was willing to spend to get whatever it was that he wanted, was underscored in late July of 2011, around the time he was being talked up as a potential candidate, when he shelled out a whopping fifty million dollars over five years, with a guaranteed twenty-four million dollars, to get just one player, the superstar wide receiver Santonio Holmes, to stay with the Jets as the 2011 season approached. Holmes's guarantee was considered the most money any receiver had ever been thrown by a team owner.

After the deal was consummated, the overjoyed and suddenly very wealthy Holmes tweeted a photo of himself in a pair of shorts, celebrating with an expensive vintage bottle of Louis Roederer Cristal, and declaring, "Big bro showed his love today."

With the nation then on the verge of financial default and the world seemingly falling apart, the editors of the *New York Post* considered Woody's deal so enormous that they plastered the photo of the goateed Holmes swigging from the nearly empty champagne bottle all over the front page, with the headline "JET FUEL."

Woody was determined to put together a team of superstars that would win the Super Bowl, whatever the cost.

For the 2011 season, he had already committed $100 million in salaries.

The head coach of Woody's Jets was the overweight, Ralph Kramdenesque Rex Ryan, in a four-year contract worth at least twelve million dollars, who often boasted about his boss's money and how he spent it in order to make the team a Super Bowl contender.

As an example, Ryan noted the seventy-five million dollars Woody had spent to build the 130,000-square-foot Atlantic Health Jet Training Center in Florham Park, New Jersey. "This wasn't like some run-of-the-mill place . . . the place is like a gleaming office structure for some high-tech company," he declared. "Heck, the weight room alone is around eleven thousand square feet."

Woody had also spent hundreds of thousands of dollars to prepare the Jets' practice fields, but when Ryan discovered that the turf wasn't level, Woody "was pissed" but went ahead and had the fields torn up and new sod put in.

Boasted Ryan: "We had a helicopter hovering all night trying to dry the field off before we could finally start using it."

Nothing ever seemed too expensive for the Johnson heir if he really wanted it.

4

Despite the growing support in some quarters for Woody Johnson to run for an elective office, it was doubtful he would ever throw his hat in the ring. He was too low-key to campaign, too secretive about his personal life, and had a closet full of embarrassing dynastic skeletons that surely would surface in the gossipy Internet age where no secrets can be held for too long.

Plus he had his own scandalous issues with which to deal—from divorce, to having two sons with his second wife prior to their marriage, to his lack of parental control involving his firstborn daughter, Casey, to the handling of his massive fortune—that in particular.

Woody's greatest political asset—his money—had at least once gotten him in an embarrassing and questionable jam. He was placed in the unaccustomed public position of being a central figure—a case history, actually—that illustrated "how U.S. citizens, with the backing of an armada of professionals, hide assets, shift income offshore, or use offshore entities to circumvent U.S. laws," according to a shocking 2006 report by the U.S. Senate's Permanent Subcommittee on Investigations into "crooked tax havens that had cost the U.S. Treasury as much as $300 million in revenue."

Woody's money issues—and his eventual naming in the Senate report of sham tax havens and the billionaires who love them—had started when he was in the process of buying the New York Jets in 2000. In order to partly finance the more than $600 million purchase—a lucrative acquisition that would more than double in value in a decade, making the billionaire even wealthier—he needed to sell securities, according to the report. Facing hefty capital gains tax on the stock sale, he began looking for a creative way to write off a good part—or possibly even all—of Uncle Sam's tax bill as an expense of doing business.

To get the ball rolling, Woody contacted his "long-term financial accountant" at KPMG, one of the world's largest firms in the audit, tax, and advisory business, who had recently moved to a super hedge fund firm headquartered in Seattle called the Quellos Group. Woody asked him "to begin looking for ways to mitigate the capital gain tax on the securities sales he was planning," according to the Senate report. In Woody's "large financial enterprise," as the subcommittee investigators would later characterize the Johnson Company, "taxes are often considered an expense."

By late December 1999, Woody had "tentatively decided" to invest in a complex financial strategy involving what turned out to be sham stock transactions—he would later claim without his knowledge—called portfolio optimized investment transactions (POINT). The base of operations for the POINT was the Isle of Man, an obscure self-governing British Crown dependency located in the Irish Sea that had no capital gains tax, or inheritance tax, and with offshore banking as one of its main economies, it was a perfect location for Quellos to set up shop.

With Woody's thumbs-up to do the deal, according to the report, one of those involved sent an e-mail stating, "Ain't capitalism great!"

Another declared, "Now I just hope Woody doesn't get cold feet or have the IRS select his return for audit!"

The deal offered to Woody by Quellos was later described by the Senate investigators "as an opportunity to purchase a tax loss for cash."

Other e-mails uncovered by the investigators during the yearlong probe made no mention "of a concern on the part of Mr. Johnson or his representatives over the profit-making aspects of the transaction."

While Woody cooperated with the Senate investigators and was interviewed by committee staff in July 2006, he claimed he couldn't remember a lot of details of the various complex transactions. He also maintained a don't-blame-me manner, and asserted that he had only followed what his trusted advisors had told him to do. Moreover, he stated that he had been advised by his lawyers in 2000 that the Quellos deal "was consistent with the tax code."

In 2003, the Internal Revenue Service had challenged that assessment, and Woody had to quietly settle up with Uncle Sam, agreeing to pay one hundred percent of the tax due—about seventeen million dollars—plus interest.

Woody should have known the old adage that if something sounds too good to be true, it probably is, but apparently he didn't think that way, trusted advisors or not.

With the IRS paid off, with no major public scrutiny at the time, Woody must have thought the tax scam scandal was all behind him.

But three years later the Senate subcommittee issued its sharply worded, highly detailed 397-page report, entitled: "Tax Haven Abuses: The Enablers, the Tools, and Secrecy," which revealed Woody's involvement along with that of a few other billionaires "who took advantage of this tax haven."

As *The Washington Post* reported about the Senate probe under a headline that declared, "Tax Shelters Saved Billionaires a Bundle," the investigation "details how these wealthy, politically connected people ducked hundreds of millions of dollars in tax payments by using secretive corporations and trusts on the Isle of Man."

When receiving word that Woody's name had surfaced in the probe, the administrator of a Web site called the Jetsinsider.com, a forum about the team, wrote: "Woody Is a Tax Cheat! Another solid move by the great businessman Woody Johnson. Will this guy ever do anything the right way and own up to his responsibilities?"

The public release of the Senate report, which made Woody Johnson appear like some greedy, fat-cat Republican tax dodger—even though he was never a target of the investigation—should have been incredibly embarrassing. But despite a few stories in the media describing the tax shelter probe, most if not all of the coverage involving Woody at the time centered on the fact that he had hired a new head coach for the Jets, and that the team was hopefully on its way to the Super Bowl.

The *Washington Post*'s Steven Pearlstein, who had covered the subcommittee's hearing, wrote, under a headline reading, "As Senate Hearing Shows,

Cheaters Ever Prosper," that "Robert Wood Johnson IV, philanthropist and heir to the Johnson & Johnson fortune," wasn't given "an old-fashioned grilling."

In September 2010, forty-eight-year-old Jeffrey Greenstein, who had put together the Quellos operation, pleaded guilty to charges of conspiracy and aiding in the filing of a false tax return in connection with the POINT, the tax shelter that Woody had unsuccessfully bet on to save himself millions in taxes. Greenstein admitted that his scam tax shelters had cheated the IRS out of $240 million. In January 2011, he was sentenced to spend the next fifty months of his life behind bars.

While Woody's platinum reputation remained intact, his hands clean, his involvement would surely become an issue if he ever did decide to run for elective office.

5

For a National Football League team owner who appeared to live and love football—and football had been very, very good to Woody financially, personally, and as a fun factor—he had been mostly a benchwarmer when he actually played the game (he wore number 81) back in prep school.

"Woody was not a world-beater of a football player," recalls Arthur Rudman, who was the head coach of Woody's team, the Mustangs, in Woody's senior year, 1965, at Millbrook School. "Woody wasn't a starter, he was our backup tight end, who played some, but probably not as much as he would have liked. We just had kids who were a little quicker. Woody did what I asked him. I'd say, 'Okay, run into that dummy, or run into that wall' and he'd do it."

Rudman had closely followed the lives of some of his Millbrook players who had had successful careers, and he especially followed Woody when he became the owner of the New York Jets. But then bad things began to happen on the team that concerned Rudman and raised in him questions about his former player's professional judgment as an NFL owner.

All of that began happening around Christmas of 2010 when the Jets' blustery, rotund head coach, Rex Ryan, and his pretty wife, Michelle, got caught in a foot fetish and swinger scandal that made national headlines. As the *New York Post* blared: "Tormented Rex Bares 'Sole' Over Kinky Feet Vids." Ryan refused to discuss his lifestyle because "this is a personal matter."

Woody—who came from a dynasty where one or another of his relatives and/or forebears were involved in some form of kinkiness—presumably had no inkling about Ryan's naughtiness until the news broke on the popular sports Web site Deadspin. Woody and his people had thoroughly checked out Ryan, presumably both his respected professional life in football *and* his private life, before he was hired—with Woody making the final decision to bring him on board as head coach.

In the wake of the scandal, Woody had private talks with Ryan, was satisfied with whatever he was told, and let the matter go.

On the other hand, Art Rudman, Woody's Millbrook prep school football coach, wasn't as forgiving. After he retired from the game, Rudman had gone from being Head Coach Rudman to Reverend Rudman of the Sebago Lake Congregational Church in Standish, Maine, and had initially been closely following with pride his onetime benchwarmer's career as the owner of the Jets.

But he was clearly upset with the personal interests of Woody's head coach, his arrogant, egotistical manner, and the fact that Woody didn't know what was going on. "As a minister, I certainly don't condone a lot of that kind of sick stuff, and I think Ryan compounds his own problems because he talks too much. And the whole affair made Woody look foolish."

Plus he was a fan of the New England Patriots, the Jets' biggest rival.

It wasn't just the fetish scandal and Woody's handling of it that disturbed Rudman.

Several other bizarre incidents had beset the Jets in the 2010 season, leaving Woody red-faced, and making the team seem like depraved rock stars.

In October, two months into the season, Deadspin.com published a report that the aging former quarterback Brett Favre had, during his 2008 season with the Jets, sent suggestive text messages and a photo—allegedly of his penis—to a onetime *Maxim* and *Playboy* model by the name of Jenn Sterger, who held the title of New York Jets "Game Day Hostess." The raunchy and boorish seduction attempts made headlines and jokes nationally, and Woody and his Jets were once again scoffed at.

The Johnson heir must have been quietly reeling. What could he possibly say in explanation? So he said nothing.

As Ryan wryly observed in a quickie, ghostwritten memoir in the spring of 2011 about his career in football and working for the Band-Aid heir, "It wouldn't be the Jets 2010 season without some weird thing happening."

There was yet another sex-related scandal during that steamy season.

Ines Sainz, a thirty-two-year-old blond stunner, was a sports reporter for the Mexican network TV Azteca and had come to the Jets' headquarters and practice field in Florham Park, New Jersey, to interview Woody's handsome young quarterback of Mexican heritage, Mark Sanchez. But Sainz's interview outfit—skintight jeans and a revealing white button-up blouse—aroused the machismo of the players when she sashayed into the locker room. Instantly, she claimed she felt sexually harassed by what she termed the "grotesque" catcalls and rude language from Woody's players, their outrageousness becoming the focus of yet another headline-making embarrassment involving Woody and the Jets.

For the team's positive public image, the owner went public, a rarity for the usually reclusive billionaire who hardly ever gave interviews and, if he did, was a man of few words. On ESPN Radio, however, he told listeners that he had personally telephoned Sainz after learning of his team's misogynistic treatment of her, and assured her that Jets officials would start questioning players and coaches posthaste to get to the bottom of Sainz's harassment charges.

"Right now, we're working with the league and we're doing all the fact-finding, checking the facts, doing the interviews," he asserted. "We certainly don't want any kind of allegations like this, or anything like this to happen. I apologized to her—if anything happened, what happened, kind of an open apology."

As the best known of the contemporary Johnson dynasty, Woody had made his mark in the high-profile, high-test, big-money world of professional football. But one must look to the distant past, and observe the brilliant first generation of Johnson & Johnson innovators, to discover where his entrepreneurial spirit was born.

PART II

GENIUS FOREBEARS

6

The first Robert Wood Johnson wasn't quite as courtly with a certain female celebrity of his generation as was his great-grandson Woody with the bombshell locker room reporter from down Mexico way.

For Johnson, it was all about business, and the business at hand had to do with what had become the company's famous logo in the late 1800s—the red cross. The female in question was Clarissa Harlowe Barton, better known in the history books as Clara Barton, the prim Civil War heroine nurse and humanitarian who had founded the American National Red Cross Society in 1881.

Johnson's problem was that he had been using Barton's red cross without her authorization, or agreement. Shrewdly deciding that the bloodred icon was the perfect symbol for Johnson & Johnson's early first-aid and health-care products, he just arrogantly went ahead and had it emblazoned. To be fair, Johnson wasn't alone. Other entrepreneurs had also used the symbol—from Red Cross Playing Cards to Red Cross Dog Collars. Anyone for a sip of Red Cross Brandy? Or a puff from a Red Cross stogie?

The list went on and on, making Clara Barton, then in her seventies, as red with outrage and frustration as the color of the disputed symbol itself.

Fed up, she went to Washington in 1895 and lobbied the U.S. Congress for a bill that would give her organization red cross exclusivity, along with the ability to license the use of the symbol, which was a way to generate income for her worthy group.

Naturally, Johnson rallied and railed against any such legislation that could take away from his company the valuable asset that the red cross had become in the marketing of his products. With Johnson in one corner, and Clara Barton in the other, they were two popular American heavyweights going into battle. She won round one when the U.S. Senate passed her measure, but the president in power at the time, Grover Cleveland, a pro–big business—think Johnson & Johnson—Democrat of whom the Republican Robert Johnson was a supporter, threw the knockout blow, by nixing the bill, and it never became law.

Subsequently, Johnson, a shrewd and charming negotiator when he needed to be, had some very private meetings with Barton, and eventually got the bargain of a lifetime. For a single crisp U.S. one-dollar bill, he had somehow convinced her to agree that Johnson & Johnson could use the red cross as a trademark. Later, the company began publishing a monthly magazine entitled *Red Cross Notes,* which was sent to physicians and druggists with much information about the latest health developments—and, of course, much subtle and not-so-subtle promotion for Johnson & Johnson's product line. However, this time, Barton was graciously made aware of the publication with "Red Cross" in the name before it was circulated, but she still was upset, admitting, "We are stupid about law"—something that Robert Johnson clearly was not.

An early issue of *Red Cross Notes* paid homage to Barton's vanity. The cover had a color drawing of an angelic Bartonesque nurse all in white holding a box of Johnson & Johnson cotton. The text read: "The only way to secure surgically clean cotton, is to demand the blue carton with the red cross and the signature of Johnson & Johnson."

$ $ $

Along with his brothers, Edward Mead Johnson and James Wood Johnson, Robert Wood Johnson had founded Johnson & Johnson in 1887 after some rough spots.

They were the sons of a poor Pennsylvania farmer, Sylvester Johnson, whose lineage went back to England and the early colonists who had settled in the Massachusetts Bay Colony, almost two decades after the Pilgrims had arrived.

Like the pioneer women from that time, Sylvester's wife, Louisa Wood Johnson, a farmer's daughter, had also descended from English stock. She was nineteen years old when she married, and right away began having babies, giving birth over the next two decades to a brood of eleven. Her first, a girl, died at birth. She was followed by four more girls and six boys.

Robert was Louisa's eighth, born a day after Valentine's Day in 1845, followed in 1852 by Mead, as he would become known, who was her tenth, and James in 1856, number eleven.

After some public school, Robert—considered the brightest of the progeny, studious and a bookworm—was sent at the age of thirteen to board at the Wyoming Seminary, established in 1844 by the Oneida Methodist Conference in Kingston, Pennsylvania, where Johnson received a classical education, according to Lawrence Foster, a onetime public relations executive for Johnson & Johnson, who self-published a book about the second Robert Wood Johnson, Woody Johnson's grandfather.

By the time Robert turned sixteen, the Civil War had started. Fearing he would be drafted in the bloody fighting between North and South, the Johnsons shuffled him off to Poughkeepsie, in New York State, to become an apprentice in a drugstore called Wood & Tittamer.

It would be the Johnson dynasty's first business contact with the world of retail health care and pharmaceuticals, and it was in this shop where the first Robert Wood Johnson was taught how to make medicinal plasters to aid in the treatment of injuries, a major turning point in his young life, as time would tell. Making the plasters properly was a difficult task, and years later, as a pharmaceutical and health-care mogul ruling the Johnson & Johnson behemoth, he was quoted in Foster's book as saying, "Probably no other branch of the pharmaceutical art has been the occasion of so much toil, anxiety, and failure . . . Expressive expletives could not be restrained."

From his experience at the apothecary, he was able to secure a job as an order clerk with a wholesale drug company in downtown Manhattan, where he spent the next four years. During that time he befriended and teamed up with a well-off, socially prominent New York City drug broker by the name of George J. Seabury, according to Foster.

In 1873, Johnson and Seabury became business partners. Their firm was called Seabury & Johnson; Seabury was president, Johnson was the firm's sales manager and corporate secretary, and together they marketed sundry medical goods—there weren't very many of any great import at the time—and plasters, which were manufactured at their plant across the East River in the borough of Brooklyn.

Always on Johnson's mind, though, was the development of a sterile surgical dressing, which would forever change modern surgery.

Seabury & Johnson was quickly expanding, and had started generating business in Europe. Five years after the firm was founded, Johnson sailed to the Continent to study the market and look for new concepts and products, traveling to Germany, England, and France.

He returned to New York enthusiastic about what he had seen in Europe and proposed expanding the business with new products, but his more conservative partner, Seabury, wasn't as excited and thought it best that they stay their course without too much sudden innovation.

Their relationship became tense and rocky, even more so when, in 1876, Seabury decided to bring his brother Robert into the business, and Johnson, not to be outdone, countered by bringing his twenty-four-year-old sibling, Edward Mead Johnson, into the firm as a salesman, although Mead was far more educated. He had studied law at the University of Michigan for a year, and had taught school for a brief time in New York State.

Two years later, Johnson proposed to bring his youngest brother, James, into Seabury & Johnson, which would, with so many Johnsons, far outnumber the Seabury siblings. In a letter, Seabury declared, "I am opposed to nepotism in business."

In time, after Johnson & Johnson was founded, nepotism would be standard operating procedure, a way of life, heralding the "Lucky Sperm Club" of wealthy heirs in later generations, which included Woody Johnson.

By 1879, the growing company distributed a hefty catalog of its products, among them numerous types of plasters for various ailments. They also hawked a new item called "Lister's Antiseptic Gauze." As had happened with

Clara Barton's red cross, Lister's name was used without apparent authorization from the great surgeon; it was the first product ever to carry Lister's increasingly world-famous name.

A year later, Seabury & Johnson production was moved to New Jersey, and set up in a leased facility in the town of South Orange.

Around the same time, the thirty-five-year-old Robert Johnson began a relationship with a New Jersey girl, Ellen Cutler, and after a quickie courtship they were married in 1880. She became the first of his two wives, and gave birth to a daughter named Roberta. The four-year marriage ended in divorce—the first of what would be many divorces in the Johnson dynasty through the generations—and Roberta was raised by Robert's brother James.

The early 1880s heralded a new, and dark era for the personal relationship between Robert Johnson and George Seabury. There were now many disagreements, their business philosophies were at odds—even though Seabury & Johnson had become increasingly successful.

In July 1885, according to Foster's account, Robert Johnson had finally had it with Seabury, and resigned from the firm. After tough negotiation by Johnson, Seabury had agreed to fork over a quarter of a million dollars—an enormous amount in late-nineteenth-century dollars—for Johnson's fifty-percent stake.

The money, per the agreement, was to be paid out over a period of time, a decision that at the time seemed beneficial to Seabury, but would come to haunt him not far down the road.

One of the key clauses was that Johnson, in exchange for the huge severance, was excluded from competing in a similar business for the next decade, which would take him into the first decade of the twentieth century.

But that noncompete clause did not include James and Mead, and what they did in early 1886 was join together with a borrowed one thousand dollars and start a new company as "wholesale druggists and drug manufacturers," according to a rather hyped announcement in the *New Brunswick Daily Times.*

The Johnsons had rented a fourth-floor loft in the abandoned Janeway and Carpenter wallpaper factory, in the industrial city of New Brunswick—halfway between New York and Philadelphia—hard by the Raritan River and along the Pennsylvania Railroad line, which made it perfect for shipping.

When Seabury learned of the Johnson brothers' operation he was livid because he suspected—and rightly so—that Robert was a silent partner, pulling the strings and supplying the capital. If he actually were involved competitively, he would be in blatant violation of their ironclad separation agreement. Johnson penned a wink-wink, nudge-nudge letter to his brothers reiterating the legality of his contract with his former partner. He also informed them that he thought they would have a tough time competing with the long-established Seabury & Johnson company and, moreover, he didn't think his siblings had anywhere near the necessary capital to make a go of it.

Still, they went ahead, with Mead as the outside man luring customers and hustling products—he was as aggressive and brilliant a businessman as his brother Robert, and that would be underscored in years to come when he would go out on his own and start a major, hugely successful company—while James handled the mechanical end of the infant Johnson & Johnson.

Meanwhile, George Seabury had shot himself in the foot, metaphorically speaking, by failing to live up to his agreement to make regular payments—he had missed several—on the quarter million dollars he had promised his former partner. Johnson, who was anxious to join his brothers in their startup, made an offer to Seabury that he couldn't refuse:

Johnson agreed to forfeit the monies due him from Seabury in exchange for his freedom to return to the business he loved, and be freed to join his siblings.

Once the deal was consummated, the aggressive and arrogant Robert Johnson let the drug trade know in a letter that he was back in the saddle, that he was becoming a partner with his brothers and, as he boasted, "taking charge of the business."

To one of his salesman, he wrote: "We have concluded to stick the knife right into the bowels of the plaster business," and to one of his distributors, the boastful and confident Johnson declared, "We guarantee the quality of the goods in every way to be equal to Seabury & Johnson or better."

On October 28, 1887, Johnson & Johnson was formally incorporated, with Robert Johnson running the show. He held forty percent of the stock, valued at one hundred thousand dollars, and Mead and James each had thirty percent.

Johnson & Johnson's first president was Robert, James was general manager, and Mead was made secretary.

They had hit the ground with serious momentum.

7

By the fall of 1888, more than a hundred employees were on the Johnson & Johnson payroll, the New Brunswick factory encompassed thirty-five thousand square feet, and a young advertising huckster by the name of J. Walter Thompson—a close friend of Robert Johnson's—had been commissioned to help make the company and its products world famous.

Johnson & Johnson, under Robert—known as "R.W."—was running full steam ahead.

Its unforgettable logo, the red cross, appeared on the first Johnson & Johnson First-Aid Kit, the Johnson & Johnson Baby Powder can, and other early consumer products from the company.

A dozen years after his first marriage had ended in divorce, Robert Johnson, looking older—and heavier at forty-seven—got married for a second time, again to a much younger woman—two decades younger. He shocked those in his social circle, in the family dynasty, and in the New Brunswick community of single women, not so single women, and widows of all ages, all of whom saw Robert Wood Johnson as a great, big wealthy catch—wealthy being the operative word.

The lucky girl, who would become a June bride and who would wear his ring, was Evangeline Armstrong, the pretty, slender daughter—one of five sisters—of a country doctor and surgeon, Edwin Armstrong, and a schoolteacher mother, Martha, from Upstate New York, the village of Holley.

Johnson, who often traveled to medical conclaves, may have been introduced to Evangeline by her father, the doctor. Knocked out by her beauty and availability, Johnson wasted no time courting her, and they immediately became intimate as would be underscored by the birth of their first child virtually nine months to the day after their quickie wedding ceremony in the foothills of the Great Smoky Mountains, in a Tennessee burg called Maryville, a week before the Independence Day celebration of 1892.

The reason Maryville was the setting for the private nuptials instead of New Brunswick, or even the bride's hometown, was probably because they had eloped. Also never squarely answered was why the angelic-looking Evangeline with her cameo-white skin and blond spit curls fell for the middle-aged, stout, mustachioed, and balding Johnson with his piercing black eyes and quick temper, who easily could have passed for her father. Moreover, as everyone knew, his real love was his company, to which he was truly wed.

The only conceivable reason Evangeline Armstrong said yes and became the second Mrs. Robert Johnson—Woody Johnson's paternal great-grandmother—was the same reason a number of women would marry Johnson men, and men would marry Johnson women, through the generations, and that was because they were rich and powerful.

Robert changed Evangeline's young life overnight; she went from upstate girl to uptown girl, the belle of New Brunswick society—although she was never fully accepted by the city's hoi polloi, and couldn't have cared less.

She also became the mistress of Gray Terrace, the biggest mansion in town, of which the hoi polloi also thought little. It was a monstrosity of a Gilded Age palace that Johnson had bought for his bride at the enormous cost in those days of seventy-five thousand dollars, and was located just a block's walk from the Johnson & Johnson complex, allowing him to come home for a hearty lunch and a cigar. While Gray Terrace was the height of luxurious living back then with its many rooms, greenhouses, and sumptuous grounds behind a low stone wall, photographs of the place before it was torn down and turned into a parking lot for Rutgers University students reminded one of the sinister-looking house on the hill where Norman Bates lived with his mummified mother.

Johnson's daughter from his first marriage, Roberta, who had been living with his brother James's family, joined her father and his bride.

And on April 4, 1893—nine months and eight days after Evangeline had tied the knot with Robert—she gave birth to a son, who was named, naturally, Robert Wood Johnson Jr., the future ruler of Johnson & Johnson—Woody Johnson's grandfather.

He would be the first of what would become the often scandalous second generation of the Johnson dynasty.

On July 14, 1895, Evangeline gave birth to her second son, who was named John Seward Johnson, who would be even more of a tabloid figure than his brother. Then, on April 18, 1897, she brought a daughter into the world, her namesake, Evangeline Brewster Johnson.

At home in Gray Terrace, Evangeline Armstrong Johnson had a staff of servants to lighten the load for the young mother of three, and stepmother of another. A colorized photograph of her three biological children—showing Robert in a sailor suit, his sister in a white frilly bonnet, and Seward also dressed in navy blue—appeared in a 1986 book called *A Company That Cares* that marked Johnson & Johnson's one hundred years in business. The Johnson siblings were sitting in a horse-drawn cart, and naturally it was Robert who was holding the reins and wielding the whip, and glaring suspiciously at the camera—a chubby, pink-cheeked vision of things to come.

By the last decade of the nineteenth century, Johnson & Johnson was turning out dozens of health-care products.

If you had a health issue, Johnson & Johnson usually had a remedy. Many were life-saving and history-making, but some had the ring of the snake oil salesman.

For indigestion and dyspepsia there was Johnson's Tablets, "Cure Guaranteed—When Directions are followed." For a time, Johnson & Johnson sold a non-habit-forming, supposedly nonalcoholic product called Vino-Kolafra, an "African-tonic stimulant" that, among other things, "invigorates the Feeble and hastens Convalescence." Despite the nonalcoholic claim, one of the ingredients was cheap sherry, which Johnson & Johnson workers had started sampling on the job—the product was soon canceled. It was a follow-up to another very successful product that had recently come on the market from another entrepreneur—a drink called Coca-Cola, which was said to have tonic potential. Johnson & Johnson, however, had their version approved by the American Medical Association.

On the plus side, the company was producing various forms of surgical sutures—catgut, twisted silk. There was the cotton that appeared in the famous blue box with the red cross on it. There were kits to aid in safe births at a time when the maternity ward was the home bedroom with a midwife attending the mother-to-be—among those products were "Dr. Simpson's MATERNITY Packet," "Umbilical Tape," and "Abdominal Binder."

There was a cream to clean the teeth called ZONWEISS—German for "white teeth"—sold for thirty-five cents. The product "is praised by dentists and refined people everywhere," declared a magazine advertisement. Bizarrely, the ad included a drawing of what appeared to be a family of ratlike creatures holding toothbrushes. Before being canceled, ZONWEISS became the first tooth cleaner in a squeezable tube.

A physician had sent a letter to Dr. Frederick B. Kilmer, a brilliant and successful pharmacist, physician, and analytical chemist, who had been appointed by Robert Johnson as the company's director of scientific affairs, and who was the father of the poet who wrote "Trees," Alfred Joyce Kilmer. The physician's letter noted that a patient had suffered from skin irritations after using medicated plasters. Kilmer thought a form of talcum powder might ease the problem and sent a can to the doctor. At the same time, corporately, Johnson & Johnson began including talc with some of the plasters it was producing. So, it was Frederick Kilmer who, in 1892, had given birth to Johnson's Baby Powder, which became a mix of talc and medicated plaster. But that was just the start.

Over time, ingredients numbering some two hundred from lands around the globe were combined to give the product and the pink behinds of a once estimated 60 percent of all babies born in America a distinctive aroma that reportedly has never been changed. Subsequent research, according to Lawrence Foster, disclosed that baby powder was linked to the love of a mother, the bond between her and her baby, through the caressing of the baby with the powder. It was more about the mother's touch than the powder's benefits, according to some researchers.

$ $ $

Of the three founding brothers of Johnson & Johnson, Edward Mead Johnson had long gone off the radar in terms of the family business by starting his own companies, completely separate from Johnson & Johnson. Still, there would be a kind of a synergy between Johnson & Johnson of New Brunswick, New Jersey, and his most successful enterprise, Mead Johnson & Company of Evansville, Indiana. While some of Johnson & Johnson's products were used to pamper the dimpled behinds of America's babies, many of Mead Johnson's products helped with their digestion.

In the mid-1890s, Mead had become fascinated with the curative powers of papaya for indigestion, which had become a growing problem related to the changing and often gluttonous eating habits of Americans in the late nineteenth century. Beyond that, he saw a market—and a need—for products in the then-infant field of infant nutrition. For some reason he was alone among his brothers in his interests, so while still at Johnson & Johnson he started his first independent company, called American Ferment—the word "ferment" referring to digestive aids—in Jersey City, New Jersey, directly across the Hudson from lower Manhattan.

In 1897, he sold all of his Johnson & Johnson stock to his ruling brother, Robert, and left the company to run American Ferment full time.

Why Mead would give up all the success and riches he had in Johnson & Johnson—despite his other fledgling interests—was still a big question mark to his great-grandson, Edward Mead Johnson III, known as Ted, a century and a decade later. "It is a mystery, but there's something that happened, either a dispute with his brothers, or something else. I just don't know," he says.

Around the same time Mead created his company, he had divorced his first wife and married a woman by the name of Helen Dalton, who operated an exclusive hat shop on fashionable Madison Avenue in New York. "She had two characteristics," says Ted, seventy-three in 2010. "One was that she was very devoted to my great-grandfather, and when his company was initially experiencing serious financial difficulties, she sold all of her jewelry to save it. The other thing, which is probably equally, if not more important, was that when there was dissention in the family all the members felt that they could go to her and talk to her—so she was the great peacemaker. She kind of rose above the male aggressions."

In 1905, in his early fifties, Mead Johnson changed the name of American Ferment to Mead Johnson & Company, moved into a new two-story factory, hired a couple of sales representatives, and business started to boom with his main digestive product, called Caroid.

Soon, Mead Johnson's line expanded, with its first major product for the feeding of infants, called Mead's Dextri-Maltose.

As it happened, Mead's firstborn, Edward Mead Johnson Jr., had been unhealthy from birth with not only a congenital heart defect—he would die at the age of forty-one—but also serious difficulty in tolerating his feedings.

"My grandfather was a very sickly person and he had that condition," says Ted Johnson, "and so my great-grandfather said, let's try to figure out something that has meaning." The nation's top pediatrician at the time prescribed a mixture on which the baby did well—one that would be similar to Mead Johnson's new Dextri-Maltose, a recipe of carbohydrate powder and milk. A scientist whom Mead had recruited from Johnson & Johnson took it from there.

One of the product's ingredients was potato starch that was imported from Germany, but the outbreak of the First World War ended such imports. Johnson needed to find a part of the United States where it was readily available, and that turned out to be America's heartland, the Midwest. He moved his operations from the Johnson dynasty's home state of New Jersey to Indiana, and in the city of Evansville, on the Ohio River, Mead Johnson & Company was established in a vacant cotton mill. His three sons, Ted, Lambert, and James, eventually were executives under their father.

Through the years Mead Johnson & Company would produce iconic—but not always tasty—products that served generations of babies and children such as cod liver oil and Pablum. There was Nutramigan, the first infant formula ever for babies sensitive to cow's milk, and Vi-Sol, the first water-soluble vitamins in drop-dosage form for infants.

In the late 1950s, the company joined the weight-loss craze that was sweeping the nation with a product for adults called Metrecal. From a chocolate-tasting diet drink to soups for weight watchers, Metrecal became an overnight sensation, with celebrities extolling its virtues.

"It wasn't what you would call a serious medical product," notes Ted Johnson, "and it probably was a fad and when the fad was over other fads came in. My father, who was extraordinarily upset by what happened to Metrecal, had to close a laboratory, cut back on facilities, and he had to lay off employees, and his stock went down."

Eventually, unrelated to the Metrecal flop, Ted Johnson's father sold the family business to another big company, and retired to Palm Beach.

$ $ $

In late January 1910, several weeks before his sixty-fifth birthday, the first Robert Wood Johnson, always healthy and driven, fell ill. He was quickly diagnosed by some of the best physicians of the time—including one who had helped try to save the life of the assassinated President McKinley—with a form of severe kidney disease that was then untreatable.

At 6:40 A.M. on February 7, 1910, in the family home, Gray Terrace, the brilliant entrepreneur and lead brother behind the founding of Johnson & Johnson, and its rise as an iconic American company, died.

"Death Calls a Captain of Industry," mourned the headline in the *New Brunswick Daily Home News*. The story noted that he had been "unconscious for some time," and at the time of his passing was surrounded by his family.

Fear gripped the Johnson & Johnson plant. Robert Johnson had been such an imposing and innovative leader that the employees—there now were some twenty-five hundred—were deeply concerned that Johnson & Johnson would die with him. The next day about half of the workforce, garbed in black, made the pilgrimage from the plant to Gray Terrace to view the boss of bosses, whose body was in repose in a mahogany casket—a duplicate of the one in which McKinley had been buried—in the drawing room of the Johnson mansion.

His obituary in the *Daily Home News* noted:

Mr. Johnson was a man of strong and pleasing personality, as well as of untiring energy. His presence was everywhere felt throughout the vast establishment with which he was always in close touch. He won the loyalty and affection of his entire force of employees . . . It is probable that along the line of surgical dressings, Mr. Johnson made his greatest success . . .

The headline of another front-page story declared: "He Built Up a System That Saved Lives . . . Helped to Make the Discoveries of Lister Practicable and Popular—A Tribute from Those Near the Man."

Johnson & Johnson essentially owned New Brunswick, and Robert Johnson had been the city's leading businessman and citizen, so he was given the biggest and most spectacular final farewell in the city's history two days after his passing, with a cortege made up of thirty carriages, untold numbers of other vehicles, and a procession of hundreds if not thousands of the town's loyal citizenry, a good number of them on his payroll.

About a year after he died, a final accounting of his estate showed he had a total of $3,372,250—*big* money in those days. Since his death, his income to his estate was more than $200,000.

The executors were his brother James; his daughter from his first marriage, Roberta Johnson Nicholas—she had been on a Florida honeymoon with her groom, Robert Carter Nicholas, later a treasurer of Johnson & Johnson, when her father died—and lastly Johnson's widow, the handsome and elegant Evangeline, who was the chief beneficiary of his enormous estate and the guardian of their three children, all of whom were still in school.

At Elmwood Cemetery in New Brunswick, an ornate mausoleum that "is like a Greek temple," according to the *Daily Home News*, was Johnson's final resting place, and what a fanciful resting place it was, replete with an artificial lake that, in the florid prose of the newspaper, "ripples at the foot of the hillock on which the splendid building to the dead rests."

The exterior walls and the columns were built of Barre granite, the most popular type of granite for the mausoleums and monuments of the rich and famous, then and into the twenty-first century. The granite from Vermont had been used in the construction of the fanciful and ornate last resting places of other generals of American commerce: Sidney Colgate, Phillip B. Armour, Walter Chrysler, and Harvey Firestone, to name a few.

Not long after her husband died, Evangeline Armstrong Johnson—now a hugely wealthy widow, still young and still quite attractive—surprised family members, company executives, and the people of New Brunswick by hastily moving with two of her three children from Gray Terrace to Manhattan, ready to begin the kind of fun social life she had always craved but couldn't have with a business-obsessed husband in the stodgy and boorish New Jersey company town where she felt superior to most everyone.

At the time of Johnson's death, Evangeline's firstborn, Robert Jr., was just a couple of months away from his seventeenth birthday, and was devastated by the patriarch's quick illness and sudden demise. He had adored and idolized his father, was closest to him of the three siblings, and planned to follow in his footsteps someday as the head of the family business—and would do so. Robert's brother, Seward, was going on fifteen, and their sister, Evangeline, the youngest of the brood, was about to turn thirteen when their father passed.

Years later Evangeline, the daughter—who would have a wild life with lovers of both sexes—was quoted by Lawrence Foster as saying, "The minute father died, my mother took an apartment in New York, and she took my brother Seward and me with her. Bob at that time sort of moved over, if you want to call it that, and stayed with my [half] sister Roberta and her husband at their home in New Brunswick."

However, a much different—and far more sinister—story involving the widow Evangeline, her lifestyle, and her children surfaced many decades later, long after her death in June 1990 at ninety-three.

As Seward's son, Seward Johnson Jr., the sculptor, tells it, his grandmother, Evangeline, "Took up with a member of [British] Parliament and she just sort of deserted her children." He says his father, then a teenager, was left with a female New York socialite who kept him as "a sexual prisoner. He was saved by his brother [Robert Jr.] who came in and got him out of there. It's a sad story, but also very significant in their relationship."

By that Seward Jr. meant that through the years when Robert Jr., a swaggering martinet, was running Johnson & Johnson, and Seward was his submissive second in command, his older brother, as payback for the rescue, would lord it over him emotionally and financially.

Moreover, Seward's sexual abuse as a teenager would have a great and negative impact on his future relationships with women, in which he was often sexually aggressive, especially with very young women, even family members. His own daughter, Mary Lea, the first baby face on the Johnson & Johnson Baby Powder container, would later claim to have been a victim.

But all of that was still to come.

With the senior Robert Johnson's death, his brother James took over the presidency. But waiting anxiously in the wings was Robert Sr.'s son, and James's nephew, Robert Jr.

8

The third brother who founded Johnson & Johnson, James Wood Johnson—slim, mustachioed, and balding—was "quiet and unassuming," respected by his employees and management team for his kind and gentle nature—far different than his aggressive late brother, Robert.

But during his watch as president from 1910 to 1932 the company greatly expanded with life-saving products during the Great War; with the company's Band-Aid showing up in virtually every American household's medicine cabinet, and with the first expansion into foreign markets—Canada, England, Mexico, and South Africa.

The trademark Johnson & Johnson red signature on many of the company's products is James Johnson's actual handwriting.

Unlike many Johnson men through the generations of the dynasty, James had had a relatively peaceful and comfortable private life. With the first of his two wives, Mary Law Johnson, he had two daughters, Helen and Louise, and the family resided in a mansion in New Brunswick called Lindenwood.

Helen—who would play a role through the years in the Johnson dynasty, and was a major stockholder in Johnson & Johnson—would go on to marry a self-made Wall Street wunderkind with the very elite-sounding name of Nicholas Gouverneur Rutgers III. His real passion rather than stocks was pipe organs, of all things, according to his octogenarian son, Nicholas Gouverneur Rutgers IV, known as Nick. "My father basically managed my mother's fortune, and he retired young to play the great organs of the world." When he was twenty, Nick, a jovial type, married the seventeen-year-old daughter of the author of *Mutiny on the Bounty,* James Norman Hall, and lived for much of his life on an island in the South Pacific.

$ $ $

Back at Johnson & Johnson, by the time he was in his seventies, James Wood Johnson's greatest threat was his ambitious, aggressive, and driven nephew, Robert Jr., who was looking to move up at a time when his aging uncle was trying to hang on to his presidency.

"What bothered James most was having to make way for his nephew, and the next generation of management. To him, it was like repelling an enemy invasion," wrote Lawrence Foster, in the self-published *Robert Wood Johnson: The Gentleman Rebel.*

Foster quoted from a letter James wrote his brother Mead, who was running his own successful company in Indiana, in which he stated what most older generations have thought: "The thing that gets my goat every once in a while, is the disrespect, if you like, or the inconsiderable estimate of ourselves on the part of the young ones." He was referring, of course, to Robert Jr.

But James Johnson didn't mind young ones when they were of the feminine variety, and especially attired in Clara Barton white. A widower for six years, he married again in his mid-seventies in 1931, to his thirty-two-year-old Scottish nurse.

They returned from an ocean voyage and were greeted by a letter bearing grim news from the Johnson & Johnson board of directors informing James that he was out as president—or, as it was put, officially retired, and without his consent. He did get a pension—what he considered a measly twenty-five hundred dollars, and he voiced his displeasure at the ill treatment, and disrespect, pointing out that under him Johnson & Johnson's revenue had more than quadrupled in his first full decade as president.

After a bit of a squabble, he formally resigned.

In late August 1932, he died while on another sea cruise.

A month and a half later, on October 15, 1932, his power-hungry nephew,

Robert Wood Johnson Jr., who had turned thirty-nine that April, was named president and general manager of Johnson & Johnson.

Under him, a new and even greater era for the company was born. It was the third year of the Great Depression.

$ $ $

If, decades later, Woody Johnson had decided to run for the U.S. Senate from New Jersey, he would have become only the second member of the Johnson dynasty to enter politics as a candidate.

The first was his grandfather, the blond and wiry Robert Wood Johnson Jr., who once claimed that he learned the most about the psychology of people—and how to manipulate and dominate them—at the age of twenty-five while serving on the Borough Council of Highland Park, New Jersey, and soon after as its mayor. His own father, the first Robert Wood Johnson, Woody Johnson's great-grandfather, had once been asked to run for mayor of New Brunswick, but after he told the Republican leadership that he would fire most of the "useless" officials, and slash appropriations, they decided to find another candidate.

Robert Jr.'s political career, brief though it was, came in the wake of some youthful wildness, including heavy drinking, barhopping, and skirt-chasing, followed by the first of his three marriages, and two scandalous divorces.

Robert Jr. had earned a reputation as a "rouster" with "pepper in his pants," and was known as a "hell-raiser." Like his grandsons decades later—Woody, Billy, and Keith, and especially Keith—Johnson was a speed freak; expensive speedboats and imported fast cars were one of his pasttimes. He'd have the car engines souped up by the mechanics at Johnson & Johnson.

"Then he'd go out and wreck them," his former supervisor, Walter Metts, recalled to Lawrence Foster. "It's a wonder he didn't kill himself."

Woody's grandfather's out-of-control lifestyle finally caught up with him when he showed up at Johnson & Johnson in what he himself later described as a "drunken stupor" and collapsed on the floor outside the board of directors' offices while a meeting was under way. His uncle James Johnson, the company head, with whom he was living at the time, was furious.

"Uncle Jimmy told him that if he didn't stop fooling around he would sell the business," Metts told Foster. "He stopped that kind of behavior almost overnight and became a very serious-minded young man."

On April 15, 1914, Johnson, having just turned twenty-one, became a member of Johnson & Johnson's board of directors, replacing one who had recently died. Four years down the road he would also possess a vast and growing fortune in company stock as provided by his father's will. Between securing his appointment to the Johnson & Johnson board and inheriting the company stock, he was promoted to head one of the company's departments.

The Johnson heir also began pursuing a local society girl, Elizabeth Dixon Ross, whose father, Millard Fillmore Ross, ran the biggest and most successful coal business in New Brunswick. Her late maternal grandfather—last name Dixon—had been a Jersey City judge. Her late paternal grandfather was Miles Ross, a Democratic U.S. Congressman from New Jersey.

In the summer of 1916, with the Great War raging in Europe, Johnson & Johnson was getting richer, producing "thousands of miles" of gauze and adhesive plaster, and "hundreds of millions" of bandages for the battlefronts, its plant running seven days a week around the clock, utilizing a large female workforce because their men were overseas fighting.

And that summer, Robert Jr., a stay-at-home captain in the army reserve, asked for Elizabeth Ross's hand in marriage. (Decades later Woody Johnson's sister was named after her—Elizabeth Ross Johnson, but known as Libet, which was how one of her young brothers mispronounced the name Elizabeth, and it stuck.)

The first Elizabeth Ross—with large breasts; a thin waist; a pretty, oval face; but a bit chunky—readily accepted Johnson's proposal, and on October 18, 1916, a Wednesday, they were married in royal style to the music of the romantic opera *Lohengrin* in an eight o'clock ceremony in the library of the bride's family mansion at 100 Lexington Avenue, in New Brunswick.

The groom's mother, Evangeline Armstrong Johnson—now Mrs. John W. Dennis of 875 Park Avenue, and also of London—attended with her new British husband. Her other son, Robert Johnson's brother, Seward, was the best man, and the whole hugely expensive affair—hundreds of flowers, pot-ted palms, magical lights, ribbon cutters, bridal attendants, groomsmen—was topped off with a gourmet dinner overseen by a popular French caterer, and the après supper dancing was supplied by an orchestra big with the debutante set.

"After the [Bermuda] honeymoon," the *New York Times* wedding announcement stated, "the couple will reside at Belleview, New Brunswick, the Johnson country home, on the Raritan River. Mr. Johnson gave his farewell bachelor dinner at the St. Regis on Thursday evening."

The newlyweds' estate actually was in Highland Park, a town of some five thousand, and that's where Johnson, a self-styled, albeit contradictory "conservative-liberal" registered Republican, first got involved in politics.

Because he was handsome, charming, rich, and powerful, plus he could talk anyone into anything, he was asked in 1918 to fill the seat—until the next election in 1919—of a Republican member of the borough council who had left town. Johnson then ran a campaign to fill his own soon-to-be vacant seat.

But just a few months before the election, tragedy struck when the matriarch, fifty-four-year-old Evangeline Armstrong Johnson Dennis—mother of Robert, Seward, and her namesake daughter, and the paternal great-grandmother of Woody Johnson—died from injuries sustained in a freak accident; she had tripped on a curb in London, broke her hip, and two weeks later succumbed to a blood clot. Young Evangeline, who had been in Europe at the time, rushed to London and was at her mother's hospital bedside when she passed away. She was buried in Noxton, Lincolnshire, where she and her husband had recently moved into a country estate.

Back home in New Jersey, life went on.

An advertisement from the Republican Committee supporting Robert Johnson declared:

"Whenever he starts anything he sticks to the finish and sees that everything goes 'Over the Top.'"

He received the most votes on the ticket, but he wasn't going to hold the council seat for long. Less than two months after the election, the council appointed him, at twenty-six, the mayor of Highland Park.

$ $ $

Highland Park was a workingman's town, located not far from the world headquarters of Johnson & Johnson in New Brunswick, and a lot of the borough's citizens worked at the plant.

One of them was a Johnson & Johnson cotton buyer by the name of Earle E. Dickson. Unlike Robert and Elizabeth Johnson, who lived on an opulent estate, Dickson and his young wife, Josephine, occupied a simple home on a small, grassy lot on narrow, two-lane, tree-lined Montgomery Street, number 326. They had recently been married and their relationship was going swimmingly, except the missus had a problem: she was clumsy when it came to preparing meals and often cut her fingers. Dickson was always responding to Josephine's cries of, "Earle, honey, guess what? I cut myself again," and he would come running with something he had jerry-rigged to cover the wound.

Finally, tired of playing Mr. First-Aid, he decided there had to be a better bandage. And there was. He gathered a long, narrow strip of surgical tape—a Johnson & Johnson product, naturally—and attached to it a few pieces of gauze, and covered the adhesive with some spare crinoline that Josephine kept in her sewing basket.

Dickson mentioned his patch at work, and as he later recalled, "The boys in the front office loved the concept," according to Lawrence Foster's account. A few weeks before Thanksgiving 1920, a virtual copy of Dickson's makeshift idea was packaged, containing a single strip, and put on drugstore shelves.

The Band-Aid, which would become one of Johnson & Johnson's biggest selling products worldwide, though it still needed some tweaks, had been born.

But the Band-Aid didn't immediately take off, probably because the consumer had to take each strip and cut it to size just like Josephine Dickson had done. Too much work, which was underscored by the first year's revenue—a measly three thousand dollars—and sales remained at such low levels for most of the Roaring Twenties, even when bathtub gin–fueled flappers cut their pretty knees falling while doing the Charleston.

But soon enough the Band-Aid became one of the most popular and purchased first-aid products in America, and the world—used in the billions to treat minor cuts and scrapes—and by then Earle Dickson, who had invented the product by chance, had been made a very well-paid Johnson & Johnson vice president.

The same year the Band-Aid was invented, there would be another birth of great import in the Johnson dynasty.

In January 1920, around the same time her husband had been named the mayor of Highland Park, and across town Earle Dickson had invented a product to cover his wife's food-preparation scrapes, Elizabeth Ross Johnson had gotten pregnant.

On September 9, 1920, she gave birth to a cute, chubby son.

To carry on the Johnson line, the infant's domineering father, rather than his submissive mother, personally chose the name.

The boy was christened Robert Wood Johnson III after his father, and he would later be known as Bobby.

But the relationship between Johnson and his wife, and Johnson and his growing son—the future father of Woody Johnson—would come to a bad end.

9

The year 1930 had been something else.

Jobless Americans were struggling through the first year after Black Friday, October 25, 1929, when, as *Variety* famously proclaimed, "Wall Street Lays an Egg," and the Great Depression was under way.

But it wasn't all that bleak for those who still had money—*big* money.

For instance, in late December of that very gloomy year, the eighteen-year-old Woolworth heiress Barbara Hutton, in a bouffant frock of white tulle—not a dime-store number—had her debut at the Ritz-Carlton Hotel at an extravagant cost of sixty thousand dollars—enough to feed, clothe, and house almost fifty Depression-ravaged families for a year.

"Brilliant Ball for Miss Hutton: Ballroom Suite Transformed into a Garden in Moonlight," swooned a headline in *The New York Times*. Some thousand swells from around the world had been invited to the affair. Rudy Vallee and the Meyer Davis Orchestra entertained. Dressed as Santa Claus, because it was just days before Christmas, was Maurice Chevalier, who, with Santa's helpers, was handing out, incredibly, such party favors as gold jewelry, diamonds, even emeralds and rubies—while outside in the street there were soup lines and hollow-eyed men selling apples from pushcarts in order to feed their families.

In the high-society crowd that evening was Robert Wood Johnson Jr., dapper and handsome in a tux, rubbing shoulders with other masters of the universe and Park Avenue matrons who were bedazzling in their priceless jewels.

Johnson was sporting his own kind of arm candy—a gorgeous, slim, and chic new number who was definitely *not* the mother of his son and namesake, Bobby Johnson III.

Besides toasting the poor little rich girl's coming out, Robert Jr. was also celebrating another very special occasion—his divorce from Bobby's mother, Elizabeth Ross Johnson, and his more recent secret marriage to the new Mrs. Johnson—petite and chic Margaret Shea, known as Maggi, who had modeled in Paris, was an actress, supposedly a fashion columnist for the French edition of *Vogue,* a budding dancer, and a talented amateur photographer.

In actuality, she was a small-town girl from Norwich, in Connecticut, and then Elmhurst, in Long Island, who had gone to New York, where she had appeared in a musical comedy called *Good News.* Scouts for the French fashion designer Jean Patou had spotted her, blond and beautiful, and after several requests she agreed, with her stage mother's permission, to come to Paris and become one of his models, and that's where she and Johnson began what would soon be an intimate relationship when Shea was twenty-five and Johnson was more than a decade older.

"I thought he was the most divine man I had ever seen," she once told Lawrence Foster, the former Johnson & Johnson public relations vice president who self-published a book about Robert Johnson Jr.

They had quietly tied the knot in September 1930 in Paris, and had honeymooned at a posh resort near fashionable Biarritz—all of which was happening while Robert Jr. was combining European Johnson & Johnson business with fun.

His divorce had been secretly granted in New Jersey's state capital, Trenton, on August 12, 1930. It had ended a mostly tumultuous fourteen-year marriage—tumultuous because of his womanizing, his around-the-clock devotion to his company, and his blatant disregard of his son.

Four years earlier, when Elizabeth Ross Johnson, known to everyone as Ruth, refused to give her philandering husband a divorce, he had gone ahead and simply left her and their son, Bobby, the future father of Woody Johnson. She then had charged the ruler of Johnson & Johnson with desertion.

"He just abandoned her and [eight-year-old] Bobby," states Nick Rutgers, who not only was Robert Jr.'s cousin but also his godson. "It was terrible."

The general consensus within Johnson's circle, according to Foster, was that he had outgrown his wife, and that he found her boring.

But the "main reason for the split was because Ruth had become fat," maintains Rutgers decades later. "She was a heavyset woman and he couldn't stand that about her. He was obsessed about his own weight and demanded that others be thin, too. He told my mother [Helen Johnson Rutgers] that he didn't like any lady who was fat. Plus, he was *the* playboy of the Western world at that time. He was absolutely a womanizer, no question about that."

The first Mrs. Johnson got a cool one million dollars, plus their New Jersey estate and other property, a huge settlement in those days, and especially during the Depression.

But it wasn't consolation for the way he had treated her and their son.

"It was especially hard on young Robert III, who was then nine but had not yet seen very much of his father. The boy was puzzled and hurt," noted Foster.

Johnson and his new bride—the second of his three wives, not to mention any number of women on the side—had moved into "Morven," in Princeton, a 1755 Georgian-style, fifteen-room mansion on five thousand acres, with an astounding history of guests, including eight presidents, among them Washington and Madison, and also the home where the creation of Princeton University was planned.

Johnson had leased the estate, which had become run down. He promised the original owners, the descendants of one of the signers to the Declaration of Independence, to renovate it to its former glory, an assignment that Maggi took on with relish.

The New York *Daily News* had broken the news of the Johnson marriage on Saturday, December 20, 1930, with a Speed Graphic photo of Johnson in a dapper derby hat, and a tabloid headline that screamed: "Johnson's Secret Wedding Follows Hushed Decree." The story described him as a "middle-aged manufacturer, a member of one of New Jersey's oldest socially-elect families," and characterized Ruth, his first wife, who had been dumped for the new model, as a "leader in Jersey society."

In boldface type, readers were told, **"The newlyweds took elaborate,**

precautions to ensure secrecy upon their arrival. They left the ship and went almost immediately to Morven, the new Johnson ménage near Princeton."

The *News* pointed out that the custody of Johnson's son, Bobby, had been divided evenly between the parents, and quoted the New York Social Register as saying the little boy was living with his father at Morven, which wasn't exactly true. Robert Jr. would have nothing to do with the boy.

The second Mrs. Johnson had a wild streak that the Johnson & Johnson mogul savored. When he was once entertaining some politicians, she and a female chum put on skimpy French maid outfits and took orders for drinks from the men while her excited husband looked on.

She had reinvented herself as a dazzling Princeton socialite and hostess, but ignored another marital duty—that of caring stepmother to her husband's young son, Bobby. And that was mainly because the boy's own father cared little for the youngster, according to Nick Rutgers, whose mother, Helen, was Bobby Johnson's godmother.

"My mother told me Robert and Maggi never even remembered his son's birthday, so my mother used to always buy him presents because his father ignored him. They ignored Bobby completely because he was fat like his mother, Ruth [Elizabeth]. His father just didn't want to have any part of him. It was a sad life for Bobby."

Instead of spending much time with his father and his stepmother, Bobby Johnson and his biological mother developed a powerful and mutual bond. As Foster noted, "Elizabeth and her son grew very close, and Bobby shared with her the pain of the divorce and the absence of his father. In later years he remarked ruefully that it was the family chauffeur who used to take him fishing and on other boyhood adventures, not his father."

Because Maggi Johnson had difficulty getting pregnant, the Johnsons adopted a newborn girl, Bobby's stepsister, who they named Sheila.

Many years later, after her father's death, Sheila Johnson Brutsch—she had married a Swiss husband, had homes in Palm Beach and Switzerland, and often sailed the world with her husband, Francois—talked with Foster about her adoptive father: "Johnson and Johnson was his wife, his mistress, his child, his friend, his toy. It was his life, much more than the rest of us of flesh and blood."

10

When Robert Wood Johnson Jr. was in high school, he had become a member of the Rutgers Prep drill team with the rank of private, and during the Great War he wore two silver bars as a stay-at-home army reserve captain. He took to military discipline—looked handsome and manly in a uniform, and he knew it—but he would never actually serve in a real man's army in actual combat.

In early 1943, a little over a year after the Japanese attack on Pearl Harbor, and with Johnson & Johnson supplying record amounts of medical supplies for the war effort—its business quadrupled—President Roosevelt, knowing of Johnson's executive abilities, appointed him to run the Smaller War Plants Corporation, created by Congress to assist the country's forty thousand small businesses to participate in war goods production.

Because Johnson soon ran into a brick wall dealing with the Washington bureaucracy, Roosevelt infuriated officers in every command by granting Johnson, on May 17, 1943, the full military rank of Brigadier General of Army Ordnance.

Without knowing what he was doing, the commander in chief had turned an already bloated ego into a strutting martinet.

Johnson, who practically carried a swagger stick in the civilian world, was in heaven.

"Oh, boy, he *loved* that—*loved* it!" recalls Nick Rutgers. "He had an office at Johnson and Johnson with all his flags and mementos."

The General had retained an Italian tailor, presumably not a fan of Mussolini, to custom make his uniforms. "The results were impressive," his biographer, Lawrence Foster, observed. "He was slender, and had a ramrod military posture. There was no better-fitting military wardrobe in Washington."

The way Johnson outfitted himself with that gleaming silver star, and the way he swaggered around Washington and New York, one would have been led to believe he had spent the duration commanding troops along the Siegfried Line.

In fact, he had served just sixty-four days—little more than two months—as a brigadier general before resigning his commission, mainly because of claimed chronic stomach problems.

But this leader of industry and egoist referred to himself until his dying day—another quarter century—as "General Johnson," and required that those who worked for him and those who knew him address him as such. With General as his new title, he dropped the appendage Jr. from his name, feeling it wasn't befitting of someone of his stature.

As his nephew the sculptor Seward Johnson Jr. asserted decades later, "My uncle dealt in fear, but he also dealt in theatrics."

The same year that the General donned and doffed his army uniform, 1943, he also decommissioned the second Mrs. Johnson, Maggi, after thirteen years of another bad marriage—during which he had a number of affairs. The future third Mrs. Johnson was a glamorous, leggy, auburn-haired, very-married Manhattan nightclub dancer by the name of Evelyne Vernon, who was part of a then-famous dance team, The Vernons, with her husband, James "Jimmy" Lewis Bruff.

It was at the fashionable Manhattan nightclub La Martinique where the General fell for Evelyne, known as Evie (pronounced Eav-ee), where she was the gorgeous performer and dance instructor. Although the General was quite a dancer, he decided to become one of Evie's star pupils, the better to get close to her, literally and figuratively.

The gossip columnist Walter Winchell had become aware of the flirtation, but never published an item because he liked the Johnson & Johnson chief, who, as Winchell saw it, was now patriotically serving his country and deserved a break; Winchell had his enemies list, but the General wasn't on it.

Despite Winchell's protection, Maggi heard about her husband's growing involvement with *that* dancer.

"People would say to me, 'Maggi, where were you last weekend? We saw Bob dancing around New York with that redheaded girl,'" Foster quoted her as saying. "Finally, he did come home one weekend in the late spring of 1943, and I said, 'Bob, I don't think you're very happy. I think you're under a strain' . . . He went to his room . . . I cried my eyes out all night long . . . I drove him to the train . . . I was in shock."

Winchell, in his popular nationally syndicated column in the *New York Daily Mirror,* finally broke his self-imposed friendship embargo on the Johnson-Vernon relationship on June 20, 1943—with the surprise revelation that Maggi also had someone new in her life and wasn't quite in the kind of mourning she had described after the General gave her the heave-ho.

General Robert Johnson (heir to the Johnson & Johnson medical supplies firm) settled $1,000,000 on his wife, now at Lake Tahoe for the divorce. Her next groom, chums insist, will be Edward Eily [Winchell misspelled it as Ely], the Egyptian from the Stork Club Set . . . General Johnson has already selected his new bride . . . She is the lovely Evelyne Vernon, co-owner of La Martinque, the night club on 57th Street . . .

On July 23, 1943, *The New York Times,* via the Associated Press, reported that a day earlier Maggi Johnson had obtained a Reno divorce from the General on "grounds of extreme cruelty."

The news of Johnson's marriage to Evie Vernon came in Winchell's *Daily Mirror* on August 5, 1943, under the headline: "Dancer Weds Gen. Johnson at Salt Lake."

One of the Johnsons with whom Evie soon bonded was Edward Mead "Ted" Johnson IV. "She was an interesting character," he said fifteen years after her passing in 1996. "There was that showgirl kind of element to her. *But,* there was also a kind of remote, grande element as well."

Ted Johnson was especially knocked out by the bling in which Evie always bathed herself, even when she was just lolling around the house.

She had an unquenchable passion for diamonds and jewels, and the General constantly fed her ravenous appetite.

"The jewelry was a *big* thing," recalls Ted, still astounded decades later in his seventies at what Evie possessed. "The General made her among the five most important collectors of major rocks in the United States, if not in the world.

"She had a sixty carat, pear-shaped diamond ring. It was a *huge* thing that Cecil Beaton had gotten for her. There was a lady of noble lineage, a woman of some stature in Britain who needed the money, and she was an acquaintance of Beaton's and she said she wanted to sell the ring quietly, and Bob said 'yes,' and Beaton told her that Evie Johnson would buy it. You looked at that ring and it was *sumpin!*" (Evie had become close to Beaton when he had painted a portrait of her that was commissioned by the General.)

"She had what was like a breastplate, and it was kind of molten gold with sharp diamond tips sticking out of it like stalactites—it looked like some sort of mining thing, and she wore that at a cocktail party at Buckingham Palace, and the Prince of Wales said, 'Oh, that's very beautiful, may I show it to the Queen Mother?' Evie said 'yes,' and she took it off and he took it over to the queen.

"She had this one ring that was many, many diamonds and it kind of puffed up near the top of the hand and it went down to the knuckle—all that distance, into kind of a point and it moved. She always used to tell me, 'Dear, it's so nice on the back of a gentleman's shoulder.'"

Along with her glamorous, bejeweled show-business persona, Evie was a staunch Catholic. She introduced her non-churchgoing Episcopalian husband to a friend, a very famous Jesuit at Oxford, Father William Slattery, and the two bonded. With her prodding, they were granted a VIP audience with Pope Pius XII at the Vatican. As a parting gift the Holy Father presented the holy terror of Johnson & Johnson with a souvenir of their visit—an almost foot-high medal honoring the patron saint of travelers, St. Christopher, a routine religious remembrance he often handed out to visiting dignitaries. But the General took the gift as something very special and very personal.

Back in New Brunswick, he had the oversize medal replicated by a Johnson & Johnson mechanic—and had it cast in bronze, which was "heart-and-ulcers time" for the employee because the boss watched over the project like a hawk. He also had Evie arrange to have a priest from the New York Archdiocese bless it, and had the copies built into the grilles of every new model of his cars, five Cadillacs and a Chrysler, according to Foster.

"I have a childhood memory of the General coming to our family home in this quite incredible Cadillac that had a St. Christopher's medal cut into the custom grille that looked like a fricking battering ram," chuckles Eric Ryan, a grandson of the General's brother, Seward. "And I thought, 'Wow, what the hell is St. Christopher doing in the *front* of the car?'"

$ $ $

The General ran Johnson & Johnson with an iron hand, expanding its product line and writing the company "Credo" that outlined its responsibilities to the medical community, the consumer, and the Johnson & Johnson employees. He also started and funded with his fortune the Robert Wood Johnson Foundation, the biggest medical foundation in American history, devoted to "people living healthy and productive lives"—unlike a number of Johnson family members themselves.

And on September 24, 1944, he took the family owned, privately held Johnson & Johnson company public on the New York Stock Exchange with an initial public offering of $37.50 per share. A $3,750 investment for one hundred shares was worth a whopping $12 million by the end of the twentieth century.

By then, with splits, those hundred shares had ballooned to one hundred and twenty-five thousand shares, and none of those huge numbers included the many dividends over the more than fifty years when the stock was first purchased. The public aside, every Johnson dynasty member—past, present, and future—who had been holding stock became wealthy beyond anyone's imagination as the value soared in the open market.

To the General, Johnson & Johnson headquarters in New Brunswick was the U.S.S. *Caine,* and he was its Captain Philip Queeg. While there would never be a mutiny, the General's crew of executives feared him, and thought him as compulsive and obsessive and rigid as the crew of the fictional *Caine* felt about their own bizarre martinet of a leader. Like Queeg, who demanded that his ship be shipshape, the General required that Johnson & Johnson's offices be pristine—not a spot of dust anywhere—when he made his frequent military-like inspections.

"Whenever he came back to the office after an absence, everyone was ready for his inevitable inspection," recalled Lawrence Foster. "For weeks before, it was customary to apply paint and polish liberally to any area of the office or factory that might not pass his close scrutiny. His obsession with neatness and cleanliness was by now widely known, and feared. To him a smudge was tantamount to treason."

The movie character Queeg was known for demoting, even court-martialing, members of his crew for minor infractions. The General, with his take-no-prisoners management style, just went ahead and gave his executives and underlings their walking papers, like he did his wives.

"He fired whole staffs at one time," asserts his cousin and godson, Nick Rutgers, recalling him with both distaste and admiration, more than four decades after his death. "He fired a lot of people just because they didn't move fast enough."

The General's obsessions and iron-clad rules carried over to Johnson & Johnson's product line, which was a big positive for the consumer.

For instance, he had decided that the one product that was most intriguing to him, and the one he believed exemplified Johnson & Johnson in the public's mind, was Johnson's Baby Powder, even though the brand itself generated a minuscule amount of revenue compared to all other Johnson & Johnson products sold worldwide.

The General had "hovered over the advertising, package design, and marketing strategy like a doting parent," maintained Foster, who worked under him for a decade. "For years he had helped to nurture the growth and success of the brand, and he wasn't about to let anyone tinker with the product without first doing battle with him . . ."

As time passed, changes were made—advertising was tweaked, packaging underwent some modifications. But Johnson oversaw it all, even down to the minute sprinkle holes in the new plastic containers.

Johnson's Baby Powder was followed by other Johnson & Johnson products for babies' bodies—lotion, soap, oil, and advertised as, "Best for Baby—Best for You."

Another product in which the General took a special interest was the sanitary napkin called Modess—how it would be advertised and marketed. He also wanted it to be inexpensive so that untold millions of women around the world could use and afford it. Johnson & Johnson wasn't the first to market a menstrual napkin, but it sold the first American disposable, called Lister's Towels, in 1896, named after Joseph P. Lister, the British surgeon and father of bacteriology, who had founded antiseptic surgery.

Because Modess—a competitor to Kotex—took off so quickly, the General formed a separate entity, the Modess Corporation, subsequently aptly called the Personal Products Company. But he was never really happy with any of the Modess advertising, so he personally conceived a revolutionary new campaign after the Second World War.

He envisioned—he *demanded*—that the advertising for the very private product that men jokingly called "the rag," and many women bought surreptitiously, come out of the shadows, and highlight ultra-femininity and high fashion instead of the monthly period.

For the campaign, the supermodels of the time—the beautiful sisters Susie Parker and Dorian Leigh, for instance, wearing gowns by Dior and Valentino, and photographed by the likes of Evie's friend Cecil Beaton, were featured in the very successful "Modess . . . *because*" campaign.

"The brilliance of the 'Modess . . . *because*' copy"—essentially conceived by Johnson—"was that it enabled each woman who read it to fill in her own reasons for wanting to buy the product," stated Foster.

While the General was in charge of virtually everything at Johnson & Johnson, his sister, the gorgeous Evangeline, had been given his cold shoulder personally and corporately. But her life was something else. She was a novelist's dream.

PART III

ECCENTRIC
EVANGELINE

11

In August 2000, a curious item went up for sale on eBay, with a minimum bid of nine hundred thousand dollars. The seller was listed as charles6@aol.com, and his location was Western North Carolina, USA.

This auction is to announce a screenplay for sale. **Attention Producers**, Directors, management companies, investors, agents . . . **TRUE STORY ACTION DRAMA FOR SALE**. Potential to be the next big box office *Titanic* hit. **UNCONVENTIONAL LOVE STORY**. Older woman/younger man.

Charles6, the seller, was actually Charles Merrill, and the listing carried with it a snapshot of him. Taken two decades earlier in Palm Beach, he was a handsome fellow, with long, streaked blond hair, wearing dark Jim Jones–style aviator sunglasses, and with what appeared to be a feathered boa around his shoulders.

Merrill, an artist, a onetime professional tennis player, also a former foundry worker; furniture refinisher; soda jerk; factory operator; horse groom; cook; photographer; Tarot card reader; charming walker of rich, elderly women—and flamboyantly gay—was the third husband of Johnson & Johnson heiress Evangeline Brewster Johnson, the General and Seward Sr.'s sister.

Evangeline and Charles Merrill, who claimed to be a member of the Merrill-Lynch investment dynasty, had shocked Palm Beach society—and most if not all of the Johnson dynasty—by getting married on Monday, September 12, 1977, on the yacht *Mazurka,* captained by Seward Sr., who had officiated at the knot-tying.

"Until the death of love!" was Evangeline's exuberant champagne toast.

The General did not attend the odd ceremony. He and his sister had been feuding for years, mainly because he had cheated her out of company stock and equal company control.

In a photograph in the *Palm Beach Daily News* on September 15, 1977, announcing the Merrill-Johnson nuptials, Evangeline looked more like her groom's wealthy and matronly great-aunt, with an AARP membership card in her Chanel purse, than his new bride—not surprising since she was more than three decades his senior. At least.

Merrill's eBay auction for his screenplay pitch ran a decade after Evangeline's death at ninety-three on June 17, 1990. She had died from injuries resulting from a fall—a fatal accident eerily reminiscent of the manner in which her mother, Evangeline Armstrong Johnson Dennis, had died in a fall some seven decades earlier.

Wrote Merrill in his eBay listing:

> In a nutshell, this is a true story of "High Society" meeting "Deliverance." It is about us, me in 1980 (46) and my late wife Evangeline (80). We made a move from a sheltered and affluent lifestyle in Palm Beach Florida to the beautiful but primitive mountains of North Carolina. Through difficult times of adjustment and living in the backwoods, we discovered love of self and a deep abiding affection for each other.
>
> She loved me and I loved her, that is why we got married. Our age difference was another cause for raised eyebrows. We discovered that our love for each other was beyond gender and age. We really didn't care about what others thought, we were happy and that is all that mattered. A year after Evangeline passed away, I was again fortunate to have found love with another companion, this time with someone of the same gender.

The pièce de résistance of Merrill's bizarre auction—which came as a shock years later to Evangeline's few survivors, especially one of her two octogenarian daughters, who were unaware of it—was his "suggested cast."

He saw either Marisa Berenson, Elizabeth Taylor, or Vanessa Redgrave playing the role of Evangeline Johnson, and the part of Merrill himself going to either Matthew McConaughey, Brad Pitt, or Jude Law.

From all accounts there were no buyers.

About a year after Merrill's unsuccessful auction, the 9/11 terrorist attack happened. To show his anger, he burned a rare antique copy of the Koran, valued at sixty thousand dollars, that had been bequeathed to him by Evangeline. He had also edited a copy of the Holy Bible with a black marker and cut out portions with a scissors as part of his protest.

"The purpose of editing and burning Abrahamic Holy Books is to eliminate homophobic hate," he declared at the time.

The final days for Evangeline Johnson Stokowski Zalstem-Zalessky Merrill, in rural North Carolina under the spell of her much younger and gay third husband, had become a virtual living hell. She was forced to live with chaos and squalor, according to her daughter, Sadja Greenwood, whose father was her mother's first husband—the late maestro, actor, and notorious womanizer Leopold Stokowski.

"It was sad," reveals Greenwood, "and I don't know why my mother went for it, but I think it was to please Charles."

Evangeline was a collector of priceless Kandinskys, Klees, and Mirós, and other iconic abstract artists—"but in the 1980s," her daughter sadly states, "things started falling apart for her."

Because Evangeline was aging, Sadja, a physician, flew east a few times every year from her home in Northern California to check up on her mother—and what she began discovering at what Evangeline and Charles had named the World's Edge Apple Organic Farm was shocking.

"There were animals, dogs and cats, everywhere, and they weren't housebroken," Sadja sadly recalls. "Charles had planted an organic apple orchard, but he didn't take care of the trees. He had a flock of chickens that multiplied, but they were not contained, and they were roosting everywhere. He had a herd of horses that were kind of wild and were multiplying out in the field. I would come and visit and try to clean up. God, it was just *so* painful."

Life at the farm was heiress Evangeline Johnson's own version of life at Grey Gardens, a decrepit mansion in East Hampton, New York, where Edith "Big Edie" Beale and her daughter, Edith "Little Edie" Beale, the aunt and first cousin of Jacqueline Kennedy Onassis, lived in squalor. The difference between the oddball Beales and the eccentric Johnson heiress was that the Beales were broke while Evangeline had millions, which made her lifestyle in redneck hell seem even more off the wall.

But Merrill was in control—her Svengali—and she was too old to protest.

The fall that caused Evangeline's death was attributable to the rocky, rough, and uneven land on the farm. Frail at ninety-three, though "very health-oriented" otherwise, asserts her daughter, she had apparently been out walking, possibly alone, with her little white dog when the last surviving child of the company cofounder Robert Wood Johnson tripped on the leash, fell to the ground, suffered serious injury, and died a few months later at the Bryan Health Care Center in Hendersonville.

Knowing her time was near, Evangeline had actually written an other-worldly missive to members of her family and friends "to be sent to you after my so-called death. I believe that there is no death, only eternal forms of Universal energies which are unending."

She signed it, "Love always, Evangeline."

After Evangeline's death, Charles Merrill sold the farm and moved to Palm Springs, California, and through a friend began meeting other rich, elderly women. "He became *very* friendly with a woman who was part of the Standard Oil Rockefellers who was in her eighties. I think she was hot for him," says the friend, Michael Grace, a writer. Merrill also regaled Grace with bizarre stories about his life with the Johnson & Johnson heiress, a marriage that lasted thirteen years.

"He said the first night that they went to bed together they fucked both thinking about her second husband, the Russian prince," Grace says.

Charles Merrill died in 2010, at the age of seventy-five.

None of Evangeline's strange life with Merrill and others ever came as a surprise to her daughter, who had spent a lifetime distancing herself from her mother *and* the Johnson dynasty and its dramas. A retired general practitioner in her eighties in 2011, Sadja's surname Greenwood was, in fact, an alias.

"Greenwood is a name I took," she says, laughing, and sounding and looking much younger than her years. "There is no Mr. Greenwood. I really enjoy saying that—*There Is No Mr. Greenwood.*"

A Radcliffe graduate, she had dropped her maiden name of Stokowski when she married and later divorced another student doctor. Sadja decided to rename herself. "For a year I thought about what name I wanted. I liked hiking in the woods, so Greenwood just appealed to me."

$ $ $

Evangeline Brewster Johnson was not your average stay-at-home soccer mom. Mostly, the heiress traveled the world with her first two husbands, Stokowski and then the Russian prince, while Sadja and her sister, Lubya, were sent away to boarding schools, six or seven of them.

Not surprisingly, mother and daughters had an odd sort of relationship, which some in the twenty-first century might consider extreme, if not possibly abusive, especially in conservative family values circles: When the girls were just toddlers, Evangeline began teaching them about sex.

"Every year beginning when we were two or three she would bring us into the bathroom and open a certain drawer and there were diaphragms and contraceptive jellies, and she would explain the whole thing about how to take care of yourself," recalls Greenwood. "It was way before I had any idea that this would be a taboo subject to be embarrassed about. I can remember saying when I was five, 'I think, Mom, I know all about this sex stuff.'"

Beyond the toddler sex education, Evangeline promoted as early as the 1920s and '30s what were then illegal abortions, and had boasted to her young daughters about her adventures in the clandestine abortion underground.

Sadja and Evangeline had a difficult relationship.

She says her mother's husbands, including her biological father, Stokowski, were never involved as parents. At the same time, Evangeline never played the role of the loving, doting grandmother to Sadja's two sons from her marriage. Regarding parenthood, she was much like her brother, Robert, the General, who had abandoned his young son, Bobby.

And Sadja never considered herself a part of the Johnson dynasty, which she was by blood. She thought little of, and about, her mother's heritage, past and present, and wanted no part of the ongoing dynastic saga.

"I checked out of that whole fancy Johnson life," she declares. "I didn't have anything to do with it."

At one point when she was working for Planned Parenthood she had applied for a grant from the Robert Wood Johnson Foundation, founded by her uncle, the General, and considered the nation's largest philanthropy devoted exclusively to the health and health care of all Americans, "but it didn't come through," she says, laughing about the irony of it all.

As her stepsister Sonya, a daughter from Stokowski's first marriage, asserts, "There seemed to be very bad relationships between all the Johnsons. My son, a psychologist, calls them a dysfunctional family. I was rather horrified by them. Those people hurt themselves so much."

There was little or no contact among Sadja, the General, and Seward, mainly because the General had cheated her mother in the family business.

Seward's son, Seward Johnson Jr., the sculptor, who, when he was in his late teens, had somewhat gotten to know Evangeline, then in her early fifties, says he became aware that she had been given "preferred stock by her father, and that Uncle Bob [the General] converted that stock to common stock [substantially reducing its value], and Evangeline felt that he really screwed her blue. In a way, Evangeline did have a very strong business mind, but it was very hard to say because her mind was also very dramatic. I remember Evangeline called her brother [the General] 'Te-De-Lo,' because it's a diminutive sounding name, and she was subtly putting him down."

Lawrence Foster once heard the General remark, "If Evangeline had been a man she would have been the one to run the company." Foster found it to be "an amusing compliment that Johnson probably did not believe—just like the time he said to her, 'Babe,'—a nickname she resented—'if you had not been my sister, you are the one woman I would have married.' Evangeline said she knew better."

12

As a young woman, Evangeline Brewster Johnson's best friend, traveling companion, roommate, (and probable lover) was Belle Baruch, the six-foot-two, masculine-looking, Junoesque daughter of multimillionaire speculator, financier, and philanthropist Bernard Baruch, known as the "Lone Wolf of Wall Street," because he had made his untold millions by buying and selling stock without being affiliated with a major firm. Overnight, he became a financial legend, a Jew who became the brunt of attacks by rabid anti-Semites such as Henry Ford.

Evangeline and Belle had much in common. Both were liberal political activists and heiresses—when Belle turned twenty-one in the first year of the Roaring Twenties her father, who she idolized and emulated in many ways, gave her a million dollars to do with as she pleased.

Belle sometimes dressed in tailored men's three-piece suits, replete with tie and dress shirt, and wore her hair cropped short. She "could outride, out-shoot, outhunt, and outsail most of the young men of her elite social circle . . . Unapologetic for her athleticism and interests in traditionally masculine pursuits, Belle towered above male and female counterparts in height and daring," according to her biographer, Mary E. Miller.

Looks-wise, Evangeline and Belle made an odd couple.

The Johnson girl was pretty, the Baruch girl was not, and if she resembled anyone in familiar twentieth-century pop culture, it was Herbert Buckingham

Khaury, better known as Tiny Tim, an oddball character who sang "Tip Toe Through the Tulips" in a falsetto voice and was often a guest on TV talk shows. Like Tiny Tim, Belle was gawky, with large feet and a pronounced nose.

Evangeline, who was two years older, had met Belle in the social whirl of debutante New York when they were in their late teens—the beginning of the Roaring Twenties—and there was an immediate physical attraction, at least on Belle's part.

As Mary Miller asserts, "Belle was in love with Evangeline."

And there was a lot about Evangeline to love.

She was tall, athletic—she was an early feminist who wore pants when a skirt was called for—sexy-looking with bedroom eyes; had a throaty, raucous voice; was a drama queen; was very smart, very rich, very rebellious; and was an activist back in the day, always ready for action and excitement.

For instance, a month before the armistice ending the Great War in 1918, an explosion ripped through a munitions depot located on Raritan Bay, not far from Johnson & Johnson's New Brunswick headquarters. It was a disaster of major proportions, many were maimed and killed. Evangeline, then twenty-one, an officer in New York City's Red Cross Motor Corps—known as the "heiress corps" because so many of the young women members were from wealthy and prominent families—drove to the dangerous and toxic scene. Even though there were still live bombs and ammunition among the flames, she remained there for several days risking her life transporting the victims and assisting doctors with Johnson & Johnson first-aid products.

Years later, Evangeline, looking back and analyzing that sort of activity, came to the conclusion that she had a "Jeanne D'Arc complex."

Her activism, though, didn't always have some great social purpose. Often zany, it still made a point.

Furious that the conservative powers in ritzy Palm Beach, where she had first visited when she was seventeen, would not permit women to wear the more revealing bathing suits that were coming into vogue in the second decade of the twentieth century, the Johnson & Johnson heiress decided to take matters into her own hands.

She donned her leather helmet and goggles, got into her hand-cranked biplane powered by a single Rolls-Royce engine—she was one of those early aviatrixes like Amelia Earhart; they both were born the same year a few months apart—and bombed the wealthy town's beaches with incendiary protest leaflets.

Years later, when she was seventy-six, she told the *Palm Beach Daily News*: "It made me so mad to have to wear stockings with my bathing costume. So, I wrote out some articles and flew in my plane, dropping the handbills on the beach, arguing against stockings. And what do you think the outcome was? The story went around that a stocking manufacturer was advertising stockings."

Belle was with her that day and congratulated her on her zany stunt. "Evangeline and Belle were angry about that [dress code]," says Mary Miller, who notes that Belle, too, would take up flying, emulating her bosom buddy, whom she adored.

While Evangeline's intimate relationships with the likes of Belle Baruch and other women were kept secret in an age when such things were not publicly revealed, many decades later another Band-Aid heiress from the Johnson dynasty—Woody Johnson's daughter, Casey—would have very public affairs with women—scandalizing her family.

Evangeline was Belle's frequent houseguest at Hobcaw Barony, a spectacular retreat on the South Carolina coast that Bernard Baruch had purchased in 1905 and where he entertained presidents and potentates. At twenty, Evangeline was photographed at Hobcaw, skeet shooting with a long-barrel rifle like a military marksman from the front yard of the estate's boat house called the Old Relick as Belle, coming into her own as a lesbian, lovingly looked on.

In the guest book at Hobcaw, Evangeline called the place "the very altar of friendship." And Belle once poetically wrote, "I am a little Hobcaw flower; growing wilder by the hour; nobody can cultivate me. Gee! I'm wild!"

The two young women were inseparable.

The headline in the November 13, 1923, *New Brunswick Daily Home News* read: "Miss Evangeline Johnson Largely Instrumental in Wilson's Great Radio Talk."

Because Evangeline was from the Johnson & Johnson family, and New Brunswick was the company's hometown, she made it in the headline, but it wasn't just Evangeline who convinced President Woodrow Wilson to deliver a highly promoted Armistice Eve message to hundreds of thousands of American radio listeners. Evangeline and Belle had put their heads together and had come up with the idea and made it fly. The two had volunteered to serve in the Woman's Pro-League Council, an organization that supported the League of Nations, of which Wilson was a major mover. Evangeline chaired the speakers' bureau, and Belle headed the council's public relations.

The two had written to the president asking him to deliver the address, but he declined at first. "Miss Johnson wrote him an urgent argument to reconsider," the *Home News* reported. "Later, Miss Johnson and Miss Baruch went to Washington, visited Mr. and Mrs. Wilson, and at that interview secured his consent to the proposition."

The radio address, on November 10, 1923, was listened to by the largest audience Wilson had ever had. The twenty-eighth president, who had served two terms, had formerly been governor of New Jersey, so he had ties to one of the state's largest corporations, Johnson & Johnson, and was close to Baruch, who was an advisor to him, so the girls had good White House connections, and a good shot at winning his agreement.

By the time of Wilson's ten-minute radio message, Evangeline and Belle had been living together for several years, sharing an opulent apartment in the exclusive, white-glove building at 515 Park Avenue. "The Baruchs were appalled," opines Mary Miller, "because young women didn't move out on their own in those days unless they were in the care of some family member, so it was rather unusual."

Evangeline and Belle were together at a time when New York was jumping with Prohibition-era nightclubs, speakeasies, and clandestine clubs for lesbians and homosexuals in Greenwich Village, which the two heiresses often explored with Belle sporting one of her butch outfits in order to fit in, and with the very femme Evangeline as her arm candy.

Beyond Belle, another very close friend and traveling companion of Evangeline's was the New York society heiress and out-of-the-closet lesbian Alice De Lamar, who had inherited ten million dollars at the age of eighteen with the death of her Dutch immigrant father, Captain Joseph De Lamar, the goldmine, copper mogul, and art connoisseur who had a spectacular Beaux-Arts mansion at Thirty-Seventh and Madison.

Evangeline had met Alice at the Miss Spence school, and the two were later volunteers together at the Red Cross where, like Evangeline, Alice was not only an ambulance driver but also a grease monkey.

Evangeline's chum was once described by a friend as "a queer girl with lots of character, but all angles and resentments and revolts."

In the spring of 1920, Evangeline, then residing at 270 Park Avenue, and Alice, who was two years older and lived near Evangeline on Park, had vacationed in Europe together, and while there Evangeline surprised everyone in the Johnson family—and Belle Baruch in particular—by claiming in a cablegram home to her brother, Robert, that shortly after arriving in London she had fallen in love and had become engaged to an Englishman by the name of Douglas Elliott Craik, who supposedly had served as an officer of the Royal Garrison Artillery during the war. She gave no other details.

On June 18, 1920, a three-paragraph engagement announcement appeared in *The New York Times.* "Robert Wood Johnson of New Brunswick, N.J. made the announcement. His sister is spending the summer in Europe with Miss Alice A. De Lamar," the notice said.

But almost a month to the day later, on July 17, 1920, the *New York Tribune* reported that the engagement of Evangeline to Craik "has been broken." Once again, no other details were given.

Evangeline, who was known as a prankster, may have fooled her brother for laughs by saying she was getting married, and in the process duped two of New York's most prestigious newspapers. By planting the engagement notice, Evangeline also was covering up her relationship with De Lamar, and her sexual preference at the time. Gossip columns would carry other unconfirmed engagement items involving Evangeline on and off until she actually did get married for the first time in 1926 to Leopold Stokowski, who happened to be a close friend of De Lamar's.

Evangeline's daughter, Sadja Greenwood, says her mother had mentioned her friendships with Belle and Alice, though she had no knowledge of them being intimate. "But it doesn't shock me at all. My mother was very tolerant of any kind of sexuality. I do know that she had a lot of gay male friends, and, of course, she married a gay guy, so she was *very* tolerant."

$ $ $

In 1925, a year after President Wilson died, Evangeline and Belle Baruch accompanied their friend, the widowed first lady, Edith Bolling Galt Wilson, the president's second wife, who was an attractive and vibrant woman in her early fifties, on a five-month summer vacation in Europe. It was Mrs. Wilson's first European trip since the president's death. He had suffered a stroke in 1919, and it was later learned that she had taken charge of a number of White House matters and was dubbed by the press "the Secret President" and "the first female president of the United States" until his death.

They had left in May aboard the ocean liner *Majestic,* arriving in France, and then traveling through Normandy to Paris, and on to Venice, Scotland, and Geneva, and returning to New York and Washington in October.

During the European holiday, Evangeline had developed an intimate bond with Edith Wilson, and they became confidantes, if not more. Edith was Evangeline's kind of woman because the first lady had what a *New York Times* writer once called "formidable determination," an attribute they both possessed and understood.

Evangeline also liked Edith because she was independent and kind of a rebel, especially for a first lady. There had been much juicy gossip in the nation's capital about Edith and Wilson, with innuendoes that they had had an affair—she was thirteen years the president's junior—and there was talk that he was cheating with her on his first wife, Ellen Wilson.

One salacious story had it that Edith had fallen out of bed when the president proposed to her, indicating that they had been sleeping together. There even had been a nasty rumor that Wilson and Edith, who were married a week before Christmas in 1915, had murdered the first Mrs. Wilson. And in the midst of all that sturm und drang *The Washington Post* was left with egg on its editorial face because of a Freudian typographical error that said the president had spent an evening "entering" Edith, instead of "entertaining" Edith.

That edition became a collector's item.

In her memoir, Mrs. Wilson wrote adoringly—almost romantically—of her first meeting with Evangeline and Belle:

> I shall always recall them as they looked that night. They were both over six
> feet tall, and were dressed in stunning velvet evening gowns of the latest

Parisian stamp. Long earrings matched the costumes. In all they were two stunning-looking creatures as I ever saw.

$ $ $

A couple of months after her return from Europe, Evangeline Brewster Johnson attended a dinner party in Manhattan and met a celebrity she had idolized from a distance—the larger-than-life maestro of the Philadelphia Orchestra, Leopold Stokowski, a brilliant musician, egotistic showman, and legendary Don Juan. She was twenty-seven, a rich and single rebel, he was forty-four, famous but not wealthy, divorced several years earlier after a decade of marriage to an American concert pianist—stage name Olga Samaroff, real name Lucy Mary Agnes Hickenlooper of Texas—with whom he had a daughter, Sonya.

When Stokowski met Evangeline, it was rumored that he had just jilted his latest lover, a nineteen-year-old Philadelphia debutante.

Still, Evangeline was open for anything.

It was love at first sight. Soon the press corps was chasing the two lovebirds, paparazzi style, staking them out, chasing them down, and getting lots of no comments. The couple secretly decided to get married, and Evangeline let her family in on the news a few days before the well-camouflaged wedding.

One of her brothers—she never identified whether it was Robert or Seward—demanded to know, "Who is he?"

Replied Evangeline, "He's a conductor."

Contemptuously, her brother declared, "In this family, one *doesn't* marry conductors."

Rolling her eyes, she responded, "Darling, not a *streetcar* conductor!"

On Saturday, January 9, 1926, one of the Philadelphia broadsheets blared: "STOKOWSKI TO MARRY N.Y. GIRL, IS REPORT . . . Marriage of Philadelphia Conductor and Miss E.B. Johnson Expected Monday . . . SHE IS LEAGUE FIGHT LEADER."

The Johnson heiress was described as "a strikingly beautiful and popular member of the younger social circles in New York and Newport . . . an enthusiastic advocate of the League of Nations . . . hostess to Mrs. Woodrow Wilson . . . and an intimate friend of Belle Baruch . . ."

Belle, hopelessly in love with Evangeline, was furious and at wits' end when told by "my golden girl," as she called Evangeline, that she was planning to quickly tie the knot with Stokowski.

"Nothing would do for Evangeline but for Belle to share her ecstasy and participate in the plans for the wedding," as Belle's biographer, Mary Miller, noted. "Belle joined in the laughter, but a cold dread was building within her as she struggled to share Evangeline's happiness. She tried to articulate her feelings but did not fully understand them herself."

A week before the wedding, Evangeline wrote a letter to her confidante, the former first lady, Edith Wilson, who was aware of the very close relationship between Evangeline and Belle, and informed her of how unsettled she felt about Belle's despair.

Evangeline said:

> Belle I hope and pray will become reconciled to the idea, though in what possible way she is "losing me" is impossible for me to understand. But I want to have her happy too for her love and devotionate [sic] friendship are among the most precious things in life.

Her words seemed disingenuous.

Miller says her "personal opinion" was that the very sophisticated Evangeline completely understood why Belle was upset. "Evangeline was a lot more savvy than what she wrote in that letter. She knew very well what was going on."

Heartbroken, Belle "reluctantly" was one of the guests at the top-secret marriage of the woman she loved to a man she hardly knew other than by professional reputation.

The ceremony took place at 4:30 in the afternoon on Monday, January, 12, 1926. The groom's secretary, Mary McGinty, prepared a press release stating that New York Supreme Court Justice R. P. Leydon had officiated, that Evangeline wore a wine-colored velvet dress, and that the ceremony was performed against a background of gold.

The wedding ring the groom gave his bride was made from a gold nugget given to him by Evangeline's friends, President and Mrs. Wilson. To keep the secrecy, it wasn't until ninety minutes after the knot was tied that the marriage license was made public. Among the dozen or so guests were Evangeline's brothers, Robert and Seward, and a devastated "Miss Belle Baruch." Wrote her biographer:

> Mourning Evangeline's marriage, Belle came to the painful realization of why no man had ever lingered in her heart. Her feelings for Evangeline far exceeded those of friendship. With agonizing insight, Belle recognized that she loved Evangeline and would prefer the affection and intimacy of other women to that of men . . . homosexuality for her, she decided, was normal . . .

After the wedding, Evangeline and Belle would visit together a few times, but their close relationship was finished. They each got on with their lives.

Belle died at sixty-five in 1964, a year before her father's passing at ninety-four, and a quarter century before her beloved Evangeline's death.

Evangeline and Stoki, as he was called, would have an open marriage within the bounds of propriety because he had a public reputation to uphold. But he'd have a number of bedmates, and then a final headline-making affair with one of the world's most glamorous movie stars and seductresses, Greta Garbo, that would result in Evangeline's first divorce.

One day Evangeline's daughter, Sadja's sister, Lubya came home from school and asked her mother the embarrassing and hurtful question, "Who is Greta Garbo? Everybody at school says Daddy is having a romance with Greta Garbo."

That was the last straw for Evangeline.

She immediately confronted Stoki and laid down the law, telling him, "Look, the children are going into adolescence and, in order to make a satisfactory heterosexual adjustment in the future, they've got to have, for at least a few years, a normal home life, a normal sort of family life."

In early November 1937, a headline in the *New York Daily Mirror* declared: "Reno Unites Johnson Kin."

In what seemingly could only have happened in the Johnson dynasty, where marriages and divorces came and went like express trains, both a Johnson wife, Mrs. Ruth Dill Johnson, the first of Seward Sr.'s three, and Evangeline, Seward's sister, were both in Nevada at the same time awaiting residency requirements for their respective divorces. Evangeline, who was ensconced at the Boulder City Hotel near Las Vegas, went horseback riding with her sister-in-law, and then moved to a dude ranch. A longtime female friend of Stoki's who was also in town to divorce her husband ran into Evangeline, who told her that she and Stoki "were ready to get a divorce anyway," the Garbo romance notwithstanding.

On December 1, 1937, Evangeline sued for divorce in Las Vegas, charging "extreme mental cruelty," a boilerplate reason. Even so, Stoki contested the charge, but not the divorce. "STOKOWSKI HITS CHARGES, Conductor Denies Wife's Divorce Accusation of Cruelty," the *New York Times* headline read. Besides demanding equal joint custody of their children, he declared, "I could not be cruel to anyone, so I certainly could not be cruel to my children or their mother. I deeply resent this untrue accusation."

The uncontested divorce was granted on December 2, 1937.

His third wife was the beautiful, eccentric, neurotic, creative society girl Gloria Vanderbilt, known as the "poor little rich girl" and the "million-dollar baby," who on her twenty-first birthday had inherited five million dollars. Her sixty-three-year-old groom, the press reported, was "old enough to be her grandfather."

On January 27, 1938, in a quickie marriage ceremony in Phoenix, Arizona, Evangeline Johnson took on the title of Princess Evangeline Zalstem-Zalessky, wife of Prince Alexis Zalstem-Zalessky, a Russian of dubious royal lineage, whom she had met in New York and Palm Beach, where he was better known in certain circles as basically a charming gigolo, good-looking, "strong and stocky," as her daughter, Sadja Greenwood, described him decades later.

"Ex-Wife of Conductor Is Bride of Russian Prince in West," the *New York Times* headline said. The story never mentioned that Evangeline was of the Johnson dynasty, only that she was "a member of a New Brunswick, N.J. family," her way of distancing herself from her roots. If the reading public didn't know better, she could have been a plumber's daughter from Hoboken.

With the marriage, Evangeline became the first and last member of the Johnson dynasty to ever become a member of Eastern European "royalty."

But most family members, like Nick Rutgers, believed Zalessky's title was phony. "He wasn't a prince," he declares. "He was a good Russian, but *not* a prince. He either gave himself the title, or Evangeline paid for it."

It infuriated members of the Johnson family that she insisted on calling herself a princess and being addressed as such. They laughed and made fun of her, especially her brothers, Robert and Seward.

Robert had once intoned, "Damned if I can understand why that woman insists on calling herself a princess, she's no more princess than the man in the moon." Her touché response was, "Well, I guess it's the same reason you call yourself a general."

In the early 1960s, Evangeline and her prince were gallivanting in Europe and had been in Zurich visiting the Bircher-Benner Clinic, a homeopathic health spa that espoused the healing power of raw fruits and vegetables and had developed Bircher Muesli. They were rushing to catch a train in the Zurich station en route to their next destination, when Zalessky, known to have aortic stenosis, suffered a fatal heart attack, and died on the spot.

Sometime in 1967, the no-longer-grieving widow Princess Evangeline Brewster Johnson Stokowski Zalstem-Zalessky was having her hair done in a Palm Beach salon by a young, good-looking gay stylist who looked half her age, and almost was. He was Charles Merrill, who became her third husband, the one with a penchant for auctioning off interesting items on eBay.

PART IV

SEWARD'S FOLLY

13

While Evangeline Johnson Stokowski Zalstem-Zalessky Merrill's life was often passionate and uninhibited, that of her brother, J. Seward Johnson, was unrestrained, narcissistic, and, at times, if accusations are to be believed, criminally immoral.

His namesake was the future well-known and often controversial sculptor J. Seward Johnson Jr., the only son of what would be a tumultuous union between J. Seward, known as Seward Sr., and the first of his three wives, attractive, titian-haired, blue-eyed Ruth Dill Johnson. She was twenty-one when twenty-nine-year-old Seward, whom she called Johnny, swept her off her feet. During their brief courtship, he aggressively pursued her and deluged her with expensive gifts—a gold Cartier cigarette case with diamonds that spelled out her initials was a typical trinket.

They were wed in true royal style in St. James Church in London on July 14, 1924. There followed whirlwind tours of the luxury capitals of Europe. Johnny treated Ruth like a princess, since he thought of the Johnson dynasty back home in provincial New Jersey as nothing less than American royalty.

Ruth, too, came from a prominent and wealthy old-line family, hers from Bermuda, where they had come to live beginning in 1620, the same year the Pilgrims, who had landed on Plymouth Rock, signed the Mayflower Compact. Bermuda was still part of the sprawling British Empire where the sun never set, and Ruth's father, Lt. Col. Thomas Melville Dill—descended from sea captains—had served as the commanding officer of the Bermuda Militia Artillery. He also was one of Bermuda's leading political figures, serving almost two decades as attorney general, and was considered quite controversial, particularly when he proposed legislation to limit Bermuda immigration, igniting death threats against the Dills because some families had to be split apart.

Ruth was named after her mother, Ruth Rapalje Neilson Dill, an American whose lineage went back to the last Dutch governor of New York, Peter Stuyvesant. But Ruth grew up in middle-class circumstances in the New Jersey industrial town of Perth Amboy—perched on the Raritan River, and practically in the shadow of the Johnson & Johnson complex in nearby New Brunswick.

Ruth Dill Johnson was the oldest of the Dill brood, followed by three brothers, Tom; Laurence, who was said to be gay; and Bayard; and two sisters, Francis, called Fan, and Diana, the youngest, born the year before Ruth married into the Johnson dynasty. Diana was not planned, as her mother was in her early forties and her father nearing fifty, she later wrote in a memoir. He was an irritable, domineering man who sported a monocle, wore a white wig, and doled out punishment with a strap to his children who, much like the Johnsons, were raised by a succession of nannies.

Unlike the Johnsons, though, the Dills, despite their wealth and power, were a family in which money "was mentioned infrequently as it was considered vulgar to dwell on the subject," as Diana later stated. When it came to money, however, nothing was too vulgar for a number of the avaricious Johnsons.

With his marriage to Ruth, Seward had become close to the Dills, and enjoyed their company. It was as if he had finally found a family of his own since, like his sister, Evangeline, and brother, Robert, he had been left in the care of others after their Johnson & Johnson cofounder father died, and their mother went off with a new man.

Ruth's first pregnancy ended in a stillbirth, the result of physical problems developed when she sailed in a storm on her husband's yacht. Her second pregnancy resulted in a beautiful daughter, born in 1926, who they named Mary Lea—the first Baby Powder can baby face, who later became one of the most troubled, vitriolic, and scandalous of Seward's brood.

That was the same year the family moved into Merriewold, the immense and spectacularly ostentatious three-story Elizabethan-Norman mansion Seward had built as a wedding present for his bride at 433 River Road, in Highland Park, New Jersey, the same workingman's town where his brother, Robert, the General, had been mayor.

The Castle, as it became known to locals, was built by Seward at the enormous pre–Great Depression cost of three hundred and fifty thousand dollars, and was sited on a private, wooded bluff where the elaborate grounds sloped down to the Raritan River, in virtual eyesight of the Johnson & Johnson plant. The spectacular land had been a wedding gift to the newly-weds from the groom's brother, the General.

Seward had then commissioned the noted Philadelphia architect Thomas Harlan Ellett to design the palatial home, for which Ellett won the New York Architectural League's silver medal. But the Johnson mansion would have a dark future that included divorce, burglaries, a suspected attempted kidnapping, and a gruesome murder. But all of that was in the future.

The construction of Merriewold and its mindboggling cost had caught the fancy of the late Roaring Twenties New York press. As Lindesay Parrott, a correspondent for the *Evening Post,* observed:

> The novel conceit of importing, all the way from England, enough slate to build a roof today has flowered into a house on the banks of the Raritan. Which is simply a more elaborate way of saying that when J. S. Johnson of Johnson & Johnson sets out to build a new home and wants English stone to crown his rooftop, he gets it—about 500 tons of it.

Seward had decided to import the slate from England on the advice of his architect because "there's nothing similar in this country," and he boasted that the particular slate covering the roof, coming from England's Cotswold District, was used on "many of the Oxford colleges." While it didn't make for a better roof, he acknowledged, "It just seemed more suitable to the house," and it was better for bragging rights.

The unique roof, though, didn't compare to the rest of Merriewold, which seemed to go on forever. There were twenty-five rooms, including six bedrooms, a ballroom, eleven fireplaces, a pair of hidden staircases, and turrets with iron steps and stained-glass windows. Many of the rooms were paneled in English oak, the floors covered in Italian marble. The 150 windows were of leaded glass. There was a guesthouse and chauffeur's quarters, a cottage for the help, and a garage for more than two dozen cars; there were stables for the thoroughbreds, and a portion of the beautiful and expensively landscaped seventeen acres included an airfield for the private planes of the Johnsons and their wealthy guests.

There were a number of oddities about the mansion, too.

For instance, over the breakfast room fireplace were Seward, Ruth, and firstborn Mary Lea's zodiac signs—Leo, Libra, and Cancer, with the crab mark being repeated at the gable. Seward also had a boat called *Zodiac*, the one on which Ruth had sailed in the rough seas that resulted in the loss of her first child during pregnancy.

The gothic ambiance of Merriewold was frightening to the Johnson children, especially to Seward Jr., the sensitive and easily upset namesake who, like his sister, Mary Lea, would have a troubled future.

"I used to be frightened as a child there, and I used to kiss my mother good night carrying a loaded twenty-two rifle when I was nine or ten," he recalled at eighty-one in 2011.

There were a number of secret passages, including what was described as an escape tunnel three football fields long that led from Seward Sr.'s personal, fully equipped barber shop in the basement to the guard booth and the garage. In another part of the castle was a circular staircase, a replica of one in Philadelphia's old City Hall. Above a balcony a lobster was carved in stone, and in front of the home were sculpted whale heads because of Seward and Ruth's love of the sea.

Oddly, dead whales would play a role in Seward Jr.'s troubled and bizarre first marriage. But again all of that lay in the future.

Behind Merriewold's library a hidden staircase went up to Seward's dressing room.

"I used to hide there and listen to people talking in the library," recollects Seward Jr.

To get to the well-stocked liquor and wine—it being Prohibition—one had to have a key to open a heavy-duty Yale lock, and know the secret of how to swing the hidden hinges of a routine-looking bookcase, holding a set of

Encyclopedia Brittanica. Inside was a full-fledged barroom that even federal Prohibition agent Elliot Ness and his crack squad of "Untouchables" would have had a difficult time discovering.

$ $ $

Everyone who visited Merriewold—tycoons, politicians, celebrities—was astounded by the mansion's grandeur.

Some years later a budding young actor with the newly branded stage name of Kirk Douglas saw the estate for the first time with his bride and first wife, Diana Dill, Ruth's baby sister. He couldn't believe his eyes. For a poor Jewish boy from the New York tenements—real name Issur Danielovitch, son of an illiterate immigrant Russian ragpicker and junkman—Merriewold was something of a fantasy place out of a storybook.

Douglas had met the very pretty Diana Dill when the two, in their twenties, were acting students at the Academy of Dramatic Arts in New York just before the start of World War II. Because of her sweet nature—Diana sympathized with Kirk and let him cry on her shoulder when their teacher criticized his acting abilities—he glibly called her "Miss Everything Is Lovely Dill."

She, too, would become an actress and a model; during the war she made the cover of a special spring issue of *Life* magazine on which she was photographed in black-and-white wearing a checked blouse and straw hat and holding a parasol.

For the Jewish Douglas, she was the ultimate shiksa, from Bermudan royalty, yet. They were married on November 2, 1943, the nondenominational service officiated by a navy chaplain in New Orleans, where Ensign Douglas was stationed at the time.

Because of a serious case of amoebic dysentery, he received an early discharge in June 1944. By then Diana was pregnant, and it was arranged that they would stay for a time at her sister Ruth's home, which the bride told the groom was just a place in the New Jersey countryside. Kirk, a tenement boy who knew nothing about the Johnsons, let alone country places, figured it was a little cottage with a white picket fence.

As they were driving down a road bordered not by white picket, but rather a high stone wall that seemed to stretch on for miles, he asked her when they'd finally reach Ruth's house.

"This," Diana told him, "is the beginning of my sister's place."

Kirk thought she was joking until they arrived at Merriewold's main entrance with gatehouses on either side of an imposing stone archway. As they rounded a curve he spotted a house that he thought was "just perfect," but Diana explained that it was only the gardener's cottage, that the Douglases would be staying in the main house.

As Kirk recalled years later in *The Ragman's Son,* his memoir, "In front of us was a gigantic, sprawling English castle with turrets and a slate roof. I was dumbfounded."

Diana told him they would be residing in the west wing, which was up a circular stone staircase, and down a hallway lined with art and suits of armor, which finally ended in their luxurious suite of rooms.

Using Merriewold as a temporary home, Douglas commuted to New York from New Brunswick by train every day seeking his first professional acting jobs, which he quickly won, appearing in a radio show, and acting in a play called *Kiss and Tell.*

He was performing on radio on September 24, 1944, when Diana gave birth in a New Brunswick hospital to a bouncing baby boy who they named Michael K. Douglas—the middle initial "K" having no real meaning. It was a compromise because Diana wanted to name the infant Kirk Douglas Jr. but Kirk explained to his gentile wife that no one in the Orthodox Jewish religion is named after a living family member, so they gave him a fake middle initial instead.

Michael Douglas spent the first three weeks or so of his life in the castle that Seward Johnson had built, and was then and forever more considered an integral part of the Johnson dynasty.

"Ruth was very gracious," Kirk Douglas remembered. "She helped us enormously and enabled us to save money by allowing us to live there." Not to overstay his sister-in-law's hospitality, the Douglases and their baby boy soon moved to their first apartment, in Greenwich Village.

"We left on a dreary fall day," he recalled. "As I looked back at the castle, I thought, Boy, I'd hate to have to build a wall around *that* and fill it with horse manure."

The Johnsons and the Douglases would forever have close family ties. But along with the Douglas dynasty's Hollywood fame and the Johnson dynasty's riches, a number of them would be plagued by divorce, drugs, tragedy, suicide, and scandal.

14

For the frigid central New Jersey winters, and broiling hot summers, J. Seward Johnson Sr. made certain that Merriewold had the most technologically advanced heating plant, which used oil and coal, and one of the first air-cooling systems. The house had to be comfortable, especially since Ruth would become pregnant every couple of years.

Two years after firstborn Mary Lea came into the world, Ruth gave birth to another daughter, Elaine, in 1928. In 1930, the namesake Seward Jr. was born, followed on January 26, 1932, by Diana Melville Johnson, named by Ruth in honor of her baby sister.

Ruth was young, healthy, and fertile and continued to get pregnant after Diana. But, on orders from her husband, she was forced to undergo illegal abortions—supposedly arranged for by his sister Evangeline—because he had the bizarre belief that additional children would weaken the Johnson dynasty bloodline.

When the infant heiress Diana was just a few weeks away from turning two months, the eyes of the nation, and the world, were transfixed on the nearby New Jersey town of Hopewell, and the family home of beloved hero-aviator Charles Lindbergh and his wife Anne Morrow Lindbergh. Around 10 P.M. on March 1—just five years after Lindbergh's epoch-making transatlantic flight—the world-famous couple's twenty-month-old toddler, Charles Augustus Lindbergh Jr., was abducted from his nursery, in what became the biggest story "since the Resurrection," as the journalist H. L. Mencken observed at the time. At the least, it was certainly *the* crime of the century.

As a massive search was under way for the celebrity baby and his abductor, a shocking kidnapping attempt occurred at Merriewold just eighteen days later, with baby Diana Johnson the presumed intended target. The apparent attempt had all the initial earmarks of the Lindbergh case, and fear gripped the nation that the same fiend had struck again.

As the lead of one local newspaper account declared on March 19, 1932, "A second kidnapping sensation in many ways paralleling the Lindbergh case, startled New Jersey today."

Declared another:

"An attempt to break into the nursery of a sleeping baby in the exact manner used by the kidnappers of Charles A. Lindbergh Jr. was made early yesterday at the home of J. Seward Johnson, wealthy vice president of Johnson & Johnson, manufacturers of surgical supplies . . . The Johnson home, Merriewold, is only twenty miles from the Lindbergh home."

It was 3 A.M. at Merriewold that Saturday morning, and Diana was asleep in the second-floor nursery, a suite consisting of several rooms where all the children slept, in the middle of the rear of the mansion, and some distance from Seward and Ruth's master bedroom. The infant was in her bassinette next to the Johnson family's dozing full-time nurse, Albertine Filiatrault.

Although the Johnson estate was well protected by an armed security guard stationed at the front gatehouse, the intruder managed to sneak onto the grounds and take a ladder from the garage, and place it under the window where Diana was sleeping.

As would soon be learned, the man knew the layout well.

When he cut a hole in the window screen and turned the window latch, the sound awakened the nurse, who spotted him framed in the window. Holding back her urge to scream, the quick-witted Miss Filiatrault grabbed the receiver of a bedside phone—a hotline connecting the main house with the quarters of night watchman John Shea—and whispered what was happening.

Shea grabbed a shotgun and headed toward the house, thoughts of the very recent unsolved Lindbergh case racing through his mind, as he would later tell police.

The man was still on the ladder, still trying to enter the room, when Shea opened fire, but missed. The intruder whipped out a revolver and returned one shot as he jumped fifteen feet to the ground, leaving deep shoe prints. Seward and Ruth, awakened by the shots, ran to the nursery, fearing the worst. Like everyone else, they had been following the Lindberghs' horrific situation, and like so many of the rich and famous, also feared being the target of a kidnapping.

Unable to reload his shotgun, Shea chased the agile intruder, who disappeared into the shadows on the sprawling grounds. Meanwhile, the nurse used an outside phone line to call police, and an all-points alarm was sounded, as a squad of Highland Park police converged on Merriewold.

Initially, New Jersey law enforcement's immediate suspicion was that the Lindbergh kidnapper had struck again, but this time had failed in snatching his target. If it were the same man, the press corps speculated, any cop who arrested the kidnapper would reap a huge reward and instant fame, and hopefully find the abducted celebrity baby alive.

In the borough of South Plainfield, about eight miles from Merriewold, police chief Cornelius McCarthy and patrolman Andrew Phillips had been alerted to the attempted kidnapping, and at 4:30 A.M. were cruising the town when they spotted an unfamiliar, fatigued-looking man stumble into an all-night greasy spoon and slump into a booth.

Their suspicions aroused, they confronted him. The chief barked, "I am an officer and you are a stranger. What are you doing in South Plainfield?"

When the powerful-looking suspect appeared to be reaching for a gun, McCarthy bopped him on the head with the butt of his Smith & Wesson. The man was found to be carrying a gun, one bullet having recently been fired.

Handcuffed, he was taken in, and under questioning would only identify himself—falsely, as it turned out—as one George Malden, giving an address, also untrue, of 518 East Sixteenth Street, in Manhattan. He said he was thirty-six years old and claimed he was an ironworker, and had just arrived in town after hitching a ride on a freight train when he was picked up. But he refused to answer any other questions during hours of grilling.

Placed in a lineup in the morning, the suspect was identified by Seward, the nurse, and the night watchman, as the same man who, on February 2, a week after Diana was born, had gotten past security, entered Merriewold, and robbed the Johnsons of three thousand dollars in their own bedroom, a case that had received no publicity at the time. The suspect's shoe also fit the imprint left in the ground during what was suspected to be the kidnapping attempt.

"I am convinced he came back to steal the baby," Seward Johnson told reporters. "It seems to me that with the Lindbergh case and incidents like this one, we ought to have some action to put a stop to this sort of thing."

Seward himself personally questioned the suspect "to get him to say something, but he won't talk," he told reporters.

Meanwhile, the man's fingerprints were rushed to the state police investigators pursuing the Lindbergh case.

A couple of days after he was taken into custody, Malden, who was being held on a concealed weapons charge while being investigated for attempted kidnapping, was identified as Richard Cowan, an escapee from the Western Penitentiary, in Rockview, Pennsylvania. After serving just ten days of an eight-to-fourteen-year term for burglary, he had walked away unnoticed from a prison gang on a wheat threshing detail the previous July. His involvement in the Lindbergh case was ruled out, and investigators concluded that another burglary at the Johnsons, rather than a kidnapping, was his motive for the attempted break-in. He was indicted, and returned to prison with an additional sentence of fourteen years.

Meanwhile, all hope of finding the Lindbergh baby alive was snuffed out when the little body was discovered on May 12, not far from the Lindbergh home, with a massive skull fracture, despite the payment of a fifty-thousand-dollar ransom.

Still fearful, Seward had turned Merriewold into an armed camp with bars on the windows and barbed wire around the grounds.

$ $ $

With the kidnap fears rampant, Robert Johnson, the General, then running the family business, convinced Seward to leave the country to protect his children.

On the surface that appeared to be concerned brotherly advice, and some of it might have been, but it also was the General's first step in a Machiavellian plan to gain majority control of Johnson & Johnson by keeping Seward away from the New Brunswick headquarters for as long as he could.

In 1944, when Johnson & Johnson became a public company and its stock soared in value, the next-to-final act in Robert's plan would be played out when he convinced his brother to take a third of his wealth and put it into trusts for his children, with Robert as one of the trustees. At the time, the brothers had equal shares in Johnson & Johnson, owning 84 percent of the company, with their sister, Evangeline, mostly out in the cold. But with a third of Seward's fortune tied up in the trusts, Robert had gotten majority control. Two years later, in 1946, he would boot Seward out of the executive suite.

Seward Jr. says his uncle's tactics back then drove him crazy with anger. "I thought he [his father] was giving up our legacies to the strong arm of his brother."

On his brother's advice, Seward and Ruth took the children to stay with her family, the Dills, in Bermuda.

"My father took us down there and my uncle managed to keep him out of New Brunswick for three or four years."

The family's stay in Bermuda was both buoyant and horrendous.

In the summer of 1933, the Dills and the Johnsons rented an enormous Victorian home, Stanhope Lodge, owned by Lady Blanche Stanhope, and that summer Seward and Ruth's brother, Bayard, representing the United States, won the Prince of Wales Cup with Seward's yacht called *Jill*.

That was the joyful part of their stay.

The horror occurred when Seward fell in love with Ruth's fourteen-year-old sister, Fan, a quarter century his junior. While the teenager had flirted with her brother-in-law, she had no further interest. But he did, and he actually fantasized about marrying the child.

Ruth was shocked when he told her, said he wanted a divorce, and left her, at least temporarily.

When Ruth and Seward finally split, the Dills were devastated. Fan, who knew the score, sobbed when she heard the divorce talk. "Secrets hung in the air," her sister, Diana Dill, who herself would be divorced from Kirk

Douglas, who had a reputation as a Casanova, after seven raucous Hollywood years, recalled later in her memoir. "Through all the summer nothing was mentioned, and it wasn't until Ruth confided in me the following year as she left for Reno that some of it was clarified for me."

What Diana didn't know when she discovered her sister crying, and what Ruth later revealed to her, was Seward's intoxication with their sister, Fan. (Fan later married a British military officer, settled in England, and in her midnineties in 2011, was said to have Alzheimer's.)

Because of Seward's scandal with Fan, "We had to leave Bermuda," recalls Seward Jr. "After we returned home, my uncle, who was hysterical to get my father out of New Brunswick again"—as part of his plan to completely take over Johnson & Johnson—"had him take us out with FBI coverage to Santa Fe, New Mexico."

There, the wandering Johnsons stayed for a time with the artist Georgia O'Keeffe and her husband, the photographer and art promoter Alfred Stieglitz.

And from there, the Johnsons went to England where, at Ruth's urging, husband and wife had a trial reconciliation, mainly for the sake of the children.

In Leicestershire, Seward, the yachtsman, had gotten hooked on hunting, and took on the pose of an English squire, purchasing best-in-breed hunting dogs, rifles and shotguns, and a country manor house similar to, or even more grand than Merriewold, replete with a large staff of servants and even its own private chapel.

Most of the time the Johnson children, now free from potential kidnappers in America, were cared for and taught in a gothic environment by icy British governesses, steely nurses, strict tutors, and housed by themselves in the immense estate's nursery wing.

Young Diana Dill, also living with the Johnson children at the time in England, where she was being educated, recalled the period when Seward and Ruth were "going through their troubles," as she put it in her memoir, *In the Wings*. Mary Lea, who was three years younger than Diana, was in awe when her cousin won a school prize. "I didn't think our family ever won anything," Diana quoted the little Johnson & Johnson heiress as saying. Looking back years later, Diana saw it as "a sad comment from a sad little girl."

With the threat of kidnapping still real back in America, Seward's sister,

Evangeline, then still married to Leopold Stokowski, also genuinely feared that her two young daughters, Sadja and Lubya, were targets for abduction, given the fame of their father, and the wealth of their mother. While Evangeline lived in Manhattan during the week, where chances for a kidnapping seemed slim, she and the children spent weekends at a better target—her isolated country estate, Cloud Walk Farm, in the blue-collar farming community of New Milford, in Litchfield County, Connecticut (later to be owned by the fashion designer Diane Von Furstenburg and her media mogul husband, Barry Diller).

Concerned about her children's security, Evangeline asked the Litchfield County district attorney for special protection. She also had her daughters under the close watch of a hired couple, and a trusted handyman by the name of Henry Perlowski, but the children were never informed about what was going on, in order to avoid frightening them.

"I think she shielded us from that," recalls her daughter, Sadja Greenwood, almost nine decades later.

Evangeline was soon the target of two extortion attempts with harsh demands: *turn over money or the kids get snatched.* The first, however, was by a crank by the name of Davis who wrote a letter demanding eight hundred dollars—the authorities never found him, or the location in the Bronx for the dropoff.

But the second caused great concern because the extortionist called Sadja and Lubya's exclusive and private Dalton School in Manhattan and demanded that Evangeline, who volunteered at the school as head of the art department, meet him with one thousand dollars in cash at Park Avenue and Eighty-Sixth Street if she didn't want her daughters abducted.

She called New York's finest, and a sting operation was set up. An envelope was filled with scraps of newspaper and, with cops staked out, Evangeline went to the location and waited—and waited. Several hours went by, but the caller never showed. There were no other threats against her, at least not any that she revealed.

It would take more than two years for the Lindbergh baby kidnapper, Bruno Richard Hauptmann, to be apprehended, charged with the federal crime, found guilty of first-degree murder at a media-frenzy trial, and executed in the electric chair at the New Jersey State Prison in April 1936.

$ $ $

A few days after Thanksgiving 1937, Ruth Dill Johnson was granted a divorce from Seward on the grounds of "cruelty of a mental nature." In front of the judge her lawyer had asked her how Seward had treated her.

"Extreme indifference," was her instant response.

In her settlement with Seward, minus alimony she got Merriewold, custody of her kids, and what amounted to a measly twelve thousand dollars annual income, chicken feed to Seward, and a drop in the bucket in the Johnson & Johnson realm.

In early December, a free woman after thirteen years as a Johnson wife in a horrific marriage, Ruth sailed for England, telling reporters gathered at the pier, "I want to be at the Isle of Wight in time to hang up Christmas stockings for my children." As part of their settlement she had convinced Seward to pass on fifty percent of his growing fortune to her brood when he died, which years later would ignite a family war over the money, the usual subject over which members of the Johnson dynasty would fight through the decades.

After all the hell she had gone through as Seward's wife, her assessment of him years later was simply, "Johnny was crazy."

Less than three years after her divorce, on June 21, 1940, Ruth Dill Johnson became Mrs. Philip D. Crockett, in a civil ceremony at Merriewold with just immediate family members in attendance. He was a Lehman Brothers investment banker, whom she had met in London.

Before her death at eighty-three, in March 1987—while she was having a colonoscopy, her colon was accidentally punctured—she and Crockett, with the main house sold off, had been living relatively modestly in what had been Merriewold's groundskeeper's cottage. It was a far cry from her former grandiose lifestyle, but also a far happier one.

Seward Jr. says his stepfather, Crockett, who had outlived Ruth and had inherited the cottage, was an old, embittered man because he always lived "in the shadow of Johnson & Johnson" wealth, power, and fame.

The stately Merriewold mansion seemed to some to be cursed, what with the acrimonious Johnson divorce, the frightening break-ins, and the once-presumed violent kidnapping attempt.

Whatever it was—a curse, or a jinx, or simply the ill fortune of the very rich people in residence—it continued into the early sixties with another marital breakup within its walls, this one ending in murder.

On September 18, 1963, Merriewold's latest owner, sixty-two-year-old Johnson & Johnson consultant Charles R. Farmer, shot and killed his estranged fifty-year-old art patron wife, Barbara, with three bullets, and then turned the snub-nosed .38 caliber revolver on himself, suffering a wound in his left shoulder, in what prosecutors had called an "apparent murder and apparent attempted suicide."

In 1968, Merriewold saw an end to its days as a private home when it was sold to a construction company for $400,000 to be renovated into offices. The price was little more than what Seward Johnson had paid to have it built back in the late 1920s.

15

Around the same time that Ruth Johnson remarried, so did Seward Sr., in 1939, to the second of his three wives. His bride was Esther Underwood, a proper, politically and socially correct liberal, and an artsy, very well-to-do Bostonian who was a descendant of William Underwood, founder in 1822 of a canned food company that became hugely successful for marketing a sandwich spread called Underwood Deviled Ham—ground ham with spices—that through generations sported a red devil, sometimes holding a pitchfork.

The company's logo somehow seemed apropos vis-à-vis the second Mrs. Seward Johnson, known as Essie, in that her husband, the second in command at Johnson & Johnson, was a demoniacal philanderer who would have many affairs during their union of some three decades that produced his fifth and sixth children—Jennifer in 1941, and James (Jimmy) Loring Johnson, in 1945—and that would end in another scandalous divorce.

Seward, it appeared, clearly enjoyed the act of making babies, but raising them in a fatherly and loving manner was a different story. They were left to their mother and the help, and given whatever they needed in order to keep them out of his hair.

Essie was an odd choice as a mate for Seward. Rather drab in looks and demeanor, she never really turned him on sexually as was underscored on their wedding night when, it was said, he spent the night with another woman. Those few who remember her decades later still can't fathom why Seward married her. He certainly didn't need her money, although it didn't hurt, and she had a good name. The speculation was that she was an agreeable beard for his womanizing.

"Essie was an old maid schoolteacher type," says Seward Jr. of his stepmother. "She definitely was not what turned him on."

Still, Seward and Essie lived the Johnson lifestyle to the fullest.

They were driven by a chauffeur when he wasn't speeding around the New Jersey countryside looking for girls to pick up in his classic Jaguar roadster; they had servants in uniform at their Oldwick mansion; they wintered at their waterfront estate in Hobe Sound, Florida; summered at their big, ivy-covered home in Essie's hometown of Chatham, Massachusetts, on Cape Cod; had a small fleet of classic sailboats designed by Seward's close pal, the noted naval architect Francis Spaulding Dunbar, also known as a womanizer who was Seward's skirt-chasing sidekick; and because Essie feared flying and getting aboard Seward's Johnson & Johnson private plane, she traveled in style in a private railroad car.

As Seward and Essie's daughter, Jennifer, once declared with grand understatement after her father's death, "We lived a nice life."

But she herself faced tragedy when just before Christmas 1980 her former husband, the father of her two sons, forty-year-old Harvard graduate Peter Gregg, a champion race car driver, shot himself in the head with a .38 caliber gun on a Florida beach. A sales slip for the recent purchase of the gun was found in his briefcase, and he had left a suicide note to Jennifer and his recent bride, Deborah Mars, stating, "I must have a right to end it." He had been suffering from what a Johnson family member described as an incurable nervous system disorder, and had been undergoing psychiatric treatment for manic depression.

Seward Sr. and his friend Spaulding Dunbar, also married, had many girlfriends—Seward boasted of a Norwegian stewardess who he dubbed his "Norwegian salmon"—and their long friendship was said to have ended over a woman who Seward chased even though she preferred Dunbar.

Meanwhile, there was talk among the Johnsons that Essie might not have really cared about her husband's philandering because her interests might have involved women.

"She had a certain masculinity about her," says her stepson, Seward Jr. "She sure wasn't feminine, and she was not my favorite person."

Seward Sr. and Essie had little in common even beyond her lack of sexual attraction. She came to think of him scornfully as a loser because he let his brother, the General, run the show at Johnson & Johnson, and she'd often give him the business in no uncertain terms, calling him "stupid."

The marriage ended in November 1971, with Essie doing far better than the first Mrs. J. Seward Johnson had, by negotiating a twenty-million-dollar divorce settlement. The then-doddering Seward—with his signature libido still active—had fallen for the couple's much younger, voluptuous, Polish immigrant chambermaid, Barbara Piasecka, called Basia, who, as it happened, had been hired by Essie.

The new servant had one hundred dollars and an interest in art when she arrived in America in the late sixties. Seward, head over fallen arches in love, married Basia when he was seventy-six years old, and she was thirty-four. That May-December relationship would, in the mid-1980s, ignite a courtroom battle royal between Seward's adult progeny—among them Seward Jr. and his sister, Mary Lea, all very wealthy from Johnson family trusts—and Basia over the $400 million fortune she had been bequeathed, after his death at eighty-seven in 1983.

During their bizarre years together, Seward would build a mansion for Basia that would make the Merriewold he had had constructed for his first wife seem like a hovel in comparison. The new palace would be called Jasna Polana, which was the name of Leo Tolstoy's Russian estate, and in Basia's Polish meant something like "bright meadow," and it certainly would be a bright place, underscored by a one-month electric bill of more than $52,000, a portion of which was due to the wattage used to air condition her dogs' kennels.

Where Merriewold cost $350,000 to build, the new Georgian-style mansion—all 54,000 square feet of it—would cost Seward a whopping $30 million to construct over four years on 170 of New Jersey's finest acres, making it one of America's most expensive homes at the time, one that when finished would soon be filled with Aubusson rugs, Empire chairs, and George III mahogany bookcases, along with a world-class art collection—Rembrandts, Titians, and Bellinis, along with tapestries, antiques, and sculpture. The immense manse would have made the *Guinness Book of World Records*, too, if there was a category for homes with the most toilets: Seward's Jasna Polana was flush with them, thirty-nine in all.

His six children's greedy court battle over their father's fortune left to his immigrant ex-chambermaid widow would have a scandalous odor of its own, and once again sully the Johnson name, imprinting it in tabloid headlines, and in at least two titillating books written about the epic case.

$ $ $

When Seward and his first wife, Ruth, divorced, their children were greatly impacted—from firstborn Mary Lea on down. "When he divorced Mom, it was the end of a chapter," she later said. "It was like he divorced us too."

Years later, she would make a startling and very public accusation about him: that over a period of years when she was a child and a teenager he had sexually molested her. This touched off a debate with some family members who refused to believe her. But all that was still to come.

Especially hard hit by the divorce was Mary Lea's younger brother, seven-year-old Seward Jr.—a tyke who then idolized his very distant and uncaring father—who was in a state of utter devastation when he walked out, just as Bobby Johnson had been when the General abandoned him and his mother. The divorce would impact Seward Jr.'s future life, especially his relationship with his father, the first of his two marriages, and sever important Johnson family bonds.

The abandonment, Seward Jr. asserted years later, made him feel "disenfranchised."

Like other Johnsons, academia wasn't Seward Jr.'s forte. One of the schools he attended was the Forman School, in Litchfield, Connecticut. Founded by young educators John and Julie Forman, the school gave personal attention to boys who had real or perceived learning problems, specializing in helping them to read through phonics. At one point, Albert Einstein, who had reading problems when he was young, became a member of the school's academic board of advisors.

Besides having learning issues, Seward Jr. was something of a hell-raiser. As he later revealed in a *New York Times* story about his time at Forman, "It was a place for dyslexics, although we weren't called that in those days. I got kicked out at one point because I couldn't pay attention. I was eventually sent back and then I used all my energy to wreck the place."

He was sixteen when he was ejected and it was actually for coming to school drunk. Disgusted with his behavior, his stepmother, Essie, refused to let him stay in the house. "She made my father make a bed for me in a boat," he says, decades later, in his early eighties, having never forgotten her ill treatment of him. "I was absolutely crushed. I hated her with a *passion*. My sisters were upset, too, and just sort of felt that my father should have stood up for me."

His teen drinking at sixteen was attributable in part to his uncle, the General, who had loved the New York nightlife, and had bought or gotten financial interests in some popular Manhattan nightclubs. "Uncle Bob said I could go to any of those clubs and sign his name." At one of them, he thinks it was the Maisonette Room at the St. Regis Hotel, he swooned over a cute singer by the name of Dorothy Shea, who would come to his table and sing a pop tune called "Park Avenue Hillbilly." Decades later he still recalls and belts out verses of the zany song.

While he drank at sixteen, he still was shy with girls and was sexually inexperienced, but his very liberal aunt Evangeline "tried to take me under her wing" with a plan to get him laid. He was having lunch with her; her then-husband, Alexis Zalstem-Zalessky; and Evangeline's two daughters, Sadja and Lubya; when, as he clearly recalls, "Zalessky comes out with, 'We have to figure out the problem with Seward's virginity.' I couldn't believe my ears."

Evangeline with her millions, and her prince with his contacts in Russia, were helping to finance the Bolshoi Ballet, and every winter they would bring a group of the leggy ballerinas to Cuernavaca, Mexico, for a vacation.

"Evangeline said, 'It's very simple. We'll just bring Seward down there and one of them's going to fix his problem.' Though I was blushing to the roots of my hair, my imagination was running wild. I pictured myself being handed from one ballerina to another until there was nothing left of me, and I *loved* the idea. But my father got wind of it and cut the whole thing off. I don't believe it was paternal concern over my teenagehood. I think it was pure jealousy."

While the orgy with the ballerinas never took place, Seward Jr. finally lost his virginity when he was twenty, courtesy of the experienced and very aggressive teenage Catholic schoolgirl daughter of Johnson & Johnson's man in Bogotá who was visiting Merriewold.

After the Forman School, the final stop on Seward Jr.'s road to higher education was in the Department of Animal Sciences at the University of Maine, where he studied poultry management—on the advice of his father, who thought chicken-raising rather than the Johnson's goldmine of a health-care business might be more of a fit. He later noted that poultry husbandry "was the only thing they'd let me into."

A family confidante was less diplomatic. "It was a way for his father, who thought him a moron, to tell him to fuck off. At school he just goofed off."

The study of poultry management didn't require the Johnson & Johnson heir to burn the midnight oil, and after some boisterous semesters he dropped out in 1951, and enlisted in the navy. Like his first-class yachtsman father and his uncle, the General, and most if not all of the other Johnson men past, present, and future, he relished boats and the sea. So, playing sailor boy for four years for Uncle Sam was a no-brainer for him, and involved much fun, adventure, and danger, such as when his ship, the frigate U.S.S. *Gloucester,* took fire from the enemy during the Korean War in a duel with shore guns; the ship took a direct hit that killed one of Seward Jr.'s shipmates and left eleven others wounded. He escaped without requiring a single Band-Aid.

Discharged honorably in 1955, Seward Jr. wanted a role in the family business. But, once again, Seward Sr. avoided his son's request.

"He bought me a farm to keep me out of Johnson and Johnson," Seward Jr. says decades later.

However, through persistence, he finally got in the door, starting at the bottom in Johnson & Johnson's surgical suture division, called Ethicon, in Somerville, New Jersey. He had to endure teasing from coworkers who scoffed that while he was a member of the ruling family, he had a low-rung, do-nothing job, but still sat at the president's table on special corporate occasions. He was bored at Ethicon, was timid and relatively unsophisticated. While shy, he had an eye for the ladies and wished he had the guts to pursue some of the pretty secretaries, but, without elaboration, he once described himself as "extremely undeveloped."

With all of his personal demons, he was absent from work more often than he was present.

16

In 1956, when J. Seward Johnson Jr. was twenty-six, he met the woman he thought would be the love of his life—fascinating, exotic (at least to him at the time), and, as the tabloids would later call her, "statuesque."

Barbara Eisenfuhr Kline Bailey Maxwell was a twenty-nine-year-old sometimes brunette, sometimes redhead dish who was raised in Germany and Switzerland—her father was variously described as a Frankfurt banker, or a lawyer, and her mother was said to be from Russia, and possibly Jewish. As it would turn out, she knew more about Seward Jr. and his roots than he did about her and hers when they first met.

Or so he says.

Just prior to meeting Seward Jr., she had spent some time in Bermuda, where she was doing what she later claimed was research for stories about the sea, and had become fascinated with whales and whaling.

She also became fascinated with another kind of catch: a Johnson & Johnson heir.

While in Bermuda she is said to have met and befriended the very important Dills, Seward Jr.'s mother's family, and she learned about the young Band-Aid scion, who happened to be a very eligible bachelor. At some point, she had settled in his hometown where, as Seward Jr. notes many years later, "the Johnson and Johnson shadow hangs over Princeton, and [did] especially in those days," meaning most everyone, including Barbara, knew about the wealthy and powerful family whose company was an American legend.

Visiting Ruth Dill Johnson Crockett at Merriewold in 1956 was David Dill, one of Ruth's brother Bayard Dill's two sons. David, who had gotten to know Barbara when she was in Bermuda, invited her to accompany him to Merriewold in order to introduce her to his bachelor cousin. That invitation was at Barbara's "insistence," asserts Seward Jr., who would believe in retrospect that she "used them [the Dills] to meet me."

In any case, she bowled him over with her looks and charm.

"She flattered me up and down," he's never forgotten, "and because my ego was about as big as a pea it kind of felt good." He also was attracted to what he calls Barbara's "street smarts." He felt that with his dyslexia and the many issues he had with his uncle, the General, and with his father, Seward Sr., "the only way I was going to survive was if I could get somebody like her to help."

In other words, he was a very mixed-up young man, but with his own agenda of sorts vis-á-vis this new woman in his life, his first serious romance.

Unlike young Seward, Barbara was no virgin when it came to a titillating lifestyle. By the time he'd fallen for her, she'd been a merry divorcee, and had a six-year-old son, Bruce, from a failed marriage, the last one ending after four years at virtually the same time the Johnson heir was hooked on her.

She was quite a potent Euro cocktail, a mix of dazzling charm, femininity, intelligence, and unbridled ambition.

When she met the Johnson scion Barbara was a successful commercial artist's agent with a client list that included the pre–Campbell Soup Can Andy Warhol, who in the mid to late fifties was doing print ads for companies like I. Miller shoes, and she also handled U.S. representation for the French graphic artist Raymond Savignac, who designed iconic advertising posters for such products as Bic razors and Yoplait yogurt. She also claimed to friends that as an agent in New York she had acquired and sold the rights to *Winnie the Pooh,* and many decades before the "Soup Nazi" of *Seinfeld* fame, she had talked about opening a chain of soup kitchens in Manhattan with a friend, the actor Anthony Quinn.

Barbara also was trying to interest Johnson & Johnson to use Savignac's work in its advertising through its prestigious Madison Avenue agency, Young & Rubicam, where she was hoping to get a shapely leg in, so to speak, for more business.

The General, who had an obsessive interest in the advertising and marketing of his company's products, was not always pleased with Y&R's research and creativity. Advertising, he felt, should be simple, and too often he was bombarded with bar charts. After one such presentation, he voiced his exasperation in one of his many harsh memos. "It was a repulsive experience," he wrote. "The copy was third-rate," and he termed the Young & Rubicam mad men at the conference table, "Flannel-headed human scenery."

There was nothing, however, third-rate, repulsive, or flannel-headed about Barbara in green and guileless Seward Jr.'s eyes and heart. She was like no other woman he had ever met—artsy, creative, with hip friends in Manhattan. She was wired, chic, and spontaneous, which was right up his alley. She owned a romantic cottage with a pool on Tyler Road in Princeton, and she had decorated the love nest herself in shades of virginal white, everything from the slipcovers to the book covers. Everything about her was irresistible, and not too long after meeting, he moved in with her—lock, stock, and trust fund, which was reportedly worth at least seven million dollars (in early 1960s dollars) at the time, and he soon gave her an engagement ring.

The live-in arrangement had triggered alarms in the New Brunswick executive suite: the brothers Johnson—Seward Sr. and the General—were concerned about who this seeming seductress really was, what she had in mind for the naïve Seward Jr., and whether their merger would ignite negative image problems and bad publicity down the road for the company.

Their worry would, in fact, prove to be warranted, depending on whom one believed.

The General ordered an intensive investigation into Barbara's background, looking for anything that might convince his nephew to bring about a quick end to the relationship.

Heading up the very secret probe was Kenneth Perry, the head of Johnson & Johnson's law department, who was, along with the General, a trustee of the Johnson family trusts. Perry's duties reportedly also included acting as a family fixer of sorts—arranging for abortions if virtuous single Johnson women had gotten pregnant, or aborting potentially scandalous relationships like the one in which Seward Jr. had now gotten himself entangled.

Under orders from the General, Perry was trying to dig up whether Barbara had a police record, whether members of her family were followers of Hitler back in the Fatherland—she claimed to Seward Jr. that she had been raised in Switzerland—or whether she was of Jewish heritage, which to Perry was the far greater evil.

"Ken Perry was very anti-Semitic," states Seward Jr., looking back to that time. "He reminded me of J. Edgar Hoover. He had a little bit of femininity to him, but he was also like a Nazi."

Perry supposedly turned up information that Barbara's Russian mother was Jewish, or might have been—and in Judaism if the mother's Jewish, her children are considered Jewish—and Perry voiced that fact loud and clear, "so I was forever protecting Barbara from his slurs," says Seward Jr. But he claims that Barbara "didn't want to admit" that "she was half-Jewish. To her Jewish was a bad thing."

Barbara was rightfully furious when she learned about the investigation. The two had a knock-down, drag-out verbal fight and Seward Jr., angry at her for blaming him when, in fact, he was defending her, walked out and left her, at least temporarily.

"She threw her engagement ring at me because they went and investigated her family in Germany," he reveals many years later. "Her father was worried he was going to lose his job in Frankfurt, so she threw the ring at me and I went into the law department and threw the ring at Ken Perry and told him off."

But that wasn't the end of it.

"Barbara kept calling me and I kept not answering the phone. I was working at Ethicon and the secretaries were getting very mad at me because I wasn't accepting her calls. Finally, she had her maid call me and say that Barbara had fainted on the bed. So I stupidly went over there and, of course, she was all made up, had her lipstick on straight, and was lying on the bed, and I just slid into it."

Because Ken Perry was accusing Barbara of lying about her background, and Barbara was accusing Perry of lying about what he had turned up about her background, Seward Jr. set up a meeting between both sides to try to set the record straight. But he became so nervous as the confrontation was about to begin that he had to rush off to the men's room. By the time he got back to Perry's office he found Barbara screaming at the Johnson & Johnson general counsel.

"She was saying that he insulted her. She said he was leering at her and then she said he said, 'You look all right for a Jew,' and I just grabbed her hand and marched her out of there."

Having kissed and made up, and once again wearing his engagement ring, Barbara had to finalize her divorce before she could marry the Johnson heir. But first she needed some expert opinion and assurance that the baby oil scion was really Mister Right.

She convinced Seward Jr. to go to Los Angeles with her to be seen by a psychiatrist she had gotten to know on the ship when she first came to the United States.

Chuckling about it years later, Seward Jr. says, "She wanted him to meet me to check me out to see if she should marry me."

Presumably the shrink gave her two thumbs up. But Seward Jr. says he wondered at the time—who was going to check out Barbara to see if she fit the bill for him.

On September 16, 1956, less than a week after Seward Jr. was given the psychiatrist's Good Husband Seal of Approval, he took Barbara's hand in marriage, to have and to hold, for better or for worse.

The latter, as it turned out, would prevail.

Knowing his father and uncle were against the marriage, Seward Jr. and Barbara (along with her son, Bruce, whom Seward Jr. eventually adopted) eloped, taking the vows of marriage in Virginia City, in Nevada, an ominously appropriate setting because Virginia City was a gold-mining boom town back in the nineteenth century, and Seward Sr. and the General suspected that the latest wife to join the Johnson dynasty was a gold digger.

As Seward Jr. observes more than a half century later, "When I went [to get married] I was so over my head. I didn't know what to do. So, it was pathetic."

In a Dear Dad letter, he once wrote, "My marriage is under threat . . . my life is hell." At the same time, the General received an Uncle Bob missive, calling upon his "sense of humanity," his "very manhood," to end the harassment.

In a note to his wife, Seward Jr. called both his father and his uncle "stupid jerks."

But he later would agree with his father and uncle's assessment that Barbara was after his fortune.

He says, "She married me for my money," and he claims, "I never loved her."

$ $ $

In the scheme of *really* bad marriages, theirs could make it into the record books.

Still, there was a sincere attempt at domesticity.

The couple went house-hunting and Seward Jr. bought for them a beautiful twenty-two-room Rocky Hill fieldstone home with six garages that was built in the 1920s at 75 Cleveland Lane, in one of Princeton's exclusive areas. It was said to have been the most expensive house sold there in 1957 when he paid seventy-five thousand dollars. One of the home's immense rooms—twenty by fifty feet—had been used in the early 1940s as a Jewish chapel and Sunday school at a time when there were very few Jews living in Princeton. Restrictive covenants and discrimination against Jews were prevalent, and they needed a place to worship. With the Johnsons now in residence, that room became Barbara's "Whale Room," where she had on display what was fast becoming a world-class collection of whaling memorabilia.

About a year after they tied the knot, sometime in 1957, during what appeared on the surface to be a relative period of calm in Seward Jr.'s constantly turbulent life, the young married couple, their son, Bruce, whom he was in the process of adopting, and Seward Sr., still quietly seething about his namesake's choice of a bride, were vacationing together in Fort Lauderdale, Florida. They seemed like one very rich, tanned, and happy family. But appearances are deceptive.

Leaving Seward Sr.'s wife, Essie, behind, they had decided to take a boat trip to an island near Bimini in the Bahamas, some fifty miles off the coast of Florida. While Seward Jr. and Bruce played together on the boat, Barbara and her father-in-law, the compulsive womanizer and philanderer, disembarked and they, too, played, claims Seward Jr. years later.

"I was on the boat with Bruce and they returned with their arms around each other," he asserts. He says he "just knew" that they had had a liaison because of how they looked together. "They couldn't keep their hands off of each other," he says. But he didn't confront his father, or his wife, because "I didn't need to hear it. I knew it. It was proved to me." When pressed, however, he could offer no other support for the allegation.

Around the same time, another bomb dropped when the trustees of a 1944 trust Seward Sr. had established for his children informed Seward Jr. and Barbara that they would not recognize their marriage. The reason: the trustees claimed to have unearthed alleged evidence that one of Barbara's previous divorces "was not truly legal," and as such she would not receive any of the millions if Seward Jr. suddenly died.

Barbara "then put tremendous, unrelenting pressure on me to correct the situation and get the trustees to give up their adamant opposition. Young and unhardened and no match for this determined, canny European woman, I cracked under the pressure . . ." he later stated.

It had all become too much for the sensitive Johnson & Johnson heir.

He fell into a severe depression, and right after the New Year 1958, some sixteen months after he married Barbara, he tried to kill himself.

His decision to take his life, he reveals decades later, "had to do with my father's relationship with Barbara."

Like he did with so many other endeavors in his young life, Seward Jr. failed to carry out his grim mission.

In a barren area of Princeton, sitting in his Edsel—a car that was as much a Ford flop as Seward Jr. was thought of as a Johnson dynasty failure—he'd brought a gun, but the wrong ammunition. More curious, the gun was one of two that had inexplicably been given to him in the recent past by a Johnson & Johnson security guard as he left the General's office where a heated discussion had taken place about his marriage. Seward Jr. was never sure that the guns were a subtle message to take some sort of extreme action.

Since he couldn't shoot himself, he chose asphyxiation, with a hose attached to the exhaust pipe, hoping the carbon monoxide would do him in and take him out of his misery.

He left two suicide notes, one "to whom it may concern . . . to certify I took my own life," the other a Dear Barbara note, stating, "I love you very much you are as beautiful inside as a saint."

He wrote he was "dying very happy."

It didn't happen.

A suspicious passerby spotted him "nearly dead" in the car, and a policeman came to his rescue, revived him, and he was rushed to Princeton Hospital.

Bobby Johnson—Seward Jr.'s first cousin (and father of nine-year-old Woody)—who was a decade older and at that point close to being named president of Johnson & Johnson, rushed to the hospital and invited him to stay at his home, which he did for a time after his release. Bobby felt sorry for his cousin because, as Seward Jr. explains, he was convinced that his own father, the General, in ordering the investigation of Barbara, had inadvertently pushed Seward Jr. into the marriage, and he believed his suicide attempt was linked to those issues—unaware of the real reason.

"Bobby knew that his father had forced the marriage," states Seward Jr. "He didn't know anything about my father [and Barbara]."

After Seward Jr. went home, he was faced with more pressure.

Barbara demanded that he adopt her son, Bruce, as soon as possible, declaring that it was "the responsible and loving thing to do."

The adoption was completed within two months.

"In my naivete, I didn't realize what was really involved."

Seward Jr. believed that his wife, "having been excluded from the 1944 trust money by the trustees, was trying to create a new claim on the trust, albeit a questionable one, by supplying me with an adopted stepson. I'd have an heir should I die. A legally adopted son, she learned, counted," he later stated.

"Even if I'd seen what her aim was, I probably wouldn't have been able to resist her. At that point in my life I was deeply confused, exhausted, and without defenses."

17

Sometime in 1958, J. Seward Johnson Jr. made a new friend, Walter Darby Bannard, a talented artist in his twenties with an Ivy League pedigree, a freewheeling manner, and a keen eye for interesting women, as his new chum would soon discover.

The two got to know each other at the Little Gallery in Princeton, which Bannard was managing and where Seward Jr. was a customer.

"He wasn't all tied up with square, Princetonian social rules," Seward Jr. notes years later. "He seemed free like an artist—he was friends with other artists—and not a guy in a gray flannel suit."

But their camaraderie would end in one of the most scandalous, humiliating, and violent divorce cases ever, and a feud that would continue for decades, into the twenty-first century, with the complex and sensitive issue of paternity at its core.

Having met Barbara Johnson, Bannard would become a central figure in the Johnsons' increasingly twisted marriage.

More than five decades later, in 2011, at the age of seventy-six, having become a noted abstract painter and a professor of art at the University of Miami, he recalled his turbulent and scandalous relationship with the Johnsons.

The son of a Pennsylvania Railroad vice president, Bannard, who at age six was drawing "realistic pictures of birds," considered himself "sort of a child prodigy," he once told a newspaper reporter. He had graduated from

Phillips Exeter Academy, and was in the class of 1956 at Princeton University, his father's alma mater, where he had earned a B.A., and where he became friends with the abstract artists Frank Stella and Michael Fried, in whose footsteps he would follow.

But there clearly was nothing artsy or abstract about Bannard's early friendship with Seward Jr.—the two acted together like a couple of frat boys at the Johnson home in Princeton where Bannard would become an ever-increasing presence—mostly, as Seward Jr. asserts, at the behest of the lady of the house.

"We used to sit and drink beer together and make notes on what beer was best," says Bannard. "Seward always had these ideas of classification of things. He decided it would be fun to rank all the beers that there were according to taste, and then we drank them and we argued about how they tasted. Seward was a very likeable guy, but he seemed very lonely and he would always constantly and compulsively complain about his family, about the General and about Bobby Jr., and it just sounded pathetic and horrible. He would mumble about conspiratorial bullshit within the company. I wouldn't call that crazy talk, but he was kind of obsessed with it."

Bannard, however, had his own family problems.

He had married young to a beautiful girl—the first of his three wives—whose goal was to become a Hollywood or Broadway star. A year or so after he had become part of Seward's circle, she ran off with his best friend from college. "Before the shit hit the fan," as he puts it, Bannard became a regular at the Johnson dinner table, and a regular at Seward and Barbara's parties.

One guest at one of the gatherings who would become infamous was Dr. Max Jacobson, as Bannard recalls. He had an Upper East Side Manhattan practice with a long list of celebrity clients, including the actor Anthony Quinn, who happened to be a friend of Barbara's. But his most famous patient was President Kennedy, whom Jacobson was injecting with amphetamines during secret White House visits. Because of his star-studded patients, many of whom were troubled emotionally and or physically, Jacobson had earned the sobriquet "Dr. Feelgood" for dispensing drugs he claimed would make them feel good.

"He visited the house and he had Dexedrine [an amphetamine] and he said, 'You have to take Dex otherwise you're always half dead. That's what I gave to Kennedy, ' " Jacobson told Seward Jr., Barbara, and others at the gathering, according to Bannard, who also was present. "He was a Dr. Feelgood and knew somebody the Johnsons knew because Barbara met all these interesting people when she would ride on the *Queens* all the time—the *Queen Mary* and *Queen Elizabeth*—back and forth to Europe, and these people would come to the house. The doctor was very intense about Dexedrine and he thought it was a cure for everything in the world. I think he was trying to suggest something for Seward I guessed because Seward was always sort of semi-depressed."

Because Bannard got to hear Seward Jr.'s horror stories about the Johnson family and his complaints about the Johnson & Johnson company ad infinitum, and got to meet a number of the Johnson family members, he came away with a very negative opinion of the lot of them, one he still held decades later:

"They are a mixed-up, weird bunch, and always have been," he came to believe. "You couldn't make them up in fiction. They are dysfunctional and just don't know how to live a normal life. The whole family is like a great big spiderweb that innocent people would drop into—normal people who get caught in the Johnson web of craziness. There were the three brothers who started Johnson and Johnson, and they were smart. By the time they got down to Seward's generation this was a pretty pathetic bunch. It's almost like European royalty."

Seward was always trying to come up with ideas that would make an impression and get him some positive notice from his uncle and father. One such concept was for Johnson & Johnson to market a roll of toilet paper that had different lengths of tear-off squares—small, medium, and large.

"He saw it as a great invention for them," recalls Bannard, whom Seward Jr. had briefed about the idea. "I said, 'Seward do *not* under *any* circumstances send it to them because they'll just think you're crazy.' I thought, Jesus Christ, if these people are down on Seward already, they're going to be a lot more down on him when he sends them that one."

After a period of recuperation following his botched suicide attempt, Seward Jr. wanted to return to his position at the Johnson & Johnson division Ethicon, but his father and uncle would not permit it until he saw a psychiatrist of whom they both approved, and who would give him a clean bill of mental health, or at least that's what they claimed needed to happen in order for him to come back to work. Over a period of months, Seward Jr., following their mandate, saw a succession of psychiatrists, but his father and uncle, he recalls years later, "kept telling me the psychiatrists I was seeing weren't good enough," and as a result he remained barred from the family business, which by then was already a public company.

One of the psychiatrists had trouble buying what he was telling him during their fifty-minute-hour sessions, so he told Seward Jr. he wanted a third party to substantiate his claims. While it appeared to be an off-the-wall request from the Freudian with a platinum-plated Manhattan practice, Seward Jr. was desperate to bring an end to his endless rounds of shrink visits.

Bannard claims Seward asked him to meet with the doctor, and that he met with the psychiatrist on two or three occasions.

But Seward Jr. says he never made such a request of Bannard.

"The psychiatrist talked to me to ascertain facts," maintains Bannard. "He wanted to know things that had happened, and to establish whether things were true or not. There was something the psychiatrist told me that gave me the creeps. He said that what Seward would do is tell stories about himself that were not about him, but were things that happened to other people. I actually witnessed that once at a party. He told a story about something he said happened to him, and it was a story that I had told him had happened to me. Now that's going to raise hairs on the back of your neck. The doctor said that kind of activity was a deeply disturbing sign. The psychiatrist analyzed Seward pretty quickly and then figured there was really nothing he could do for him, except for Seward to keep out of trouble."

Seward Jr. eventually came to the realization that his father and uncle's demand that he see a psychiatrist who had the Johnson & Johnson seal of approval was actually a ploy to force him out of the company.

And it worked.

After he saw the last unapproved shrink, he received his pink slip in the form of a letter from Johnson & Johnson executive Richard A. Sellars, who one day would become chairman and CEO of the company. Sellars informed him that his services would no longer be needed, because, says Seward Jr., "I'd been gone so long that they filled my place, so I never could go back."

Seward Jr., however, had started to agree with his father and uncle about Barbara, especially when she began pushing him, he claims, to get as much money as possible out of his trusts. If he didn't, he alleges she later said, she hoped he would be more successful the next time he tried to kill himself.

The gun under the bed contretemps was another warning sign of big trouble in the marriage.

Seward Jr. says he had discovered that Barbara had hidden an automatic pistol under the marital mattress, on Seward's side of the bed, "and it used to bother the hell" out of him. He had complained to Barbara about the gun, but one day it had suddenly vanished.

"She said, 'Where is it?'"

"I said, 'Where's what?'"

"She said, 'You know what I mean.'"

"I said, 'What the hell are you talking about?'"

"She said, 'Where's the pistol? Where did you put it?'"

"I said, 'It's probably under the mattress where *you* stupidly put it.'"

"She said, 'No it isn't, and you know it isn't there.'"

"I said, 'I know nothing of the sort.'"

"She said, 'You probably were so frightened that you've forgotten what you did with it.'"

The war of she-said, he-said over the missing gun went on ad infinitum for weeks, he claimed.

Barbara finally came up with a plan to get to the bottom of the mystery, or so it seemed.

"She said 'There's just one thing you're going to do,'" recalls Seward Jr., about the missing gun. "'You're going to go to a psychiatrist and get him to give you sodium pentathol so you can remember what you did with it.'"

Seward Jr. followed Barbara's edict—he knew he hadn't taken the gun, or at least *thought* he hadn't—and had a psychiatrist put him under with the psychoactive truth drug, popular in Hollywood melodramas that resembled the kind of life he was now living for real.

"When I came up [from the drug] I said, I didn't take the gun, did I? He said of course not, all you did is talk about your father and how upset you were with him. Then he said, 'Do you think *she* took the gun?' And the thought had never occurred to me, and I just sat there as though somebody had shot me, and I was *terrified*." To Seward, it was like *Gaslight* with Charles Boyer where he's trying to drive Ingrid Bergman crazy. "Barbara was gas-lighting me. I said, 'What the hell am I going to do?' The psychiatrist said, 'When the time comes you're going to know what to do.' "

18

Like Greta Garbo, whose signature movie line was, "I *vant* to be alone," Barbara Johnson told her husband, Seward Jr., that she, too, needed some quality time alone, which meant a first-class cabin for herself and without him aboard the *Queen Mary* to Europe.

Barbara had carefully packed for the round-trip transatlantic crossing, and included in her luggage a variety of Johnson & Johnson products gotten gratis in the company store, and that she would give out to other passengers—a bit of self-promotion that secured her an invitation to the captain's table. After all, she was part of one of America's most iconic corporate families, which she always liked to make quite clear. It was there, at dinner, that she met a dashing—and very married—Englishman by the name of David Proudlove, a World War II Royal Air Force ace, some fifteen years her husband's senior.

Proudlove's father-in-law owned an aircraft company in Great Britain, and he had hired the ex-fighter pilot to be his firm's U.S. sales representative. When Barbara met Proudlove, he, his wife, and daughter were in the process of settling into a home in the upscale New York City suburb of Scarsdale, about ninety minutes from Princeton.

"Proudlove was saying that his family hadn't moved in properly yet and they were going back and forth to England. He was giving me a lot of garbage," says Seward Jr., recalling that personally horrific time decades later when "Barbara brought him home with her, and he moved in with us. His wife filed for divorce."

When Seward Jr. complained about how unseemly cozy the Johnson abode had become with Proudlove in residence, he remembered Barbara stating, "How could I be so mean, with poor David going through his nasty divorce. When poor David lost his job that became still another reason for not asking him to leave."

Darby Bannard also was starting to spend a lot of time in the Johnson house—he had since been hired by Seward Jr. as Barbara's "secretary" to help her catalogue her whaling collection.

In short order, the original man of the house—the Band-Aid scion—was reduced to being a virtual voyeur in his own home, watching as Barbara, allegedly clad in sheer lingerie, played hostess to live-in guest Proudlove.

"She received many intimate notes and love poems from Proudlove," Seward Jr. would later claim in titillating divorce papers. Moreover, he would charge that Barbara "frequently permitted Proudlove, while in their home, to fondle her amorously while she was scantily clad, and kiss her lips, legs, thighs, and other parts of her body."

Proudlove seemingly began playing the man-of-the-house role, taking on the tasks of interviewing prospective servants, overseeing Barbara's book-keeping and check-writing, while Seward Jr. became the household's chief cook and bottle washer, or, as he later put it, "baby sitter, chauffeur, and errand boy."

Just before New Year's Eve 1959, the Johnsons and Proudlove went to England, leaving Bruce with the help. Barbara told her husband she wanted a divorce, and planned to marry Proudlove. Furious, Seward Jr. returned home. Not only was he feeling angry and foolish, but he needed to rush back to Princeton because he had errands to perform, including putting Bruce, then twelve, back in school.

Barbara returned home a few weeks later.

She had good news, and she had bad news.

The good news was that she had decided not to marry Proudlove.

The bad news was Barbara's insistence that Darby Bannard spend a lot more time in the house helping her to catalogue her collection of New England's early whaling industry.

Her relationship with Bannard had clearly grown fonder.

And Bannard was taken by, and intrigued with, the lady of the house.

"She looked like [the French novelist] Françoise Sagan," he observes admiringly many years later. "Barbara had a sort of filling-the-room kind of personality . . . She was just a tremendously energetic—a typical Sagittarius who just goes off in a direction. Off the wall? Well, maybe. But in all sorts of positive ways."

Seward Jr. would later charge that Barbara committed adultery first with Proudlove, then with Bannard. At one point she allegedly demanded that her husband sleep on a sofa and not in the marital bed, he claimed, and he said that he also was forced to spend a month in the dressing room adjoining the locked master bedroom occupied by his wife and allegedly Bannard. Another time she invited him to join her and Bannard—three in a bed, the tabloids gloated, because "it would be cozy," an invitation that Seward Jr. declined, or as a legal complaint later stated in his eventual divorce case, "Plaintiff refused such a tripartite arrangement."

Bruna Szaloky, a forty-year-old Hungarian seamstress who worked for the Johnsons, would later testify that she often saw the lady of the house stripped to nothing more than her bra and panties while Bannard ogled her. At times, she alleged, Seward Jr. also was present with Bannard in the bedroom when Barbara tried on different outfits.

Seward Jr. would later contend that Barbara had "on many occasions permitted herself to appear nude or scantily clad" in front of Bannard, and had permitted herself to be "kissed and fondled" by him. He further swore that Barbara requested Bannard "to dress and undress her."

Besides the claimed erotic clothing changes, a Johnson maid, Mrs. Queenie Knowles, would testify about seeing Barbara bathing in Bannard's presence. Later, Seward Jr. would insist, "She permits him to watch her while she goes to the toilet and takes baths and showers."

Barbara and Bannard spent more and more quality time together.

"They worked continuously day after day and into the nights," stated Seward Jr. "Though the [whaling] collection was extensive, I began to wonder as the months passed how long they were going to take to finish the job."

Bannard, at least six years Barbara's junior, claims it was Seward Jr. who had brought him on to assist Barbara with her whaling project, and he vehemently denies Seward's allegations that he had essentially moved into the Johnson home.

"I was there to some extent. One of the reasons I was there a lot was because the whaling project was kind of like a second job, and I got to be quite an expert on the subject." So much so that while working alongside Barbara he produced a four-hundred-photograph scrimshaw book called *Scrimshaw* that was eventually published years later.

Seward Jr. claimed that in February 1960 Barbara had wanted to get away to a cabin in the Pocono Mountains of Pennsylvania to work up a compendium of the whaling logbooks she owned, which she hoped would be used in some sort of TV series, and had arranged to spend a week there in solitude.

"Darby Bannard," he says, "would drop her off, then drive on to New York to meet his father. I was to drive up near the end of her stay and bring some supplies. When I arrived, Darby was there. He'd been 'snowed in,' they said. I was deeply troubled by this obvious, careless, contemptuous deception and withdrew."

That week in the Poconos and what may or may not have occurred there, depending on who was telling the story, would incredibly reverberate into the twenty-first century, four decades hence.

More than a half century later, Bannard denies he ever was there, or says he doesn't remember being there, and claims it was Seward Jr. and Barbara who had spent that week together in the mountains. "He's just trying to make a case, so let him make a case."

The case is an important one because Barbara had become pregnant, and the blessed event would later be timed by Seward Jr. to that Poconos escape, the one in which he alleges that Bannard was in residence, and which Bannard denies.

When Barbara became pregnant, Seward Jr. asserts, "I was not having intercourse with her for a full year."

A month or so after what would become the much-disputed Pocono Mountains getaway, Seward Jr. maintained that Barbara "suddenly became amorous. That surprised me. We hadn't had any sort of sexual relations for a long time," he avowed. "She was challengingly seductive and I tried to comply but in vain because it seemed so awkward and repelling. We never related sexually again. I was fuzzy on obstetrical matters and the timing of child-bearing, but I do remember being surprised when, in August, I saw not only that she was pregnant but that her state seemed so advanced.

"All that summer into the autumn and winter," he asserted, his wife and Darby "were very close. They'd share a private joke or a little intimacy and then, as an afterthought, suddenly remembering I was in the room, they'd make a show of including me."

$ $ $

When the stork arrived on January 10, 1961, Barbara Johnson was taken to the maternity ward at Princeton Hospital by her husband—with Walter Darby Bannard anxiously tagging along like he, too, was the expectant fa-ther. Seward Jr. has never forgotten the scene. "There were two fathers pac-ing the waiting room floor," he has stated. And he quoted Barbara telling him, "Isn't it good of Darby to come give us support?"

Barbara became the proud mother of a healthy girl on January 11, 1961, her second child. When it was time to show the newborn to the father, the maternity nurse was greeted by both Seward Jr. and, Seward claimed, Darby Bannard.

Unlike most new fathers who hand out cigars to celebrate the blessed event, the very suspicious Seward Jr. held on to his Cohibas and Montecristos.

On the day Barbara left the hospital to return home with the infant, Seward Jr. "stayed to pay the bills and it was Darby" who drove the new mother home, and it was Bannard who, in the following weeks, "was so insistent" on changing the baby's diapers, and heating her bottles that "it somehow became less and less necessary for me to involve myself," he claimed.

With all of that happening, it would be a few years and much legal wran-gling before the child's birth certificate was signed. She was named Jeniah Anne Josephine Johnson, as in J A J, as in Johnson & Johnson. Seward Jr. says it was Barbara who had chosen the name.

When Jeniah was two months old, in March 1961, Barbara flew to Bermuda and "begged" Seward Jr.'s uncle, Sir Bayard Dill, to "persuade" the Johnson family to attend the christening of Jeniah, then scheduled for May in Princeton. "She especially wanted my father to come," declared Seward Jr. "She knew he had very strong reservations about her . . . had opposed our marriage . . . and had kept away from me almost entirely since the wedding four and a half years earlier. She asked Uncle Bayard to help her mend this rift between my father and me."

Barbara had made elaborate preparation for Jeniah's christening ceremony in order to honor her baby and impress the Johnson family and especially Seward Sr., and to bring him around, hopefully with the help of Bayard Dill, who was a brother of Seward Jr.'s mother, Ruth.

Barbara's grand plans included importing to New Jersey from London the entire world-renowned Westminster Boys' Choir, who had performed for potentates and royalty. For tiny Jeniah's christening gown, she had commissioned the noted designer Mr. John, whose clients included the Duchess of Windsor, Gloria Vanderbilt, Lauren Bacall, and Joan Crawford. An Episcopal minister was being flown in from Kansas to perform the ceremony, which was scheduled to take place at the Johnson home rather than in church for reasons of privacy.

After Barbara's return from Bermuda, Seward Jr. noticed a stark change in her attitude toward him: she had suddenly begun treating him "as the father, requiring me to do all the baby duty. I was pleased but confused."

He said he later realized that "the shift" from Bannard to himself had come about because of the upcoming christening and that Barbara "wanted me to act like a father in the presence of the Johnson family. She told Darby to make himself scarce during the christening."

While he didn't attend, at Barbara's urging—"I was around but I didn't go"—Bannard remembers the event as "quite a do. It was done in the backyard and the place was absolutely jammed, and there were all kinds of high-powered people. The christening dress designed by Mr. John was beautiful."

One of the christening gifts that baby Jeniah received, he recalls, was a solid gold "piss pot, a chamber pot" that was inscribed.

The May 20, 1961, christening was a huge success and had come off exactly the way Barbara had planned it.

"Uncle Bayard [Dill] made the speech that he'd been asked to make about mending the family break," Seward Jr. stated.

Even Seward Sr., who had shut himself off from his son, had made an appearance, which was a major family breakthrough, or so it appeared.

But once the service had ended and the guests had left, Bannard once again returned to the Johnson household's daily life and, according to Seward Jr., "immediately relieved me of daddy duty . . . it more and more became evident that I was unwanted" in Jeniah's room.

Looking back, he felt "the exclusion grew so intense" that by the end of 1961, he "just gave up. I packed a bag and hid it." And in January 1962, while Barbara and Bannard were spending a day together in New York City, "I took the opportunity to leave for good."

Free of what he termed Barbara's "intimidating personality," he did the "unpleasant" math, counted back nine months from Barbara's full-term pregnancy to determine the date of conception, and concluded that it had occurred when she was snowed in in that cabin in the Poconos, allegedly with Bannard.

Seward Jr. had visited his father, from whom he had been long estranged—the christening of Jeniah, though, had helped to break some of the ice between them. But now he was forced to tell his father that he "suspected" that Jeniah was not his after all. He later quoted Seward Sr. as responding, "Damn! Two weeks ago I set up a trust, and I included her name in some way. It seemed in the spring things were finally going well with you." Believing his son's claim, and wasting no time, Seward Sr. telephoned one of his lawyers, told him about Seward Jr.'s suspicion, and was advised that it didn't matter because the trustees had "absolute and uncontrolled discretion" as to who would benefit from the trust.

Seward Jr. claimed many years later, "I was not having intercourse with [Barbara] for a full year prior to the child's birth," and alleges that Bannard was Jeniah's biological father. Bannard calls Seward Jr.'s allegation "ridiculous."

So if Seward Jr. denied that he was Jeniah's father, and Darby Bannard denied that he was her father—"I denied it a million times and I still deny it," he declares in 2011—then who was her father?

"Maybe it was an immaculate conception," offers Bannard glibly. "Certainly by the time we went through all those [future court] procedures, it wasn't very immaculate anymore."

In January 1962, a year after Jeniah Johnson's birth, Seward Jr. filed for what would become a nasty, rancorous, very public and humiliating divorce that would put a harsh spotlight—not for the first or last time, however—on the unconventional world of one of America's wealthiest families.

He claimed "extreme cruelty and adultery" and sought a blood test to prove paternity.

Seward Jr. later claimed that Barbara responded by asserting that he had actually "condoned" a "sexual relationship" between her and Bannard. She also claimed that Seward Jr. had "connived to throw" the two of them together as a way of securing "evidence for a divorce."

19

The very secretive Johnson dynasty had closely guarded the scandalous goings-on in J. Seward Johnson Jr.'s home, but that changed a week before Valentine's Day 1963 when shots rang out in the Princeton mansion where Barbara had continued to reside, and was receiving nine hundred dollars a week in temporary alimony.

The gunfire shot Seward Jr. and Barbara's marital mess onto the front pages and into the Princeton police blotter. For the well-to-do residents of the placid Ivy League community, such louche and scandalous behavior was unheard of within its bucolic and manicured boundaries.

The Johnson scandal became the talk of the town, and made headlines around the nation.

What ensued in the predawn hours was a nightmarish film noir scene that even Raymond Chandler couldn't have invented, and at the same time it had the sense of a comedy of errors like the Keystone Kops.

It was around 3 A.M. on February 8, 1963, " a date that shall live in infamy," declares Darby Bannard, recalling what happened—when a raiding team of seven men, some of them armed *Hollywood Confidential*–style with camera equipment, gained entry to the Johnson home at 75 Cleveland Lane, seeking evidence of adultery for Seward Jr.'s divorce case against his estranged wife.

His hope was that they would find and photograph Barbara and Bannard in flagrante delicto.

Bannard had moved into the Johnson home "to some extent" and had even set up an art studio there, he acknowledges. But he says he's innocent of anything more.

Years later, he says: "When Seward moved out there was a lot of animosity and I identified with Barbara's situation. She was getting telephone threats on her life from somebody calling himself Mr. X, and Mr. X was going to do things to her. She was scared to death. So sometimes I'd just stay over there. He then sent that gang of thugs in. I was there that night. He wanted to catch me in bed with her, but I wasn't in bed with her."

Before the private eyes could find out who might be in bed with whom, they had to get past Barbara's ferocious-looking and snarling white English bulldog, Ebenezer, so the team leader, forty-year-old Harold Purcell, president of the Essex Investigating Bureau, fired a five-and-dime plastic water pistol filled with ammonia into the dog's eyes, temporarily putting him out of commission.

Meanwhile, hiding in a car outside the house was Seward Jr., closely watching the not-so-clandestine action that was unfolding.

"I had to go with them on the raid to let them in the house, quote unquote," he says many years later, chuckling at the memory. "I said, if I'm going to go, my lawyer's going to go, too, so he went and he was scared to death."

Once inside, a fifty-year-old Philip Marlowe wannabe by the name of Harvey D. Blount quietly climbed the stairs and entered Barbara's bedroom. Wearing skimpy pajamas she jumped out of bed and confronted the intruder—Blount was black—with a gun.

Sounding like a tough-talking Chandler-style tomato, the estranged Johnson wife—dubbed "an attractive red-haired Princeton socialite" by the press—later told a packed magistrate's hearing in Princeton what had happened:

"I was awakened simultaneously by noise and also the sense of someone being present. I saw a man . . . a colored man . . . coming toward me.

"I pushed him real hard. He fell. I got my gun in the lower drawer of the cabinet. I looked up and told him to get out. He kept coming and I shot him. He kept coming and I shot him a little higher."

Two-year-old Jeniah, in her crib, was yelling "bang, bang, bang" as the reports from her mother's gun reverberated through the house, Bannard clearly recalls.

Outside in the car, Seward Jr. and his lawyer panicked.

"I said, 'Someone's been shot!' He said, 'Let's get out of here!' There was a car that was supposed to pick up everyone, but the rest of them got arrested. We left and drove back to Newark."

Blount, taken to Princeton Hospital, was critically wounded—shot four times with Barbara's .22 caliber target pistol. The bullets hit him in the face—he would lose an eye—in the right shoulder, left hip, and neck.

During the bedroom melee the photographers fired away, too; their popping flashbulbs and blast of lights mixing with the sound and sight of gunfire was almost psychedelic.

Not surprisingly, a shootout involving one of the country's wealthiest families became daily tabloid headline fodder: "Redhead Tells of Shooting 'Eye,'" screamed the *New York Daily Mirror*. The *Daily News* proclaimed, "Rich Wife Tells of Shooting in Her Bedroom."

One of Blount's colleagues, Lorann R. Pike, a twenty-five-year-old carpenter who participated in the raid, would later claim in court that he saw Bannard running out of Barbara's bedroom.

He was, Pike claimed, "dressed in his skivvies."

Barbara, however, had a different version of events.

It was a whale of a story.

She stated that Bannard was, indeed, with her in the bedroom, but only because the bedroom was also where her whale cataloguing and research was being conducted and, besides, she asserted that Bannard wasn't in the bedroom at the time Blount forced his way in, despite what Pike claimed, when the private dicks showed up. At one point there was even a scuffle between Bannard and the raiders, and while all that was happening, Barbara climbed out of her bedroom window, ran to a neighbor's house, and called the cops.

One of the Johnson raiders, Joseph S. Pelusio, reportedly held Bannard, his helper, Irving Potts, and Barbara's then-fourteen-year-old son, Bruce, at gunpoint against a wall and threatened to shoot them if they moved.

"We were innocent bystanders and got beat up," maintains Bannard. "What a bunch those guys were. They were just sort of hired off the street.

They came into that room where I was calling the police and they lined everybody up with guns—the raiders had guns, and then they kicked us down the stairs."

Seward Jr., who had instigated the disastrous raid, and who had fled the scene when the bullets started flying, had holed up in a room at the Nassau Inn in Newark, waiting to be summoned by authorities about his role in the almost fatal fiasco. He was awakened the next night by New Jersey Democratic Party political power Balfour Bowen Thorn Lord, known as Thorn, who was married to his second wife, Nina Underwood McAlpin Lord, one of Essie Underwood Johnson's sisters, and the ex-wife of an heir to the McAlpin hotel fortune.

In a classic understatement, Thorn says, "Seward, you're in a big pickle. I'm going to see what I can do to help you."

Figuring the cops were on the Johnson & Johnson heir's trail, Thorn told Seward, " 'I'm driving by the hotel. I have a Lincoln, get in, but get right down on the floor as soon as you get in,' so I got in the car, and Thorn said, 'Get down!' I thought, what's with him?" recalls Seward Jr. "And he drives all around Princeton. Every time we pulled up to a light, Thorn says 'Get down!' I thought, Holy Mackerel, I'm not a criminal."

Seward Jr. soon learned that Lord, who a couple of years earlier had been New Jersey's unsuccessful Democratic nominee for the U.S. Senate, was in the midst of a nervous breakdown, was in a troubled marriage, and had been acting oddly. It only got worse. Lord subsequently committed suicide at the age of fifty-eight by strangling himself with an electric shaver cord wrapped twice around his neck. His body was discovered sitting in an armchair at a friend's home.

As a result of the raid, there were some eighty charges and countercharges filed by the state of New Jersey against Barbara—one was a technical charge of atrocious assault and battery—and against the investigators, against Bannard, described as Barbara's "bookkeeper and secretary" in the court papers, and against Irving Potts, a twenty-one-year-old clerk who worked in a local Princeton bookstore and who was assisting Bannard and Barbara as curator in the whale project, and also cataloguing her collection of porcelain birds.

With all of the participants and all of the wild charges, the Princeton magistrate who was assigned the case for a preliminary hearing, Theodore T. Tams Jr., declared it was developing into a "Roman circus."

In the end, the grand jury, after hearing a dozen witnesses, declined to indict Barbara and Seward Jr. However, two of the detectives, Harry Purcell, who had spritzed Ebenezer with the ammonia, and Joseph S. Pelusio, who was employed by Purcell, were indicted on charges of assault. As a result of the bizarre late-night events at the Johnson estate, the grand jury also recommended stricter license rules for New Jersey private detectives, in order to keep clowns like the raiders out of the P.I. profession.

"One might have thought the exposure of the adultery and the photographic evidence that the raid produced would have been sufficient evidence to justify a blood test" to determine the paternity of Jeniah, Seward Jr. later stated. "But the sensational shooting somehow clouded the situation."

In a postscript to the whole outlandish affair, the New Jersey Society for the Prevention of Cruelty to Animals attempted to go after the detectives for knocking out Ebenezer, but that case was eventually dismissed. Barbara, however, claimed the dog had suffered psychological scars in the wake of the incident. "He used to wag his tail," she said sadly. "Now he hides under the table whenever anyone appears at the door."

20

As J. Seward Johnson Jr.'s divorce case slowly moved forward after the disastrous raid, he "lived not only with frustration but also in fear," as he later observes.

"We had an affidavit from a woman who said that after I left [Barbara] had hired a man, the woman's husband, as a guard and gave him a gun to shoot anyone who came into the house."

The bodyguard wanted to make certain he didn't shoot Seward by mistake so he asked for his description.

The affidavit described Seward Jr. as weighing 370 pounds, twice what he actually weighed—"which meant that if I'd shown up and the man had done as he was ordered, I'd have been shot," he claimed in a letter to his father.

Meanwhile, Barbara Johnson's attorney decided that Seward Jr. required more "psychiatric, psychological, and psychoanalytical assistance."

In one of the many depositions in the case, Seward Sr. reportedly was asked whether he recalled Barbara once telling him that she thought her husband required psychiatric treatment "for some very unusual tendencies" that he had. Under questioning, it was revealed that those tendencies reportedly involved "frequent masturbation."

In response to another question, Seward Sr., the second in charge of the nation's largest health-needs conglomerate, said he did not recall saying to Barbara, "If that's the way he derives his pleasure, that's for him to determine."

A week before Christmas 1963, some ten months after the raid, a Mercer County judge, George H. Barlow, ordered that Jeniah Anne Johnson undergo blood tests after Seward Jr. once again maintained that he was not her father, and that Darby Bannard was her father. Seward Jr.'s prominent New Jersey attorney, Warren W. Wilentz, in asking for the tests, charged that Barbara had slept with Bannard.

Barbara, however, insisted that the publicity might cause psychological harm to the toddler. Seven months later a New Jersey appellate court ruled that such tests should be administered only as a last resort. Judge Milton B. Conford said that the child "is entitled to protection from the threats in respect of its legitimacy and property rights involved in the taking of blood grouping tests in these circumstances unless and until no alternative is left."

Conford recommended that lower court hearings be held on the issue of adultery, and if Barbara had committed adultery the court should determine whether Seward Jr. condoned it because Barbara's lawyers argued that Seward Jr. permitted Bannard to reside in the Johnson house long before he made the claims that Barbara and Bannard had slept together.

As for Jeniah, there never would be a blood test administered to determine paternity.

For ten days in November 1964, all of the juicy bits about the horrific Johnson marriage were made public in a packed Trenton courtroom with New Jersey Superior Court Judge Charles F. Paulis presiding. The titillating divorce trial was covered in all its salacious detail, in particular by New York City's high-circulation, straphanger daily tabloids, and by the international wire services.

Headlines roared: "J&J Heir: Story from Bed to Verse," and "Drug Co. Heir Wins Divorce, and Wife Wins a Big Wad."

Barbara denied all of the allegations made against her by Seward Jr.—the lovers, the chicanery, the adultery, the mental cruelty, all of it—and she filed a countersuit, claiming that not only had her husband deserted her when he left in January 1962, but that *he*, in fact, was the partner in the volatile and violent marriage who had violated the Seventh Commandment, *Thou shalt not commit adultery.*

The alleged paramour was a homely intellectual college student in her mid-twenties by the name of Joyce Cecilia Horton, who Seward Jr. had met at the zenith of his marital troubles (but with whom he maintains he did not become intimate while he was still living with Barbara), and who would become his second wife.

During the divorce trial, the two women lashed out at one another like mean schoolgirls. At one point, Barbara walked up to Seward Jr. and said, pointing to Horton in the gallery, "She has a face like a pizza," and at another point Horton stood up in the packed courtroom and barked, "That's not true," about something to which Barbara had testified.

Almost a half century later, Joyce Cecilia Horton Johnson considers Barbara "a liar."

In December 1964, Seward Jr.'s uncle, the General, fed up with the whole matter, wrote a letter stating his opinion that Seward Jr. and Barbara—the pair of them—"are abnormal."

In order to pay his high-priced divorce lawyers, Seward Jr. desperately needed cash, money that was tied up in his trust. He knew there would be a quid pro quo because his uncle was one of the trustees, and there was: Seward Jr. was required to resign as trustee of his sisters' trusts because the General wanted control over them.

"My uncle drove a hard bargain," Seward Jr. declared. "On the pretext that no Johnson who could get himself into such a marital mess was qualified to be trusted with other people's money, he declared that if I wanted money for my divorce, I must resign."

While he got the funds, he apparently lost millions in future trustee fees.

Another aspect of the case that seemed to have no end involved Seward Jr.'s effort—his first of what would be a number of them going forward for decades—to disinherit Jeniah, once again claiming she was not his. Under a trust fund, the disputed child was to have received an annual payment of more than $135,000. But Seward Jr. had, on orders from the judge as part of the divorce settlement, reluctantly signed a document on March 3, 1965, which was witnessed and notarized, stating he *was* Jeniah's biological father.

That document, entitled "Acknowledgement of Paternity," stated: "The undersigned, John Seward Johnson, Jr., hereby unequivocally acknowledges paternity of Jeniah Anne Josephine Johnson, born of Barbara E. Johnson at Princeton, New Jersey, on January 11, 1961."

As a colleague, Patrick McCarthy, later observes, "Seward essentially had a gun to his head. He was trying to pursue a divorce and they wouldn't grant him the divorce unless he acknowledged paternity. If someone wants out of a marriage, especially someone in Seward Johnson's position, they are going to do whatever it takes to get out of that marriage."

Most birth certificates are filed shortly after a child comes into the world. But Seward Jr. claims that Jeniah's had not immediately been filed by Barbara. In fact, he asserts, it happened as long as four years later, only after he accepted paternity as part of the divorce settlement.

After about two years of fierce and passionate litigation, the nine-year marriage from hell of J. Seward Johnson Jr. and Barbara Eisenfuhr Kline Bailey Maxwell Johnson ended on March 8, 1965, on the grounds of desertion. Barbara got custody of Jeniah, of course, and her son, Bruce, whom Seward Jr. had adopted. Beyond that, she got one million dollars in Johnson & Johnson stock and cash in addition to the Princeton estate, and financial support for the children until the age of twenty-three.

Moreover, Seward Jr. says, the deal involved "that I would acknowledge Bannard's child as mine."

In June 1969, Seward Jr. won still another case, that one to have his trust changed so that Jeniah and her half brother, Bruce, could never benefit from his estate when he died. At the time, that estate was worth some twenty-eight million dollars. Under the new trust, his second wife and children would be the beneficiaries.

Darby Bannard, accused by Seward Jr. of being Barbara's lover and Jeniah's father, never testified at the divorce trial, but he was deposed, as he recalls, in part about his relationship with Barbara.

"There were certain things that were factually based that were obvious, and other things that were just lunacy and fantasy," he says years later. "If I was going to see Barbara in the nude, I wasn't going to see her in the nude when Seward was around. That kind of stuff just didn't make sense." And he calls Seward Jr.'s charges of adultery "just bullshit."

21

As he waited for his divorce to be finalized, J. Seward Johnson Jr. took extreme, often melodramatic measures to avoid being spotted with his girlfriend and future wife, Joyce Cecilia Horton.

"I was worried about being followed," he says. "I had a whole bunch of cars and drivers and escape routes. I had a car with us [him and Joyce] in it, and a car following us so if someone else was following us my [backup] car would radio us and we'd pull off all of a sudden so they couldn't follow. We didn't know [if anyone was following]. I wanted to make sure they couldn't."

Joyce, who had " an incredibly sheltered life" growing up, she avows many years later, never told her parents that the man she intended to marry was a member of the famous and, in some circles, infamous, Johnson dynasty, a troubled heir who had just been entangled in one of the messiest headline-making divorce cases. "I think if they had known more about the Johnson family they would have maybe *not* been happy and they would have wondered why [she would marry into the family], but they didn't."

A week or two after his divorce was finalized, Seward Jr. and Joyce were married in a small, simple ceremony at the historic Homestead Resort hotel in Hot Springs, Virginia. Those *not* in attendance were the groom's father, Seward Sr., still displeased with him, and Seward's mother, Ruth Dill Johnson, and her second husband, who despised the Johnson family.

Seward Jr.'s second wife and first wife were from entirely different worlds.

Joyce, a Philadelphia girl with a twin sister, was a descendant of the wealthy Hortons who had arrived in 1632 on their own ships from Horton, in England. While most Hortons in the United States were educators, Joyce's father, a Wharton School graduate, was a government accountant who testified as an expert witness in tax cases, and spent his weekends at home reading Plato and Shakespeare.

She had graduated from Ravenhill Academy in Philadelphia, the same prestigious Catholic girls' school once attended by a budding actress named Grace Kelly. When Seward Jr. met Joyce, she was finishing her junior year at George Washington University, with aspirations to be a writer.

Joyce had closely monitored Seward Jr.'s divorce trial, and had married him when his life was in major turmoil, so her initial shock at becoming a Johnson wife didn't change for a long time.

"It still is [a shock]," she firmly states in 2011, even after a half century of marriage, and just months after more Johnson dynasty scandal was in the headlines with the tragic death of Woody Johnson's troubled daughter, Casey. "It's all a shock, anything to do with the Johnsons," she declares. "It's negative and unbelievable for me."

After they were married, Seward and Joyce moved to Cambridge, Massachusetts. She had a son whom they named John Seward Johnson III, who later became the liberal supporter of Barack Obama when Woody Johnson was pitching McCain-Palin, and a daughter, Clelia, who started calling herself India Blake when she did some acting. With the stage name, this fourth-generation Johnson distanced herself from the family dynasty.

It was Joyce who first spotted Seward Jr.'s artistic talents and who he credits with being his muse. Away from the Johnson dynasty drama and out of his dreadful first marriage, he had started dabbling in painting and sculpture.

He had tried to get admitted to Boston's School of the Museum of Fine Arts, but was rejected. It was then that Joyce convinced him to take sculpting classes at the Cambridge Adult Education Center, and the first piece he ever finished, a stylized nude woman he called *Stainless Girl*, won first place, among some seven thousand entries, in an art competition sponsored by U.S. Steel.

Seward Jr. never made it into the upper echelon of the family business, stymied by his father and uncle, and had thought of himself as an utter and complete failure. But he was now on his way as a sculptor of often controversial, lifelike, three-dimensional statues, a calling and career in which he would finally succeed, gaining international fame and sometimes infamy. He found joy in his work, and even financial success beyond his Johnson & Johnson trust fund millions, inheritances, trusteeships, Johnson & Johnson stock ownership, real estate holdings, and private ventures.

Some of his pieces would sell for as much as one million dollars each.

In a 1970 "Dear Dad" letter he wrote, "I cannot help but hope that I may, through this occupation, give you, as well as myself, something to be proud of me over."

Critics, though, weren't always in his corner.

By the twenty-first century, his work was considered important enough to be given a show and an entire floor at the prestigious Corcoran Gallery of Art in the nation's capital, focusing on his curious lifelike renderings of Impressionist art, which the curator of the show, Jacquelyn Serwer, had noted "are clever and witty and beautifully executed."

But the exhibit was immediately panned by Blake Gopnik, the *Washington Post*'s long-respected art critic, who, in the lead to his September 12, 2003, poison pen review observed:

> Don't you hate the way it feels when you've had a couple of rotten-egg and sardine milkshakes, and then you get stuck going backward on a roller coaster for an hour or two, and the only music you've got for your Walkman is an accordion version of *Carmen*? You know that feeling? No? Then go see "Beyond the Frame; Impressionism Revisited: The Sculptures of J. Seward Johnson, Jr."

He added, "But let's not mince words: This show is really, really bad."

Seward Jr. was still getting a laugh out of Gopnik's sarcasm years later, and boasting that despite the repugnant review, or because of it, "my show ended up being the most popular show in the history of the museum. I was going to send him a thank-you note but I haven't gotten around to it yet."

The Corcoran's director who had green-lighted the exhibit would later be dismissed, and Seward Jr.'s show reportedly was one of the reasons for his dismissal, along with more major financial difficulties that the gallery was having.

But a number of other critics disagreed with the naysayers, including Richard Lacayo, writing in *Time* magazine, who declared that Johnson "is not to be dismissed . . . Johnson's work is a very welcome relief from what is called plunk art, mediocre abstract sculpture plopped down in public places."

One of his hundreds of life-size, real-life sculptures called *Double Check*, which portrayed a businessman reviewing a contract, was among some one hundred million dollars in art that had been part of the horrific damage inflicted in the 9/11 attack on the World Trade Center. While works by the likes of Miró and Calder were ruined, only Seward Jr.'s piece completely survived, although covered in the dust of what had been one of the towers, and it became an improvised memorial to the dead on which memorial notes and flowers were placed.

Spending more than twenty million dollars, Seward Jr. had created and established the Grounds for Sculpture, turning what had been the old New Jersey State Fairgrounds into a sylvan setting for dozens of his sculptures for public viewing. He also established the nonprofit Johnson Atelier to cast bronze, and artists such as Marisol and George Segal have used the facilities to cast some of their works. Seward Jr. fondly recalls how Segal, the painter who later became best known for his own life-size sculptures, first visited his New Jersey studio, and saw his three-dimensional renderings. "He looked around and said, 'Holy shit!' and then he copied it and did it in his style."

One of those who also had become transfixed by Seward Jr.'s work was the "King of Pop," Michael Jackson.

In the early nineties, out of the blue, Seward Jr. was invited by Jackson's longtime plastic surgeon, Dr. Steven Hoefflin, to Jackson's home, Neverland, in California, to confer about a sculpture that the entertainer wanted done of himself, and to teach the art of sculpting.

To break the ice, Jackson offered to take Seward Jr. to see the animals in his zoo.

"He drove me out in the golf cart to the giraffes, and we went up on a high platform so I could be up with the giraffes' heads. Animals somehow take to me and all the giraffes came over and started licking my face. Michael was so impressed he started to dance. Apparently I passed some sort of test.

"I turned to him and I said, 'Michael, if I'm going to teach you how to sculpt, you've got to teach me how to do the moonwalk.' I was studying as he did this thing, examining his legs, and I swear they were like they weren't attached to his body. But I could *not* follow what he was doing, and I fell on my face. He marched off. He had enough trying to teach me."

Arrangements were made for Jackson to come to Seward Jr.'s home in Princeton—wearing a disguise—to take sculpting lessons. However, a month or so later Jackson telephoned Seward Jr., who was staying with his family in a hotel in Key West, Florida, where he was buying another home.

"He got my daughter India's room by mistake, and she answered the phone and in his high-pitched voice he said, 'This is Michael Jackson.' And my daughter said, 'Oh, come on Dad, quit kidding!'" thinking her father was impersonating Jackson. "Then he got hold of me and he said, 'Oh, God, you recognize my voice,' and I was wondering, how the hell I wouldn't."

Jackson informed Seward Jr. that a long-planned world tour was about to begin and he'd have to put off the lessons.

"That was truly the last time we were in contact."

He later received an autographed photo from the Gloved One, with the words: "To Seward, Thanx to a genius, Love Michael."

Seward Jr. says that one of his great regrets in life was not learning how to do the moonwalk.

$ $ $

Joyce Johnson, who had kick-started Seward Jr.'s sculpting and was his toughest critic and biggest booster, crows many years later that he is "an incredible innovator. I used to say to him early on, 'I don't know if you're an artist, but I know you're a genius.' Seward was the first person to take sculpture off the pedestal."

Some people in Chicago didn't agree with the muse's assessment in midsummer 2011 when Seward Jr.'s giant Marilyn Monroe caused a critical cyclone on Michigan Avenue in the Windy City.

Seward Jr. had made an exact replica of Marilyn in her iconic pose in the film *The Seven-Year Itch* in which she's standing above a subway grate with her Frederick's of Hollywood–style dress billowing up and exposing her legs and her panties. But his version was a Godzilla-like twenty-six feet tall, and in the eye of a number of beholders—parents who had brought their kids to see the statue—Seward Jr.'s Marilyn seemed almost pornographic.

As the *Los Angeles Times* observed, the statue "has been called 'creepy schlock' and 'a giant, silent avatar of nonconsent.' Some observers are appalled at the seemingly endless stream of tourists hugging her legs and voyeurs young and old unabashedly shooting upskirt photos with their cell phones."

Back at home in Princeton, Seward Jr., who loved controversy and confrontation, savored it all, including the hubbub over erotic statues commissioned by Prince Jefri Bolkiah, the brother of the Sultan of Brunei. The statues figured in a lawsuit not involving Seward Jr.

"They make me blush," a lawyer involved in the case said at the time.

But Seward Jr. says he never laid his fine sculptor's hand on the statues, and didn't have any idea who had commissioned them for the one million dollars he was paid.

"Actually," he says, "I didn't do them. I did the *maquettes*," which were the eighteen-inch models of what was to come. "I had my people do them. I took the Kama Sutra and picked three of the most outrageous positions and I sent them over [to the people who worked in his foundry] and said, 'Give these back to me life-size, and hire some models and do what's necessary.'"

When they were finished, Seward Jr. never signed them.

The sculptures had been commissioned by an intermediary, an Asian woman representing a company called Silvercrest, with whom Seward Jr.'s associate, Paula Stokes, who handled his lucrative sculpture business, had met with no more than twice. After delivery, the woman and the firm she represented vanished. "It was all very on-purpose mysterious," Stokes told her boss.

Despite all the controversy about his work, or because of it, Seward Jr. says at eighty-one in 2011, that he wants to be remembered as an artist, not a Johnson.

"My art is how I present it, how I fool people."

22

When Joyce Horton married J. Seward Johnson Jr., she didn't feel a fit with the Johnson family and wasn't particularly taken with his mother, Ruth Dill Johnson Crockett, or his stepmother, Esther "Essie" Underwood Johnson, who Seward Jr. himself despised.

Curiously, of the three women who her philandering father-in-law, Seward Sr., had taken as his wives, Joyce most liked the one who would become the most loathed by her husband and his five siblings, loathed mainly because of money and greed. The object of her fondness and the target of the Johnson siblings' wrath was Barbara "Basia" Piasecka, the bodacious, curvaceous Polish refugee and former chambermaid, the farmer's daughter with a college degree, who at thirty-four had married Seward Jr.'s seventy-six-year-old father in 1971, just a week after the old man divorced Essie.

The same Basia who once poignantly asked, "Is it a shame in America to be a maid and work hard?"

At Seward Sr.'s death of cancer at the age of eighty-seven, in May 1983, "the Cinderella chambermaid," as she was dubbed by the press, inherited the bulk of his fortune, more than $400 million, leaving five of his six children—four with Ruth, and two with Essie—out of his final will, dated August 3, 1973. Only Seward Jr. received some money and property, one million dollars and a home on Cape Cod.

Led by him, the furious siblings, claiming undue influence and elder abuse by Basia—they also charged that she had "bewitched" the wealthy and eccentric geezer—ignited a scandalous courtroom battle over the will in 1986 that even made Seward Jr.'s divorce trial from his own Barbara a decade earlier seem mild by comparison.

"Basia to me was a European experience," says Joyce, who had naturally sided with her husband and his siblings during the court battle, but nevertheless had respect for the onetime housekeeper who in time would become one of the world's richest women, parlaying her Johnson winnings into an even bigger fortune by buying and auctioning off rare art while living the good life in Monte Carlo. (In September 2011, *Forbes* reported that the seventy-four-year-old Johnson & Johnson widow had a net worth of $3.1 billion.)

Joyce says that she admired Basia's candidness, even when Basia was critical of the Johnsons, and would confide to Joyce, "Oh, you know, the Johnsons, they're not very bright. Some of them are *stupid* . . ."

"Basia seemed to favor me. She said, 'You are so much smarter than the Johnson family.' She sort of related to me in a very personal way."

Joyce's esteem for Basia, who married Seward Sr. six years after Joyce married Seward Jr., grew the more the daughter-in-law got to know her.

But Joyce also saw craziness.

"She was almost two different people. In a way, she could be genuine and sincere, and in another way there was something screwy."

Less than a month before his father died and before his shocking will was read, Seward Jr. and Joyce were spending time with Basia, who then resided in the splendor of Jasna Polana, the spectacular New Jersey *über* mansion brimming with art and antiques that she had had built with her doddering husband's millions when he was still alive. (She later sold it after his death. It was turned into a fancy golf course.)

"Joyce and I were sitting there with her, and [Basia] was thumbing through a Park-Bernet art auction catalogue like she was a kid with an FAO Schwarz catalogue and checking off things for four hundred thousand dollars," Seward Jr. says. Recalling the moment, Joyce claims Basia declared, "I have two mottos. Strike when the iron is hot, and when you see an opportunity take it."

Even though Seward Jr. was in the forefront of his siblings' court battle with Basia—he convinced them to sue her to try to get some of those hundreds of millions she had been bequeathed by his father—he reveals more than a quarter of a century later that he actually had liked and respected Basia, particularly her pugnacious, combative style.

But before the trial, when her lawyer asked him, "Where do you stand?" his immediate chilling response was, "I haven't seen the will yet but if it's a cold fish in the face I'm going to lead everyone against you."

$ $ $

Before the start of what would become the most costly, outrageous, and bitterly fought will contest ever at the time, another vicious battle, known only to the plaintiffs, was being quietly waged outside the courtroom.

Inside Manhattan's Surrogate Court, the trial, which would last four months, cost untold millions in legal fees, and have an anticlimactic denouement, was docketed as *Johnson v. Johnson*; the other shootout might have arguably been designated *Johnson v. Margolick v. Goldsmith*.

David Margolick was the ambitious thirty-three-year-old legal correspondent for *The New York Times*. With a law degree from Stanford, and well-tuned journalistic skills, he saw the forthcoming Johnson trial as much bigger than a daily hard-news story for the Gray Lady, and decided to write a book about the case.

With visions of a big bestseller, he approached Seward Jr., the fifty-five-year-old leader of the litigious siblings to secure the family's cooperation.

All seemed copasetic.

But on June 12, 1985, as a prelude to the start of the trial, *The Times* published a story by Margolick headlined: "A Famous Fortune Entangles Family in a Bitter Fight Over Bequest."

While the headline was tame—splashed across the paper's prominent B1 section, known as the second front—Margolick's story wasn't.

Quoting Basia's lawyers and court papers filed by them, Margolick ravaged Seward Jr. and his siblings, especially his sister, Mary Lea. He also gave the Johnsons' side, but not nearly enough to placate Seward Jr., who wanted it *all* pro-Johnson and anti-Basia.

Seward Jr. read the piece and turned purple with rage.

A quarter century later, in 2011, he still feels intense animosity toward Margolick.

"I tried to be really straight with him, and boy, oh boy, that trial thing he wrote showed me . . . that he was a slime bag from *The New York Times*," he declares. "I dislike him *so* much."

After Margolick's story ran, Seward Jr. says, "I decided we must stop this [Margolick's book]. I said to the family, 'Who the hell knows someone who's had a bestseller?' "

As it turned out, Mary Lea and her third husband, the gay and Jewish Hollywood and Broadway producer Marty Richards, knew the perfect author: a Park Avenue socialite and writer, Barbara Goldsmith.

Goldsmith, who covered the trial and was given interviews with the siblings and relatives, came up with one major revelation, which became the book's big hook, which was Mary Lea's shocking—and, as it turned out, very questionable—disclosure that her father, Seward Sr., had molested her when she was growing up.

Mary Lea clearly had an agenda to sully her father after his death, because she held a huge grudge against him: the two had often feuded, and had gotten into a heated dispute after she sued him in the 1960s in an effort to get more money out of the family trust. He fired back in a toxic letter, declaring, "You are turning out to be a troublemaker beyond my imagination."

What greater revenge than accusing him after his death of molesting her?

Just as Seward Jr. was apoplectic over Margolick's *Times* story, he was knocked for a loop when he got an advance copy of Goldsmith's opus and saw what was written about his sister and his father.

"I didn't think it was true," Seward Jr. declares for the first time a quarter century later. "I was *appalled* because I had driven the family to teaming up with Goldsmith. I even gave her the title for her book."

Seward Jr., who acknowledges that he and Mary Lea were a lot alike emotionally, finally began to believe her claim and "felt very badly" for her.

Looking back many years later, he first "assumed" that Mary Lea made the revelation because she had a vendetta against her father. Later, he convinced himself, "It was a way of feeling right about herself, and setting the record straight. It was a way to try to get rid of the scar."

On the one hand, he believes his late sister's story to be true, on the other he acknowledges that she could have invented it.

"I can't say it's not possible."

$ $ $

Two decades after their mother Mary Lea's death in 1990, brothers Eric Ryan and Quentin Ryan seriously questioned the veracity of her charges of sexual abuse against their grandfather.

They voiced their opinions separately because they, too, had been feuding for a number of years.

For his part, Quentin emphatically disbelieves his mother's story and claims it was instigated by her flamboyant, publicity-hungry producer husband, Marty Richards. "Marty sold her on it," he firmly maintains. "I questioned my aunts and there is *no* truth to my mother's allegation whatsoever. My mother was not a stable person. She was heavily into alcohol and painkillers."

States Eric Ryan, "It's easy for me to spin out a lot of positions on whether my mom was delusional, or whether she was projecting, or whether she was seeking attention. There are lots of arguments to say that it never happened. That's really why I object to my mom having gone public with it because I think that's an exploration that was really only appropriately done between my mother and her therapist, if it was going to be done after her father's death."

Like his brother Quentin, Eric believes Marty Richards had pushed Mary Lea into making the charge, true or not, against her father, for publicity purposes.

"Marty was the driving force in seeing a benefit to creating—to cloaking—the Johnson name in celebrity, even if that celebrity has an aspect of notoriety about it," Ryan avows. "One has to remember that my mom and Marty were in show business, so it was kind of like trying to promote my mother as a celebrity, and a way to promote their shows, and their business, and to attract investors."

With Mary Lea's Johnson & Johnson wealth and the Bronx-born Marty Richards's show business chutzpah and flamboyant style, the pair had formed a very successful production team, and in 1976 they had founded the Producers Circle Company—a winning combination that won them many Tony Awards and a Pulitzer for films like *The Boys from Brazil*, and Broadway hits like *La Cage aux Folles*.

Eric believes his mother's role in show business—even just as the financial angel—may have had some influence on her shocking story of incest.

"As a producer her job was to help raise money to put shows together, and part of that was trying to create personal celebrity for herself so that people would want to be in her company," Ryan observes. "And part of this personal celebrity was embracing victimhood. She wanted people gathering around her, and have them wanting to be with her, and have them be sympathetic to her."

$ $ $

In 1993, David Margolick's book was published. If he was upset that he'd been refused cooperation by the Johnson siblings, he showed it by exacting revenge with painful and belittling descriptions of the principals.

Calling Seward Jr. "the ringleader" of the lawsuit, he painted him as "a man of pale skin, yellowed, stubby smoker's teeth, the jowls of a walrus, and the drooping eyelids of a *Doonesbury* character," and pictured his wife Joyce as "one of those haggard, haunted characters from the paintings of Edward Munch."

Mary Lea and other family members fared no better. While Barbara Goldsmith described Mary Lea as "a quiet, generous, gentle blond woman with intense blue-green eyes," Margolick, who sat near Goldsmith during the trial with a contingent of other reporters, described a completely different persona. "Mary Lea," he wrote, "was a large, disassociated androgynous woman who looked eerily like the character Zaza in *La Cage aux Folles*," and he characterized her husband, Marty Richards, who sat protectively next to her through the trial, as looking "more like an escort than a spouse . . . boyish, diminutive, immaculately coiffed."

In his caustic epilogue, Margolick wrote that Marty Richards had been "peddling privately" the story about Seward Sr.'s claimed molestation of Mary Lea, and he emphasized that Goldsmith "was traipsing a doddering

Mary Lea around the talk-show circuit to decry child abuse and, incidentally, to help hawk her book."

After all the sturm und drang and circus-like atmosphere, the trial had ended anticlimactically with an out-of-court settlement, an agreement in which the Johnson siblings reportedly received $40 million, and $25 million was paid for the legal fees of both sides. A Seward Johnson Sr. charity that had also been left out of the will received about $20 million, and Basia was left with a staggering $350 million nest egg.

Not long after the settlement, she demurely invited a contingent of reporters to Jasna Polana, her orange and pink stone mansion, declaring she wanted to show off "not the quantity of my money, but the quality," and that included a museum's worth of Rembrandts, Titians, and Flemish tapestries. When she escorted reporters into the living room she boasted that they were standing on what she called "a king's carpet" that had once been the possession of Louis XIV. Then they moved on to her prize piece—a Raphael drawing of an apostle's transfiguration: price tag, five million dollars. All of this was just the tip of the priceless stuff she had accumulated during the marriage, and that now was all hers.

She concluded the tour with a comment about the trial and all of the name-calling she had endured from the Johnson plaintiffs.

"The whole thing was envy," she declared. "Envy causes hate. Hate causes war."

When Judy Garland's daughter Liza Minnelli, upset by Mary Lea's disturbing account of Seward Sr.'s alleged incest, began soliciting funds for a group battling child abuse, she wrote to the wealthy Basia, seeking a contribution. Basia's response was pure unadulterated vitriol.

She advised Minnelli to "contact Barbara Goldsmith, who made so much money from her false accusations that my husband was a child abuser. He was as much a child abuser as I am Liza Minnelli."

Having become a billionaire, Basia died on April Fool's Day 2013, at age seventy-six, near her childhood home in Poland.

23

After her divorce from J. Seward Johnson Jr., the former Barbara Eisen-fuhr Kline Bailey Maxwell Johnson lived the life of a Princeton socialite. She would always keep the famous Johnson surname, but much later began calling herself "Kristina."

Barbara's sprawling fieldstone home that her ex-husband had bought for them, which she got in the divorce, was filled with whaling and nautical memorabilia. Entranced with the hobby, she had even once considered purchasing a dead whale—all sixty-five feet of major mammal—to put on the roof, but was concerned about what the neighbors might think, so she dropped the idea.

Still, a fourteen-foot-high whale's jawbone greeted visitors to her garden.

"I tried to decorate it the way a sea captain's wife would have done when her husband brought home all this scrimshaw and gear and she wanted to put it somewhere so she wouldn't hurt his feelings," she once explained.

At one point, she had a staff of servants, one of them a butler named Kerche who was required to wear a morning coat when guests were present, and who sported a monocle like the characters played by the actor Erich von Stroheim in the movies. Her household also had a number of pets, among them a fierce German shepherd who stood alert for trespassers, and a giant tortoise, described as being as big as a boulder, who roamed the garden, and who supposedly was born around 1800 and was claimed to have belonged to Queen Victoria.

"She actually got it from a descendant of Queen Victoria," says Darby Bannard, who was still in the picture. "Some aristocratic lady who married a decorator gave it to her." With Seward Jr. out of her life—at least for a time—her relationship with Bannard had solidified.

While he never tied the knot with Barbara, Bannard acknowledges that marriage was, indeed, discussed. But, he notes, "Barbara was a lot to handle, and I really needed a wife who was going to give me fifty percent of the deal. But Barbara certainly has all of what it takes. She's an original."

The two, he says, "pretty much" began living together with Jeniah and Bruce as one happy family in the Princeton estate that Johnson & Johnson trust fund money had bought. They often traveled together. One destination was Mexico, where she was treated by a homeopathic doctor for severe sciatica and where Bannard bet on and owned race horses for a time.

Three years after the Johnson divorce, Bannard and Barbara celebrated with champagne when he was awarded a prestigious Guggenheim Fellowship for his art, and later a grant from the National Endowment for the Arts. Over the subsequent years his abstract paintings would have hundreds of solo and group exhibitions.

He even once wrote a murder mystery entitled *Two Dead Men in Rock Creek Park*, which takes place in 1970s post-Watergate Washington.

Among the characters is a woman whose lover is a famous sculptor.

$ $ $

Having become a savvy folk art collector, Barbara Johnson had aggressively networked with the rich and noteworthy in what was becoming the booming folk art collector's field. In 1969, with the help of some of those insiders, the wealthy divorcee with the prominent Johnson name was made a trustee of the American Folk Art Museum in New York, and in 1971 was appointed president of the board of directors.

At the time, the museum, operating out of a converted townhouse on West Fifty-Third Street, was going broke and Barbara, like a latter-day Joan of Arc, rode to its rescue and hoped she could save it.

With the museum in dire financial straits, with serious questions being raised about how it was being operated, and with Barbara Johnson in a key position, the museum became the subject of an investigation by New York State Attorney General Louis J. Lefkowitz.

The financial problems had started after the museum's founder, biggest sponsor, and president emeritus, Joseph B. Martinson, the fifty-nine-year-old scion of the Martinson's Coffee fortune, died suddenly in late October 1970 of a leg infection he got while skin-diving in Singapore. The flow of money then wound down to a trickle.

"Ailing Folk Art Museum Is Under Inquiry by State," read the headline in the Thursday, April 30, 1974, edition of *The New York Times*.

The investigation was started when the museum's retiring director, Joseph O'Doherty, who was resigning to run for the U.S. Congress from New Jersey, sent a report to Lefkowitz's office that raised serious questions about the museum's operations and finances.

"The museum was totally down financially, practically bankrupt, and we were about to be closed, and so I put all my efforts together to get the right kind of board of trustees and money to put it back on a stable foot," Barbara Johnson says many years later. "But the Internal Revenue Service agent came to the place and tried to close it up."

Despite her efforts, leading museum members claimed that Barbara had been making "vital decisions without consulting the board," and acerbically described her style of running things as "one-woman rule," *The Times* reported.

One serious accusation was that Barbara Johnson had engaged in nepotism. After O'Doherty became the fourth director of the museum in four years to resign, an acting director was named who had absolutely no previous museum experience. That person, who had come aboard in 1971, was none other than Barbara's son, and Seward Jr.'s adopted son, twenty-five-year-old Bruce Johnson, a recent Wesleyan University graduate. In 1974, he was named as the museum's full-time director despite Barbara's promise that a search committee had been formed to find a different, experienced permanent director.

Oddly, *The Times*, in mentioning the nepotism issue, described Bruce Johnson simply as Barbara's "relative," not her beloved son.

Besides her son, her reported lover, Darby Bannard, had also become involved unofficially with the museum's operations.

As he had with Jeniah Johnson, Bannard had also developed a close, seemingly fatherly relationship with her half brother.

"Bruce was a kid who could have been president of the United States," says Bannard proudly. "I remember walking up Madison Avenue with him one day and we were talking about the museum, and we were seriously trying to figure out what to do about this problem [the issues facing the museum], and we turned left and we see the Metropolitan Museum of Art, and Bruce opened his arms and says, 'Today the Folk Art Museum, tomorrow the Met.'"

In attempting to get the museum back in shape, Barbara recruited new trustees—including quite a New Jersey contingent—among them the wife of James E. Burke, a top Johnson & Johnson executive who became the company's board chairman and CEO, the other the wife of a former New Jersey governor. Also brought into the fold around 1973 was another friend of Barbara's, a Princeton University graduate by the name of Ralph O. Esmerian, a fourth-generation Manhattan dealer in rare jewels, who under Barbara's rule became the museum's treasurer.

When the issue was raised of Barbara choosing her son, Bruce, as the museum's director, Esmerian came quickly to his and her defense. "He's fantastic—perfect for the situation," he told the *Times*, and noted, "We have to forget the nepotism factor."

Five years after Esmerian left the museum's chairmanship he was arrested on federal fraud charges. According to the U.S. Attorney in Manhattan, the dapper, white-haired Esmerian "allegedly lied and looted to maintain his personal and financial status by tricking his lenders, stealing from investors, and deceiving the bankruptcy court," all relating to his ownership of Fred Leighton, a high-end jewelry business. Prosecutors charged that more than $210 million in loans had been used to finance his business and lifestyle. In July 2012, Esmerian was sentenced to six years in prison for wire and bankruptcy fraud.

$ $ $

Seward Jr.'s adopted son, Bruce, was a handsome young eligible bachelor with a prestigious Manhattan career, thanks to his mother, and he had a number of attractive women at his beck and call.

"There were a bunch of girls *always* after him," boasts Darby Bannard, like a proud father.

One who Johnson was seeing fairly regularly was Eleanora Walker, who was thirteen years his senior—she was forty, he was twenty-seven—and who was an agent representing a group of folk art painters. Johnson was planning an exhibition at the museum on the cat in American folk art, and Walker, a cat lover, began working on the project, generating publicity for Johnson's January–March 1976 show. Johnson had written the catalogue, entitled *American Cat-alogue.*

Before long Johnson and Walker were an item.

"He was very nice, very bright, had a good heart, a good mind, very straightforward, and had a good sense of humor," she remembers with enormous fondness in 2011. "He was enjoying being director of the museum."

He never made her aware of the nepotism issue, she says, or the other problems facing the museum. While he introduced her to his mother, he made no mention of her hellish marriage, scandalous divorce, or his dysfunctional upbringing.

"It's not the kind of thing he would discuss," she observes. "He was just enjoying life, and we were romantically involved."

On the sunny Sunday morning of June 6, 1976, Bruce Johnson asked Eleanora Walker to jump on the back of his motorcycle and get out of the city for the day; he needed a break, having been working hard on an upcoming show of baby and doll quilts. Their destination was bucolic Bear Mountain State Park, near the Hudson River about one hundred miles north of Manhattan. They spent the day hiking, and had lunch, but by late afternoon a light rain had started falling and they decided to head back to the city.

It was pouring by the time they exited the Bear Mountain Bridge around 6:30 P.M. The road was slick and Johnson lost control of the motorcycle, skidded across the yellow line, and slammed head on into a car driven by a fifty-eight-year-old local man.

Years later the memory of the accident still haunts Walker. "I remember we skimmed a car coming in the opposite direction and the next thing I knew I was sitting on the road and Bruce was lying on the road beside me."

The two were rushed to Peekskill Community Hospital. Incredibly, Walker and the motorist survived the horrific accident with just bruises, but Johnson was pronounced dead.

A memorial service was held at the Princeton University Chapel. Bruce Johnson's adoptive father, Seward Jr., did not attend. Years later, he says, "My stepfather [Phil Crockett] always hated the Johnson family so much that anything he could do he did, and he catered to Barbara. When Bruce died Crockett insisted on going to the funeral and my mother went along, and I said, 'Considering what has transpired between us I cannot go.' I thought a lot of Bruce as a young man. But this [attendance at the funeral] would obviously undo everything. There was so much blood flowing through the bridges."

24

Sometime in the mid-1970s, Seward Johnson Jr.'s ex-wife, Barbara, had decided to go to law school in Boston. In some quarters, it was thought she did this in order to better deal with Johnson family legal matters if and when they surfaced, and they usually did.

"She became a lawyer because I guess she thought she did so well screwing me. Anyone who has that mind-set would want to have whatever tools would work the best," Seward Jr. says, looking back.

But Walter Darby Bannard, who had remained close to Barbara, maintains, "She suddenly felt the need to do something serious, to show her worth in something solid, like Seward did when he decided he had to make sculpture."

Barbara moved into a beautiful house on exclusive Beacon Hill—near the home of then-Boston mayor Kevin White. She had two servants at her beck and call, and was probably the richest and chicest future attorney enrolled in classes at Suffolk University Law School.

On June 12, 1978, almost two years to the day of her son Bruce's death, Barbara graduated, and shortly thereafter, she began taking a course to prepare herself for the bar examination, and that's when she met and quickly fell for her next soul mate.

Lloyd Williams, son of a New York City fireman, was a coffee-colored, freckle-faced African-American, one of five children from a middle-class black family from St. Albans, in Queens, New York. When he and Barbara became involved, he had a huge red Afro hairstyle, and he sported the cool African nickname Kamau (pronounced "Kam-ou"). Bright and outgoing, Williams had graduated from the highly competitive law school at Boston University, had earned a master's degree at Brown University, and he was something of a celebrity as a percussionist in Boston's avant-garde improvisational jazz scene.

When they began dating, Williams says years later, he noticed that Barbara seemed "very frightened of people and the world. She was too nervous to even sit and have lunch on the Charles River, and I would have to tell her, 'Nothing's going to happen to you.' "

When he asked her what was bothering her, she told him something that "shocked" him—that about a year before they met, she and her daughter, who was living with her in Boston, had been kidnapped, that they "were saved without ransom money having to pass hands," but that no one was prosecuted because "she was very interested in keeping it under the radar. I think they [the kidnapper, or kidnappers] were let go because she didn't want to testify. That's what she told me."

Williams says he did his best to ease her anxiety, noting, "I think part of our attraction for each other was that I was sort of protective and calm."

While they had a strong attraction, others in Williams's circle viewed them as one of the oddest couples anyone could imagine.

"It was a bizarre matching because Barbara was his senior by at least twenty or twenty-five years, possibly even thirty years—it was hard to tell how old she actually was because she claimed one thing and it was always something else," says Williams's close friend back then, Miles B. Neustein, also a Boston University Law School graduate. Along with Williams, Neustein was an improvisational musician, who had "hit it off as kindred spirits" with Williams in Bean Town's jazz scene. Neustein later became a New Jersey civil trial attorney, and joined the Johnson dynasty when he married the sister-in-law of Seward Jr.'s nephew Eric Ryan.

"Barbara and Kamau were two completely different personalities," Neustein observes. "It wasn't the race thing, but their age difference, their socioeconomic backgrounds, the fact that Kamau was a rather brilliant street-savvy musician-cum-lawyer—and Barbara Johnson had all the affectations of an heiress. She seemed to have reinvented herself after divorcing Seward, and acted like someone who had *old* money, and gave the impression that she was an heiress from Europe, a descendant of European aristocracy. I just didn't see them having a thing in common other than the law, which is nothing you want to talk about over dinner."

Williams himself had also questioned the difference in their ages.

"Barbara was very attractive, very impulsive, and a very brilliant person in a lot of ways. But I didn't know she was as old as she was. She claimed to be *much* younger. I sensed she was cheating a little more than she said but nowhere near as much."

Still, he found her intriguing and beguiling—as had Seward Johnson Jr.—at least at first.

"For a young guy like me it was fascinating to be dating someone who was so well connected," he notes years later. "Barbara used to have a saying that there are *only* four hundred people in the world and all the rest are extras. What she meant by that was the Fortune 400. What bothered me about her was that connection to power and celebrity—and *always* networking."

In September 1978, several months after they met at that bar exam course, they took the vows of holy matrimony in a very simple ceremony officiated by a Boston justice of the peace.

Their marriage came as a lightning bolt out of the blue to Williams's friends because he had never given any indication that marriage to the wealthy former Johnson wife—with a mansion in Princeton, a spectacular place in Nantucket overlooking the sea, and more—was even in the cards.

Neustein's reaction was, "What? Are you out of your fucking mind? But I didn't question him. That was an internal reaction. He was getting flack from everywhere. But I wanted to be the one friend he had that wasn't being judgmental."

No one could figure what the attraction was. If anyone in Williams's circle of friends thought he had married her for her money, that he was a gold digger, something she herself had been thought of a couple of decades back when she married Seward Jr., they were way off base.

"If anything, he wasn't materialistic," says Neustein. "For the life of me I couldn't say what the attraction was, but he fell head over heels for her. They were both such eccentric individuals that maybe the differences were the attraction."

Darby Bannard, too, was surprised that Barbara had once again tied the knot. "I thought, 'Oh, God, *more* trouble.'"

Now that they were married, Williams says he was "often thought of" within the dynasty as "The Black Johnson."

Despite Barbara's rancorous divorce a decade earlier from Seward Jr., she continued to remain friends with a number of Johnsons, including Woody's sister, Libet. And in that curious familial situation, Williams became friendly with Seward Jr.

But Williams claims he knew very little early on about Barbara's Johnson dynasty history because she didn't talk about it, and he didn't know what to ask. "I would get into a cab in Princeton and people would assume that I worked for her," he recalls. "People would say, 'You work for that woman who shot her husband.' People would have these weird half-truth stories, and then I'd say to Barbara, 'Somebody said you shot your husband.' And then she would tell me what really happened."

Most average couples go on a honeymoon for a week or more and then return to their everyday lives. For Barbara and Kamau, however, "It was a constant honeymoon," he observes. "We had a jet-set lifestyle. For me it was an incredible lifestyle."

One of their first stops after they tied the knot was a visit to Barbara's close friends Pete and Jeanette, who lived in the nation's capital. She never explained to her groom who Pete and Jeanette were until they arrived at their posh Georgetown home. Jeanette, as it turned out, was the second wife of Peter, more formally known as U.S. Senator Harrison Arlington "Pete" Williams, a powerful and popular New Jersey Democrat.

Several years after Barbara introduced her groom to the prominent Garden State politician and his wife, the senator was convicted for taking bribes and conspiracy in what was known as the FBI's Abscam sting operation. He was secretly videotaped telling a phony Arab sheik that he could get him lucrative government contracts in return for a piece of the action. He served a prison sentence, and before his death in 2001, he tried for one of the many presidential pardons Bill Clinton was handing out, but was turned down.

With the honeymoon over, Barbara and Kamau returned to her estate on Cleveland Lane in Princeton. During the first two years he commuted to the University of Pennsylvania in Philadelphia, where he earned an MBA at the prestigious Wharton School. Then, the two of them set up a law practice in the house.

According to Bannard, Barbara's daughter Jeniah, in her late teens at the time, wasn't very happy about the marriage.

"Jeniah was disapproving and definitely not thrilled," he claims. "She just thought it was a bad idea. If the subject of the marriage would come up, Kookie would just say, 'Well, she screwed that one up.'"

Williams, however, didn't see it that way, and says he and the girl got along "great. I don't know when, or at what point she might have felt that." One thing he did notice about Jeniah, he says, was that she looked remarkably like Bannard, and "there was a lot of behavior in which Bannard acted like her biological father. Early on I might have said to Barbara, 'Kookie looks a lot like Darby,' and that was nipped in the bud. But I had my suspicions."

Because she was so very social, charming, and wealthy—Barbara seemed to know everybody who was anybody because of her past ties to the Johnsons and her own high-level networking—she had wangled through her New Jersey Democratic political connections, most likely Senator Williams, an invitation to a dinner party at the White House then occupied by President Jimmy Carter. For Barbara it was one of the great moments of her life, to be seated with her husband in the presence of the commander in chief.

However, the big evening with a liberal southern president who backed civil and human rights didn't come off at first as she had planned.

Recounts Neustein: "They go to the White House and Kamau drops her off, parks the car, and they take a look at him, assume he was her chauffeur, and he was ushered into the chauffeur's area. To the embarrassment of whoever made the mistake, they verified that he was on the guest list, and he did attend. Kamau told me what had happened, but there was an undercurrent in that he indicated, look what racism has done now."

Williams remembers that evening all too well, asserting decades later, "That sort of thing happened a number of times, and it happened on that occasion."

But Williams was an enigma when it came to matters of race as evidenced by his subsequent appearance on the outrageously sacrilegious *Howard Stern Show* on radio that often used crude racist humor satirically, usually eliciting big laughs from Stern's millions of white blue-collar bridge-and-tunnel listeners, and also from his black cohost and foil, Robin Quivers. At Boston University—where Neustein and Stern were undergraduates together, and both had campus radio shows—Stern was suspended from his very first program on WTBU for a skit called "Godzilla Goes to Harlem."

Knowing both Stern's humor and Williams's feelings about racism, Neustein was dumbfounded when he learned from his brother-in-law Eric Ryan that Williams had actually made an appearance on Stern's show.

"At one point because he had some notoriety being married to a Johnson, or a pseudo Johnson, [and being black *and* law-degreed], Kamau was on *Howard Stern* as part of a gag game show, and they called him 'F. Lee Buckwheat' after [famed defense attorney] F. Lee Bailey, who was also a Boston University alumnus," says Neustein. (Bailey, who was white, had been part of the controversial O. J. Simpson defense team, and Buckwheat was the nickname of a black child character—a "pickaninny" stereotype—who was part of the *Our Gang* movie comedies of the 1930s and 1940s.)

"I was surprised that Kamau went along with it," observes Neustein. "It was so out of character for him, but maybe he did it as a spoof, or he did it just to do it because he had very eccentric ways, and he would do things for shock value on occasion."

Actually, Williams promoted his appearance on the Stern show, he acknowledges years later, and believes he had good reason to do so.

"I was in the midst of the divorce, and I was losing," he says. "My lawyer could have cared less about me. Legal battles can often be about money and Barbara had so much money and she could just continue with motions, and run it on, and I was running out of money.

"So I went on the *Howard Stern Show* to say I had this famous legal case, but the case only became famous because I was on the show and that piqued the world's interest and most importantly embarrassed my lawyer into taking the case seriously when her phone started ringing off the hook, so that was motivation for her to go forward."

Williams readily admits that through the years he's been highly eccentric.

When Williams drove on the toxic New Jersey Turnpike he had begun wearing a gas mask "because he was afraid that the fumes were carcinogenic. He was germophobic, but not to the extent of a Howard Hughes," notes Neustein.

Eric Ryan recalls hearing that Barbara and Williams were spotted in Nantucket and Princeton riding in an antique European sports car, garbed in white linen jumpsuits like beekeepers' outfits, which were believed to be intended to ward off germs. "It was like two nutjobs hooking up," opines Ryan. "As long as their hormones were in balance, they were probably fine. When the bad chemicals took over, they probably couldn't stand each other."

Bannard says he never knew Barbara to be phobic about germs, but he had inklings about Williams. "I went to an antique show with him and I had to go to the restroom, and as I was going to wash my hands he said, 'Don't do that!' I asked why, and he said, 'The water's got AIDS in it.' If he was joking I would have taken it as a joke, but he was serious."

In 2012, Williams still gets a kick out of the way people perceived him and his sometimes outlandishness ways—and his marriage to the former Barbara Johnson.

He says he was never afraid of germs but rather of "pollution" because "I'm very connected to nature." He claims he wore a gas mask "maybe once" on the turnpike in order to make a point.

The beekeeper-like outfits he and Barbara were spotted wearing were, he asserts, actually white decontamination jumpsuits "like you'd wear after a nuclear attack." And he claims they wore them not to ward off germs, but rather because the suits "were cool-looking and offbeat."

As for AIDS in the water supply, he says that was all tongue-in-cheek. "I would say to people, 'Don't use a public toilet because AIDS can travel up the stream of urine.' That was a joke."

Seward Jr., always keeping tabs on his ex-wife, Barbara, and Jeniah, the daughter whose birthright he long disputed, had become friends with Williams, who had many complaints about her. "She treated him terribly," Seward Jr. claims Williams told him. "He probably wanted my help in dealing with Barbara. She treated him insultingly. She wouldn't give him the key to the house and things like that."

Williams says that toward the end of the marriage things got "ugly. Things happened. There were certainly long periods of time when I did have a key to the house. When things started going south, I cried on people's shoulders, like Seward."

After ten roller-coaster years of marriage, he and Barbara Eisenfuhr

Kline Bailey Maxwell Johnson Williams were divorced in 1988 in New Jersey.

"It was pretty predictable," observes Bannard. "Barbara told me stories about how he was running off with some blonde, all this kind of hysterical stuff, and I just said, 'Well, you just gotta get rid of the guy.'"

Women, especially wealthy Princeton women, sought him out as a lover, he acknowledges, but he denies cheating on Barbara. "That's nonsense, "he says. "The reason the marriage ended was because we grew apart . . . I was no longer content to live in her shadow as 'Mr. Barbara Johnson.'"

In 1993, Williams remarried, and helped raise a son, a future Princeton University graduate, from his wife's first marriage, and he remained living in Princeton, and took on a new career as a respected film and book critic for mostly black publications and Internet sites.

Every so often in town, he says in 2012, he bumps into Barbara "and we'll smile at each other. She lives very much under the radar."

$ $ $

Around the same time that Barbara graduated from law school with her LL.B, Walter Darby Bannard had remarried, to a woman at least a dozen years his junior who, he says, resembled the voluptuous fictional superheroine Sheena, Queen of the Jungle. He says, "She was really something else—a real California girl with long blond hair, and an hourglass build."

Some months into the marriage, Mya Bannard gave birth to a son, whom they named Billy. Seward Jr., who was still keeping a close watch on Barbara and Bannard in an effort to get evidence about Jeniah's paternity, found out that the Bannards often socialized with Barbara, and that Bannard always attended Jeniah's birthday parties, bringing along his son.

On one such occasion, claimed Seward Jr., Billy Bannard said, "Kookie is my sister," which caused Barbara to get "very upset and said that wasn't true. Billy started to cry and said, 'Daddy told me so.'"

Seward Jr. stated that the information about the child's outburst, which he viewed as more ammunition supporting his theory that Bannard was Jeniah's father, was part of a sworn affidavit from someone who was present at the party, heard the children talking, and informed on them.

Bannard says it didn't happen exactly the way Seward Jr. claimed, although he acknowledges, "We used to have elaborate birthday parties for Kookie. Billy would go to those parties, but Billy wouldn't cry. He'd just shrug it off.

"It just sounds like another Seward fantasy."

25

In the late 1980s, J. Seward Johnson Jr., still desperate to get a sample of his daughter Jeniah Johnson's DNA through a blood test in order to prove he was not her biological father and keep her from benefiting from rich family trusts, reached out to a private detective in Hollywood with quite a reputation. His name was Anthony Pellicano, and he billed himself as the "PI to the stars."

His client list included high-priced Beverly Hills lawyers whose own red-carpet clients encompassed the likes of Tom Cruise, Michael Jackson, and Elizabeth Taylor, and his Rolodex listed superagents like Michael Ovitz and others on Hollywood's A-list.

Pellicano, with skullduggery that ranged from telephone-bugging—Sylvester Stallone reportedly had his phone tapped—to harassing a *Los Angeles Times* entertainment reporter who once found a dead fish with a rose in its mouth on her car as a warning to get off his back—had a reputation for getting the goods, despite his devious methods.

In one case, the ex-wife of the billionaire MGM mogul and Las Vegas hotel sultan Kirk Kerkorian claimed that Pellicano had tapped her phone conversations in an effort to show she was lying when she claimed Kerkorian was her daughter's father. Later, DNA tests proved he was not and that a film producer was the actual biological father.

Seward Jr. was impressed with Pellicano's success and flew out to

Hollywood to meet with him. He outlined the Jeniah story and said he wanted help to get a sample of her DNA.

According to Seward Jr., Pellicano had an immediate answer:

"He said, 'Well, Jeniah is just going to have an accident,'" After the accident, which someone would have to arrange, the private eye explained, Jeniah would be taken to a hospital where a DNA sample would be secured.

When he informed his lawyer, a former district attorney, what the private eye had advised, the attorney told him to "get away from him, dump this guy. He said, 'If Jeniah has an accident the first person that I would look for would be you.' He meant me because I had motive."

Seward Jr. took his lawyer's advice.

In 2008, the sixty-four-year-old Pellicano was sentenced to fifteen years in prison, convicted on a total of seventy-eight counts, including wiretapping, racketeering, and wire fraud, stemming from two separate trials.

But Seward Jr.'s efforts to prove, or disprove, Jeniah Johnson's paternity didn't end with the rogue detective's imprisonment.

$ $ $

Jeniah "Kookie" Johnson had a seemingly full and happy life in Princeton in the wake of all the scandal and legal wars and ongoing skirmishes over the identity of her biological father, issues she declines to discuss.

"It was a big strain that went on forever about her inheritance, and that got her down," Walter Darby Bannard states. "But, Kookie's a very normal, practical, realistic person and she just dealt with it. She's not like the Johnsons, who are totally nuts and neurotic."

After private school, Jeniah attended Georgetown University, where she earned a Bachelor of Arts degree in art history and English, and later studied landscape design and horticulture at Rutgers University.

In the entrepreneurial spirit of the Johnsons, and with the artistic flair of both Seward Jr. *and* Darby Bannard, she created two imaginative businesses. Her first was a landscape firm called Glorious Gardens, and she was its chief designer for some fifteen years. Later, she became a jewelry designer for a couple of years, selling under the business name Kooka Jewelry.

All through her life, though, Jeniah continued to embrace the famous—

and, in some circles, infamous—Johnson surname, even after she got married—just like her mother, Barbara, had done after her divorce from Seward Jr.

Jeniah had married a talented decorative painter, muralist, and musician by the name of Thomas Sheeran, the son of a prominent Princeton physician, Dr. Archibald D. Sheeran. With her husband, she had a son, Henry Bruce Sheeran—his middle name after her deceased half brother. She was active in her son's private school, and became a part of the Princeton social scene, volunteering and working mostly in the artsy sector.

As Bannard observes, Jeniah became "a socialite."

She and her husband were among the sponsors of the "Pino to Picasso-Vintage 2008" event, described as "one of the hippest and liveliest art happenings" in Princeton. And they were members of the "Mozart Circle" of wealthy contributors—$50,000 to $99,999 (all tax deductible)—to the Arts Council of Princeton's campaign to build the Paul Robeson Center for the Arts. Ironically, among the contributors in the "Rembrandt Circle"—$100,000 to $499,999—was Woody Johnson's mother, Betty Wold Johnson, and the J. Seward Johnson Sr. 1963 Charitable Trust (which years earlier had specifically banned Jeniah as a beneficiary).

For some seven years, Jeniah had been a volunteer for the prestigious Princeton Arts Council, serving on the board and working as a marketing and development consultant, before becoming its full-time director of community relations.

Her mother, Barbara, using the name Kristina Johnson, was a member of the board of trustees, and both she and Jeniah served on the board together at one point. Among the funders—strange bedfellows since Jeniah wasn't thought of as a biological Johnson—were the J. Seward Johnson 1963 Charitable Trust, the Robert Wood Johnson Foundation, the Johnson & Johnson Consumer Companies, Inc., and Woody Johnson's mother.

$ $ $

In September 2002, Seward Jr. sent an emotional and caustic letter to Jeniah, who had just turned forty-one, spelling out in great detail his tumultuous marriage to her mother, his knowledge of her mother's relationship with

Darby Bannard, his questions about her pregnancy, and Jeniah's birthright.

With a heartfelt, albeit hard-edged tone, he ended the seven-page, single-spaced letter by writing:

I have often wondered how you've felt about this elaborate fiction your mother has required you to live. On the most obvious level, you must have noticed that, as photographs demonstrate, you and Darby Bannard share a remarkable resemblance, and that, from pictures of me you must have seen in the newspapers, you look nothing at all like me. How have you managed to deal with this stubborn fact? How have you explained to yourself Darby's attitude and behavior toward you, consistently paternal rather than merely sympathetic—his officiating at all your birthday parties, his presence at all the important times, and so on.

I'm sure you could cite countless other ways Darby has demonstrated his true relationship with you, his natural bond with you. Yet you and Darby both have had to deny that bond and veil that relationship. It's truly sad.

You may have a wholly different view of it, but to me it seems clear that before your birth your mother, driven by extraordinary cynicism, conducted a false structure around you and, over the years, trained you to live in it. As much as you may love her and as dutifully as you may have learned to play your part, you must have become troubled on some level that your mother's grim scheme had become your reality. It doesn't take a Shakespeare or Chekhov or a Tennessee Williams to recognize your plight for the moving tragedy it is.

Despite all these indications, all the questions that must have come into your mind, you yourself have continued to use the Johnson name in preference to your married name or the name Bannard. You call yourself Johnson, but you have never in forty years contacted me or any other member of the Johnson family.

The fact that there is a lot of money involved does not excuse your living this deception. I hope you find the strength of character to renounce the whole sorry thing.

$ $ $

Four decades after Jeniah Johnson was born into a very dysfunctional and disturbed family situation, the heated battle over her paternity had escalated even more—incredibly into the new millenium—with the highest court in New Jersey, and that state's legislature, being brought into the conflict.

The twenty-first-century battle over Jeniah's paternity and whether she should benefit further from Johnson family trusts was ignited when Seward Jr.'s two children from his second marriage, John Seward Johnson III and Clelia Constance Johnson, known professionally as India Blake, joined with two of their cousins, the late Mary Lea's sons, Eric and Hillary Ryan, to appeal the decades-old divorce court ruling that held that Seward Jr. was Jeniah's father, and that a trust worth a fortune that included her could not be challenged.

Their ultimate goal was to see that Jeniah never received one red cent from that trust. If she did, they and their siblings would presumably get a smaller piece of the money pie—not earned through jobs or professions, but left to them as part of the immense Johnson & Johnson fortune.

The New Jersey Supreme Court heard the case in the fall–winter session of 2000–2001. After all of that legal wrangling, most likely costing hundreds of thousands of dollars in attorneys' fees, the court decided in Jeniah's favor. She had roundly won, without ever having to take a blood test (or later a DNA test) to prove or disprove the identity of her biological father.

Much of the court's decision was based on New Jersey's 1983 Parentage Act, which held that a child born in wedlock is presumed to be the legitimate offspring of the husband. The fact that Jeniah was born while Seward Jr. was married to Jeniah's mother, Barbara, meant that he was the father, whether he agreed or not, and that no blood or DNA test would ever have to be administered as Seward Jr. had sought in hopes to disprove paternity.

After the defeat in New Jersey, the Johnson cousins asked the U.S. Supreme Court to hear their case, but were refused.

But that didn't stop Seward Jr., who began a big-money lobbying campaign, giving more than $280,000 in contributions to New Jersey politicians and party committees, in an effort to change the Parentage Act in his favor and for other men in similar situations.

In 2001, New Jersey's Senate Judiciary Committee approved a bill to change the controversial Parentage Act in such a way as to benefit Seward Jr. in his war to prove he wasn't Jeniah's biological father.

But Robert Singer, the state senator who had sponsored the measure, soon went public declaring he had been misled by a Johnson lobbyist and attorney. Singer claimed Seward Jr.'s representative had given him the impression that the bill would fix a major inequity in the law, rather than simply help the Johnsons in their battle with Jeniah over paternity and trust fund money.

In 2004, with Singer out of the picture, a pair of then–highly respected New Jersey assemblymen, Anthony Impreveduto and Neil Cohen, became the primary sponsors of Seward Jr.'s legislation.

But the Garden State being what it is—long a haven for corrupt politicians and real-life Tony Sopranos—it turned out that the Band-Aid heir's supporters were a couple of bad apples.

Impreveduto, a teacher by profession, subsequently pleaded guilty to state charges of having spent tens of thousands of dollars in campaign contributions on personal expenses—clothing, travel, even paying his income taxes. Meanwhile, Cohen, who had been talking up Seward Jr.'s proposed measure dealing with child legitimacy and paternity, would later be indicted on charges of possession of child pornography—reportedly viewing the many sick images on his computer in the state office building. He eventually pleaded guilty to distributing child pornography.

After years of fighting, Seward Jr. eventually gave up his battle, but not his belief.

And Jeniah came out on top when a secret agreement was reached between the Johnson trustees, who were three top executives at Johnson & Johnson, and the lawyers for Jeniah, then in her early fifties.

"She ended up getting seventeen million dollars out of the trust as a settlement," Seward Jr. reveals.

He calls the deal "a deep wound," and describes the settlement as being "upside down. It's wrong is right. When you have something that's totally indigestible, what the hell do you do with it, and the only thing I can do with it is preoccupy myself with trying to accomplish what I want to accomplish, and concentrate on that and not allow myself to sink into bitterness."

On April 18, 2013, Barbara Johnson died. Her obit made no mention of Seward Jr.

PART V

WOODY'S SECRETS

26

It was one of those steely gray overcast afternoons in usually sunny Palm Beach, near the end of the 2010–11 winter social season, when Woody Johnson decided to rent a bicycle and take a leisurely ride along a scenic stretch of North Lake Way in the very private and posh far north end of the fabulously wealthy resort town.

For Woody, the Gold Coast of South Florida held many memories, both happy and sad. Like most other members of the Johnson dynasty, his parents, Robert Wood "Bobby" Johnson III and the former Betty May Wold, had spent most winters in the Sunshine State, where they owned spectacular homes, first in Pompano Beach along "Millionaires' Mile," and later some miles south in Fort Lauderdale's exclusive Bay Colony, where Woody and his brothers, Keith and Billy, always had flashy convertibles and nifty speedboats from the time they were in their early teens.

Moreover, Woody's early business career after he received his first eight-figure trust fund payment when he turned twenty-one was as a real estate developer and cable television entrepreneur in South Florida beginning in the mid-1970s, and it was there where he had met his first wife, Nancy Sale Frey Johnson, and where she had given birth to the first of their three daughters, Sale Trotter Case "Casey" Johnson.

Florida also held dark memories for Woody. It was where his father had died from cancer in 1970, in the prime of life at the age of fifty, following his humiliating and very public firing as the president of Johnson & Johnson by Woody's grandfather, the General. And it was in Florida where one of Woody's three brothers, Keith Wold Johnson, had died of a drug overdose five years later, just a little more than a month before another brother, Willard "Billy" Trotter Case Johnson, was killed in a motorcycle accident.

Still, with all of that hurt in the far distant past, Woody enjoyed the luxury of life whenever he visited Palm Beach.

In the afternoon of March 3, 2011, just a month before his sixty-fourth birthday, and days away from the thirty-sixth anniversary of his brothers' tragic deaths, the New York Jets owner and Republican power broker had shown up at the Palm Beach Bicycle Trail Shop, at 233 Sunshine Avenue, a three-decades-old landmark for bike sales and rentals, located just a football field away—one hundred yards—from a safe, authorized bike trail.

He rented a tan-colored Trek for fifteen dollars an hour, didn't bother with a helmet, and rather than taking the bike trail, he rode north on two-lane, well-trafficked, undivided North Lake Way.

It was about ten minutes after four, as he was pedaling on the wrong side of the road, without the protection of a safety helmet, when Woody collided with a vehicle driven by one Shawn P. Brett, a forty-four-year-old West Palm Beach resident, who was exiting the driveway of the estate at 1486 North Lake Way.

Knocked off the bike, Woody was in serious pain and was rushed by Palm Beach Fire Rescue to Good Samaritan Hospital, according to the police report. Brett, uninjured, was released from the scene, and no charges were filed.

"When the cop brought the bike back, I asked if everyone was okay," recalls the bike shop owner, Mark Quinn, some months after the accident, "and he said, 'Oh, no. He [Woody] went to the doctor's, but the accident was his fault. He was on the wrong side of the road.'"

Quinn says he never heard from Woody after the accident, and was never paid for the rental, or the cost of the minor damage to the bike. He also noted that his shop recommends helmets and the traffic-free bike trail, both of which Woody ignored.

At the split second that Brett's car and Woody's bike connected, it was as if two American dynasties had collided.

As it turned out, Brett was the personal chef of Ogden Mills "Dinny" Phipps, a hugely wealthy financier, legendary Thoroughbred owner and breeder, and vice chairman of the board of his family's Bessemer Trust, headquartered at 630 Fifth Avenue, in Rockefeller Center, in Manhattan, just floors above where the Johnson Company, Woody's suite of offices, was located. This was the address that Woody had curiously given as his residence (which it wasn't), according to the police report.

From a family of longtime loyal Republicans like Woody, Phipps was a contributor to, and supporter of, John McCain's 2008 presidential campaign, of which Woody was a key backer and national fundraiser.

Phipps says he had no idea why the Johnson & Johnson scion was riding outside his gated mansion, and he was shocked that Woody was pedaling on the wrong side of the road and without a helmet.

"He was lucky he wasn't seriously hurt."

Woody was, indeed, lucky.

When he fell off the bike, he didn't hit his bare head, but suffered a badly bruised and fractured left ankle that required surgery seven days after the accident. His injury, initially kept quiet as per his modus operandi of extreme privacy and secrecy regarding his personal life, only became known several weeks later when he publicly surfaced on crutches on March 22, 2011, at the National Football League's annual meeting in New Orleans.

When spotted limping like an injured wide receiver, he glibly told the *New York Post*, "I took on a car, and the car won . . . I wasn't wearing a helmet and all that stuff. You are supposed to do all that stuff. Luckily, I didn't hit my head or anything."

When asked who was to blame, Woody declared, "A driver's not supposed to hit bikes."

He also told Gang Green Nation, a Web site that was devoted to news about the Jets, "The car was coming out of a driveway, I was just kind of lulled into complacency, maybe. I wasn't paying as much attention . . ."

As the owner of a professional football team, Woody, more than most anyone, was aware of the importance of helmets to avoid head injuries.

Just three months before the accident, in early December 2010, he had stood beside National Football League commissioner Roger Goodell, and Woody's close friend and Republican ally Chris Christie, in the New York

Jets' and the New York Giants' shared stadium, when the New Jersey governor signed into law a comprehensive concussion bill to protect high school and college football players from head injuries.

Woody told the gathering that Goodell was "trying to get every state in the union to pass legislation" regarding helmet safety and head trauma.

As a member of the exclusive club of thirty-two NFL team owners for more than a decade in 2011 when his bike and the car collided, Woody had taken seriously the controversial head injuries and concussions suffered by players on the field as a result of purposeful brain-jarring helmet-to-helmet contact. He was an ardent proponent of penalties and fines levied against players who were violators, and he always favored even better helmet protection.

So it was shocking that Woody Johnson, a billionaire in his midsixties with much personal and professional responsibility, would get on a bike without a helmet, ride on the wrong side of the road, and be "lulled into complacency" and not be "paying as much attention" as deemed necessary.

But Woody Johnson had always been a chance-taker, and the Florida incident wasn't the first time he had been involved in a serious accident. At least twice before, his life had been at risk and he had been lucky to survive.

As John Vicino, a retired Florida policeman who along with his brothers, Neil and Guy, was a close friend of Woody and his ill-fated brothers, Keith and Billy, since childhood, observes:

"Woody was the carefree, jocular, accident-prone guy. It always seemed Woody was breaking something, or he'd have an accident, or he'd turn over a motorbike, or something like that."

$ $ $

While high school and college kids from working-class families were taking their spring breaks back in the 1960s in beach towns like Fort Lauderdale—made popular by such drive-in movie films as *Beach Blanket Bingo,* starring former Mouseketeer Annette Funicello and South Philadelphia teen idol Frankie Avalon—the scions and heirs like Woody Johnson who attended the elite Millbrook School partied in the breathtaking island nation of Bermuda.

In 1964, Woody, then still known as Bob by most of his classmates, was

27

When Woody Johnson graduated from Millbrook School in June 1965, he hadn't made much of an impact academically or socially during the four years he was there, other than that near-fatal impact when his head hit that windshield in Bermuda, a horrific event that was still remembered as his Millbrook legacy by some classmates years later.

Before the Bermuda accident, he had also suffered a broken arm while at Millbrook, and was in a cast and sling for some months. Jack Mills, his roommate who also played on the Millbrook football team with Woody, says it might have happened when Woody was hurt on the field, or back at his home in Princeton, but it was yet another accident in what was becoming a streak of them, and they'd only get worse.

During his four-year Millbrook matriculation after spending his primary schooling at the private and fancy Princeton Country Day School, Woody played one season, mostly as a benchwarmer, on the football squad; had been a member of the Wednesday Night Cook Squad; was on the A.A. Committee; served up candy bars at the Milk Bar; and headed the Grounds Committee in his senior year, which basically meant cleaning up leaves and mowing lawns. Such menial jobs were required of all students at Millbrook by the headmaster, Edward Pulling, who had founded the school, and whose retirement came with the graduation of Woody's class.

The June 1965 class yearbook, the *Tamarack,* said of Robert Wood Johnson IV:

Bob Johnson and Jack Mills formed an impulsive and somewhat enigmatic team on the Millbrook campus. Bob was the quieter of the two, yet one could not help but wonder if this quietness did not mask the more diabolical mind. When the Guest House groaned under the weight of restless, elephantine-sounding Sixth Formers, one could be assured that Ronson was avidly involved in the fray. There was more to his fiendish machinations in the dorm than mere physical rebellion. Bob had also a mild dosage of cunning. Did not anyone ever wonder why Bob, with his seemingly endless knowledge of television, never happens to appear with the rest of the gang in the Milk Bar in order to view his most popular programs . . . hmm?

A Princeton man, Bob pursued the country-club life by vigorous participation in the squash program. Bob was responsible for keeping the quads clean this year as head of the Grounds Committee.

The reference to television was a nudge-nudge, wink-wink way by the yearbook editors of revealing that Woody had sneaked a set into his dorm room, had hidden it in a closet, and watched it surreptitiously, which was against Millbrook's strict rules and was reason for expulsion. But he was never caught, says Mills.

While Mills, a bright, easygoing young man, was much the opposite of Woody in terms of social station, personality, academics, and interests, the often tongue-in-cheek *Tamarack* described him as "the other half of the 'me-and-my-shadow' team of Johnson and Mills"—mostly because they were roomies, were usually together, and weren't part of any Millbrook clique.

Mills, according to the yearbook editors who wrote the blurbs, Tom Doelger and Noah W. Hotchkiss, was an "ebullient character" who "spent many of his waking hours quietly bemoaning the rape of the American frontier, the demise of the Buffalo and Indians, and the steady, slow pillage of our nation's natural resources," which later explained his career as a dedicated environmentalist for the federal government.

Together while at Millbrook, Woody and Mills went on a camping trip in the woods of Minnesota near where Woody's maternal grandparents, the

Wolds, had a country home, and the two chums made the grand tour of Europe in a rented VW Bug.

$ $ $

While many of Woody's classmates went on to elite colleges and Ivy League universities such as Dartmouth, where Jack Mills matriculated and from where he graduated, Woody, not the brightest in the 1965 class of some forty students, managed to get into a completely different kind of school that had a certain singular reputation: the University of Arizona topped the list as one of *Playboy* magazine's ultimate party schools.

Woody gave the reason for his college selection many years later.

"When I first visited Tucson with my father—to be exposed to mountains and sunshine—I had never seen anything like it," he told the University of Arizona's *Alumnus* magazine in the Fall 2009 issue. "Then I saw all the girls from Southern California coming out of the home economics building, and I said, 'Dad, this looks like a pretty good spot here.'"

Besides the pretty girls, there was a life-and-death reason Woody signed up at the University of Arizona: Like many privileged men of his generation, he was there to avoid the Vietnam War draft. As his cousin Eric Ryan, who also attended there for a time, notes, "The University of Arizona was our haven from Hanoi."

With the escalating combat in Southeast Asia, the Band-Aid heir needed the safety net of an easy-to-get-into, fun-loving college, and the draft exemption that went with it. Moreover, he is said to have gotten into Arizona with the help of his uncle, Dr. Keith Wold, Woody's mother's brother, according to longtime friend John Vicino.

"That time in American history the draft was nipping at everybody's tails, and Dr. Wold had a good connection at the University of Arizona to get Woody in," says Vicino.

His influential source, according to Vicino, was Barry Morris Goldwater, the conservative and powerful five-term U.S. senator from Arizona, and the Republican Party's nominee for president in 1964. In his unsuccessful bid to be commander in chief, Goldwater had the vigorous support of most, if not all, of the voting members of the Johnson dynasty.

"Woody was close to not getting into Arizona," Vicino asserts. "I can re-member because it was a panicky day. Woody wasn't a real studious guy, but he had gotten in, and Dr. Wold was the one who was friends with Barry Goldwater."

Known as "Mr. Conservative, " Goldwater was a highly respected figure and a major influence at the University of Arizona, which had been his alma mater for one year before he dropped out because his father was ill. As a senator, the university was one of his constituents.

Years later Woody, as a billionaire Republican power broker, would team up with his cousin, Dr. Wold's son, GOP bundler Keith Wold, who had also gone to the University of Arizona. The two worked closely in support of the presidential campaign of the U.S. senator from Arizona who had succeeded Barry Goldwater when he retired—John McCain, who had been a prisoner of war in Vietnam.

When Woody enrolled at Arizona, safe from the draft, more than 125,000 U.S. troops already were on the ground in Vietnam—by the end of the war, two and a half million American men would have served—but not one of them would be a member of the influential and privileged Johnson dynasty.

Woody began classes in September 1965 and easily morphed into the ul-timate hard-partying frat boy reminiscent of characters in *National Lam-poon's Animal House,* the comedy about the alcohol-besotted misfits in Delta House.

During "rush week" in his freshman year Woody made the rounds of the various fraternities, but chose to pledge with Delta Chi, known as the "Intra-mural House," mainly because many of its members were jocks who won most of the sporting events with other frats, including football. Delta Chi was considered, at least by its members looking back years later, as *the* animal house of all animal house fraternities on the campus of the party school of all party schools back in the Swinging Sixties.

Delta Chi, located in a two-story redbrick building, was a frat that had seemed to always be on one form of university probation or another—usually for excessive drinking, but there was pot smoking, debauched par-ties, and academic failure.

At one point, remembers Phil Calihan, son of a wealthy Phoenix businessman, who was president of the frat during the first year Woody pledged, "We rented a hangar down at the airport and had a whole bunch of kegs of beer delivered, and we invited all the fraternities and sororities and, of course, hundreds of people showed up, and then the school got there and said, 'You can't do this!—You can't have a party off campus,' so they put us on probation."

But that wasn't half the story of life in Delta Chi.

Kent Muccilli, who arrived in 1965 along with the class of 1969 that included Woody Johnson, wasn't told when he pledged that Delta Chi was already on strict alcohol probation.

"There were some crazy people in Delta Chi," he recalls. "Most of the house was drunk by noon on Friday, so nobody went to classes in the afternoon. On a Friday night, there would be beer bottles lined up in the hallways. Unfortunately, I didn't have enough self-control. I was like the other pledges. We weren't going to class half the time."

Because there was just too much partying and not enough stress on academics in Delta Chi, Muccilli didn't make grades, got his letter of "Greetings" from Uncle Sam, and left after just one semester. To avoid the draft, he joined a military reserve unit.

"We were just a good 'ol bunch of young guys just having a good time, a crazy time," recalls Woody's pledge brother, Walter "Bucky" Lovejoy. "Grades were kind of the last thing we were thinking about."

And that appeared to be the case with Woody, who never was formally initiated and remained a lowly Delta Chi pledge for as long as two years because, as Lovejoy and others recall, the Band-Aid heir never scored the frat's minimum grades required to be inducted into their brotherhood.

As a Delta Chi career pledge, Woody was required to help clean the frat house and, during Hell Week, carry with him a paddle and get active members' signatures on it. "In order to get a signature, they got to swat you on the butt," says Lovejoy.

Woody stayed with Delta Chi through his freshman and sophomore years, even though his only claim to fame was helping the frat win the Greek Week chariot race.

Unlike other college campuses where angry demonstrations against the Vietnam War were happening, where young men were burning their draft cards and others were fleeing to Canada, the University of Arizona had little of it, as if it were under a dome in the desert. Bob Dylan's popular mantra during Woody's matriculation was "The Times They Are A-Changin'," except apparently at U of A.

A classmate and future fraternity brother of Woody's, Steve Rempe, says, "We weren't protesting anything. We were like little Bush [President George W.]. If somebody had to go because they failed and got drafted, they got into the National Guard by hook or by crook because they knew someone."

Lovejoy recalls one evening watching *The Huntley-Brinkley Report*, NBC's then-popular evening newscast with Chet Huntley and David Brinkley, when the program closed with a feature about life on the University of Arizona campus.

"I'll never forget it," says Lovejoy. "David Brinkley said something like, 'We're going to Tucson, Arizona, Chet.' And they showed pictures of thousands of guys standing out in front of their dorms screaming, 'Pants! Pants! Pants!' and marching up the street and having a good ol' time, and Huntley and Brinkley pointed out that this wasn't over Vietnam, but was an old-fashioned panty raid. 'Good night, Chet. Good night, David.'"

Woody, as everyone knew, was an active participant in those collegiate frolics.

28

Woody Johnson wasn't the only young member of the Johnson dynasty who had gone west to have fun at the University of Arizona and avoid the draft. J. Seward Johnson Sr.'s grandson Eric Ryan, whose mother, Mary Lea Johnson, was the first baby face on the Johnson & Johnson's Baby Powder container, had also enrolled there along with Woody's ill-fated younger brother, Billy.

"It was the Vietnam era and I was involved in the antiwar movement as a high school student and had filed for conscientious objector status, which was denied," says Ryan. "I had no idea that I was even going to get into college because I was near the bottom of my class [at the elite Canterbury School, in Connecticut]. But I had Vietnam inviting me to come over and shoot people in rice paddies. I fully expected to be drafted, and I fully expected to be a draft resister, and I was considering going to Canada."

Instead, he headed to the Tucson campus where the booze flowed, the pot was primo, and, as Woody had acknowledged when he first visited the school, the girls were hot.

"The attraction was that Woody was already there, and having a great time, and sending home stories about what good times could be had there," says Ryan. "It was a great place to escape the draft. There were many people at the University of Arizona who viewed it as a safe haven from Hanoi."

Ryan, who later went to law school and became a prosecuting attorney in New York City for a time in the 1980s, says Woody was a perfect fit for the university's Vietnam War–era zeitgeist.

"He was the ultimate frat boy," observes his cousin. "Woody fit in to the beer parties and the frat house scene pretty readily. And certainly at Arizona there was a ton of weed. He was a party-hearty kind of guy."

Ryan left the university within a year because his mother and his father, William Ryan, the first of her three husbands, were divorcing and there was "total chaos, lots of tension, and tons of fighting" at home. Woody's brother Billy soon followed, and both began attending classes at New York University. Woody's uncle—his mother's brother, Dr. Keith Wold—would refer to the school as "Jew York University," Eric Ryan recalls.

After two years of failing to be initiated into Delta Chi, Woody pledged and was initiated into another fraternity with an even more ominous reputation for Animal House craziness, Sigma Alpha Epsilon.

"SAE was definitely *not* community service oriented," says Texas attorney Martin Muncy, who was an SAE fraternity brother of Woody's and also a member of his class of 1969.

Among Woody's other SAE cohorts were the Shadegg brothers, John—a future conservative Republican U.S. congressman from Arizona and an attorney, and David, who became a builder. Their father was ultraconservative Stephen Shadegg, described by *The New York Times* as Barry Goldwater's "alter ego." A veteran political campaign manager who came from Betty Johnson's Twin Cities hometown, Shadegg had helped Goldwater win his first term in the Senate, and was instrumental in Goldwater's future political career.

Steve Rempe, another SAE brother of Woody's who, like Shadegg and Muncy, also became a lawyer, a public defender, says, "Anything *Animal House* did, we did better. We weren't much of a social organization—other than drinking."

As a pledge during SAE's "Hell Week" of hazing, Woody, twenty years old at the time, was required to carry a brick with his name written on it. A fraternity brother would write an obscene limerick on the brick, and Woody was then required to recite it whenever anyone on campus spoke to him. The coup de grace was when he was forced to submit to having his body covered with molasses, and then ordered to roll around in a bed of corn flakes mixed with hot sauce. So covered, he had to wear the molasses and corn flakes gunnysack around campus, looking like the campus idiot.

When Woody was finally accepted as a brother in good standing, SAE wasn't open to just anyone.

"There was a general racial discrimination policy against blacks," states Muncy, "and in 1966 we pledged a guy by the name of Goldstein. Other than him, I can't remember any other Jews. The fraternity was a Christian-based organization, which was long lost, I'm sure, by the time it had been adulterated by all the alcohol and drugs."

Because the university was just some sixty miles north of the Mexican border town of Nogales it was, says a frat brother, "pretty easy to smuggle" high-quality marijuana into the country and onto the campus, where it was widely smoked and sold.

The other toxic substance bought in Mexico and brought to the school was high-test, 190-proof alcohol dubbed "Pure Al," which was readily consumed within Sigma Alpha Epsilon, and at the frat's parties.

From a keg in the kitchen, the alcohol, diluted with punch, came through an intricate system of rubber tubes to on-and-off taps in ten or so locations in the house—a delivery system designed by the frat's engineering school brothers. "You could get the booze anywhere in the house," states Rempe. "Everyone was a binge drinker."

If the alcohol from Mexico, freely available throughout the house, wasn't enough, the boys from SAE had blank Illinois birth certificates they used to get false Arizona driver's licenses to illegally buy liquor in bottle stores.

An SAE brother and a friend of Woody's, Pat Lynch, says that parents of the silver-spoon kids who came to the university—many like the Johnson & Johnson scion who couldn't get into better schools—thought it was safe because it seemed far from places where they could get into trouble. "Me and quite a few of Bobby's contemporaries were spoiled little rich kids who their parents sent off to get them away from the East Coast and bad influences, and the worst place to send them was to a party school in Arizona. They thought it was safe because it was out in the desert. Oh, God, were they ever wrong."

They didn't call SAE the "country club fraternity" for nothing, because Woody wasn't the only scion from a hugely wealthy or scandalous dynasty ensconced in the house.

Among them was the grandson of another billionaire who owned a major sports team and vast real estate holdings in California. A few years before he arrived on campus, his mother, one of the daughters of the magnate, made headlines and shocked society when she ran off and married the rector of the family's church.

Fraternity brothers of Woody and the other member recall that both of them stayed under the radar as much as possible regarding their family affiliations, scandals, and money—although Woody drove around campus in a British racing-green Jaguar XKE. "Not many people knew Woody was from Johnson and Johnson," recalls Steve Rempe. "I never would have thought he came from that family because he just didn't play that role, and wasn't a snob."

Unlike the traditional blowout Delta House toga party featured in *National Lampoon's Animal House,* the SAE brothers threw a traditional blowout luau party at the beginning of every fall semester (and a Hell's Angels party in the spring), serving a punch made with the virtually pure alcohol bought in Mexico during pot and booze runs.

The year Woody was a freshman the SAE luau almost turned fatal. A pretty coed who was a member of Delta Gamma, who had never drunk before coming to the university, became critically ill from swigging too much of the high-octane punch. "She passed out and was rushed to the emergency room to have her stomach pumped. She did not die, but she was knocking on the door," recalls Muncy. Coeds—they had to prove they were virgins to get into the SAE house—would get so inebriated they'd be found passed out on the floor of dormitory elevators.

One year the financially well-off frat brothers put together a big chunk of change and hired Ike and Tina Turner and the Ikettes to perform. Tina sang from atop an old piano in the house. Some years later an SAE frat brother ran into her in Las Vegas and reminded her about the performance. He's never forgotten her response. "It was," she said, "the lowest point in my career as an entertainer."

29

One of the memorable scenes in *Animal House* was when some of the frat brothers, facing expulsion by the insanely frustrated Dean Wormer, who had put Delta House on "double secret probation," decided to take a road trip.

And it was on such a collegiate excursion at the beginning of his junior year that Woody Johnson, for at least a second time since his near-fatal brush with death in Bermuda, almost lost his life.

But this time it would be far more serious than requiring thirty stitches to close a head wound.

Woody's closest friend and roommate at the time was a "free spirit" by the name of Gary Johnson. As another Sigma Alpha Epsilon brother, Dan Fick, notes, "Bob and Gary lived together. They hung out together. They were Johnson and Johnson, but they weren't related." Even their mothers were both named Betty.

One story involving Woody and Gary that was still being recalled by SAE brothers more than four decades later involved an incident that easily could have been exaggerated in its telling through the years, and might even have been apocryphal. As Martin Muncy heard the story, Gary, Woody, and a couple of other friends, returning from Mexico in a VW van, were stopped at the border. "The Border Patrol asks whether they had anything to declare, and Gary says, 'We got forty pounds of pot, but you'll never find it.' So the cops took that van apart into small pieces, didn't find anything, and then said, 'Have fun putting it back together, boys.' The Border Patrol could do that."

Everyone had a nickname in SAE. Because of Johnson & Johnson, Woody was called "Band-Aid, " or "B.J." for Bob Johnson. Some joked that B.J. also stood for "Blowjob."

His bosom buddy, Gary, from Southern California, was dubbed "Beachy," because of his blond, tanned surfer look. And together, the team of Woody and Gary were known as the "Dupree Brothers." They had taken the name from two brothers, Ronnie and Paul Dupree, who back in the mid- to late 1960s were professional wrestlers, and former Hell's Angels.

"The Johnson boys—Bobby and Gary—they were the money boys, the party guys," recalls Muncy, the attorney. "They would drink the whiskey and have some fun, and I imagine they smoked, too."

Gary was said to have graduated from Hollywood High School, and was the playboy son of a wealthy Southern California developer, Raymond Johnson, who reportedly was involved in the building òf Marina Del Rey in Los Angeles, according to Gary's friend and SAE brother, William Culver White. The Johnsons had moved to Phoenix and lived in a beautiful home on the edge of the elite Phoenix Country Club.

As those involved recall, it was early September 1968, the start of Woody's junior year, when he and his girlfriend at the time, Diane Vonderahe, along with her Kappa Alpha Theta sorority sister and roommate, Debby Sceli, and another friend, an SAE brother by the name of Kim Lockwood, were invited to one of Gary's popular bashes at his parents' home. Whenever Gary threw a party, Woody was always the guest of honor.

It was already dark when Woody and his pals hit Arizona Interstate 10 westbound through the desert for the ninety-minute drive to Phoenix. Diane and Debby had just come from a ceremony for their sorority's new pledges, and all four of them in the car, Diane recalls years later, were drinking.

"Oh, my God, who knows what we had, but yes, we were drinking alcohol, and I don't know what it was. Of course, we were *celebrating* as we do in college."

At exit 226, which leads to the small town of Red Rock, about eighty miles from Phoenix, they stopped.

"We pulled off one of the off-ramps because we all had to go to the bathroom, and it was pitch-black outside.

"So B.J. and Kim Lockwood went on one side of the overpass and Debby and I went to the other side of the overpass.

"Even all these years later it kind of gives me the creeps talking about it because it's not a very happy story. My heart's still beating. I was in total panic."

In the dark, Woody, who had been drinking, was urinating, and when he was finished he took a step or two backward "and as we quickly came to find out," says a still horrified Vonderahe, "it was like an eighteen-foot drop, and B.J. just stepped off of it.

"We heard Kim screaming for us, and my roommate, Debby, was actually in the nursing program, luckily. So we ran over and she went down to try to help B.J., and I ran onto the highway. I finally flagged down a trucker, and he said he would go to a phone and call for an ambulance."

They were completely without communication in the middle of nowhere, and their friend, Woody, appeared near dead.

Woody had broken his back and was virtually paralyzed.

"It took a half hour to forty-five minutes before the ambulance showed up," recalls Vonderahe. "Debby was able to get B.J. in some kind of position, and Kim held him up. It was kind of dangerous, and Debby kind of knew that, but in those days you just kind of did what you thought you needed to do, and so the emergency people went down the embankment and put B.J. in the ambulance and, of course, he was in excruciating pain."

The ambulance took twenty-one-year-old Woody to the closest hospital, which was located in the small desert town of Casa Grande. But the little hospital there didn't have the facilities to care for him.

"So they had to put B.J. back in the ambulance, and I guess by now it was maybe one o'clock in the morning, and they took him to Phoenix."

Luckily, one of the best hospitals for treating Woody's kind of critical back injury was located in the "Valley of the Sun City"—the Barrow Neurological Institute of St. John's Hospital and Medical Center, which had been founded in 1962, and was recognized internationally for dealing with spine and brain disorders.

Woody underwent surgery and was in intensive care there for three or four months.

"They told him he would never walk again," says Debby Sceli Peacock, the former nursing student. "That was the prognosis after his surgery."

News of Woody's accident quickly got back to the SAE fraternity house.

"The first news we had was that he probably was paralyzed, or he was going to die, and that he fell off a bridge," says Martin Muncy. "I remember someone saying, 'Man, I wonder how screwed up Band-Aid was to step off that bridge? I wonder how messed up he was to do something like that?' But it didn't surprise anyone because he was known to party."

When word of Woody's accident reached his longtime friends the Vicino family, who had known the Johnsons for years and had moved from Princeton to Fort Lauderdale in 1965, where Bobby and Betty Johnson had built another home, they were devastated, but not surprised.

"It was always like, hey, Woody's here!" says John Vicino, Keith Johnson's best pal, recalling Woody's wildness. "He would be doing J-turns on his speedboat. He would be saying, 'We're going to sneak out late at night and ring people's doorbells.' With Woody, it was—we're going to do something stupid.

"But when we heard that he broke his back, my mother got us all together and we went to church and we prayed for him because they thought he wouldn't make it, or he'd be paralyzed."

After several hellish months at Barrow Neurological, he was released and taken to Gary Johnson's family home where he underwent more therapy before he was moved back east to undergo intense rehabilitation and learn to walk again.

"At Gary's house, Bobby was placed in a gurney of sorts and had to be turned over by full-time attendants several times a day to avoid bed sores," says SAE brother Pat Lynch. "He was completely immobile, completely rigid, and *very* depressed."

Woody's mother, Betty, had left a hellish situation at home where her husband, Bobby Johnson, was critically ill to come to Phoenix and be at the side of her firstborn. "She was the mother hen," states Lynch, who was there beside her offering to help as best he could. "Her focus on Woody was tremendous. Her love was just incredible."

30

Brought up by his mother and nannies after the General left them for another woman and with the family chauffeur as a father figure, Robert Wood "Bobby" Johnson III wanted more family life for his own children, especially his sons. When Bobby was a youngster he had been sent away to board at Millbrook School, where he graduated near the end of the Depression. Hoping to establish a tradition for the next generation, he had sent his first two boys, Woody and Keith, there.

After Millbrook, Bobby Johnson spent two years, from September 1939 until June 1941, at small, rather isolated Hamilton College, in Clinton, New York. There were just 158 members in his freshman year, a number that diminished each semester as the boys enlisted, or were drafted. The 1940 *Hamiltonian* yearbook had a photo of a serious-looking Bobby Johnson with his Psi Upsilon fraternity brothers.

Hamilton's motto was "Know Thyself," something with which Bobby Johnson would always struggle because of his lack of self-confidence inculcated by his father's odious treatment and abandonment of him.

Despite the General's resentment, Bobby wanted to prove himself, and went to work at Johnson & Johnson when he was twenty in the summer of 1940. The best job he could secure—even though his father ran the family business, and probably because of it—was as a laborer in the dusty mill where plaster casts were manufactured, according to Lawrence Foster. Bobby's coworkers were mostly second-generation Hungarians, and the struggling heir to a great fortune received the same low hourly wage and was treated no better and no worse.

After the Japanese sneak attack on Pearl Harbor, he was drafted into the army and received his training on the campus of Ohio State University. Unlike his father, who had pressured President Roosevelt into making him a brigadier general, Bobby always remained an enlisted man, and never received a promotion higher than sergeant.

At some point just before or after the United States entered the fighting, Bobby had met his future wife—slender, attractive blonde Betty May Wold, the daughter of well-to-do Saint Paul opthamologist Dr. Karl Christian Wold and Maybelle Lundgren Wold. Betty's father was the foster son of a Swedish-born St. Paul physician, Dr. Olof Sohlberg, who had married Helvina A. Wold in 1886.

Betty's family—she had two brothers, Keith and Sidney, who also became physicians, and a sister—lived in a Gilded Age Victorian at 1157 Summit Avenue, considered one of the city's finest streets at the time, and located in the prestigious Summit Hill neighborhood that was once home to the city's robber barons, and the rich, famous, and infamous—ranging at times from F. Scott and Zelda Fitzgerald to the Ma Barker–Alvin Karpis gang that had terrorized the Midwest.

Because her father had a thriving practice, Betty was sent to the exclusive, all-girls Summit School during the Depression when many such elite private schools couldn't afford to remain open. At Summit, she became close chums with several other girls from well-off St. Paul families, among them Jean Schilling Chockley Ricketts, whose father was the president of a large paper products company, and the two remained lifelong friends. They were among just eleven graduates in the Summit School class of June 1939.

Betty, as Ricketts recalls her in their school days, was "blondish, very attractive, *always* slim."

Attractive, yes; academically bright, well . . .

"Betty was *not* the greatest student," maintains Ricketts, who at the age of ninety in 2011, and also three times married like her friend, had a clear memory of their school days together.

Betty's lack of academic achievement at Summit was underscored when the girls graduated.

"Out of our class of eleven, two went to Wellesley College"—Jean was one of them—"two went to Smith College, two went to Vassar, one went to Wheaton College, and one went to the University of Minnesota. They were all very bright," she observes. "But Betty went to Pine Manor Junior College, which then was a two-year finishing school for girls from moneyed families who could bring their horses and ride. Betty wasn't stupid, she just wasn't much of an intellectual."

Betty Wold had chosen fashionable Pine Manor because it, too, was in Wellesley, Massachusetts, where she could continue her friendship with Jean. Also in the town of Wellesley, a bicycle ride away from Pine Manor, was what was then a two-year business school for men called the Babson Institute. Its founder, Roger Babson, hired executives as instructors, and the curriculum mostly involved on-the-job training rather than academics, practical experience rather than lectures.

One of the students at Babson when Betty Wold was at Pine Manor was Bobby Johnson, according to Jean Ricketts. "That's where they met and Betty dated him. The boys from Babson, which was a school for the sons of very wealthy men who couldn't get into Princeton, Yale, or Harvard, dated girls from Pine Manor."

Betty May Wold began her finishing school career in a class of about one hundred young women who had come from twenty-four states and five foreign countries, and was the largest new class the school had ever had. They were there to learn social and personal etiquette, and the salient points of being prim and proper, while preparing for their coming out in society, eventual membership in the Junior League, and the country club set—all with the goal of that generation of meeting a handsome, wealthy husband of good lineage to take care of them in the manner in which they had been raised.

In September 1940, when Betty returned for her second and final year, the world was in crises. The Luftwaffe was dumping tons of bombs on Britain, killing thousands. Japan had joined the Axis powers. In Washington, the first draft number was drawn by Secretary of War Henry L. Stimson.

And in Tokyo, a top-secret plan was being finalized by Emperor Hirohito and his henchmen for a fatal sneak attack on a U.S. Naval base in the Pacific. With the world seemingly in flames and getting worse by the day, Betty's class began a war relief program, and with proceeds from various school events—the French club carnival, a fashion show, tickets sold by the Mimes and Masques players—a rolling kitchen was sent to blitzed London.

Betty graduated from Pine Manor in June 1941—the same month Bobby Johnson left Hamilton College—five months before Pearl Harbor.

Twenty-two months later, on April 4, 1943, the wedding page of *The New York Times* carried a two-paragraph item, with a St. Paul dateline, and the headline: "BETTY WOLD BETROTHED, Fiance Robert W. Johnson, Jr., Is Son of WPB Vice Chairman." It also said said that the intended groom, who was "of the Army"—he was then a private—and the daughter of Dr. and Mrs. Karl C. Wold "of this city" had become engaged. The item noted that Bobby was the "son of Mrs. Ross Johnson of Belleview Farm, New Brunswick, N.J." and "son also of Colonel Robert W. Johnson, vice chairman of the war Production Board and chairman of the Smaller War Plants Corporation." There was no mention that the future groom was the grandson of one of the founders of Johnson & Johnson, which was then booming—supplying medical supplies to our boys and allies in combat zones around the world—or that he was the heir to a great fortune.

By the time they tied the knot that October 7, in St. Paul, Betty was serving as a navy technician in the WAVES, the acronym for "Women Accepted for Volunteer Emergency Service." Private Bobby was then stationed at Camp Campbell, in Kentucky.

During his service, he reportedly spent four years in England, France, and Germany with the First and 14th Armored Division. But he may have been out of harm's way. He once told his son Billy's friend John Vicino that his job in the army was documenting and cataloguing pistols that were turned in by officers, and that at the end of the war he had been given a captured German Luger that he had brought home as a souvenir, a prized possession that he showed visitors.

Because of the war, Betty and her friend Jean lost track of one another. "But I eventually heard she had married Bobby Johnson. We were all very,

very surprised and happy for her and said, 'She wasn't the smartest one in the class, but she married the best.' She ended up extremely wealthy. *Extremely.*"

Because of her separation from Bobby Johnson caused by the war, Betty didn't give birth to the first of her brood of five until April 1947 when Woody was born, followed by Keith in 1948, and her only daughter, Libet, in 1950, with Billy and Christopher still to come.

At Bobby and Betty's nuptials, her brother Keith, then at the University of North Dakota Medical School, met Bobby's cousin Elaine Johnson, the second-born daughter of Seward Johnson Sr. and his first wife, Ruth Dill Johnson.

That meeting was like hitting the lottery for him, for he became the second Wold sibling to marry into one of the world's wealthiest and most powerful families.

On the afternoon of July 2, 1949, in Christ Protestant Episcopal Church in New Brunswick, Keith and Elaine tied the proverbial knot. Betty, who had played Cupid for her brother, along with Elaine's older sister, and Mary Lea, were matron and maid of honor, respectively. Dr. Wold was the lucky groom's best man, and the ushers included Keith's brother, Dr. Sidney Wold, Seward Johnson Jr., and Elaine's cousin Bobby Johnson, Woody's father.

When Betty's brother, Keith, married into the Johnson dynasty, their staunchly Republican father, the doctor—Woody Johnson's maternal grandfather—had become embroiled in a heated national controversy. He had written a controversial book entitled *Mr. President—How Is Your Health?* that charged that the late President Roosevelt and his doctors had been involved in a shocking cover-up of his health during the crucial war years.

But the Roosevelts came out fighting, calling Wold's accusation a bald-faced lie. The president's daughter, Anna Roosevelt Boettinger, declared that Wold's claim was "absolutely and completely untrue." The late president's son, Elliott Roosevelt, called Wold's book "dirty journalism," and the Roosevelts further asserted that Wold had never even met F.D.R., and had never talked to his White House physician.

31

After Bobby Johnson's honorable discharge from the army in 1945, he was determined to earn the respect of his father, the General, and to prove himself as an executive and a leader. He returned to Johnson & Johnson and began moving up the ladder, working in various departments, from personnel to manufacturing, and in the process getting a good overview of the company. His main interest was advertising and merchandising.

When he turned twenty-seven in 1947, the same year Betty gave birth to Woody, Bobby was elected to the board of directors, mainly because he was the boss's son, and the grandson of one of the founders. Whatever his feelings were about Bobby, the General wanted to keep it all in the family. In the mid-1950s, he activated a seven-member executive committee that included thirty-four-year-old Bobby, which put father and son in offices practically next to each other.

They began having petty disagreements over such things as whether Bobby's office should be contemporary or traditional, or whether his secretary should eat in a private dining room or the cafeteria. "It soon became apparent to the General that Bobby was going to stand his ground on issues both large and small, but because both men had a distaste for open conflict, they managed to keep their differences from flaring into arguments, for the time being," according to former Johnson & Johnson public relations head Lawrence Foster.

Moreover, in the highly competitive upper echelon of Johnson & Johnson, Bobby faced constant backstabbing from other executives who weren't part of the Johnson family, but who dreamed of one day succeeding the General when he retired, or as many said, when he was carried out in a box. Envious executives rarely gave the General commendations about his son, and usually had sniping things to say about him.

Still, he continued to move up the ladder. In 1955, he became executive vice president for marketing, a promotion that received coverage in the business section of *The New York Times*, which reported that he would be in charge of "marketing, field sales, merchandising and advertising." At the time, Johnson & Johnson was doing business in more than one hundred countries.

Five years later, at the age of forty, he was named executive vice president and general manager, and a year after that, on January 1, 1961, he reached his goal: president of Johnson & Johnson.

That same year the General established hugely lucrative "spendthrift trusts" with increasingly valuable Johnson & Johnson stock for his grandchildren, Woody and his siblings—which was the first time he had made any sort of generous gesture toward them. The General had previously established similar trusts for his two children—Bobby, from his first marriage, and Sheila, who was adopted during his second marriage.

The trust fund money was doled out based on age and would make Woody and his siblings very wealthy—tens of millions of dollars wealthy—beginning when each of them turned twenty-one, and with bigger increments thereafter. With the gift from their grandfather who they never really got to know, Woody and his brothers and sister became members of the lucky sperm club, and could live like royalty without ever having to raise a finger to do anything. Among his siblings, Woody would be the one the best known for actively pursuing a business career, mainly as the owner of the New York Jets, but that wouldn't happen until he was in his fifties.

Spendthrift trusts were usually established to protect the beneficiary from his or her own extravagance, or inability to wisely manage his or her finances. When the trusts were established, Woody was just beginning his schooling at Millbrook. He received his first check when he turned twenty-one in April 1968—about ten million dollars—but didn't get to enjoy any of it immediately because about five months later he broke his back and was laid up for many months.

His next payment was at the age of twenty-five and was said to be in the range of twenty-five to fifty million dollars. That's when he went into business as a condo and land developer in Florida. The next payments kicked in when he turned thirty, around the time he married his first wife, then at thirty-five when he had children, and the final payment was when he turned forty-five in 1992.

As he once told his first business partner, Michael Spielvogel, after receiving his second big trust fund check, " 'If I blow this, I still have the next chunk of money coming to me.' He was always complimentary about how brilliant his family was when it came to doing things like trust funds," says Spielvogel.

$ $ $

Bobby and Betty's home, where Woody and his four siblings spent their childhoods and some of their teen years, was a sprawling, redbrick, center hall colonial-style mansion with a circular drive with a big tree in the middle that virtually hid the house at 108 Edgerstoune Drive, in one of Princeton's most exclusive neighborhoods. The grounds were impressive and included a greenhouse for Betty, who enjoyed gardening, and an Olympic-size pool, with a pool house. There was a three-car garage for Bobby and Betty's Cadillac Eldorado convertibles, and his pride and joy—a restored Packard.

They also owned a winter mansion in Florida and a summer place at the Jersey shore.

The Johnsons' home was staffed by two Scandinavian maids who also did cooking and cleaning, and assisted as nannies. Betty and Isabel lived in a room above the kitchen, had a close relationship, and were believed to be lesbians. "To an extent they helped raise the Johnson kids, and they were disciplinarians," says Neil Vicino, who spent much time in the house as one of Keith Johnson's best friends.

Neil's brother John, who was Billy Johnson's close pal, says the two women were "very protective" of the Johnson children. He recalls that when Keith raced down the driveway in his go-kart and into Edgerstoune Road where he skidded and overturned, breaking both his legs, it was either Betty or Isabel who rushed to his aid. "The police tried to keep her from the accident scene, so she jumped into her little Sunbeam and drove over the sidewalk around three cops and jumped out of the car to help Keith." A photo of Keith, his legs in casts, was prominently pinned on the wall of the Johnson kitchen.

The other regular member of the household was a man named Jimmy, who acted as a bodyguard for the Johnson children. He also was said to have been the longtime family chauffeur who had become a virtual surrogate father for young Bobby when the General abandoned him and his mother. He later became Bobby Johnson's bodyguard, and there was family lore that he had even gone into the army with Bobby to watch over the Johnson heir.

Bobby Johnson's prized room in the Princeton house, the den, was the ultimate macho man cave. On the walls were the mounted heads of wild animals, among them a Cape Buffalo that he claimed he had shot in Africa after it had charged him and driven him up a tree.

The thing was, Bobby Johnson didn't seem the sportsman type. Always very heavy and out of shape, which infuriated his father, and laid-back with soft features, there was nothing about him that screamed great white hunter, so there were those who questioned the veracity of his big-game stories, and believed that the display was strictly for show. Another reason for doubt was that there didn't seem to be much of a window in his life to have gone on such hunting expeditions, what with his going away to prep school, then to college, followed by his army service, marriage, fathering a brood of five, and his driven devotion to Johnson & Johnson.

Still, there were many believers, particularly among his young sons and their pals, whose eyes widened whenever they entered Bobby Johnson's trophy room domain. "It impressed me as a young kid. I'd never seen anything like it. I had no reason to disbelieve any of it," says Neil Vicino, who spent his adult life as a broadcast journalist, a career where cynicism is the rule rather than the exception. "Maybe the hunting was his way of proving to the General that he was the guy that the General wanted him to be."

John Vicino viewed the den as "our little fantasy place. It was like being in a Johnny Weissmuller movie. We were once talking and I said to Mr. Johnson, 'Boy, one day I want to go do this,' and he says, 'Johnny, they are beautiful animals. It's better to shoot them with a camera than a rifle.'"

Woody's cousin Eric Ryan saw Bobby Johnson as a Hemingwayesque character and had no reason to disbelieve his adventures in the bush. He, too, recalls seeing the Cape Buffalo head, and leopard skin rugs, and a certain photograph of Bobby Johnson on the trophy wall.

"He's in a fishing camp in Alaska, and he's pulling his shirt up and patting his belly. And what you can read from the picture, not necessarily knowing all of the circumstances, was that he was proud that he had lost some weight. In the picture, he's still a big, rotund guy, but he's a big, rotund guy with two weeks' growth of beard, and had been out in the woods doing manual stuff."

32

A long with Bobby Johnson's relatively rapid rise to the upper echelon of Johnson & Johnson, there came another change in his life that seemed as uncharacteristic as his earlier big-game hunting. His marriage had become endangered when he was said to have begun seeing other women, something not unheard of among Johnson men through the generations; his father, the General, and his uncle, J. Seward Johnson Sr., had had six wives between them, and untold mistresses.

While Betty Johnson had delivered her first four of five children within the first six years of marriage, she had still managed to retain her Scandinavian beauty; she was described by a male admirer back then as "a willowy blonde who looked Diane Keatonish."

Nevertheless, Bobby had grown bored and developed a mid-life crisis in the form of a wandering eye.

He had revealed his secret to a most unlikely source, his drama queen cousin Mary Lea Johnson, when they were getting drunk together, which was said to have been frequently.

"My mother and Bob were very close friends, and her idea of a really good time was to sit down with him, mix up a pitcher of martinis, and chat for hours about family sagas—and all kinds of [personal] things would come out," says her son, Eric Ryan. "They were just telling the truth while being drunk. She would tell him things like how she lost her virginity."

And Mary Lea had also passed on to her son, Eric, her cousin Bobby's bleary confidence that he was involved with another woman.

"My mother referred to it as an affair, and that Bob threatened to leave Betty and chase after this woman, who was described to me as a model."

The reputed affair had happened in the late 1950s or early 1960s. Mary Lea claimed that "Betty found out about the woman, about Bob's infatuation, whatever it was, and told Bob that she would not grant him a divorce and would not go quietly to slaughter," recalls Ryan.

At the time, the Johnsons had been married more than a decade. Woody, the oldest of the four children, was a preadolescent, and the fifth and last child in Betty's brood, Christopher, was born in 1959, just before or just after Bobby's claimed fling. "Given the size of the Johnson family—Betty and the kids—a divorce would have not been just messy, but hideously expensive for someone who suddenly found himself cast adrift by family," observes Ryan.

The "other woman" was a bathing suit model who Bobby was believed to have met at a boating event. Mary Lea called her "Miss Budweiser" because there had been a number of speedboats by that name in honor of the beer. After Betty learned of her husband's involvement, she gave him an ultimatum that she would not go quietly, and that she would play hardball to keep the marriage together. Bobby subsequently ended the relationship was the way Mary Lea explained it, "and they resolved it," says Ryan.

Mary Lea, however, wasn't the only one who claimed knowledge of an extramarital fling by Bobby Johnson.

Mariann Strong, a New York literary agent whose brother-in-law was the first cousin of Mary Lea's mother, Ruth Dill Johnson, and who had close ties to the members of the Johnson dynasty's third generation, claims that she, too, knew of an affair that Bobby Johnson was having.

"The woman I knew about was definitely *not* a Miss Budweiser," states Strong. "She was a very good-looking girl, slender, medium height, a brunette, who had a very good job in New York and lived in New Jersey, and was married. She told me she had an affair with him because she knew my husband's family was related," states Strong. "I sometimes rode on the train with her coming from New York and once after she told me about him she got off at the New Brunswick station, and I saw him meet her on the platform. I can't swear that she went to bed with him, but she certainly fraternized with him," continues Strong. "I don't know if she was *the* one, or one of many, but she was one."

$ $ $

The stress of Bobby Johnson's position as president of Johnson & Johnson—the competition he faced from backstabbing executives, the ongoing skirmishes with his father, and whatever marital problems existed at home—finally caught up with him in late 1964.

He was admitted for tests at Middlesex General Hospital, in New Jersey, later to be renamed Robert Wood Johnson University Hospital. The results were not good. "When he came out of the hospital," stated Lawrence Foster, "he reported to his colleagues that he had several health problems, including a peptic ulcer, high blood pressure, and his excessive weight."

As he went off to Florida to attend a company business meeting and relax a bit through the Christmas holidays at his winter home, he had no idea that he would soon be sacked. But the day after Valentine's Day of 1965, he received a not so loving missive from Johnson & Johnson that he had been placed on an indefinite leave, and at half of the compensation he had been receiving. The decision was his father's and was like a punch in the stomach, and an indication of more dire things to come.

In the subsequent weeks efforts were made by company intermediaries to bring about a peace between the General and Bobby, to maintain, as Foster noted, "the continuity of the Johnson family policy and leadership in the company," and to avoid losing the family's "influence on the business" if Bobby never returned.

In mid-April, Bobby sent an emotional "Dear Dad" letter to the General, according to Foster, refuting criticism of his leadership that ranged from cronyism for hiring executives he liked and trusted, to pursuing products that had failed, and to overseeing advertising strategies that had been considered unsound. Moreover, he angrily disputed allegations that he had become an alcoholic, and called what was being said about him nothing more than character assassination.

He asked his father to allow him to return to "our company" but without losing "my self-respect."

But by the time he finished the letter, and without his knowledge, his position as president of Johnson & Johnson was abolished, and a new one was created, president of Johnson & Johnson Worldwide, and given to the chairman of the executive committee of the board of directors.

Bobby termed his removal "a tragedy."

"[H]is lifelong dream of someday running Johnson and Johnson was shattered. So was the relationship with his father . . . Bobby felt that he had been destroyed. His father believed that the decision he had made was in the best interest of the company," according to Foster.

This drama was unfolding as Woody was graduating from Millbrook School, and embarking on his ill-fated college career at the University of Arizona. Woody had had a very formal and mostly distant relationship with his grandfather, who had now essentially castrated his father by cutting off his career. Sometimes when Woody was a youngster he'd get a note from the General, but mostly it was about the family business that Woody didn't understand.

Betty, who had stood by and cheered her husband's rise in Johnson & Johnson over the years, was both devastated and furious about how her father-in-law had dumped her husband, and she made her feelings known in what Foster described as "a sternly worded letter" expressing that Bobby had been "victimized at the company." Foster reported that the General had put the letter, which he marked confidential, in a safe-deposit box, and did not let anyone else ever read it.

After Bobby was axed, Betty became aware that longtime friends and acquaintances, people they had known from the time Bobby had started at the company after they were married—all Johnson & Johnson people—had suddenly given them the cold shoulder, had blacklisted them socially. It was extremely difficult for her to take since Johnson & Johnson had become as much her life as it was his.

As a female friend notes, "Betty had been a captive of Johnson and Johnson. She didn't do anything that wasn't involved with the company. She was wrapped up in Johnson and Johnson politics, always the corporate wife."

Members of the Johnson dynasty, such as Edward Mead (Ted) Johnson, whose father and the General had a close relationship, were outraged and revolted by the General's treatment of Bobby and felt that his firing was contemptible.

Afraid to do the actual firing of his son, the General enlisted his brother, Seward Sr., to do the distasteful deed. Ted Johnson says he was told by his father, "The General felt badly about having to fire Bobby and he told Seward, 'Just tell him he's finished.'"

$ $ $

The last few years of the decade of the sixties were a dramatic, dire, and devastating time for the Johnson dynasty.

In early 1967, the General's health, too, had become the subject of growing consternation. Despite his obsession with being slim and staying in shape, he had been a smoker and had developed a persistent cough that was growing worse, on top of a heart condition.

So both father and son were dealing with major health issues.

After his firing, Bobby had made a valiant effort to begin a new career. He started a business in Menlo Park, New Jersey—where Thomas Edison had first conducted his experiments—called Johnson Industries, Inc., with the goal of developing an aloe-based skin cream called Vedra.

But his work was in vain because, like his father, his health had worsened. Taken seriously ill, he was once again rushed to New Brunswick Hospital, where doctors were considering a diagnosis of cancer and discussing surgery on his colon.

Not long after Bobby's emergency hospitalization, the General himself went for a checkup at Roosevelt Hospital in New York and a routine X-ray showed a tumor on part of one of his lungs. It was in a difficult position that made a biopsy all but impossible, so it wasn't known whether it was malignant or benign. In June 1967, he began thirty days of radiation therapy at Pennsylvania Hospital in Philadelphia.

The son and father—two different generations of the Johnson dynasty, one the leader, the other the namesake, two men who had battled for decades from the time one was abandoned as a child by the other—would both be diagnosed with incurable cancers.

The General's wife, Evie, the onetime nightclub dancer, had tried to cheer him up, but to no avail. He knew his end was near, and so did she. The days of the General and Evie being the golden couple of New York café society were behind them, and they had long ago stopped sleeping in the same bedroom.

In discussing the General later, Evie was quoted by Lawrence Foster as saying, "He could, on occasion, be very warm and sentimental, but you didn't see that very often . . . We had a very honest and friendly relationship. He would say that most of the men he knew had outgrown their wives. That wasn't the case with us. He would ask what I thought about this and that— not that he ever paid attention."

The day after the start of the New Year 1968 the General was admitted to Roosevelt Hospital in New York. "Johnson's skin began turning yellowish. He was losing weight rapidly and looked emaciated," Foster recalled.

The General had been diagnosed with liver cancer.

There now were two health crises happening at the same time. Across the Hudson River from New York, at Middlesex Hospital in New Brunswick, the General's namesake, Bobby, was also being treated for cancer—cancer of the colon.

The General's longtime private nurses thought now was the time to have father and son end their feud. The two very sick men had a meeting in the old man's hospital room, spent a half hour together after several years of not speaking. The deathbed rapprochement lifted the General's spirits and made him happy in his final days.

As Seward Johnson Jr. observes many years later, "It really meant something to his father, but it didn't mean anything to Bobby." That, he says, was also the opinion of Betty Johnson. Foster, too, stated that the meeting "had not erased all the bitter memories Bobby had of his departure from the company."

Obsessive even to the end, the General had written specific instructions on how his body should be handled. He wanted a simple funeral, with no viewing, no flowers, and no eulogy, and wrote that he would be "deeply pleased" if his family and his closest coworkers would be present at the service at Christ Church in New Brunswick, the industrial town where Johnson & Johnson made its first dollar near the end of the nineteenth century.

Except for family bequests, his immense fortune of hundreds of millions of dollars in Johnson & Johnson stock was left to the Robert Wood Johnson Foundation.

General Robert Wood Johnson Jr.'s last words to one of his nurses before he died shortly after six P.M. on January 30, 1968, at the age of seventy-four, were:

"I have millions and I would give everything I have if someone could make me well."

$ $ $

After the death of his father, Bobby Johnson, himself dying from colorectal cancer, which is often linked to obesity and excessive alcohol consumption, spent the remaining months of his life mostly at the family's Bay Colony estate in Fort Lauderdale.

Located on yacht-festooned canals close to the palm-tree-lined blue waters of the Intracoastal Waterway, Bay Colony was the perfect place to live and, in Bobby Johnson's case, the perfect place to die. It was considered so incredibly luxe that the television news magazine *60 Minutes* had once sent correspondent Morley Safer to do a feature story about what a wealthy and exotic enclave it was, an ultra-exclusive community where the homes even had, as Safer wryly pointed out, kumquats growing on the trees.

The Johnsons' property had a main house and a guesthouse with a pool in between where Bobby Johnson spent much time, seeking energy from the Florida sunshine. In September 1968, nine months after the General died, more tragedy struck when Woody broke his back in Arizona. Because Bobby was too ill to travel and was undergoing rugged cancer treatments, it was decided that Betty would go to Phoenix to attend to their son during his long recovery from his near-paralyzing injury.

At first Bobby Johnson was to receive cobalt radiation treatment, but one of the top researchers at Johnson & Johnson told him that cobalt was "going to burn the hell out of him," a family friend recalls, so it was suggested that his cancer be treated with the use of a newly developed type of X-ray machine, called a linear accelerator, to quickly and more safely beam radiation at his cancerous tissues and tumors.

The matriarch, Betty, kept a stiff upper lip as her husband slowly slipped away. "Betty's extremely tight-ass, suppresses her emotions quite well, and manages to keep a game face in place through any kind of adversity," observes Eric Ryan. "As Bob was dying, I don't remember outpourings of emotion from Betty. What I remember is her saying, 'We got to be tough, we got to be strong to get through this,' and there was a lot of stuffing down emotions rather than allowing them to show."

With little or no hope to survive his cancer, Bobby decided to live it up as best he could. To enjoy whatever time he had left, he found pleasure in buying two expensive automobiles, which, of course, he could well afford.

He had always wanted a Rolls-Royce like the one his father had had, but at first he debated buying one. He had conferred with friends in Fort Lauderdale who were aware of his cancer and knew that he was dying, so they told him to just go for it.

But first he bought a Mercedes Benz 600, which back in the day was a competitor to Rolls-Royce and Bentley and, at the time, was the world's fastest sedan, owned by the likes of John Lennon, Elizabeth Taylor, Elvis Presley, and even Fidel Castro.

But Bobby hadn't lost his desire for the Rolls, and finally, when he knew his chance of surviving his cancer was slim to none, he ordered a convertible, dark green in color, with a dark beige top.

"He didn't suffer a lot in the mornings, the mornings were pretty good for him," a family friend recalls. "So Bobby would get behind the wheel of his Rolls with the top down and just cruise around."

In mid-December 1970, his condition became far more critical, the beginning of the end, and he was admitted to Holy Cross Hospital in Fort Lauderdale. All of his children were there, including Woody, who had by then recovered sufficiently from his accident to be with his failing father.

Three days before Christmas, three months after his fiftieth birthday, Robert Wood (Bobby) Johnson III died.

The family held a private memorial service in Fort Lauderdale where he was interred, rather than in one of the traditional Johnson family plots or mausoleums in New Jersey. Some viewed this as a snub aimed at the family for how badly he and Betty felt he had been treated by his father, and the powers at Johnson & Johnson.

Bobby Johnson was the last known member of the Johnson dynasty to work in what had been the family business. Woody Johnson and his siblings would have nothing to do with the company, career-wise. But each collected the untold tens of millions of dollars in company stock left to them in Johnson dynasty trust funds.

33

When the doctors felt Woody Johnson was well enough to be transported, he was flown from Phoenix and admitted to the Rusk Institute of Rehabilitative Medicine, part of New York University Hospital, for a number of months of more rehabilitation for his paralyzing back injury. The Johnson family had rented an apartment near the hospital to be close to him.

It was an excruciating ordeal that seemed to go on forever. "Woody spent eight months at Rusk on morphine," says his first wife, Nancy Sale Frey Johnson Rashad. "He always needed more drugs and he told me after we were married that he would throw his fork out into the hallway to get the nurses' attention. The muscles on the front of one of his feet atrophied, so when he walks it's almost like he has to swing his leg to get his toe to come up to take a step forward, but it's almost impossible to notice."

A friend from Princeton, John Bigelow Taylor, recalls Woody "hanging upside down in some kind of traction. He was able to talk, but in a terrible position."

When Woody was finally ambulatory enough in 1970, he attended the wedding in Vermont of his Millbrook School roommate, John Stewart Mills, who was then in his first year of graduate school, studying urban planning in the School of Public Administration of New York University. His bride was twenty-year-old Laura Freeman, a pretty, bright junior at the University of Vermont, where she was a member of the women's ski team.

Unlike twenty-two-year-old Woody, Jack Mills was moving forward with his life, taking on responsibilities, preparing for a career, while Woody was still at loose ends, recovering from his accident, floundering about, still needing to finish college. The only difference between Robert Wood Johnson IV—one of the four ushers in the Mills's wedding ceremony—and the other young people celebrating Jack and Laura's marriage, was that Woody was a multimillionaire who had collected his first trust fund payment of about ten million dollars.

Mills hadn't heard from Woody—he still called him Bob, the name he knew him by at Millbrook School—since a year or so after they had graduated in 1965, and wasn't aware of his accident until he arrived at the wedding "kind of stiff and had a little difficulty walking. He told me they had been out in the desert and had been drinking and he fell into a dry wash, or something like that. He didn't go into any great detail. But his mother called and said he needed to be very careful. There had been some talk about all of us going out that night on toboggans and his mother tried to convince Laura to discourage Woody from any of that kind of activity."

Of the two, Mills had been the "shy one" and Woody the "far more gregarious" one through their prep school years. Mills was also the better student, while Woody "was average, not extraordinarily academic. He didn't seem driven," says Mills. "He was just fun to be around. He had a pretty nice stereo in our room at Millbrook and he had all the Beach Boy albums, he *loved* the Beach Boys, and Barbra Streisand—and that's an interesting combination."

While Mills's father was a Republican politician most of his life—he once ran unsuccessfully for the U.S. Congress and had received a contribution from Bobby Johnson—the Mills family was financially middle-class and modest. What Jack liked about Woody was the fact that "he was down to earth, and with his family background he could have been a supreme jerk, and he wasn't." During one of his visits to the Johnson estate in Princeton, Mills asked Woody who some of the people were socializing with his parents. "'Oh, those are the DuPonts,' he responded, but he didn't think it was any big deal."

The last time the prep school roommates had been together before the Mills's wedding was their grand tour of Europe during the summer of 1966, after their first year in college. Neither had been there before. The Johnsons had rented a Volkswagen for the boys, and they racked up some six thousand miles traveling around. The only hitch occurred when Woody lost his passport as they were about to enter Italy, causing a delay in their trip. But a local Johnson & Johnson representative helped to expedite their passage over the border with a new passport.

When they were in Norway, above the Arctic Circle, they didn't have the proper outerwear. Woody, wearing a raincoat and sneakers, decided to trek across the ice on a glacier where he had found reindeer antlers. "He's holding these antlers in his hand," recalls Mills, "and he's jabbing them in the ice to stop from sliding into a crevice. It could have been a total disaster."

$ $ $

Woody returned to the University of Arizona sometime in 1970 to finish his junior and senior years that were interrupted by his back injury (and finally was awarded his degree, a BA in history, in February 1972, almost seven years after he graduated from Millbrook.)

Despite the seriousness of his back injury, his partying resumed to some extent, especially when his brothers, Keith and Billy, and cousins, Eric Ryan and Clint Wold, and other friends began showing up on the Tucson campus, either to take classes, or to just hang out and party. Woody also began dating Debby Sceli, the nursing student who was with him the night of the accident and who had come to his aid.

For a time, while working on his degree, he rented a condo apartment at 941 North Euclid Boulevard, some five blocks from the campus in a complex that was as much an animal house as were his former frat houses.

"The place was just a madhouse, absolutely insane, and full of crazy people," recalls another resident who had graduated from Millbrook and was a pal of Keith Johnson. "There was *tons* of pot and a lot of beer. We had a roommate who brought home a gun one day and shot and wounded himself, a fool trying to show off to his girlfriend."

Despite the fact that Woody had gotten his first big trust fund check, "he wasn't living" what Eric Ryan remembers as "a particularly flamboyant lifestyle." After Euclid, he had rented a small stucco house at 232 North Vine Street, in Tucson, one of a row of similar places, each having two small windows with a door in the middle, with absolutely no curb appeal.

"Woody was driving a beat-up VW bus, had shoulder-length hair, and was just trying to fit in like a regular guy," says Ryan.

Woody had also started drinking again and doing crazy stunts that risked getting him reinjured.

During a bout of boozing with Ryan, Woody initiated a wrestling match, and had gotten Eric in a headlock. "It was a whole physical tussle, two guys having a little too much to drink and goofing around," recalls Ryan. "And Woody falls over and rolls on his back and I was suddenly aware of other people in the room who are yelling, 'Oh, my God!' and they intervened to stop the horseplay because they were really concerned that Woody should not have been doing that."

Remembering that scene, Ryan said he was concerned about Woody's willingness to take chances.

Ryan and Billy Johnson, taking classes at the university, had rented a thousand-dollar-a-month three-bedroom house at 3001 East Helen Street in Tucson for the half year Ryan took classes, and the full year Billy stayed, and the place became a crash pad for friends and relatives from the East Coast.

Eric and Billy had gotten motorcycles. Not to be outdone, Woody bought a Norton Commando, a high-performance, big bike that was considered the Porsche of the motorcycle world. "It was definitely the motorcycle of choice," observes Ryan, "of someone who was walking a tightrope in terms of risk."

Billy, considered more creative and brighter than Woody, or Keith, was also something of a risk-taker. He had driven out to Arizona in one of the presents his father had given him for his eighteenth birthday, a very fast, bright red Mercury Cougar XR7 convertible powered by a big 390 horsepower V8 engine, with a four-barrel carburetor and fast Hurst shifter.

When he arrived on campus he saw that Ryan had already bought a Kawasaki 500 motorcycle with the one-thousand-dollar transportation allowance his mother, Mary Lea, had given him. "One thousand dollars in those days would have bought me a pretty nice secondhand VW Beetle," says Ryan, looking back, "but being young and stupid I went down and bought the motorcycle, which was really hot."

The Kawasaki, one of the fastest production cycles at the time, was dubbed the "widowmaker" among bikers because so many people had been killed on them due to its dangerous handling characteristics.

That was dramatically—and almost fatally—underscored when Billy Johnson convinced his cousin Eric to loan him his "red, fire-breathing death wish." While there was no helmet law in Arizona at the time, Ryan talked Billy into wearing his. He must have had a premonition.

Within thirty seconds, Billy had run a stop sign and driven the motorcycle into the side of a VW bus, with his head hitting the air intake right above the rear wheel, pushing it in.

"All of this was happening right outside of Woody's house, and so Woody and I *run* out and we see Billy lying in the street and we run up to him, and he's taken to the ER, and he's treated and released and, incredibly, has no serious injuries. He bought the wreck of my motorcycle from me that day. But, he had no business whatsoever on a motorcycle."

Not too long in the future that would be proven.

Billy had also wrecked the blood-red Mercury Cougar, almost killing himself and Ryan.

"Billy tried to get across train tracks before a freight came, and he took a turn too fast and the car flipped," says Ryan. "I still thank God he did because we never would have beat the train. He just kind of walked away like, Oh, well, no big deal. I felt lucky I wasn't killed."

$ $ $

Like his brother Billy, Keith Johnson had become a regular visitor to the Arizona campus, mainly to hang out and to party with his siblings and cousins.

But back in New Jersey, he had recently gotten into trouble for the first, but not the last time, with drugs.

Keith had been part of a triumvirate with John Bigelow Taylor and another friend—boys who had grown up together in Princeton, went to Princeton Country Day School, and later Keith and the friend had been part of a rowdy and wealthy group of boys from PCD that went to Millbrook School for a time when Woody was in his senior year there.

A jock who played football and soccer at Millbrook, the friend, like the Johnson boys, was a scion of an iconic dynasty.

"We were just sort of three buddies running around Princeton in 1968, 1969, 1970," says Taylor, who was from a far less wealthy and powerful family. One summer day the threesome, in their late teens, had driven from Princeton to the New Jersey summer resort town of Seaside Heights on the Atlantic Ocean. To more thoroughly enjoy the boardwalk's amusement park rides, says Taylor, they had smoked marijuana and gotten stoned.

"It was the three of us, and we'd been on some ride and we were laughing and having a good time and carrying on, and some plainclothes cops were watching us and just thought we looked like we were high, and so they asked for identification, and wanted to know how we got there, and when we said by car they made us go back to the car, and they found pot in the glove compartment," says Taylor, who later became a noted photographer.

One of his photographic projects was for the 1995 book *The White House Collection of American Craft,* assembled with the encouragement of first lady Hillary Clinton and her husband, the president, who once famously claimed "I didn't inhale" when the issue of his youthful pot smoking came up.

After the marijuana was found in their car, Taylor says, the three of them were arrested.

Looking back years later, he says, "It was just a little misdemeanor thing. In those days marijuana was almost legal, it was everywhere, and there was so much of it around Princeton because it was a university town."

Nevertheless, the three had to go to court, and they were sentenced to a thirty-day suspension of their driver's licenses, he recalls. (The record of their arrest and adjudication has long ago been expunged from police and court files.) But the boys were boastful about it at the time. "John or Keith told me about it just in the sharing of war stories," recalls Ryan.

While the boys might have viewed their bust as something cool in that age of sex, drugs, and rock 'n' roll, their parents didn't—in particular, Betty Johnson, who had just gone through hell with Woody's accident attributable to his own night of heavy partying.

Betty blamed the drug activity and Keith's arrest on Taylor, and banned him from the Johnson home.

"She *assumed* that it was somehow my influence on Keith, which is something I always resented, and her view was wrong in fact. I was much more of the follower, but she was saying, 'It can't be *my* son.' If any one of us lived a reckless life and could be a bad influence it was Keith. He thought it was all a joke. It didn't mean anything to him."

Keith was cut from different cloth than his pals. The latter two, friends say, were macho and athletic, while Keith was considered effeminate—even gay—by people who knew him from the time he entered Millbrook School until his death a decade later in 1975 from a cocaine overdose.

The marijuana arrest wasn't the first time Taylor was with Keith Johnson when the Band-Aid heir got into trouble.

The second time was far more serious and nearly fatal.

It was the night of June 4, 1972, Taylor's twenty-second birthday, which was being celebrated with lots of drinking at a bar and dance club called Goodtime Charley's in the small town of Kingston, New Jersey, near Princeton.

Since the pot arrest Taylor and Keith hadn't seen much of each other, going off in different directions. Keith had received his first trust fund millions—like Woody, about ten million dollars—and was spending crazily on exotic cars, fast boats, designer clothing, five-star restaurants, and every other luxury imaginable, and that included primo drugs.

"We were living very different lives," says Taylor. "I was trying to make my way in the world and Keith was investing in cable companies and taking cocaine."

But while their lives diverged, he and Keith had kept up, and Keith, then twenty-three, had showed up at Taylor's birthday bash in a fast, new Porsche, one of many exotic cars he bought and usually wrecked. Then living mostly in Fort Lauderdale in the Johnson family estate's guesthouse, Keith had arrived at Goodtime Charley's with pretty Barbara Miller, who was nineteen, and lived in Yardley, Pennsylvania, not far from Princeton.

After drinking and getting high, Keith, who was developing something of a reputation for being rough and abusive with women, had gotten into a loud argument with his date, Eric Ryan had heard, and the two, having a yelling match, raced off in his Porsche.

"I was behind him and he just zoomed off at an amazing rate of speed and we eventually caught up with him down the road," recalls Taylor. "Unfortunately, his car was upside down and he and my friend, Barbara, were thrown out of the car and spilled out all over the road, and the car was basically upside down and a total wreck. They had *terrible* injuries. She was in really bad shape. They came real close to dying, and it was just Keith's typical craziness and irresponsibility that caused it."

The headline in the June 7, 1972, issue of the weekly *Princeton Packet* newspaper read: "2 Injured As Car Hits Rt. 27 Tree."

The story reported that Keith's 1971 Porsche was headed west on the Princeton-Kingston Road at 1:07 A.M. "when his car left the pavement and hit a tree. The car was totally wrecked."

Keith and his date were taken to Princeton Medical Center. She had received lacerations on her right arm and contusions on her forehead, while Keith suffered a fractured jaw and neck, according to the Princeton Township Police department's initial report.

A subsequent newspaper account in the *Town Topics* newspaper on June 8, with the headline, "Sports Car Totaled," said that Keith's Porsche had actually hit two trees that were forty feet apart after missing a curve in the road. Keith had suffered a fractured vertebra and fractured jaw, and his date had suffered multiple head injuries. The impact was so intense that the Porsche's right rear wheel was sheared off and found fifty feet away.

Taylor remembers that the girl "was in really bad shape. It took her years to recover, and a lot of surgeries."

It was believed that the Johnsons were sued by her family.

After Keith was released from the hospital, his jaw was wired shut for a number of months.

"At one point he could hardly eat, and that's what started him on pain pills," says Anita Tiburzi Johnson, who had married a Johnson dynasty cousin, Stephen Johnson. "Keith told me how he got hooked on pain pills after the accident. He could only eat soft foods, and he talked about how much pain he was in. He looked like he was wearing braces."

Keith had given others a different story about his wired jaw, boasting that he had his jaw *intentionally* broken for cosmetic purposes, and then rebuilt so it would look like the signature chin of a famous actor closely related to the Johnson dynasty: Kirk Douglas.

With millions of trust fund dollars at his disposal, Keith had purchased a twelve-cylinder, signature red Ferrari Daytona, of which a limited number were ever produced. The car was considered so iconic and rare that a replica of it was featured in the popular 1970s TV program *Miami Vice*. Keith's was a true racing car, and not easy to handle.

There was just one problem. Keith couldn't drive it.

"He'd stall it at every traffic light because of the clutch pressure," says Ryan. "He would buy things that he had no use for, but he bought them because they were icons of wealth, prestige, and status."

Evangeline Brewster Johnson, sister of Johnson & Johnson's chauvinistic leaders—Robert Wood Johnson Jr., known as the "General," and playboy J. Seward Johnson Sr.—was cheated out of prime company stock and power. She had two daughters in the first of her three marriages, the last to a homosexual, and was herself considered bisexual. *(Sadja Greenwood)*

Belle Baruch (left), lesbian daughter of Wall Street titan Bernard Baruch, fell in love with Evangeline Brewster Johnson, and the pair was inseparable until Evangeline's first turbulent marriage to famed maestro and roué Leopold Stokowski. Here, the two young women flirt and play at the Baruch estate. *(The Belle W. Baruch Foundation, Hobcaw Barony)*

Evangeline Brewster Johnson with her third husband, the gay one-time hairdresser and artist Charles Merrill, her junior by several decades. Her last years were spent in Grey Gardens–style hell before her death at 93 in 1990. Merrill later tried to auction their bizarre love story as a screenplay on eBay. *(Sadja Greenwood)*

Troubled heiress Mary Lea Johnson Ryan D'Arc Richards, the first baby face on the Johnson & Johnson Baby Powder can, with her third husband, the gay showbiz maven Marty Richards, who played a controversial role in dynasty dramas and was detested by certain family members. After the death of her father, Seward Johnson Sr., she claimed he molested her, which was later questioned. (© Globe Photos/ZUMAPRESS.com)

After a troubled childhood and a horrific and scandalous first marriage that included a failed suicide attempt and a shootout, Seward Johnson Jr. (far right) became a prominent sculptor. Pictured here at the Corcoran Gallery, his exhibit (left) was lambasted by the *Washington Post* art critic. Johnson also spent years questioning the paternity of a daughter. (© *The Washington Times*)

obert Wood "Woody" Johnson IV, billionaire owner of the New York Jets, and great-grandson f one of the Johnson & Johnson founders, was mostly a bench warmer as backup tight end when e played for Millbrook School, pictured here, number 81, to the left of roommate Jack Mills. Woody joined *Animal House*–style frats while in college, and nearly died in a drunken fall.

Young Keith Wold Johnson, one of Woody's four siblings, became troubled in his teens and began using drugs, including LSD, and once was arrested for possessing marijuana. Thought to be gay, he died in his mid-twenties of a cocaine overdose, leaving behind an immense fortune to his three brothers and sister.

After graduating from college, Woody Johnson (center, background) took his father's advice and teamed up with "a Jew who wasn't a silver spoon"—Michael Spielvogel (foreground)—to learn "bidness" and develop condos and land in South Florida, a partnership that ended badly. Here, they pitch a Fort Lauderdale high-rise.

Nancy Sale Frey, a jock from a prominent Jewish family in St. Louis, elected herself captain of the newly formed women's tennis team at her alma mater, the University of Miami. She met her future husband, Woody Johnson, working for a company marketing one of his Florida condo developments in the 1970s.

In June 1978, on the grounds of his parents' estate in Princeton, New Jersey, Woody Johnson, 31, married Nancy Sale Frey, 29, in a very private ceremony— after she converted from Judaism and after signing a prenuptial agreement. She would give birth to his three daughters during a sometimes turbulent union.

On September 24, 1979, at a hospital in Hollywood, Florida, Woody Johnson became a father when wife, Sale, gave birth to cute, chubby heiress, Sale Trotter Case Johnson, known as Casey. At eight she would be diagnosed with life-threatening diabetes, and later in life diagnosed with the mental illness Borderline Personality Disorder, which seriously impacted her behavior.

When she was about four, Casey Johnson was hamming it up with a child's exuberance. Years later that wildness would turn into scandalous gossip column fodder when she became a Hollywood vixen, embarrassing her family, especially her father, who essentially washed his hands of her.

Before Woody Johnson and troubled daughter Casey went to war, stopping all communication because of her scandalous behavior and failure to seek proper help, the two cheerfully posed together at a glitzy event in New York City. (©PatrickMcMullan.com)

In happier family times, circa 1990, Woody and Sale Johnson and their brood posed for artist Geoffrey Geary for this 41-by-50-inch oil on canvas, entitled *Johnson Family at the Farm*. It depicts Casey, a horse named Christmas, and sisters Jaime and Daisy with their parents and family dog, Butter. Their elegant New Jersey farm had every luxury amenity. *("Portrait of Robert Wood Johnson IV and family, painted by Geoffrey Geary, Johnson Family at the Farm")*

In 2006, Casey Johnson gave a tell-all to *Vanity Fair* entitled "Heiress vs. Heiress," about her aunt—her father's sister—Elizabeth Ross "Libet" Johnson (far left) that infuriated the dynasty. Casey's mother, Sale (center), advised her daughter against cooperating, but she didn't listen. *(©PatrickMcMullan.com)*

In the mid-1990s, the five-times-married mother of four Libet Johnson commissioned the society portraitist James Childs to paint her lying seductively on a chaise, part of a set she had built in his studio. The frame alone cost her a cool $60,000. She didn't like the way he painted her nose, so he changed it. But he refused her request to pose in a negligée. *(James Childs, "Portrait of Elizabeth Ross Johnson," oil on canvas 21½ x 29¾, 1998)*

In 2007, against the advice of family and friends who felt she wasn't emotionally and physically fit to be a mother, Casey Johnson adopted a baby girl from Kazakhstan, who she named Ava-Monroe Johnson after her movie star idols. She showed off her latest acquisition at a luncheon for a new book by actress Joan Collins. *(NPX/starmaxine.com 2008)*

In the weeks before Casey Johnson tragically died at age 30 in January 2010, her life, spinning out of control, included a bizarre relationship with the TV reality show celebrity Tila Tequila, who claimed the two were planning to be married and that Casey, who she called her "wifey," had given her a ring. But family members say Casey wasn't gay. *(© Hellmuth Dominguez, PacificCoastNews.com)*

After Casey Johnson died from diabetes-related issues, her mother, Sale, and second husband, former football player Ahmad Rashad, both in their sixties, took on the responsibility of raising adopted Ava-Monroe, and thought she was "the most beguiling creature." But, in early 2013, Sale and Rashad appeared headed for a divorce. (©PatrickMcMullan.com)

Nancy Sale Frey Johnson Rashad's divorce from Woody Johnson was finalized in November 2001 and her stockbroker father joyfully boasted that his daughter received a whopping $100 million settlement. (© Globe Photos/ZUMApress.com)

After Woody's divorce from Sale, he dated a number of women before becoming romantically involved with pretty Suzanne Ircha, two decades his junior. She gave birth to two Johnson heirs— Robert Wood Johnson V, and another son called Brick—before she and Woody were wed in June 2009. (John Barret–Globe Photos, Inc. 2010)

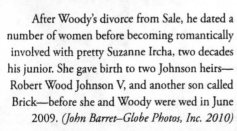

34

Keith Wold Johnson had had little formal education beyond high school. For primary school and part of junior high, he had followed his brother Woody and gone to Princeton Country Day, which was aptly described by one graduate as "an exclusive school in a privileged community, which meant that kids got Porsches for their first cars."

Famous and infamous PCD graduates through the years included Christopher Reeve, the singer Mary Chapin Carpenter, and the parent killers Lyle and Erik Menendez.

Because at least two of her sons and their father went there, Betty Johnson was a big supporter of the school. She was later named trustee emerita.

Keith began classes at Millbrook School on September 18, 1964, with four of his PCD classmates, when Woody was starting his senior year there.

According to Millbrook's 1965 *Tamarack* yearbook, which carried a blurb and photos of Keith's freshman class of some forty students, ". . . it was apparent that this form was definitely unique—a fact which foreshadowed an extremely interesting year . . . In the dorm they fell prey to a ceaseless barrage of reports" that resulted in punishments, dropouts, and expulsions, and ". . . they met the hardy resistance of upper formers . . ."

Because Keith had such low grades at PCD, he and a few, if not all, of his Princeton clique were admitted to Millbrook with a special condition.

"We all were accepted if we did ninth grade all over again," says the de facto leader of the Princeton pack, James Field Delano, known as Jeff, whose father was a principal in the Applied Science Corporation of Princeton, which developed and advanced airplane telemetry. "We did one ninth grade at Princeton Country Day, and we did the ninth grade again at Millbrook."

Keith desperately required tutoring help. His academic underachievement had come to the attention of Millbrook's founder, Edward Pulling, then in his last year as headmaster before taking his retirement. With a wealthy and powerful family like the Johnsons on the books for future endowments and contributions, Pulling took a special interest in seeing that Keith made it through by having him tutored.

He had asked a bright sophomore, Fred Lowell—the future head of the political law department at a prestigious California law firm—to tutor him. "The Johnson family paid me, and I would spend time with Keith, helping him. It was kind of unusual, that sort of tutoring, but apparently he needed help. Keith just struck me as very average, very quiet, kind of shy. I wouldn't know how he would turn out."

With his blondish hair, pale white skin, and a bad case of acne, Keith had an ethereal Warholesque countenance, and to many of his classmates he was an enigma. To classmates like ski team captain Brian Sisselman, Keith seemed like a hollow shell. "There was nothing there. There was no *there*, there. There was absolutely no personality," he recalls.

"Keith was skinny, not muscular, and he was somewhat soft," states one of the few boys in Keith's class with whom he had bonded. "I wouldn't call him necessarily manly. Some guys shaved early, some guys had hair on their chests. He didn't have any of that."

To Jeff Delano, who had quickly earned a reputation as the Millbrook "class clown," Keith "was a little effeminate in the way he walked, the way he talked. I was a big athlete. Keith was different."

The image people had of the Johnson heir was underscored very publicly, and with hilarity, by the entire school one evening early in his freshman year.

One of Millbrook's long-standing traditions for "bennies," as the third-form freshmen were called, required them to participate in a lighthearted evening of skits produced and directed for the most part by the sixth-form seniors. The skit that senior George Nathan Cowan Jr. directed, which featured Keith Johnson and two other third-formers, was considered the laugh riot of the show.

"It was about a vampire who comes to a guy's house and steals his wife," recalls Cowan. "The punch line is, as the vampire is running away with the wife, he says to the husband, 'Don't worry. I'll bring her back when she's empty.'"

The scene got lots of laughs, and especially raucous cheers for Cowan's diabolical casting because it underscored something about Keith's persona that many had perceived.

"The guy who played the wife was this really big guy, and I specifically cast him as the female because he was *so* big," says Cowan, scion of a Wall Street family, still chuckling about the skit and the players more than four decades later. "The wife was played for laughs and the vampire was played for laughs. And Keith played the straight guy, the husband. Keith had effeminate mannerisms, especially in his speech, and that's the main reason I cast him as the husband, because it was definitely funnier than if he played the wife."

Keith became the brunt of some teasing—the sophomoric but hurtful slang terms "faggot" and "queer" were whispered, or hurled in his direction.

Millbrook was a far different place in the 1960s than it had been in the 1940s when William F. Buckley Jr. was a student, the editor of the *National Review* later claimed in an essay about his alma mater called "God and Boys at Millbrook." Published in *The New York Times Magazine* on Sunday, October 4, 1981, he wrote, "Millbrook encouraged a civility among its students. There was practically no bullying, and when an instance of it was uncovered Mr. Pulling dramatically announced at the morning prayer session that he would close down the doors of the school rather than tolerate such stuff."

$ $ $

Drugs had entered the scene at Millbrook, and Keith Johnson and a couple of other boys had started getting together to smoke marijuana. It would only get worse for him.

Like some Stephen Kingish nightmare, the staid and cloistered Millbrook School had also suddenly found itself at ground zero of the sixties psychedelic revolution when, in the fall of 1963, Dr. Timothy Leary, the former Harvard professor who was the leading proponent of the hallucinatory drug LSD, moved to the bucolic town of Millbrook, and became a neighbor of the school when the Johnson scions, Woody and Keith, were students there.

Leary's anthem was "turn on, tune in, drop out," and Keith Johnson, with a budding serious addictive personality, along with a few other Millbrook students, became quasi adherents.

At least one of Keith's classmates, with whom he was said to have turned on at Leary's, later succumbed from too much tripping. Another committed suicide. And Keith himself would have a fatal drug overdose.

In his essay about his alma mater, Buckley noted that "Timothy Leary ran a kind of anti–Millbrook School for drug users until the elders finally ran him out . . ."

Leary's Xanadu was set behind gates at the edge of town, not far from the Millbrook campus. "I remember seeing the flashing lights," recalls Keith's class president Mark Smith, one of the first two black students admitted to Millbrook. "Leary's house was right over the hill."

With Leary in residence, the party was nonstop under the guise of studying the effects of LSD. One of the great snake oil salesman of the twentieth century, Leary, who Richard Nixon termed "the most dangerous man in America," named the Millbrook estate the Castalia Institute, which was part of his "League of Spiritual Discovery," its acronym, LSD.

Along with the LSD there was sex—lots of it. One, it seemed, couldn't be consumed without the other. Leary and his acid attracted scores of beautiful, liberated young women, many of them chic high-fashion models—one of the most beautiful of all was five-foot-nine Eileen Ford model Nena von Schlebrugge—a *Vogue* cover girl who married Leary. She was the mother of Uma Thurman, who was one of four children fathered by another husband after Leary.

The drugs, the free love, all of it was a natural aphrodisiac for young people, virginal teens like Keith Johnson and a few of his more rebellious, druggie classmates.

At Leary's place, they were the kids in the candy store.

Pulling, the headmaster, proclaimed Leary was "off-limits to everybody," recalls Keith's classmate Phil Ross. "He said something like, 'Nobody is allowed to be there, and they will be dealt with harshly if they're found out to be there.'"

It didn't take long before the national press, learning of the goings-on in the small Hudson Valley New York village, began running stories about the guru and his drug. *The New York Times* ran a lengthy piece in a column called "The Talk of Millbrook" that was headlined "Leary Drug Cult Stirs Millbrook, Uneasy Village Fears Influx of Addicts."

The townspeople were angry and scared and had wanted to march on the Leary estate like the torch-bearing frightened peasants in the Frankenstein story.

Millbrook was an easy getaway from the fashionable Manhattan avenues of Park and Fifth, and the manicured estates of Princeton, and for as long as anyone could remember, the town had been on the high-society map for the horsey set, the foxhunt crowd, and the gentleman farmer. The Johnsons would always keep close ties to Millbrook. Woody and Keith's sister, Libet Johnson, bought an immense estate in the town. From the air in her private helicopter, her property resembled a small town, as one of her many boyfriends later remembered it, because it was so sprawling, and there were so many buildings on the land beyond the spectacular main house.

In mid-April of 1966, local authorities, convinced all kinds of laws were being broken, raided the Leary estate, an assault that in part was orchestrated by the Dutchess County, New York, assistant district attorney, G. Gordon Liddy, a onetime FBI agent, who would gain infamy and a prison sentence as one of President Nixon's Watergate burglars. In his 1996 autobiography, *Will*, Liddy stated that, "Local boys and girls had been seen entering and leaving the estate. Fleeting glimpses were reported of persons strolling the grounds in the nude. To fears of drug-induced dementia were added pot-induced pregnancy. The word was that at Leary's lair the panties were dropping as fast as the acid."

At the time of the raid, more than two dozen men and women were found lolling, or more, on mattresses.

Among some of the Millbrook boys attending Leary's trippy bacchanal

JERRY OPPENHEIMER

to turn on along with Keith was the co-editor in chief of the 1968 *Tamarack* yearbook, Christopher Reilly Praeger. His yearbook page had a psychedelic drawing of a face with a tulip growing out of its right eye, a quote from Bob Dylan, and the LSD-related line, "Our first trip together was a real goof!" Another was Sigourney Thayer of the yearbook's literary department, who had Mansonesque glaring eyes on his page, and the identical "first trip" caption under his photo.

After he was caught smoking marijuana and booted out, Praeger, the son of the architect who had designed Shea Stadium, the original home of the New York Jets, went mad from too many LSD trips and was later found dead in a pond in Colorado. His family placed the blame on Leary for turning him on. Two years after attending Woodstock, Thayer blew his brains out with a shotgun "because he was hearing voices, and he had been doing acid," according to his Millbrook classmate Sherwin Harris.

Around the time the local authorities led by Liddy were planning to raid Timothy Leary's headquarters, Keith Johnson had suddenly vanished from Millbrook School before he completed his second year there.

"He just took off, and was gone," recalls classmate Stephen Gidley, who was himself expelled from Millbrook for infractions. "Christmas vacation ended and there was no Keith. It was *so* unusual a disappearance. There was no good-bye, nothing. When he took off and didn't come back I thought to myself, he is one of *the* strangest people, and I think the whole class reacted similarly. He just left like he was never connected."

Keith completed his remaining high school years in Florida, where his father was ill. He graduated in June 1968 from the six-year-old private Saint Andrew's School, an Episcopal academy in Boca Raton that was named for the patron saint of Scotland, and was mainly attended by rich kids who played lots of sports and drove expensive convertibles. Most of its notable alumni were jocks—golfers and tennis players such as Jennifer Capriati, who spent just one term there. Its campus during Keith's matriculation was used by the Miami Dolphins of the National Football League as the team's training camp.

Sherwin Harris, art editor of the class of 1968 *Tamarack* yearbook, included an "In Memory" page of all the people from the class "who had been tossed out," or had quit, and the montage included a snapshot of Keith Johnson, seen reading a paperback copy of Harold Robbins bestseller *The Carpet-baggers*, which the critic for *The Times* complained "should have been inscribed on the walls of a public lavatory," noting that it was filled with "a collection of monotonous episodes about normal and abnormal sex."

35

Betty May Wold Johnson was considered one of the most attractive and eligible widows in the town of Princeton in the very early years of the 1970s. In her early fifties, still slender after five pregnancies, blond and coiffed, she was a millionairess many times over, possessed a huge block of Johnson & Johnson stock, and had a lovely estate in town, as well as another on Florida's Gold Coast. And while she had problems with some members of her brood—Woody and Keith in particular—life for her was returning to normal after the torturous death of her husband, Bobby, in late 1970.

In the wake of his passing, she was said to have traveled on cultural trips to such places as China and Venice through a Princeton University program that arranged educational excursions for wealthy potential donors as a way of cultivating relationships.

Then she met a man.

Eugene P. Gillespie, tall, good-looking, charming, was one of the most eligible widowers in Princeton. His artist wife, George Ann, had died of cancer in the summer of 1972. The father of three—two young adult sons, Peter and William, and a daughter, her mother's namesake and also an artist—Gene Gillespie had been a Princeton University graduate, class of 1940, of which he was president, and a high-ranking career army officer. After a year at the University of Virginia law school, the Second World War came along and he served with distinction with the Artillery Corps, and then as a pilot in Africa, Sicily, Italy, France, and Germany. At one point, he was General Mark Clark's personal pilot. After the war he earned a regular army commission.

During the Kennedy administration, when the buildup for the Vietnam War began, he and his family were sent to Cambodia for a two-year hardship tour, and lived in Phnom Penh as part of MAG, the Military Advisory Group. At Fort Sill, in Oklahoma, he was commander of the Target Acquisition Department of the army's missile school. He was awarded the Legion of Merit medal for "outstanding achievement in the most cherished traditions of the United States Army."

Having risen to the rank of full colonel, he subsequently was offered the position of aide to George Samuel Blanchard, a four-star army general, who also was the godfather to Gillespie's daughter. Gillespie turned down the post because it involved long days and much travel, and he wanted to settle in one place after years of military service, and that place, when he retired in 1964, was Princeton.

That was the official story of his esteemed career. A family confidante had a somewhat different take, which was that Gillespie ended his career mostly because he had become opposed to the Vietnam War. "They told Gene, 'You're going to be a general and it's going to be wonderful, and we're going to make you [Secretary of Defense Robert] McNamara's desk officer.' But Gene said, 'I've been to Cambodia, I know what's going on.' He said, 'I will not do that,' and they said, 'Well, you'll have to leave the army.' "

Whichever way it happened, Gillespie honorably retired and returned to his alma mater, Princeton, as an administrator and fundraiser, and became active in the Princeton community as trustee of the Medical Center at Princeton, helping bring in contributions for the McCarter Theatre, and was active in the Princeton Club of New York.

All in all, Gillespie seemed to have all the right stuff for a strong woman like Betty Johnson, herself in the military during World War II as a WAVE.

"When he worked for Princeton, he was doing alumni relations, which was basically fundraising and planning, so he got back in touch with all of his classmates at reunions," says his son Peter, who became a home builder. "One of them knew Betty and introduced them, and they went out together for several months and decided they would get married."

As a woman friend of Betty notes, "She was on her own after Bob died, and the next thing we knew Gene and Betty found each other. Gene was attractive to Betty. He had traveled all over the world, he was charming and elegant, and he was very social—and she fell for him. The two went out a number of times. Gene wasn't wealthy, but Betty sure was, and when he married her, it was, well, *la de dah*, and the rest is history."

But Betty's marriage to Gillespie was never really a part of the Johnson dynasty's history, at least publicly.

It had always been kept very quiet.

There was never a wedding announcement in *The New York Times*, such as one would expect for such a marriage, because, as Peter Gillespie says, "Betty and the Johnsons guard their privacy." Betty was not known to have even used the Gillespie surname during the marriage. Gillespie's obituary in the October 25, 2006, issue of the *Princeton Alumni Weekly*—he died May 31, 2006, at the age of eighty-seven—made no mention that he had even been married to the Johnson & Johnson heiress and mother of New York Jets owner Woody Johnson. "Gene lost his first wife, George Ann, to cancer in 1972," the obituary states. "He found 'a new life companion' in Sara Tiedman, his second wife. Golf, bridge, and travel, including winters spent in Florida and Antigua, were their pastimes."

His life with Betty Johnson—and it was turbulent—had all but disappeared from his biography. And even more so from hers.

Only his obituary in one of the local Princeton newspapers, which had heard the news of his marriage to the Johnson & Johnson widow through the grapevine but never published anything about it, did report, "His second marriage, to Betty Johnson, ended in divorce." That was one of the very rare times that the two had been linked publicly.

Betty's very quiet second marriage took place in July 1973. While she had waited some thirty months after Bobby died to take the big plunge, Gillespie tied the knot with her just twelve months after the death of his first wife and mother of his children.

"My dad liked being married, so I wasn't shocked that he did it so fast after my mother died," says his artist daughter, George Ann Gillespie Fox. "I was very pleased he had found somebody to love, and who loved him enough to marry him. I was just happy for him."

But Betty's decision, and especially her choice for husband number two, had little, if any support from members of the Johnson dynasty to whom she had always been so loyal. In fact, a number of them, like the sculptor Seward Johnson Jr., were shocked by her decision.

"Betty married somebody who they all *hated*," Seward Jr. asserts. "Gillespie was an aggressive, social-climbing guy. He was *distasteful* and I could not understand her vulnerability to him. I was vice president of the McCarter Theatre in Princeton and they"—Betty and Gillespie—"supported one of the plays, and I went there with them, and he kind of steered me by the shoulder and I just reached up and took his hand and threw it away. I found him *so* repelling."

Even worse, according to Seward, Betty's children—Woody, Keith, Libet, Billy, and Christopher, but especially Keith—"hated him," he asserts. "They hated him, and they called him Hitler."

Rather than move together into a new home free of the memories that Betty had with Bobby Johnson for some three decades of marriage—the good and the bad—she invited Gillespie to move into her estate at 108 Edgerstoune Road, which he did, selling his own family home in Princeton.

By the time of his mother's marriage, Keith was living large with his trust fund millions and mostly on his own in the guesthouse of the Johnson's Bay Colony estate in Fort Lauderdale. But he was furious at his mother, irrationally so, almost as if Gillespie had stolen her away from him. Of her four sons, he was considered a mama's boy.

It became a family psychodrama of immense proportions.

"Keith hated Eugene Gillespie—hated, hated, hated him—and it created a great deal of tension between he and his mother, and Keith was the ringleader of his siblings' hate, too," says his cousin Eric Ryan. "He felt it was inappropriate for his mother to remarry so quickly, and Eugene had children by a prior marriage and there was a sense on Keith's part that the Gillespie children were displacing the Johnson children in the household, and that did not go down well with the Johnson kids."

In fact, Betty was being *overly* protective of the pre-Gillespie Johnson domain. When Gillespie's daughter, George Ann, in her teens, returned to Princeton from France where she had been staying with family friends, working on her art, she butted heads with Betty, according to Betty's woman friend. "Gene's daughter came home from France to see her dad and his new wife and Betty gave her a very nice room. I know George Ann said to Betty, 'Oh, this is so nice, I'm going to call my friend, a girlfriend, to show it to her.' But Betty said, 'This is *my* house, and you *won't* have anybody in here who I don't know and approve of.' Betty was very private and possessive in that way, and tough, so tough she scares me."

Still, Keith seethed at his mother's marriage, and their relationship had become resentful.

"Before Betty married Gillespie, there was already tension between her and Keith because of his lifestyle, because of his not being gainfully employed, because of him being sort of profligate in his spending," asserts Ryan.

But her marriage to Gillespie sent Keith over the edge.

"I remember Keith saying that he couldn't stand it that Gillespie was sitting in his father's chair, and sleeping in his father's bed," recounts Ryan.

And when Keith, who was car-crazy, learned that Gillespie was driving one of his late father's prized autos, the Mercedes-Benz 600, he actually tried to destroy it.

"He went out and wrecked the car when they were in Florida early in the marriage," says Ryan. Feeling guilty and fearful of the consequences, "he managed to get all of the body work and repairs done without his mother being aware that the car had been damaged."

$ $ $

Keith Wold Johnson had become even more of a menace to himself and to others, doing more drugs, destroying more cars, and having even more bizarre relationships with women than ever before.

Betty, then beginning her new life with Gene Gillespie, wasn't aware, or chose not to get involved.

Keith's near-fatal accident in his Porsche in Princeton, which left him and his date seriously injured, was the only one that had ever become public. On another extraordinary occasion, in Florida, he drove a new BMW coupe onto the beach in Pompano while he was on an apparent LSD trip. He was with a girl at the time and had dropped the acid to watch the sunset. But the new car had gotten mired in the sand and when the tide came in, the expensive German import was swept away, and he was too stoned to do anything to save it.

"Keith wrecked innumerable fast cars," Eric Ryan says, "something over a dozen. The cars were practically disposable in Keith's case. There was a canary yellow Mercedes roadster that he had and within weeks, it was turned upside down on one of the back roads in Princeton. That inability on his part to do effective risk management in his life seemed to me to forecast his [eventual] drug overdose."

According to Fort Lauderdale Police Department records Keith received two traffic warrants on the same day in February of 1972, and in July 1974 he was charged as an "incompetent driver." The cases, with no details given, were listed on an arrest card with an FBI number of "802712J2," and an arrest number of "ID*80159." The card gave his description and noted that he had "braces on top and bottom teeth," probably related to his broken jaw from the accident in Princeton.

When Keith was seen with women they were usually spectacularly beautiful and mostly on his arm in order to show them off.

At the same time, he also had a lot of rage toward women, according to people in his circle.

"Keith became aggressive with women at parties after having ingested drugs and alcohol—the women's clothes torn, that sort of thing," asserts Ryan. "It was his misdirected sexuality, his anger towards women, his feeling that he was in a public role where he had to be amorous, but feeling repulsed by the women themselves. It was a whole complicated thing. There was a whole self-destructive spiral that was manifesting itself in his relationships with women, his relationships with automobiles, and his relationship with wealth."

At one point, around 1973, when his mother was getting remarried, Keith invited a pretty young woman to accompany him to France—all first class, all expenses paid, in one of the best cabins—aboard the luxury ocean liner SS *France,* the flagship of the French Line, sailing from New York to Le Havre. The girl, who expected a romantic voyage, and might even have had visions of marrying into the young Band-Aid heir's dynasty, was vastly disappointed. The first night out, Keith drank himself into a stupor and threw up on her shoes, and they never slept together the entire voyage.

"My understanding is that he ended up having to get his own cabin, and when the ship landed in Le Havre, she got the train to Paris and got on a plane home," says Ryan. "Keith had these grand romantic gestures, but they weren't really based on wanting to have arm candy."

Of the ill-fated trip Keith later boasted how many glasses of Rémy Martin he had that had made him ill—and how that "damn bitch didn't understand, and got all upset over a little vomit on her shoes."

For a time Keith dated the glamorous sister, Jane, of his best friend from childhood, Neil Vicino, whom they all thought had movie-star looks. "Keith's feelings for Jane were stronger than hers for him, and of course Jane was something very nice to have on your arm, like a Liz Taylor lookalike," observes Neil many years later.

Jane was well aware of Keith's troubles with cars, drugs, and women. When they were dating he once took her to the elegant Club International in Fort Lauderdale, the city's first true society hangout that had yacht slips and catered to stars like Johnny Carson and Paul Newman when they were in town. But instead of a romantic candlelight dinner Keith got smashed and when they got out to the parking lot someone had flattened the tire on one of his many exotic cars. Because he couldn't figure out how to change it, Jane had to get on her knees and do it.

Her gay brother, Guy, also the brother to John and Neil Vicino, actually stepped in and ended the relationship. "He was very intuitive to problems that were occurring with Keith," recalls John. "We all smoked a little pot back then, but Guy could see that more was happening with Keith in terms of drugs."

Jane had started seeing a distant Johnson cousin, Stephen Johnson, who was her date the evening of her brother Neil Vicino's 1972 wedding party at Windows on the World on the 106th floor of the World Trade Center.

When Keith arrived, offending Neil and his bride by not bringing a gift, he was infuriated to find Jane with Stephen. Keith stormed out, bringing a few members of the wedding party with him with a promise of getting high, and they got stoned in a car parked in a nearby lot. One of them, however, soon returned to the party and was asked by another guest, "Did you guys smoke a J?" The one who had accompanied Keith said, "No, he wanted to turn me on to cocaine and I just shook my head and walked away."

Like his brother Woody, Keith had developed a very close friendship with the tall, dark, and handsome Guy Vicino.

Woody had met Guy at Princeton Country Day School and they had become lifelong friends. When Woody went off to Millbrook, Guy prepped at the exclusive Lawrenceville School near Princeton where one of his housemates was Prince Turki bin Faisal al-Saud, who later became Saudi Arabia's ambassador to the United States. It was a relationship that Guy often boasted about later in life.

When Woody went out to Arizona, Guy Vicino went to Boston College, then transferred to the University of Miami, class of 1968, where Woody's first wife, Nancy Sale Frey, also matriculated, class of 1971. After college, and to escape the Vietnam War draft, he joined the U.S. Coast Guard, where he had homosexual encounters during his two-year enlistment. When he returned from active duty, he began living what his brother John termed "a sheltered gay life. He wasn't out there with Rainbow Coalition stickers."

Keith and Guy had much in common—dandified clothing, exotic cars, decorating, all expensive and fashionable. "From the time he was a kid," says his brother Neil, "Guy always wanted the best. He was very much into keeping up with the Johnsons as opposed to keeping up with the Joneses. It caused strife within our family."

Guy also had a very curious relationship with his sister, Jane, which especially intrigued Keith, and may have been one of the reasons why he was attracted to her beyond her good looks. Of the four Vicino siblings, Guy was closest to Jane and, says Neil, "Guy wanted to be seen with her on his arm. Guy would literally dress Jane when she was in her teens so she looked like she was twenty-five, and he would take her out on dates."

But Guy, described by Neil as "flamboyant but not effeminate," wasn't simply dolling up and glamorizing his sister to use as a beard in order to make people believe that he was straight; he had a far different and twisted motive.

"He would take her out to show her off because it might be a way for Guy to attract young men [to him, not her]," asserts Neil. He was convinced that Guy was using his sister as bait. "It was a gay thing to do," observes Neil. "Jane went along with it because she was treated like a princess."

Keith Johnson had found Jane and Guy's kinky relationship right up his alley, and he emulated it in his own way. He dated attractive women so they'd be on his arm for show-and-tell.

$ $ $

Looking back years later, Eric Ryan thinks it "fair" to describe his cousin Keith as a closeted homosexual.

Keith's supposed sexual preference was "generally accepted" by his parents and siblings, but wasn't discussed. "Maybe," Ryan suggests, "there was some belief that if he met the right girl, she would straighten him out."

Not everyone thought like Ryan, however, including Keith's sister-in-law-to-be, Nancy Sale Frey Johnson Rashad, who years later says, "He was definitely not gay, and that never occurred to me in a million years." But she knew Keith for only a short time before he died while she was dating Woody. She considered Keith a "fabulous renaissance man, far ahead of his time and age, and he *definitely* was into girls. Woody and I went on trips with him with dates. I knew the girls, we talked, and there was definitely a sexual relationship. Maybe he was bisexual and I never realized it."

Keith once boasted to a friend that his first heterosexual experience, during which he lost his virginity, was with a Parisian prostitute while he was taking his grand tour of Europe after finally graduating from prep school.

In dress and style, Keith resembled a 1970s version of the character Waldo Lydecker, a pretentious dandy played by Clifton Webb in the 1944 film noir *Laura,* in which the divaesque gossip columnist is so obsessed with the character Laura Hunt, played by Gene Tierney, that he attempts to murder her—twice—because she desires more masculine men.

Keith dressed expensively like the Lydecker character. In the 1970s era of shaggy-haired twenty-somethings wearing ragged bellbottoms and denim work shirts, he had closets full of handsomely tailored clothing—most, if not all of it, of the bespoke Saville Row variety. But there were several pieces that stood out that only Liberace might have been caught wearing. One was Keith's one-of-a-kind Burberry-style trench coat that was lined with the skins of some 150 hamsters.

The other piece in Keith's closet that raised eyebrows was a pretentious and costly motorcycle jacket designed for him by Pierre Cardin, not Harley-Davidson.

If anyone was ready for the Front Row, it was the Band-Aid heir.

With his trust fund money, Keith bought silver cigarette cases, Cartier lighters, Tiffany cuff links, and didn't even think about spending hundreds of dollars on a simple cotton button-down shirt as long as it had a fancy designer label, items that most young people weren't thinking about when they were mobilizing back then against the war, or yelling "Black Power!"

Like the fictional Lydecker, who was obsessed by the beautiful Laura Hunt character, Keith had become consumed by another gorgeous fantasy: the glamorous French actress Catherine Deneuve, who was six years his senior, and had appeared in such kinky films as *Repulsion,* in which she played a woman who had LSD-like hallucinations, and *The Hunger,* which has a lesbian love scene.

Deneuve was a gay icon of sorts, in the realm of Liza Minnelli and Judy Garland. She once provocatively posed on the cover of a French gay male magazine with a nude male model, and reportedly was the sexy inspiration for a lesbian publication actually called *Deneuve.*

Keith had become so fixated on her that he had planned to throw a fancy dinner party for some fifty guests at his private dining club if she attended. He began making plans for her arrival and had purchased a white tuxedo for his fantasy evening.

"Keith thought she was gorgeous, beautiful, stylish," recalls Eric Ryan. "It was never quite so overt as him saying, 'Oh, what a great outfit she's wearing, I wish I could wear that kind of outfit, too,' but kind of along those lines."

Whether Deneuve ever responded to Keith's invitation, or whether the party was ever held, was never made clear.

But Keith's brother Woody and their gay pal Guy Vicino had disparagingly branded him with the nickname "Catherine Deneuve-Nanette Fabray," according to Sale Johnson.

Not all of Keith Wold Johnson's desires and acquisitions were completely frivolous.

Aside from the exotic and fast cars that he bought and usually wrecked, he had purchased a classic sailing ketch that he named the *Sea Prince*, which was usually anchored in Fort Lauderdale. Keith had bought it with the help of Guy Vicino, who had been working as a yacht salesman and interior decorator of yachts for Charles P. Irwin Yacht Brokerage, in Fort Lauderdale.

But it was on Woody rather than Keith that Guy always focused.

"Guy talked about Woody *all* the time—'I was at his house for dinner, I was this with Woody, I was that with Woody, or we did this, or Woody did that.' They were *very* close," recalls Irwin.

Keith had staffed the *Sea Prince* with an experienced captain, whom Eric Ryan met and says was gay. Keith made certain the captain looked the nautical part, and had him outfitted in a crisp white uniform—a shirt with epaulets, white shorts with a sharp crease—that was appropriate for the waters off of Florida, the Caribbean, and the British West Indies, where Keith liked to sail.

Ryan had sailed with Keith and was knocked out by the *Sea Prince*'s detail—all burled wood—construction, and the decorating. "The cabinetry below deck had bird's-eye maple, teak joinery around the bunks, and strips of mahogany held the foam mattress pads in place. It was a gorgeous boat that would have been in a lot of cocktail table picture books of sailboats."

Ryan had conversations with the captain, who told him that Keith "had no real desire to learn to sail," and that he was "never going to attempt to steer the *Sea Prince* into a harbor. Keith didn't care about that. What he cared about was that the *Sea Prince* was *his* boat."

Keith had also put as much as seven million dollars of his trust fund millions into a more speculative enterprise, the search for gold bullion and treasure from Spanish galleons that were sunk off the coast of Florida. The treasure hunt was a good investment and supposedly paid off to the tune of about thirty million dollars in bullion that was discovered in a sunken galleon. A court battle reportedly ensued with the state of Florida, which wanted part of the take because the treasure had been found within the state's territorial waters, and a fifty-fifty split was said to have been negotiated.

On the advice of his financial advisors, Keith also invested wisely in a budding new consumer communications business in South Florida. It was called cable television, a business his brother Woody later inherited and parlayed into many millions of dollars in value and profit.

36

Betty Johnson's marriage to Eugene Gillespie was in trouble almost from the start. Not only did her children and members of the larger Johnson dynasty despise him—unjustifiably for the most part—but Betty herself had come to the realization that she had not gotten over the loss of Bobby, and had clearly made a mistake leaping again so quickly into a second marriage.

"She was still *so* wrapped up in Johnson and Johnson and still clearly in love with Bobby, and Gene was saying that it was driving him crazy," says a person who was close to the couple. "He told me, 'I can't get Betty to come out and be social. I can't get her to move, and I can't get her to stop thinking about the fact that her husband died.' He also was concerned because Betty would not cry, and Gene said that if she just let all that emotional stuff come out she might heal. He felt she was still emotionally paralyzed. He was just trying to make her part of his life, but was getting sort of fed up."

For Betty, it would only get worse, much worse.

In the third week of March 1975, around St. Patrick's Day, her sons, Woody, now twenty-seven and involved in a land and condo development business in South Florida, and twenty-six-year-old Keith, who was still doing drugs and living self-indulgently, were together on a ten-day cruise aboard the *Sea Prince* in the British Antilles where Keith had a small circle of friends, some of whom were thought to be involved in the drug trade.

On Sunday, March 23, Woody would later tell the police, the brothers returned by plane through Miami, and Keith rented a car to drive them back to Fort Lauderdale where Woody was now living.

The next day, Monday, March 24, Keith, who had decided to move back to the mainland presumably at Woody's behest, drove to an apartment complex at 90 Isle of Venice Drive—one of the palm-tree-lined fingers of land surrounded by water with docks off of Los Olas Boulevard, in Fort Lauderdale—to look at a small, furnished first-floor motel-like apartment. With Keith was a well-to-do friend, Roger McMullen, who suggested that he rent the unit from the owners, Tracy and Catherine Geiger. He signed the lease on the spot rather than move back into the guesthouse at Bay Colony because he was still very much at odds with his mother over her marriage to Gene Gillespie.

The following Thursday, March 27, Keith and McMullen returned the rental car to Miami and picked up Keith's Mercedes that he had stored in a warehouse in Port Everglades.

That night, Woody, whose twenty-eighth birthday was just a few days away, had dinner with Keith.

It was the last time he would see his brother alive.

The next morning, Good Friday, March 28, Keith moved into his new rental.

During the day on Saturday and into the early morning hours of Easter Sunday, Keith's television could be heard blaring nonstop. Concerned, his landlady, Mrs. Geiger, and her husband knocked on his door, asking if he wanted to go out for breakfast. When they got no response they tried to enter but saw that the door was bolted with a chain lock, which they removed from its hinges, and entered the apartment. What they found caused Mrs. Geiger to let out a scream, like a scene in a television crime drama.

The "narrative summary of circumstances surrounding death," as documented in the "Report of investigation by medical examiner, Seventeenth District In and For Broward County, Florida," stated that "Keith Wold Johnson, age 26; race, white; sex, male; marital status, single; occupation, executive; home address, 108 Edgerstoune Road, Princeton, N.J., was found dead lying on his face, completely nude.

"Rigor had set in. Lividity was on the front of the body. There was [a one-inch by one-third inch] abrasion on the chin. A syringe was found lying on the floor in a closet [off the living room] with a spoon containing white powder. A plastic bag with white powder was also found near the syringe. The body showed [at least three] injection marks [that appeared to be fresh] on the antecubital fossae [the elbow pit of both arms.] Nothing was missing from the apartment."

A local newspaper, the *Sun-Sentinel*, reported that "Robert Johnson"—Woody—had been questioned by police, and he had told them that "he did not know his brother used drugs," which was not true. As Sale Johnson notes years later, "Woody knew Keith smoked pot. I don't think he knew he did drugs like cocaine, and that's what killed him."

With his denial, Woody was clearly making a valiant effort to protect the Johnson dynasty name and his brother's legacy.

In the recent past, he had expressed anger about Keith's use of drugs, and might even have known, or suspected, the identity of his drug connection, according to Michael Richard Spielvogel, Woody's business partner in Woodric Enterprises, their fledgling South Florida investment and development company. "Bob [Spielvogel never called him Woody] was *always* so violently upset about his reckless brothers doing drugs, especially Keith. It ate up Bob. I once saw him put his hand through the solid wood door in our office, he was *so* mad. It happened to do with whoever supplied Keith the goods, and it was somebody that maybe Bob knew. He was *furious*.

"Before Keith's death," continues Spielvogel, "there was talk on more than one occasion about him going into rehab. I know Bob tried. It wasn't that Keith died and the family said, oh, we didn't know he was doing drugs. They knew it. I would have thought he could have been saved because of all the family money, and put in rehab, and coveted more, instead of letting him loose on society."

But Betty Johnson's marriage to Eugene Gillespie two years before Keith's death was said to have created such a "wedge" between Keith and his mother that, asserts Eric Ryan, "Betty lost whatever influence she had over Keith's behavior, and would not have been able to do an intervention or offer him professional help."

It was Woody who was given the horrific responsibility of identifying his brother's body. "It was devastating for him," notes Sale Johnson.

According to the medical examiner's report, Keith had died at approximately 11:15 P.M. on Friday, after having dinner earlier in the evening with his uncle, Dr. Keith Wold, for whom he was named. The wealthy ophthalmologist who had married into the Johnson family and was Keith's mother's brother told investigators that his nephew "was apparently all right" when he last saw him, which was the last time Keith was seen alive by anyone.

$ $ $

Dr. Wold, acting for his sister and the broader Johnson family, immediately used his influence with the right people around Fort Lauderdale to keep the story of his nephew's troubled life and tragic death as contained as possible, thus reducing the chance of yet another very public scandal within the dynasty, and he was quite successful with his cover-up.

As Eric Ryan notes some thirty-five years later, "Dr. Wold was instrumental in keeping the lid on. He was pretty well connected in Fort Lauderdale society. He knew the right lawyers to call, the right politicians to call, the right journalists to call, to make sure the wishes of the Johnson family were respected."

As a result, there were just a few short wire service dispatches about Keith's death that ran mostly in small Florida newspapers and in the New York–New Jersey region where the Johnson family was well known.

A headline in the *New York Post* over an eight-paragraph story buried on page twenty-four read, "J&J Drug Heir Dies of Overdose." The lead paragraph reported that Keith had been found "with a blue belt tied loosely around his forearm and a sack of cocaine nearby . . . Officers said the quantity of cocaine was small enough to be considered the average amount bought for personal use and not for resale."

A three-paragraph United Press International story ran in *The New York Times* on April Fool's Day with the headline, "Johnson & Johnson Heir Dies; Drug Overdose Is Hinted."

The New York *Daily News* quoted a spokesman for Johnson & Johnson as stating that Keith "had never worked for the company and apparently lived on his investments."

The dearth of coverage was remarkable, especially compared to the international headlines and commentaries after the death of Woody's troubled daughter, Casey, some thirty-five years later.

When the Vicino family learned about Keith's death, they were in a state of shock. "I can remember that I walked into the kitchen and my sister was crying, my mother and dad were all crying, and my dad kept shaking his head and saying, 'I knew something was going to happen to that kid,'" recalls John Vicino.

If there was anything at the last dinner shared by Dr. Wold and his nephew that had caused Keith to go back to his newly rented apartment and put a fatal needle in his arm, it was probably related to Betty Johnson's marriage. A well-connected family friend heard that Wold had heatedly lectured Keith and ordered him to control his anger regarding his mother's second marriage, and that Keith was furious about being told what to do and had stormed off.

Eric Ryan, who was well aware of Keith's use of drugs, maintains years later that Keith hadn't been injecting cocaine for very long, just about three months.

On that Easter holiday weekend of the overdose, says Ryan, Keith had reached out to some people, saying that he had acquired a quantity of cocaine and wanted to party. But Keith had made himself persona non grata in that community because of his history of bad behavior, so he was left sitting home alone, depressed, and with his stash of toxic white powder.

"I believe it really was an accidental overdose on the basis that the coke that Keith had shot previously was street-quality coke, and the coke that he was able to buy in Florida—Miami then being the cocaine capital of the world—was much stronger and Keith really didn't know how to do dosages, how to figure out what was going to give him a rush, but not kill him. I've always believed that it was death by misadventure, that Keith was just naïve about how to handle drugs."

Others had different theories.

There was talk in law enforcement circles that Keith had gotten involved with a bad crowd in the British West Indies—that the *Sea Prince* was being used to transport drugs—and there were whispers that his overdose was actually a case of murder by one or more bad guys with whom he had become involved. And there was chatter among people who knew him well that he had actually committed suicide because he was unsuccessfully trying to deal with his sexual identity.

Keith's death sparked a series of complex issues involving Occidental Insurance Company of California, which had written a "key man" policy on him for seven million dollars, and the Union Commerce Bank of Cleveland, which was the beneficiary for loans made to Keith's company, American Video.

According to Woody's business partner at the time, Michael Spielvogel, who had a background in the insurance business, "Keith didn't disclose that he was a druggie and the insurance company found out about it and they didn't want to pay the claim. If Keith had said he used drugs, he would not have gotten the policy. The contention was prove it—prove he used drugs. Everyone knew he did drugs, but that wasn't proof—being arrested for drug use was proof. The burden of proof was on the insurance company."

In the end, however, Occidental paid the bank $4.2 million.

Still later, there was a related case involving the Internal Revenue Service and Keith's estate involving taxes.

After the autopsy, Keith's body was returned to Princeton, and a couple of days later, a very private funeral service was held involving members of the Johnson family, some of Keith's cousins, and a few of Keith's friends.

Ryan, who was present with some of his siblings, says, "There was just so much shock over his death that nobody really knew what to do or say."

Another family member observes, "It was so strange because nobody cried. The Johnsons are very stoic. They don't show their emotions."

37

Keith Johnson's death was naturally shocking and traumatic for his mother. Less than five years after her husband's demise, Betty was emotionally paralyzed, but remained stoic. Hoping to help her get over this second blow, Eugene Gillespie suggested that they begin traveling and get out from under the dark cloud that now hung over the Johnson mansion on Edgerstoune Road in Princeton.

"They were trying to get over Keith's death and they were trying to not go places where Keith had been," says a person who was close to the couple. "Gene had friends who were in England and were taking care of a large, very beautiful estate and they invited them to come and stay as long as they wanted. Keith's death was very traumatic for Gene, too. But he did convince Betty to come away with him and go to Europe. They left shortly after Keith's funeral."

Betty's fourth-born, Billy, who had mourned at his brother's funeral, was about to leave, too, to return to Hollywood, where he was living. Like everyone else in the tight Johnson circle, Billy was shattered by Keith's tragic end. The two had been close even though Billy, born in 1952, was younger by four years.

The siblings had done drugs together but, unlike Keith, Billy had his limits. Like Keith, he drove expensive cars like a lunatic and wrecked at least one of them, and was a speed demon when it came to powerful motorcycles and speedboats. But, unlike Keith, he had set goals for himself. He wanted to do more than just live off of his trust fund inheritance. Billy had big dreams of getting into the movie business and, if one listened to his claims, he seemed close to succeeding around the time Keith overdosed.

Of Betty's three eldest sons—Woody, Keith, and Billy—Billy was considered the best and the brightest, the most artistic and the most creative. Physically, he stood about five-foot-ten, was skinny, weighing around 130 pounds, wasn't very athletic but was physically strong. Some thought him to be socially awkward, which was underscored by the fact that he had difficulty meeting women, and was not known to ever have had a serious girlfriend, even after he entered his twenties.

After he left the University of Arizona Billy began taking film study and production courses at New York University. He was living in his sister Libet's Upper East Side apartment when he turned twenty-one in late 1973 and received his first trust fund check of an estimated ten million dollars. Practically the next day, he quit school with the goal, he told friends and family, of securing the film rights to an Ernest Hemingway novel that he liked and to which he related called *Islands in the Stream*.

The novel was first published in 1970, nine years after Hemingway, a depressive, had committed suicide, and the same year that Bobby Johnson died of cancer and Billy had turned eighteen. The story is about a Hemingway-type character, an artist by the name of Thomas Hudson, who lives on the island of Bimini in the Bahamas, some fifty miles off the coast of South Florida—a locale that Billy knew well from his childhood, and where Keith, cruising on the *Sea Prince* with Billy aboard, often sailed. Hemingway's plot line resonated even more with Billy's own past experiences, which was one of the reasons he was inspired to secure the film rights.

Hudson, for instance, has three sons who suddenly appear in his life one summer—he had earlier abandoned his family—and they have a bittersweet reunion that includes a deep-sea fishing trip for marlin—a favorite sport of Bobby Johnson—who sometimes took his own sons with him on such excursions.

"In a lot of ways, Billy viewed the book as autobiographical," says John Vicino, who was close to Billy from childhood. "Hemingway's story of the character in the Bahamas bonding with his kids was exactly what happened in the Johnson family. The best times I remember was when we used to go to the Bimini Big Game Fishing Club and there was a big, black guy there named Percy. He'd take us out and get us drunk and we'd go fishing for sharks, and wrestle with sharks while we were drunk, and *Islands in the Stream* is about all of that kind of activity."

Billy later claimed to his cousins and close friends that he had flown to Ketchum, Idaho, where Hemingway had moved in 1959 from Cuba, and where some members of the author's family were still living, and successfully secured the Hollywood rights to *Islands in the Stream.*

He also boasted that while he was in Ketchum, he had developed a personal friendship with the Nobel Prize–winning "Papa" Hemingway's granddaughters, the future actress and author Mariel Hemingway, who was then just twelve, and her troubled sister, Margaux, a supermodel at twenty then married to her first husband. Like Keith Johnson, Margaux died of a drug overdose—she at the age of forty-two in 1996, just one day before the anniversary of her grandfather's suicide by shotgun. In 2011, Mariel, through a representative, says she had no memory of ever meeting Billy Johnson, and knew nothing about him securing any rights to her grandfather's novel.

But those were the claims Billy had made and no one had any reason to doubt him. They still were convinced many decades later that what he had told them was the truth.

"I certainly remember Billy told me he had the rights," says Eric Ryan, "and that *Islands in the Stream* was going to be his film project. He told about being in the Hemingway family home and maybe dealing with Hemingway's widow."

However, when *Islands in the Stream* was released in 1977 as a major motion picture starring George C. Scott, David Hemmings, and Claire Bloom, there was nothing in the credits, or in Paramount Pictures' archives, to indicate any involvement by Billy Johnson. While he told some people that he was going to be the film's producer, the actual producers were Peter Bart, Max Palevsky, and an associate producer, Ken Wales.

In his review, the *New York Times* film critic Vincent Canby noted that an American journalist and novelist by the name of Denne Bart Petitclerc "apparently has had the blessing of Hemingway's widow, Mary, in adapting the novel." Again, there was no mention of the Johnson heir's involvement.

He must have been fantasizing about it all because Petitclerc actually had a real-life relationship with Hemingway, had become a protégé of sorts, and had the inside track to *Islands*.

In the 1950s, working in Florida as a young reporter at the *Miami Herald*, he had written a letter to Hemingway, who responded with an invitation to go fishing with him in Cuba. On one of their later get-togethers, Hemingway mentioned *Islands* and thought it was perfect for the big screen, and Petitclerc, wholeheartedly agreeing, ran with it. Their friendship resulted in Petitclerc adapting Hemingway's novel for the film.

Billy also had boasted that he had bought a famous boat that had once belonged to Hemingway—the thirty-eight-foot motorized fishing vessel called *Pilar* that the writer and soldier of fortune had bought in 1934 at the height of his career.

"Billy showed me photographs of it that he took," says Eric Ryan. "It was my understanding that it was the actual boat, and that he had it in Marina Del Rey where he was living."

But according to an October 3, 2007, article in *Yachting Magazine* entitled, "Saving *Pilar* and Hemingway," his widow, Mary Hemingway, had actually given *Pilar* to her late husband's "beloved Cuban captain," Gregorio Fuentes, who turned the *Pilar* over to the communist government of Fidel Castro, where it had been a tourist attraction since the early 1960s, and was still in Cuba at the time the article was written.

Billy Johnson was clearly fibbing about owning the prized boat, clearly had some sort of an obsession with Hemingway, and was quite successful in convincing everyone in his close circle that he was making a success of himself in Hollywood with the Hemingway project. At twenty-two, with his vivid imagination and powers of persuasion, he certainly had lots of chutzpah, which is often all it took to be successful in the movie business. He might have had a bright future.

Sadly, he never would get the opportunity to genuinely prove himself.

Late in the evening of May 19, 1975, the phone rang in Eric Ryan's Manhattan apartment. Calling was his cousin, Libet Johnson, Billy's sister, who was then twenty-five and into the second of her five marriages. She had horrific news. Billy had just been in a serious motorcycle accident in Santa Monica. He had been rushed, she told Ryan, to Santa Monica Hospital and was undergoing emergency surgery. She and her brother Woody had divided up the important calls to announce yet another family tragedy.

"Libet was saying to me, 'It really doesn't look good.' Then I got another call a couple of hours later saying that Billy had passed," Ryan vividly recalls. "It was an oh-my-God moment. It was kind of disbelief, then acceptance and then a feeling of what a waste of a life, in a pretty rapid cycle. I felt that Billy had tremendous potential and I had looked forward to a future of professional involvement with him. I just always knew our friendship was such that we would be doing stuff together."

Billy had died in the operating room three hours after his powerful motorcycle sped out of control at high speed, slammed into a parking meter, and threw him some sixty feet through the air after it crashed.

His death came just fifty days after his brother Keith had injected a fatal dose of cocaine into his arm.

The next morning John Vicino was called out of his history class at Emory University, in Atlanta, by a dean and told there was an important telephone call. "My mother told me Billy had been killed, and I said, 'Oh, my God!' I went out in the quadrangle and I just started crying like a little boy. I know that he was affected by Keith's death to the extent of recklessness."

Vicino recalls that one of the last conversations he had with Billy had to do with speed. At the time, Billy had a fast mid-engine Porsche. "He told me, 'I'm just taking more chances driving than I ever have,' and I told him to take care of himself and he said he would.

"If he had lived," speculates Vicino, who firmly believed Billy's Hollywood success stories, "he would have been another Scorsese."

There was talk that Billy was either stoned, or had had a few drinks before rolling, and that he had been traveling at an incredible rate of speed at the time of the crash. And as had been the case with his brother Keith, there was chatter that his death was a suicide. "Billy had a lot of unresolved anger that was expressed in self-destructive tendencies," asserts Eric Ryan.

"Cycle Crash Kills Heir to a Drug Firm," said the headline over the four-paragraph New York *Daily News* wire service and staff story the next day.

"Johnson Scion Killed," read the headline over the three-paragraph report in the *New York Post*.

Both stories offered basic details about the accident, and both mentioned the tragic irony of two heirs to a great American fortune dying within weeks of one another.

A search was immediately begun to find Betty and her husband in Europe to inform them of the latest tragedy, and a Johnson family attorney quickly tracked them down on a layover in Geneva.

"They were actually in the airport waiting for a flight and there was an announcement that said would Mr. and Mrs. Gillespie please come to the office," recalls a friend of the couple. "They were there to get over Keith's death and they were given the phone and told that Billy had been killed. Betty was in a state of shock. Gene was paralyzed. They immediately got on a flight back to New York and home to Princeton for the second funeral for one of her sons in just a few weeks."

Back in Princeton there was a very private church service, and Woody offered the eulogy for his brother.

"It was pretty emotional," remembers Ryan. His brother Quentin Ryan recalls, "I was with our father and my brother Roderick in Hilton Head and we got a call from Seward, or Eric, and Rod and I drove up to New Jersey for the funeral. It was just horrendous."

The death of his two brothers was "crushing" on Woody, recalls his onetime business partner, Michael Spielvogel. "He basically disappeared, went underground, and there was very little communication. He was totally in shock, consoling and being with his family, and the family went very quiet. It was a very sad time."

Billy left $100,000 to the Lawrenceville School, his and Guy Vicino's New Jersey prep school alma mater. The Willard T.C. Johnson Foundation, Inc., was also established regarding his inherited fortune.

Betty was said to have later endowed a section of the Central Park Zoo in Billy's name because of an animal there that he loved as a child.

Meanwhile, the high drama of the two recent tragic events had put a permanent pall over Betty's second marriage.

"That was really a hard blow for her," says Gene Gillespie's son, Peter, looking back. "Not too many mothers and wives could deal with the death of a husband and then five years later the deaths of two sons. Betty had a really hard time and that put stress on their marriage, and it was just impossible for my father to help her. He just couldn't deal with it."

Within months of Billy's death, the Gillespies separated and a divorce action was started after just three very difficult years of marriage.

"I really didn't talk to my father about the divorce," says the daughter, George Ann Gillespie Fox. "He was very private, and I just respected whatever his choices, or her choices, were. We all went our separate ways. It was a part of my life that I don't think about very much."

While most thought Betty's decision to get a divorce resulted from the tragedies, that wasn't the reason she gave to some others.

"I hadn't seen Betty for some time and when I next saw her she was married to her second husband, and the next thing I knew she was divorced from him," says Betty's longtime friend from childhood, Jean Schilling Chockley Ricketts. "When I next saw her she told me that he had just married her for one reason, and one reason only, and that was for her money, and she told me it was a big mistake on her part marrying him."

Both Betty and Gillespie each got married for a third time.

He married Sara Tiedeman Davies, a longtime friend with whom he had once worked. Later, the third Mrs. Gillespie introduced Betty to a neighbor, the man who became her third husband, Douglas Fountain Bushnell, a well-to-do widower with two sons and a daughter—the same as Betty—who had worked for many years for the American Express Company. Bushnell was a New Jersey native, had gone to Rutgers University, and during the Second World War had served in the navy in a bomb disposal unit.

Sara Gillespie had known that Bushnell had lost his first wife, Margaret, in 1970—by coincidence the same year Betty had lost Bobby. She was also aware that Betty was now a divorcee. Playing Cupid, she had invited them both to a dinner party. There was an instant attraction, they began dating, and before long, in the kind of Hollywood ending her late son Billy might have appreciated, Betty and Bushnell were married in a very quiet and very private service in 1978, and lived happily ever after.

Unlike Gene Gillespie, Bushnell was well liked by Betty's surviving children—Woody, Libet, and the youngest, Christopher, who was then nineteen, and by the wider Johnson dynasty. Bushnell was credited with helping Betty come out from under the dark cloud of the tragedies she had bravely endured, and the two became very social. Betty, with her Johnson & Johnson millions, became philanthropic, and was known in news accounts, despite being Mrs. Bushnell, as "New Jersey philanthropist Betty Wold Johnson."

She had become a supporter of a number of arts institutions, such as the Metropolitan Museum of Art in New York City. In 2001, she and Bushnell received an annual award from the New Jersey Performing Arts Center (NJPAC) for being significant benefactors—Betty had donated one million dollars in 1999 and again in 2000, and had made other gifts totaling one hundred thousand dollars.

And both were active contributors to Republican candidates and causes.

In December 2007, the same month Bobby Johnson had died almost four decades earlier, Bushnell passed away at the age of eighty-seven. His obituary stated, "Life for him was a great adventure. He enjoyed everything he did. He will be remembered for his kindness and thoughtfulness. Equally at home on his tractor or the dance floor, he was a consummate gentleman."

The next year, Betty, widowed twice, divorced once, continued with her philanthropy, and gave eleven million dollars to NJPAC, which at the time was the single largest individual gift in the Newark arts center's history. The center's president at the time, Lawrence P. Goldman, said that Betty had asked him "a question that I never get asked: 'What is the hardest category for which you're seeking money?' I said, 'Nobody wants to support keeping the building in "like new" condition,' and she said, 'That's exactly what I want to give the money for, then.'"

Betty had a tough façade but could be sprightly in her old age. Many years after she divorced Gillespie, she ran into his widow, Sara, at someone else's memorial service in Princeton and, according to an observer, Betty said to her, 'Let's give everybody a good laugh and let them see us together since we both were married to the same guy and no one would believe we'd be speaking to each other." Betty then walked down the church aisle with her.

"She got a good giggle when she saw the other women whispering and pointing at her."

PART VI

TROUBLED MARY LEA

38

Around the time Betty May Wold Johnson Gillespie Bushnell was coming to terms with the tragic deaths of her two sons, and was securing a divorce from her second husband—all handled discreetly—a very public and quite bizarre drama involving another member of the Johnson dynasty was being acted out on the world's largest media stage, to wit:

"Jury Told That Heiress Was Target
of Murder Plot Husband Planned"
The New York Times

"Husband Gay, Hit It Off With Hitman,
Heiress Tells Court, Says Spouse was Homosexual"
New York *Daily News*

"$20M Will Cited in 'Plot' on Heiress"
New York Post

All through New York City's long, hot summer of 1977—when a power failure blacked out all five of the city's teeming boroughs for twenty-five hours during a heat wave; when the "44-Caliber Killer," better known as "Son of Sam," continuing a murder spree begun a year earlier, shot six and killed two more before he was caught, and when some optimistic Mad Men came up with the iconic, and ironic for the times, slogan, "I Love New York"— the Big Apple's bedraggled straphangers also were gripped by news stories about the latest titillating scandal involving a member of the dynasty that had brought the world Tylenol and Modess.

The heiress in the headlines was Mary Lea Johnson, whose picture, as a cute infant, was the first on the can of Johnson & Johnson's Baby Powder. The inheritor of a trust fund estimated at upward of one hundred million dollars, she had gone to the office of Bronx District Attorney Mario Merola with a doozy of a tale—"my husband's plotting to kill me"—that sounded like it was spun out of James M. Cain's Underwood.

This was the same Mary Lea Johnson who would later claim that her own father, Seward Johnson Sr., had molested her from childhood and into her teens—a tale that even some of her own children were convinced she had invented after his death to gain sympathy and attention.

In terms of pure shock value and sheer outrageous wickedness, Mary Lea's hit-man case even surpassed the titillation factor of her brother Seward Johnson Jr.'s earlier divorce battle with his first wife, Barbara.

Now fifty, Mary Lea had accused her second husband, Victor D'Arc, a prominent fifty-three-year-old Upper East Side child psychiatrist, of wanting her dead so he could cash in on the twenty million dollars that she had bequeathed to him in one of her many wills.

She claimed that D'Arc had asked thirty-two-year-old John Fino of the Bronx—Mary Lea's trusted chauffeur, handyman at her New Jersey estate and Manhattan apartment, and a struggling actor (who reportedly was Robert De Niro's double in the 1974 film *Godfather Part II*)—to arrange for a contract killing, and to make it look like a mugging gone bad. As much as two hundred thousand dollars were to have changed hands if Mary Lea suddenly became a corpse.

She further claimed D'Arc had gone to Fino to get the job done because the two were lovers.

Despite the seriousness of her allegations against D'Arc, he was never charged in the case, or even called to testify.

"There were insane accusations flying around," says Karen Scourby D'Arc, one of two daughters from his first marriage many years later. "If they were true, something would have come of them, and nothing came of them regarding my father."

To combat Mary Lea's tale of murder, and since D'Arc wasn't facing any formal charges, he took his case to the press, telling a *Times* reporter:

"My wife is very naïve. She has so much money she's like a Howard Hughes, and those around her will tell her anything she wants to hear. All they want is her money."

Moreover, according to the *News,* he claimed his life, too, was in jeopardy.

"I keep getting these threatening phone calls," D'Arc stated, "and once I received a voodoo doll stuck with pins."

The doctor, who had instantly given up his fifty-thousand-dollar-a-year practice to manage Mary Lea's multimillion-dollar financial assets, then proceeded to claim that Mary Lea had "a menopausal problem."

D'Arc maintained that his estranged wife wanted to use the money to invest in Broadway plays and films. When the two separated and filed for divorce a year earlier, Mary Lea already was involved with the gay Jewish show-business maven Marty Richards, who would become her third husband, and a major player, one not always beloved, in the Johnson dynasty dramas. She had already invested about a million dollars in a few of Richards's big-name productions on the Great White Way, including *Chicago,* and later Hollywood productions like *The Shining,* all of which they were doing through their Mary Lea–financed company called The Producer Circle.

$ $ $

Mary Lea had fallen for Vincent D'Arc, who was affiliated with the psychiatric department at St. Luke's Hospital, in Manhattan, when he was treating her troubled teenage son Seward Ryan, "who had a significant substance abuse problem," says his brother Eric. "Seward was talking to him about how he has this mother who is a trust-funder and that she's in a bad relationship with his nut-job father and Victor invited my mother to come up to New York to discuss my brother's case and then they ended up dating."

Her mind-boggling story that D'Arc planned to have her bumped off became public for the first time in a Bronx courtroom—and on the pages of every New York City daily, and in wire service stories across the country. The shocking revelations began on June 1, 1977, at Fino's trial for contempt of court, and then in Mary Lea's New Jersey divorce proceedings, all happening around the same time.

When Fino was called before a Bronx grand jury and questioned about her charges, he refused to answer and was charged with contempt. Despite the spate of headline stories about a murder plot and other crimes and misdemeanors, contempt was the only charge ever formally lodged in the case, and Fino was the only key defendant.

The prosecutor in the case, Donald Levin, an assistant Bronx D.A., said there was evidence to show that Fino, who was friends with Mary Lea, had actually told her about the murder plot, not because he was looking out for her welfare, but rather because "he knew where his bread and butter was."

Fino's lawyer, Stephen Weiss, claimed his client was fearful of testifying because D'Arc "wouldn't hesitate to snuff out two lives for his own gain . . . there's a large bounty on her head."

Mary Lea's allegation that her husband and Fino were lovers was made by her lawyers during a divorce action in Somerset County Court, in Somerville, New Jersey, where D'Arc had filed for divorce in September 1976. Mary Lea had filed her own divorce action that November in Manhattan Supreme Court.

Mary Lea claimed that beginning in mid-December of 1973 the bespectacled, mustachioed D'Arc pursued "an open, notorious, continuous course of deviant homosexual intercourse" with Fino, a swarthy and tall ex-Marine with a bent nose, who sported a mustache, mutton-chop sideburns, and a pompadour hairdo. Moreover, she claimed that D'Arc "repeatedly requested" her to "engage in sexual intercourse with various men" of his choice, and in his presence.

The court papers stated that D'Arc had made "arrangements to liquidate her through a paid assassin."

If D'Arc's sexual activities were being exposed, so were Mary Lea's.

D'Arc had filed a complaint with the New Jersey court charging that on a vacation in March 1975 on the tony island of Saint Martin in the Caribbean, Mary Lea had gone barhopping with a male friend of hers, without her husband, and had ended the boozy night swimming nude with her friend and one of the "local natives" at a town beach at dawn.

Her lawyers also released a transcript of a phone conversation between D'Arc and Fino's father, Ted Fino. In it, D'Arc was quoted as saying, "Tell him, Teddy, I'd like it to be, you know, a mugging . . . And if it comes up and costs a couple of thousand more, okay . . . and I'll give you fifty thousand dollars over the next year after the operation."

As John Fino's contempt trial played out, Mary Lea, a frustrated diva who loved drama, and had once in her late teens studied for a time at the American Academy of Dramatic Arts, said that because of D'Arc and the plot on her life, she had had "a year of sheer torture." To protect her life, she had hired bodyguards to be with her around the clock. At one point, when she learned of the purported relationship between D'Arc and Fino, she claimed that she had tried suicide by pinning a note to herself, taking what she asserted was enough prescription and over-the-counter drugs to "kill an elephant," and positioning herself in bed waiting for death to come, but that all she suffered was an upset stomach. Like her brother, Seward Jr.'s earlier suicide attempt, hers had failed, too.

Mary Lea's son Eric says the whole case was "so unclear and so charged with drama that it ushered in the start of an era in my mother's life where she traveled with bodyguards. My mother was never a picture of mental stability, and she took on the role of a hunted victim."

John Fino was eventually found guilty of contempt.

He received an indeterminate sentence of up to four years in prison—with a minimum of a year behind bars for refusing to testify before the grand jury probing Mary Lea's charges of a contract killing plot—and he actually served twenty-six months.

He soon broke his silence and gave his side of the story. And it was as much of a whopper as the one Mary Lea had told that ignited the whole case in the first place.

Fino denied there ever really was a plan to kill her, and he dismissed her claims that he had had a homosexual relationship with D'Arc, stating, "I don't know where that came from. There was one little scene."

He claimed it all had to do with helping D'Arc scare off Marty Richards, who was stealing Mary Lea's affections. He said he refused to testify before the grand jury as a way to protect D'Arc's two teenage daughters.

"I just couldn't see any reason for making myself look like a rat, ruining the doctor's reputation . . . hurting his children in school upstate, just to make a big smear case in the papers or to help Mary Lea get her divorce."

He characterized the Johnson & Johnson heiress as "gullible" and said she was the target of influence of "a bunch of gay guys." He acknowledged that Mary Lea's Merriewold West was the setting for kinky sex and much drug-taking, which only intensified, he maintained, when Marty Richards became a player in the scenario.

By late summer 1977, Mary Lea had written D'Arc out of her will. By year's end, she and D'Arc's no-fault divorce was granted.

With Fino behind bars, the Bronx D.A. dropped the whole case.

D'Arc died in 1995, according to his daughter, Karen Scourby D'Arc.

Eric Ryan says he "heard from more than one source" that the cause of D'Arc's death at seventy was AIDS-related.

$ $ $

Despite her claims that her husband wanted her dead, Mary Lea Johnson Ryan D'Arc (soon to be Mrs. Marty Richards) was living life to the fullest.

She had four homes, was chauffeured around New York City in a gleaming tan and black Rolls-Royce that had been built for a maharaja, wore silk caftans and feather boas along with rare pieces of jewelry from Africa and the South Seas.

Her sprawling high-rise co-op apartment, 19H, in the Sovereign in Manhattan's tony Sutton Place neighborhood, was more like a ranch house in the sky, and decorated in an eclectic mix of priceless English antiques and contemporary pieces. Her gay beau, Marty Richards, also had an apartment, 41G, in the Sovereign, where he was living with a business partner before Richards and the Johnson heiress moved in together.

Richards once said that he was "terrified" of Mary Lea's "wealth. It's been one of our major problems."

Still, he went along for the ride because even more terrifying was "[t]he thought of living without her."

And living without her fortune.

With Richards, she had bought a lavish estate in Beverly Hills, originally built for Ruby Keeler by Al Jolson, and while it was being refurbished and furnished, she rented a huge suite at the Beverly Wilshire Hotel. She soon bought a mansion that she named "By the Sea" on fashionable Gin Lane in chic Southampton on Long Island where the Cristal and cocaine flowed. She had an immense art collection, some two hundred works, most of them by the early-twentieth-century Danish artist Antonio Nicolo Gasparo Jacobsen, who was known as the "Audubon of steam vessels." Many of them decorated the production office she shared with Richards.

She invested, and lost a small fortune, in an art gallery, the M. L. D'Arc Gallery, on Manhattan's Upper West Side. It was a losing proposition mainly because she had a small stable of artists on stipends ranging from thirty to fifty thousand dollars a year, with guarantees that she'd buy their work, and some took advantage of her generosity and naivete about the business.

"In some cases their money went into good wine, and in some cases into their arms in the form of drugs," maintains her son Eric, who was in his mid-twenties at the time. He says she also had sponsored some extreme performance art in the gallery.

One live piece in front of an audience involved two actors standing at two lecterns and pretending to be in a debate. "But, inside one of the lecterns was a girl giving one of the actors a blowjob, and the audience was watching on a monitor. It was all sort of being staged against the backdrop of my mom being an enthusiastic supporter and patron of the arts."

Mary Lea never understood the concept of restraint. The poor little rich girl had grown up without it, and she wasn't alone; restraint had never been part of the Johnson dynasty genes. While the headlines blared embarrassing and scandalous stories about her bizzaro world, her father, J. Seward Johnson Sr., then in his late seventies, was ignoring it all, and living it up with his decades-younger Polish housekeeper wife, Basia, and they were building their thirty-million-dollar dream mansion in New Jersey.

39

Mary Lea Johnson was just twenty when she got married for the first time. The date was November 22, 1950, the place St. Paul's Roman Catholic Church in Highland Park, New Jersey—where her uncle, the General, had once been mayor—and the groom was William Kendall Ryan, a Jersey boy, a radio journalist at a small station, a devout Catholic, and later a right-wing Goldwater Republican who was not well liked by her siblings. Her brother, Seward Jr.—the best man at her wedding—says Ryan had turned Mary Lea "into a baby-making machine. He was a psychotic from what I was told by his children."

During two difficult decades with Ryan, Mary Lea had five sons and a daughter; her first child, Eric, in 1951, her last child, Quentin, in 1958.

The Ryans' first home was a one-hundred-acre spread in Bedminster, New Jersey, where Mary Lea raised her kids and where they lived like the Beverly Hillbillies with millions of dollars, along with six hundred chickens, four pigs, and two cows. During the marriage, she bought another farm—four hundred chickens, eighty sheep—in Easton, Maryland, where Ryan owned a small weekly newspaper, the *Mid-Shore Times,* for a time.

Ryan had a violent streak, and his children were often his target. "My father was a rager," says Eric Ryan, recalling his childhood. "While I never saw him be physically violent toward my mother, he was certainly physically violent toward his kids—he used belts, hairbrushes, and shoes."

Because of his Catholicism, Ryan had sent most of his sons to the Canterbury School, an exclusive Catholic boys' boarding school in rural New Milford, Connecticut, the same blue-collar town where their aunt, Evangeline Brewster Johnson, once had her estate, Cloud Walk Farm.

Eric soon discovered that Canterbury was a breeding ground for homosexual activity. "I saw blowjobs in the shower. I saw a guy come into my room one night and pull down my covers and attempt to suck my dick. I waked up and the guy freaked out and left the room to go try the same thing with somebody else down the hall. I had the quintessential Catholic experience where I went to the headmaster about the incident and was told that it could not have happened."

The Ryans were divorced in 1972, with Mary Lea then headed into her second marriage, the bizarre and frightening union with Vincent D'Arc.

Bill Ryan got a one-million-dollar settlement and one of the farms. Years later, after Mary Lea died, Ryan went to court unsuccessfully seeking 10 percent of each of his children's inheritances. But she had already disinherited them, igniting yet another battle to restore the wealth they felt was their due.

As her son Quentin observes: "There were so many lawsuits and battles and crap that flew around in the Johnson and Ryan families. It was just one mess after another. There was just tremendous bitterness."

Bill Ryan, who had been estranged from his children for years, died in October 2010, in Hilton Head, North Carolina.

While Mary Lea claimed that her second husband, D'Arc, was a homosexual, and she was open to the fact that her third husband, Marty Richards, was gay, Eric Ryan says his biological father's "sexuality was also pretty tortured," and that he thinks he was "a repressed homosexual."

Ryan says he learned posthumously that his father had become "very friendly with the gay community" in Hilton Head, "and very supportive of gay rights. He even spent some time working in an AIDS hospice on a volunteer basis."

But Eric was unable to discover whether his father had ever been involved with another man.

$ $ $

When Mary Lea Johnson Ryan married Vincent D'Arc in 1972, just a few days after divorcing her first husband, she bought a spectacular 140-acre estate in Far Hills, New Jersey. The main house had been a Revolutionary War inn, which she named Merriewold West, in honor of her father Seward Sr.'s estate, Merriewold. She also used her mansion as an art gallery where she sponsored several shows, including outdoor exhibits of sculpture by the likes of Louise Nevelson and Alexander Calder.

Her youngest son, Quentin, says many years later that because of all of the homosexual, bisexual, cuckolding, and sometimes even heterosexual sex going on there during the D'Arc era, "Merriewold West was a circus, a freak show. D'Arc was gay and had his boyfriends out there on the weekends. The contractors working there used to refer to the house as 'Mirror World West' because the master bedroom was floor-to-ceiling—*and* ceiling—mirrors."

As a licensed psychiatrist D'Arc had legal access to all kinds of drugs—painkillers, barbiturates, uppers and downers—and made them freely available, dispensing them like M&M's on Halloween to Mary Lea and her sons.

"He literally would write prescriptions in my name and my brothers' names for everything—Seconal, Demerol, Tuinol, you name it," Quentin Ryan says. "He had all kinds of pills in his medicine cabinet and my brothers would steal them, and he never complained, or even raised an issue. I once told my mother and Dr. D'Arc that my brother Seward had a drug problem, and told them they had to deal with it, and they were like, 'yeah, yeah, yeah, we know.' My mother's house, Merriewold West, was out of control. The police had a map of the place, they knew it so well."

Mary Lea Johnson Ryan D'Arc (and soon Richards) would never be voted mother of the year.

"She let us use drugs," says Quentin, fifty-five years old in 2011. "For my eighteenth birthday, she gave me a blank check, and a quarter ounce of cocaine. I was like, 'God, Mom, this is what you're thinking? It's really pathetic.' She had a very bizarre and twisted personality. Dealing with her was like dealing with a fourteen-year-old. She certainly was not maternal."

His brother Eric says that on occasion he smoked marijuana with her, and claims that Quentin and Seward both had dealt with drug problems. "My brother Seward for years and years struggled with it, so it was just really prevalent," says Quentin. Eric says Seward was once arrested for holding up a New York cabbie and served a one-year custodial sentence in drug rehab in lieu of incarceration "after a deal was worked out with the court." He later contracted hepatitis, Eric says, "from being an IV drug user," but was successfully treated by a psychic healer in Brazil. Married with four children, Seward was studying sculpture and living off his Johnson family trust fund in 2011.

Quentin, also a Johnson & Johnson trust-funder, became a "glass blower," according to his wife, Dale, whom he married in 1983. In 2012, she self-published a picture book about living in their Litchfield, Connecticut, farmhouse with her husband, two sons, and five dogs.

40

In October 1978, on a plane headed for Hollywood, Mary Lea Johnson Ryan D'Arc told her companion and business partner, Marty Richards, that it was about time that they tied the knot. The Band-Aid heiress and the gay producer soon had a quickie, private ceremony in a lawyer's office without any family members in attendance.

At the Stork Club in Manhattan, they threw a glitzy wedding reception. Afterward, her son Hillary Ryan, her fourth-born, furious that his mother had married someone he considered to be yet another leech, was said to have gone to the trustees who held the pursestrings to her fortune, and reportedly told them that she had tied the knot with "a Broadway Jew fag," and to keep his mitts out of her pot of gold.

"For Marty, meeting and marrying my mother was a win-win situation," says Eric Ryan, looking back many years later. "He went from being a small-time casting agent to being a big-time producer overnight with her financial backing. The place Marty lived in when he first met my mother was a shared apartment on Central Park West, ground floor, with a bedspread hung up on the windows to create some privacy. He went pretty much directly from there to the penthouse in the Sovereign, and on from there [in the early 1980s] to the River House."

The fourteen-room, nine-thousand-square-foot River House duplex that cost in the neighborhood of three million dollars, and was appointed and furnished for about the same amount, underscored Marty Richards's overnight affluence due to Mary Lea, whose own fortune was attributable to the sale of lots of baby powder and Band-Aids.

The maisonette, in what was considered one of Manhattan's most luxe buildings, a gated co-op with spectacular views of the city and the East River, was so exclusive that Gloria Vanderbilt sued when she was turned away. When Joan Crawford wasn't considered the right caliber for a River House residence she reportedly arranged to have a big, bright sign advertising Pepsi-Cola placed on the other side of the river in hopes it would piss off another resident of the building—the president of Coca-Cola.

But Marty Richards, with the Johnson & Johnson heiress on his arm, got in, and he put his mark on the place.

"Marty had his own bathroom that had a tile ceiling with his initials like a monogram," recalls Ryan. "It was probably six feet high and it was all done with a royal blue background and his initials 'MR' were in gold leaf. Marty could lie in the tub [that could bathe four at a time] and look up at his monogram."

Visitors had compared the lavishly decorated place to Versailles. There were gilt-edged mirrors and the rooms were arranged with French and English furniture from the seventeenth and eighteenth centuries. Everywhere were marble sculptures, such as a Greek male torso, and priceless antique china in beautifully carved cabinetry. In the powder room hung a painting by Jean Dufy.

The initials over Marty Richards's tub could have read "MRK" because his real name was Morton Richard Klein and he was one of the first Jews to become a member of the very un-Jewish and, at times, anti-Semitic Johnson dynasty. Unlike Mary Lea, who had grown up very much unloved, but with great wealth and in grand style, Marty was the progeny of Sid and Shirley Klein of little money, and of the Grand Concourse in the Bronx.

He had gone to Taft High School with another neighborhood kid, Stanley Kubrick, who years later as a famous director was quoted as saying, "When I heard we would be working together on *The Shining,* I called him in Scotland and started singing 'Hail Taft High.' [He said] 'Who the fuck is this?' and hung up."

Richards's parents had once sent him to the Marie Moses School of Dance and Singing because, at nine, he had a wonderful little voice, and it was there he became friends with some other future showbiz types such as Rita Moreno and Donna Reed. When he was about to enter adolescence he got a part as a newsboy in a Broadway show called *Mexican Hayride*. In his late teens, he sang in clubs.

In the mid-1950s, when Mary Lea Johnson Ryan was giving birth to her fifth, her future third husband's name appeared in a show-business item in the *Daily News* about "young baritone Mart Richards, a teen-aged sensation. This Bronx-born buddy of Sal Mineo [who was gay and murdered years later in West Hollywood], first became popular when he did commercials for a candy bar."

In the early 1950s, he had a brief marriage that ended when he concluded he liked boys more than girls, but never told his parents. "It was the fifties, you didn't talk about those things then. My mother would have jumped out the window, she would have thought she did something terribly wrong," he acknowledged in a *New York* magazine profile. "I never walked around in a tutu. The only difference was I liked guys."

The fact that he was gay and they mostly slept in separate beds didn't faze Mary Lea, because she was overjoyed that she finally had a marriage partner who, she felt, really cared for her, and who loved show business as much as she did.

Like the gay Charles Merrill with Evangeline Brewster Johnson, Richards would claim that he and Mary Lea "had a totally normal sexual relationship," and that she made him feel "handsome and virile."

The only real issue, supposedly, was that she had millions, and he had nothing.

Mary Lea often voiced the Johnson dynasty mantra: "You never know if people are being nice to you because of the money or because they really respect you as a person," she once told a journalist. "But you have to trust somebody, and while you rule out the ones who are obviously opportunistic, you take everybody at face value until they disappoint you."

To the poor little rich girl, Richards was suspect at first but proved himself, at least in her eyes, as one who wasn't opportunistic. "Sure, I feared

Marty was only interested in me because I was rich," she once said. "I'd be stupid not to think about it. As it turned out, he was interested in me *despite* the fact that I was rich."

No one in the Johnson-Ryan axis believed a word she, or he, was saying when it came to her fortune.

Says Quentin Ryan, "I never completely trusted him. She and Marty were spending gobs of money, just unbelievable amounts of money, and I was like, 'Mom, you can't buy your friends. These people are destroying you,' and Marty had his bodyguard drag me to the other room and slap me around. My mother made roughly three and a half million dollars a year after taxes from her trust and they were spending on the average between nine and thirteen million dollars a year. When Marty married her, he won the Powerball."

On the first day of June 1988, two years before Mary Lea died, five of six of her progeny who were furious with the mad money spending of their mother and Richards—and mostly fearful that there wouldn't be any millions left in her Johnson & Johnson trust fund coffers for them—took their whining to the press.

"Johnson Heirs Battle over Trust Fund," ran the headline across the Page Six gossip column of the *New York Post*. The lead said: "Johnson & Johnson heiress Mary Lea Richards has been spending an $80 million trust fund faster than most people can go through a box of Band-Aids. And if she keeps on at her present rate, her children by William Ryan—Quentin, Alice, Hillary, Roderick and Seward—claim they won't have enough to buy that box."

The trust in question had been established in 1944 by her father, J. Seward Johnson Sr. From the trust Mary Lea was getting the income, some three million dollars a year, and upon her death, her children understood that they would get what was left, which they estimated to be about sixty million dollars. But if the Ryan gang were to be believed, she had spent almost eighteen million dollars just between 1983 and 1988, with "no rhyme or reason," Quentin Ryan, then thirty, told the *Post*.

He claimed that his mother spent more than three million dollars for just the furnishings in her River House apartment. His brother Hillary chimed in that his mother and Richards had spent one hundred thousand dollars in just one twenty-four-hour period entertaining dignitaries while on a trip to China. On a cruise aboard the *QE2*, they blew a half-million dollars.

"I'm convinced that Marty Richards is doing everything he can to make sure he gets it all," declared Hillary Ryan, who claimed that Richards's "dry-cleaning bill is larger than my annual income."

Moreover, he charged that Richards had put up a wall between Mary Lea and her children.

"He has painted us in a bad light. He's shut us out of her life. He has an insatiable appetite for money."

Five of the children—not including Eric, who was his mother's favorite, her principal heir among the siblings, and who was in her will to the tune of seventeen million dollars, give or take—had recently lost a case before the New Jersey Supreme Court to prevent Mary Lea's trustees from giving her whatever she asked for, thus allowing her to spend like a drunken sailor with Richards happily assisting. Hillary declared that his mother was "easily swayed by the people she's surrounded herself with, and it's a pretty cutthroat cast of characters."

Around the time the gossip item appeared, Mary Lea's health was beginning to seriously fail. She had liver cancer, and her doctors determined that she required liver transplant surgery. "She had shingles. She had diabetes. Her skin had a distinct yellow caste. Her eyes had a yellow cast. She was in bad shape," Eric recalls. "This was a whole period with a lot of drama and desperation over her health issues and drama over legal issues, and how the trustees would react to the publicity that was being stirred up by my siblings."

In late April 1990, Mary Lea was admitted to Presbyterian University Hospital in Pittsburgh, where she underwent the transplant surgery. Two weeks later, on May 3, seventeen days before her sixty-fourth birthday, she died.

After her passing, fierce battles erupted in and out of court involving her children; her third husband, Marty Richards; and her first husband, Bill Ryan.

Even in death, Mary Lea's Johnson & Johnson money was what everyone cared about. Two trusts, both of them established by her father, Seward Sr.—one in 1944, the other in 1961—had become the objects of fierce combat.

The 1944 trust, all of it in Johnson & Johnson stock, was litigated in the early 1990s, and resulted in Richards getting about forty-four million dollars, almost half of the ninety million dollars that Mary Lea had in her estate. The remainder was eventually divided among her children, but not equally.

Mary Lea's will provided for Richards to receive the bulk of her estate and for Eric to receive about seventeen million dollars, and his siblings were to get just one million dollars each. Moreover, there was a clause that stated if any of them, except for Eric, contested her last will and testament "they would lose what they were otherwise given at the point of my mother's death," says Eric. "I was the only one who was immunized from that clause."

In order to make the division of money a bit better for his siblings, Eric, who had a law degree, says he acted as a sort of big brother/Robin Hood and entered "into a negotiation with Marty on the one hand, and with my siblings' attorneys on the other hand, where I got Marty to move about twelve million dollars from his side of the pile into my siblings' side of the pile and, at the same time, I moved about two million dollars, or three million dollars from my inheritance, so I enriched each of my siblings' take from my mom's will from about one million dollars to about three million, five hundred thousand dollars, and the question of there being a will contest disappeared."

However, the battle over Seward Sr.'s 1961 trust was a classic.

"Ultimately, everything boiled down once again to Mary Lea Johnson's money," observes Richard Collier, the Princeton attorney who represented two of her children, Roderick and Alice, in the litigation.

The case dragged on for a mind-boggling twelve years, involved a number of high-powered lawyers—one of them being Ken Starr, who had written the "Starr Report" charging that President Clinton had lied about his relationship with Monica Lewinsky—thousands of pages of testimony and documents, and all of it was focused on trying to determine the definition of just a single word.

"It's extraordinary," says Collier, "that we spent a dozen years on the word 'spouse.' You wouldn't think that you would need a six-day trial and more than a decade of litigation up and down the New Jersey Supreme Court twice to determine what the word 'spouse' means—but that's what happened."

In early 1997, Mary Lea's children and others filed a lawsuit in New Jersey to keep her spouses (by then her widowers)—Marty Richards and Bill Ryan—from benefiting. And there began the strange legal argument over the meaning of the word "spouse."

"The only position that concerned me and the court," says Collier, was "should Marty be, or not be, eligible for distribution from that trust. There was a lot of money in that trust, so it was worth a lot of people's efforts to determine that issue."

On April 3, 2008, the New Jersey Supreme Court, in a five-to-two ruling, decided that seventy-six-year-old Richards was still considered a spouse even though Mary Lea had died some eighteen years earlier, and that he could share in the huge trust fund along with other family members, among them great-grandchildren. The court left it to the estate's trustees how much he would receive from the trust, valued around $350 million. While he won the role of spouse, he was not considered a distributee by the trustees and received no financial reward, according to Eric Ryan. Some of the other beneficiaries began getting anywhere from seven hundred thousand dollars to $1.5 million annually, which was to stop in 2014, and continue with the next generation of the Johnson dynasty.

Richards, who wore two wedding rings, his and his late wife's, naturally was overjoyed, telling a reporter for *The New York Times*, "I've always wanted to be part of the family. It hurt me terribly when they said I was not a spouse. What do you mean I'm not a spouse? I wanted to be treated respectfully as Mr. [Seward] Johnson had suggested I be treated."

After battling liver cancer and undergoing surgery in 2011, Richards celebrated his eightieth birthday, on January 17, 2012, in grand style at the Rubin Museum of Art in New York City. Looking slim and tanned, his hair white with a bald spot in the middle, he gaily posed for photos with the likes of close Johnson family friends Michael Douglas and Catherine Zeta-Jones, she who had starred in Richards's film adaptation of *Chicago*.

"Marty always liked to keep it in the Johnson dynasty," a close friend says. "He saw himself as a Johnson through and through, and would until his dying day."

That day came ten months later, on November 26, 2012, some twenty-two years after the death of Mary Lea. Richards was buried next to her in Locust Valley Cemetery in Long Island, not far from where he and the heiress had once constantly partied on her Band-Aid– and Baby Oil–financed Southampton estate.

They were not alone in death, though, as they rarely had ever been alone in life.

Curiously, their burial site was a private grove also occupied by the graves of at least five close friends and theatrical associates, among them a one-time hairdresser who helped produce two Producer Circle plays in the early seventies and again in the early eighties—a "strikingly handsome" homosexual who had photographs done of himself in studios "to make him look like an Adonis," a Johnson family member says. He had died of AIDS a couple of years after Mary Lea's passing.

Another buried there was Mary Lea's longtime protector in life and then in death, the celebrity bodyguard to the stars, Tony Maffatone, an ex-cop from Paterson, New Jersey, whom she had hired back in the mid-1970s when she claimed her then-husband had put out a murder contract on her. Maffatone, who died in 2000 at age fifty-seven in a scuba diving accident, had also done security work for Dolly Parton, and for Sylvester Stallone, whom he taught fighting and weapons use for the film *Rambo: First Blood Part II*."

While chums of Mary Lea and Marty were buried in the cemetery grove, no provision had ever been made for the burial there of Mary Lea's five sons and one daughter from the first of her three marriages, who had survived their mother.

"When my mother married Marty, there was sort of a gradual displacement with my mother's relationship to her kids," says first-born, Eric Ryan, who had had a "combative history" with Richards over the years. "I think this [the burial place] was kind of a metaphor for all of that, and it's curious from a psychological point of view, and from a family dynamic point of view.

"In a lot of ways Marty was the child my mother always *wished* she had, and she really enjoyed making him happy in material ways by giving him carte blanche with interior decorators or tailors. Marty's closets were like something out of *The Great Gatsby*—row upon row of two-thousand-dollar suits. At their social events I would meet people who would introduce themselves as, 'Oh, I dress Marty.' They were people from Upper East Side boutiques."

Regarding the burial grove—which is surrounded by bright rhododendrons, with shiny brass plaques marking the graves of Mary Lea, Richards, and their friends, and a stone bench inscribed with an eloquent quote from *Romeo and Juliet*—Ryan sees it all as very appropriate, and observes: "If life's a party, why couldn't death be a party."

One of the several viewings for Richards, Ryan says, "had the feeling of a cocktail party without the booze." A rabbi gave a brief prayer and then friends like Chita Rivera shared remembrances. She called him a "genius of the theater."

While Richards had become a millionaire many times over during his curious marriage to the Johnson heiress, had been bequeathed millions more in inheritance after she died, and presumably made millions more as a successful partner with her in their theatrical business, people close to him at the end of his life believed he had gone through most, if not all of it, living the good life. As Michael Riedel, a longtime friend and theater critic for the *New York Post,* noted in an appreciation column, "He had millions and burned through millions."

That fact was underscored by Maryanne Dittman, an associate of Mary Lea and Marty's, who had run into Eric Ryan when she attended his funeral. She told him, "They did not want to pay for the death announcement in *The New York Times* because they were trying to be conservative. She told me that they preplanned and prepaid for the funeral and that they had been able to save a great deal of money that way, so there was definitely a sense of trying to carefully manage what funds he had."

It was thought that, at best, Richard's estate might be worth $10 million.

But Ryan didn't think he or his siblings, or their children, would be beneficiaries of any of it.

"I would be totally shocked," he says. "I would cash the check, don't get me wrong. But it would be a total shock."

PART VII

ACQUIRING IDENTITY

41

Almost four decades before Woody Johnson spent $635 million of his vast Johnson & Johnson trust fund fortune to buy the New York Jets football team, he and his aggressive young business partner and idea man, Michael Richard Spielvogel, tried to snap up the Tampa Bay Buccaneers.

At the time, 1976, Spielvogel, a skinny, wired, good-looking Jewish *macher* from Long Island, didn't even know what a down was, but Woody did, even though he wasn't a rabid football fan. The last time the Band-Aid heir had tossed the pigskin was back in prep school when he was mostly warming the bench.

Woody had high hopes that owning a National Football League team would give him his own identity, one that had nothing to do with his family's eponymous health-care business. Spielvogel, whose job it was to teach Woody about business, look for new venture opportunities, and broker deals for him—they were both just twenty-eight years old—had heard that the new Buccaneers franchise was going up on the block, and was open for bidders. He called the NFL and started the ball rolling.

"I had the authority from Bob [he never called him Woody] to make a deal and I made an offer of fourteen million dollars to be in the name of Robert Wood Johnson IV," Spielvogel says many years later. "Trying to get the Bucs was just one of those crazy things we did. We were just kids buying land and building condominiums."

As it turned out, Woody lost his bid for the team, which became part of the American Football Conference West. Ownership went to a more established high roller, Hugh Franklin Culverhouse, a hugely wealthy attorney and real estate mogul from Jacksonville, who paid four million dollars more than the team of Woody and Spielvogel had offered.

"It was all politics," Spielvogel asserts. "We played off Robert's name, the Johnson and Johnson name, figuring we'd have a real good shot. We were just kids and the National Football League was dealing with more sophisticated people. When it fell apart it was like, okay, so what, no big deal, what's next?"

Woody would have to wait until the new millennium to have his dream of owning a professional football team come true—and finally earn his own identity at the age of fifty-three—when he bought the Jets many seasons after superstar quarterback Joe "Broadway Joe" Namath was gone from the team. Woody then got the chance to feel some of the pain of what it was like to own another often mediocre team—"the same old Jets," was the long-heard refrain from the fans. The Jets hadn't won the big game since Super Bowl III, when Richard Nixon was in his first presidential term, and Woody was recovering from his broken back.

Still, Woody had never forgotten his first shot at becoming an elite NFL owner. When a sports reporter asked him in 2010 whether he had ever shown interest in another team in the past, he named the Bucs, but ignored, or twisted, some important facts:

"When I was about thirty, they had put a bid out for Tampa Bay . . . I'd just sold a cable company down there. So I looked at that for a while. And that involved building a team, building a stadium, moving to Tampa, all those things. That's a bit much for me. Plus, living in Tampa is not living in New York."

What he failed to mention was that the cable company he sold had actually been his brother Keith's, inherited by Woody after Keith's drug overdose; that he had seriously been actively looking forward to building a team and everything that went with it; that living in Tampa was never an issue because he was already residing in Fort Lauderdale, just a twenty-minute private plane flight away; and that while Tampa wasn't New York, he didn't move there from Florida until the early 1980s. Most important, he hedged on the fact that he had definitely made a very serious bid with very serious money and had been shut out.

And ignored altogether in Woody's curriculum vitae was Michael Spielvogel's important role. He had become a nonperson in Woody's scenario.

In 2011, twenty-nine-year-old Jaime Johnson, one of Woody's two pretty, blond heiress daughters—his firstborn, Casey, had died a year earlier—told a *New York Times* fashion reporter that it was her billionaire father who had inspired her to do something positive with her life. She had begun dabbling in the photography world, shooting subjects like her father's Jets' 2012 cheerleader calendar.

"My dad worked every day since graduating college," stated Jaime with sincerity. "He told me, 'I put on a suit and tie every day because I wanted to stay in the game.' "

But that's not how Spielvogel remembers Jaime's father the very first time they met at the Fort Lauderdale home of a friend, the heir to a fortune in IBM stock, one Sunday afternoon in 1973.

"We were watching a Miami Dolphins game on television and the doorbell rang and I go to the front door and there's this guy with long blond, scraggly hair down to his shoulders, wearing sandals, and his zipper was pulled down and I could see his underpants through his Bermuda shorts," Spielvogel vividly recalls. "He was disheveled. I thought, who is this beach bum?"

As they sat in front of the television watching the game, Woody made conversation by asking Spielvogel what he was up to, and learned that the guy was involved in building apartment houses in South Florida, had a successful insurance business back in Long Island, and was driving a flashy Cadillac Eldorado convertible. In other words, Spielvogel came across as a successful, fast-talking, likeable hustler who was "making a lot of money" at a young age, and who had done it all on his own.

"I got the impression that was kind of impressive to him," says Spielvogel. "I had made it the hard way on my own. I hadn't inherited a dime. Those guys had stock certificates. I didn't have family money."

The meeting was "kind of a non-event" for Spielvogel, who, after his brief Florida visit, had returned to his base of operations in Port Jefferson, New

York, having no idea who the bedraggled fellow was with whom he had chatted, and couldn't have cared less.

Several weeks later Spielvogel, who claimed to be the youngest agent at Guardian Life Insurance Company of America, was sitting in his office, in a small, one-story professional office building he had built and leased back to Guardian, when his secretary, a high school intern, told him there was a call from a Mr. Johnson. Spielvogel didn't know a Johnson and had to refresh his memory. Woody said he was now in New Jersey, in Princeton, and wanted to come up and meet with him.

"I gave him a Jewish invitation," recalls Spielvogel. "Come anytime."

Ninety minutes later Woody was on the phone again.

"I'm here," he says. "I'm at the airport."

This time he was zipped up and wearing a suit and tie, but his sandy-blond hair, in the fashion of the time, was still scraggly and down to his shoulders.

"He started the conversation and said, 'My dad told me that I have to learn business from somebody who made their own money without inheriting it, and preferably he should be a Jew. That's why I'm here.'"

It was a pitch that Spielvogel, who was one of the Chosen People, has never forgotten. He tried to keep himself from laughing, or throwing the guy out.

Woody went on to say that he and his mother had "checked out" Spielvogel and learned that he was legitimate, had fit his late father's criteria—a Jew with no family fortune—and was "the kind of guy that could teach him 'bidness,' and that's how he said business, he called it 'bidness,'" says Spielvogel, still getting a laugh at Woody's pronunciation years later, but believing he was just trying to "sound cool."

Woody then told him that he had millions of dollars at his disposal, that he wanted to invest some of it, and that he was willing, if Spielvogel agreed, to have him as his business partner.

Woody then made quite an offer that Spielvogel eventually could not refuse.

He told him, "I'll give you ten percent of the first deal we do just to feel each other out, and twenty-five percent of everything thereafter."

Woody said, "I'll be responsible for the finances and the money and you be responsible to teach me 'bidness' and what to do and how to do it."

Processing what he was hearing, Spielvogel says he was flattered, still didn't really know to whom he was talking, but his gut feeling was it all sounded off-the-wall, unreal, and "very, very naïve." Who, he thought, makes an offer like that on the spot? "It was bizarre, but he was unsophisticated in business," recounts Spielvogel. "He had no street smarts. He didn't know how to do anything in business, or even in life, but he tried to look and sound important."

Spielvogel told Woody, "I'll get back to you," and offered to drive him back to the nearby Long Island airport for his return flight to Princeton. That's when he started to become a believer.

"On the tarmac was an impressive private plane. I waited with my mouth open while he took off."

Spielvogel returned to his office, called their mutual friend in Fort Lauderdale—"a rich playboy"—to check out his shaggy-haired visitor and to get the scoop. "I said, 'Who is this guy, Bob Johnson?' and he told me he was the heir to Johnson and Johnson, and he said, 'Michael, can I get in on this partnership, too?' "

The two met again in Florida and afterward Spielvogel was convinced that Woody "could deliver whatever we needed financially." At the time, Woody had access to as much as fifty million dollars (in mid-1970 dollars), which was quite a handsome sum, and he was due to get his next trust fund check when he turned thirty several years later.

Things moved quickly after that meeting.

Woody arranged for a partnership agreement to be drawn up by a Fort Lauderdale attorney, Alex A. Dow, a friend of the Johnson family, and their company, Woodric Enterprises—for the "Wood" in Robert Wood Johnson IV, and the "Ric" in Spielvogel's middle name, Richard—was incorporated. Beyond the generous percentage deal Woody had promised, Spielvogel also was given a salary of seven hundred dollars a week, and, he says, the title of executive vice president of Woodric. They rented an office suite with seventeen hundred square feet on the seventeenth floor of the fairly new Landmark Bank Building, then the tallest building in Fort Lauderdale, and outfitted it with custom-made office furniture purchased in Miami.

They were on their way.

They bonded fairly quickly. Woody's pet name for his new business partner was "Michael-ito," but Spielvogel called him Bob, or Robert. At the time, he recalls, only family members and very close friends used the nickname "Woody."

Until he found a place of his own, Spielvogel was permitted by Woody to stay in the guesthouse at the Johnson family's Bay Colony estate in Fort Lauderdale, Woody's mother's house, but only when she wasn't there.

"Bob was actually scared of his mother, and I don't mean that in a negative way. But he didn't defy her. If she said something, that was it."

Years later, the very private owner of the Jets spoke briefly about his mother to a reporter, saying in part, "She's pretty hard-core. She doesn't complain about anything. Her advice to me always was, 'When you're cold, put a jacket on. Stop complaining. When you're hot, take it off.' She's a pragmatic person. She's kind of like I am. She's on the side of fiscal responsibility. You've got to pay your bills."

Early in the partnership, Woody "had left tons of money in the bank and went away," says Spielvogel. "He said, 'Don't spend it all at once.' Robert was flying around the country for two or three weeks at a time, and enjoying himself. I bought into that. My job was to do the job, and Robert's job was to be Robert."

Spielvogel would later come to believe that Woody wasn't in business with him to actually make money.

"I don't think money motivated him. Woody was in partnership with me to learn business and play the game, and be able to grow up and be able to look sophisticated. He already had a fortune."

42

The Woodric partnership's first acquisition was five hundred acres of raw land in Melbourne, Florida, for two hundred and fifty thousand dollars, purchased with the idea of developing it, or selling off lots. A bigger deal was a one-hundred room Sheraton Inn in Boca Raton that had gone into foreclosure and that they got for a bargain price of three million and one dollars in an auction. The twelve-acre property included a helicopter, a small golf course, shops, and other amenities. It was soon converted into a Holiday Inn. "It was," says Michael Spielvogel looking back, "quite a property."

The moneyman and lead partner, Woody Johnson, liked the deal Spielvogel had made—it was his biggest in terms of investment—but he wanted no part of the helicopter. "He didn't want his name attached to it," says Spielvogel. "He didn't want the liability in case something happened, and someone would come after his money.

"Woody would think more about the consequences of how the family would think, and he was overprotective of who he was, almost to the point of not letting it be known that he was the one behind the development. He was afraid people would steal from him, or hurt him, paranoid that people were going to take advantage of him."

By holing up in Florida, by having Spielvogel as his front man, and remaining virtually anonymous under the Woodric corporate umbrella, Woody was insulating himself emotionally and professionally as best he could from his brothers' shenanigans, from the family scandals up north, even from any repercussions from his mother's divorce.

However, Woody couldn't keep his name or reputation completely pristine during the midseventies when he and Spielvogel were hustling business in South Florida. There were a couple of lawsuits involving fraudulent or misleading sales activity, and another involving Woody's personal failure to pay his own condominium association dues for a four-thousand-square-foot penthouse he had bought in the newly-built Corinthian on the Intracoastal in Fort Lauderdale. He was held in contempt of court.

After Woody became nationally known as owner of the New York Jets, *The New York Times* made mention of the two cases in a 2004 profile of the football mogul headlined: "Behind the Jets, a Private Man Pushes His Dreams," which described him back in the midseventies as an "unorthodox" risk-taker who "could be tough." He declined to be interviewed when the paper contacted him.

$ $ $

Despite all of the hustling, it wasn't all business for the young Woodric Enterprises partners.

The two spent many nights haunting South Florida's clubs and bars—favorites were a place called Brothers Three where major groups like Frankie Valli and the Four Seasons had gotten their start, and a babe-magnet spot called Bachelors—looking for women, and doing well.

"Bob and I were pigs. We were whoremasters," maintains Spielvogel. "There wasn't a day that we didn't have women at the house. Bob could get any woman he wanted. If you drove around in a Rolls-Royce Corniche convertible, and a rust-color Porsche Carrera that was his pride and joy, and lived in a multimillion-dollar house in Bay Colony, and had a guesthouse, and you were who you were—a Johnson heir—well, once the girls knew that they were putty in Woody's hands."

There was one young woman in Woody Johnson's life in the early to mid-1970s who didn't fit in any way, shape, or form in the bimbo, pickup, or one-night stand category.

Her name was Bonnie Tiburzi.

"They were in a hot and heavy relationship," says Spielvogel. "She was very pretty and a great catch, but Bob was also seeing other women."

Like Woody's great-aunt, the eccentric Evangeline Brewster Johnson, who had been an early-twentieth-century aviatrix, Tiburzi had a love of flying. And when she was twenty-four, she broke into the aviation all-men's club by becoming America's first woman commercial pilot for a major airline, American.

Tiburzi became famous at the time. Her promotion during the pro-feminist era of the midseventies became a major media story with cheeky newspaper headlines like: "She Flies by the Seat of Her Panties," and "American Beauty Is Rose in the Cockpit."

After an almost quarter-century career of piloting, Tiburzi retired in 1998.

Along the way, she had had one bad marriage, to another pilot, and then a good one—to Bruce Faulkner Caputo, who had been a one-term Republican U.S. Congressman from Yonkers, a New York City commuter district, and later a U.S. Senate candidate. But his political career crashed and burned when it became public that he had made inaccurate claims about his Vietnam War service.

In her 1984 memoir, *TAKEOFF!* Tiburzi reminisced about her career, and also chronicled her romance with Woody, who she identified as "Bob," because, as she emphasizes years later, "I didn't want to use the name Woody. Everyone would know who he really was. I wanted to protect his privacy."

Among a number of references to him in the book, she stated (with the help of a professional writer):

Bob was an attractive, unassuming, thoughtful guy who was trying hard to establish his own identity and career . . . He was ingenious, he had the resources and he needed to go places . . . Yet he could not completely understand that what I wanted was right for a woman. I'm not sure I even cared . . . I was obsessed with airplanes . . . Bob was his usual steadfast self, encouraging me to do what I felt I should and yet not wildly enthusiastic about my goals.

Reminiscing about Woody and Spielvogel in 2010, she says: "Woody was just an all-around great guy who had a beach boy look and was playful and fun. I always thought of Michael as being more serious than Woody. He was a let's-get-the-job-done business-type person who didn't laugh or joke like Woody. I saw him as a finger-snapping, gum-chewing guy, though I never actually saw him snap his fingers, or chew gum, but that was kind of his persona. Michael was *very* pivotal to Woody, getting him into business because Woody had ambition to do something different other than Johnson and Johnson."

Before she dated Woody, she had become a "buddy" of his brother Keith; they had been introduced by Guy Vicino, who was running one of his chic fashion boutiques in Fort Lauderdale. "I adored Keith but he was a bit bizarre and had an affected way, but with a lot of flair."

Keith knew class and style and recognized it when he saw it, and he saw it in Bonnie, who was then teaching flying at an airport in Pompano Beach. "I had a Cartier watch and I remember Keith pointing it out and saying, 'Oh, a flight instructor with a Cartier watch! Hmm. How fancy.' Most of my flight instructor friends, or my students, didn't know a Cartier from a Timex, but Keith certainly knew the difference."

Bonnie knew Guy was gay—"he was very flamboyant, I mean you just knew it, and he didn't hide it"—and she suspected Keith was, too, from his mannerisms and style. "He certainly had those airs," she says. But she was unaware, though, of his drug problem, she claims, and was "shocked"—*shocked*—when she learned he had overdosed and, as she understood, "they found a needle in his arm."

She had also heard "through one of the lawyers" that when Keith died he had left "an astronomical amount of money. It was just amazing—it was seventy million dollars."

She never got to know Woody and Keith's other ill-fated brother, Billy.

On one occasion, playing Cupid, Keith asked her if she wouldn't mind if he brought his big brother Woody along for dinner at a Chinese restaurant in Fort Lauderdale. "Woody showed up, and he was *so* cute, and the next day he called and asked me whether I was dating his brother, and I said no, and he said, 'Oh, then can I ask you out?' and I said yes. I adored Woody, and thought he was wonderful, a good all-around guy, just kind of *uncomplicated*. We pretty much dated for two or three years."

Bonnie was a tomboy growing up and a jock of sorts when she and Woody were seeing each other. They played tennis, went boating, and she learned to scuba dive in the Johnson's Bay Colony swimming pool. It was while they were in bathing suits that she first saw the glaring scar on his back. "It was huge—*huge*. He told me he had broken his back when he stepped off a ledge, or a rock, when he was in college, and he told me just because I had said, 'Oh, gosh *what* happened to you?" (Years later, she ran into him as he was walking toward his office in Rockefeller Center and she recognized him from behind because of his gait. "He sort of lists a little bit to one side. It was a permanent injury.")

Woody, she says, wasn't much of a romantic, never gave her gifts, or wrote her love letters, or brought her flowers. Because of his very private nature, he never opened up about the death of his father, which loomed large with him, his troubled brothers' escapades, or any of the other embarrassments and scandals of the Johnson dynasty. "We just had fun."

Bonnie had no expectations about a future with Woody, either, because her sole goal in life was to become a commercial airline pilot.

"I never thought, 'Oh, goody, if I marry this guy I'm going to have lots of money. I never thought, I'm sorry I didn't [marry him] because from the time I met him I was really so focused on flying, for good or for bad that was my direction, and I think Woody was trying to be on his own and do something with his life. Marriage was not in the cards."

Once she won her wings at American Airlines, they lost touch.

"I hope he was fond of me," she says decades later, "because I was certainly very fond of him."

One of the last times she was with him, he showed her a magazine, and in it was a photograph of Woody, Spielvogel, and an attractive young woman named Nancy Sale Frey.

"Everybody was wearing black T-shirts and wearing construction hats, and it had to do with one of their developments," Bonnie recalls. "He could have been dating her at the very same time he was dating me. He was a cute guy and I'm sure sparks probably flew."

43

When the construction of Woody Johnson and Michael Spielvogel's massive high-rise Runaway Bay condominium project in downtown Fort Lauderdale was completed, they required experts to help with the marketing, advertising, and sales of the apartment units.

Herbert A. Tobin & Associates, with an in-house staff of about twenty-five, was in the business of handling such projects "from womb to tomb," as its founder, Herbie Tobin, liked to boast. The firm had good genes.

Tobin's father, Ben, a Jewish immigrant from Russia, was a shrewd entrepreneur who, along with his partners, Alfred R. Glancy and Roger L. Stevens, the founding chairman of New York's Lincoln Center, acquired controlling interest in the Empire State Building in 1951, and had projects all over the country.

Spielvogel says he personally checked out the Tobin company before he brought Woody in for a meeting because "one of my functions was to insulate Robert from business deals."

To see what he was dealing with, Tobin toured Runaway Bay but wasn't impressed. As a funny promotional gimmick in the mid-1970s, Tobin's parent company, Ryerson & Haynes, had commissioned the comedian Henny Youngman to do his shtick on a record album entitled, *Take My Project, Please,* a play on Youngman's signature line, "Take my wife, please." The album cover showed Youngman fiddling while a row of high-rise buildings burned behind him.

After his inspection, Tobin thought Runaway Bay was a disaster waiting to happen, too, sales-wise.

"It really was a building that was not well conceived in terms of marketability," he says in 2010. "Their problem was there really weren't a lot of water views—the water was far off. It was a B-player in terms of an investment. The other problem was that the building needed to be sold in a rough real estate market. My business was *thriving* because there were people like Woody and Spielvogel in trouble."

When construction of Runaway Bay—named after a location in Jamaica—was started "it was a good market," maintains Spielvogel. "But it takes two to three years to complete. You have to have a good crystal ball."

Along with the complex, Tobin didn't think much of Spielvogel, who was generating bad reviews from everyone except Woody—that was still to come. "He was a nightmare, so I didn't think Woody always surrounded himself with the smartest people," observes Tobin. "He was a pushy kind of New York Jewish guy who did not reflect what you'd expect of a partner of a Johnson and Johnson heir. He was not the ambassador to St. James Court. He probably felt he caught a fat hog in the ass with Woody and that's pretty much what he had done. He was a real putz."

Not knowing the two well, Tobin was under the impression that the fast-talking Spielvogel had glommed on to the seemingly mild-mannered Woody, when it was really the other way around. What Tobin also didn't understand was that Woody was living vicariously through Spielvogel's bravado and his bluster just as he would decades later through Rex Ryan's Ralph Kramden bombast and braggadocio.

It took Tobin a while before he actually learned who Woody really was because he kept such a low profile, with Spielvogel out front.

"I never put together the Johnson part of his name with Johnson and Johnson. I eventually learned at some point after he became our client that he was an heir, and I thought, 'Holy shit!' For a kid who's been carried in a trust fund situation like him to have any kind of entrepreneurial fire in the belly was unique to me."

But Tobin quickly noted that Woody left mostly everything in Spielvogel's hands, acting more like a playboy than a businessman who had a lot of serious money riding on their Runaway Bay project. "Woody would take off into the wild blue yonder. He was never going to be the guy who was the day-to-day, do-the-job guy. He was going to have people doing all the work for him."

After Tobin had toured Runaway Bay and had met with the principals and had decided to take on the project, he called a staff meeting to brief his people about the job and what needed to be done.

Instantly, one of his most aggressive employees jumped up and volunteered to oversee the whole deal. Her name was Nancy Sale Frey, "a tiger woman" in her midtwenties "who got things done" and who had recently been promoted as one of Tobin's several young thirty-five-thousand-dollar-a-year vice presidents.

Tobin had hired Sailee, as she called herself, a year or so earlier when she was job-hunting after she had been laid off by her previous employer, Leadership Housing, said to have been her first job after she graduated from the University of Miami in 1971, where she had majored in education and psychology and played lots of tennis.

Job-hunting, she walked unannounced into the office of Herb's brother, Steve Tobin, who was then the sales manager for a project called Aventura, billed as Miami's version of Beverly Hills. While Steve Tobin didn't have any openings, he was impressed enough with her style, aggressiveness, ambition, and the experience she had in her previous job to recommend her to Herb, whose firm he, too, soon joined and where he worked closely with Nancy Sale Frey.

"She was very driven to be successful," says Herb Tobin, looking back, "and she achieved a very high level of financial success as a result of the events that took place in my company, meaning she met Woody Johnson, and she immediately pushed herself onto that project. I always thought she was *very* opportunistic *and* smart. She knew how to get what she wanted, and she got it. She said, 'I would like to work on that account.'

"She found a way to find out who Woody was," continues Tobin. "She saw an opportunity, she knew how to read situations, she saw vulnerability, and moved in and filled a void. I saw her interest. She *pushed* herself into that job. She hooked on to Woody, and the relationship grew legs. Somebody had to go hold hands with the client, and she did it—literally."

Many years later Nancy Sale Frey Johnson Rashad claims that it was Spielvogel who got her involved in the project because of how sexy she looked, and that she didn't jump in on it on her own, and had no agenda. "He saw me go into Herb's office and I was wearing a long chamois skirt with a slit up the front and I had long blond hair, and high platform shoes, and he told Herb that they wanted me to be the account person. I had no idea, really, who Woody Johnson was."

If anyone could get Runaway Bay up and running in terms of marketing and advertising, it was Sale Frey, a jock from a prominent Jewish St. Louis family who did her job as aggressively as she attacked opponents on the tennis courts at college. Sale's job was to shepherd Woody and Spielvogel's account, coordinating everything to make sure it would all happen, which she did, and Woody was duly impressed with her professionally and personally.

Tobin, however, was somewhat surprised that Woody had fallen for her, at least the physical aspect.

"She was not a knockout," in Tobin's eyes. "She put herself together, and she always dressed nicely, but she was kind of tomboyish. Today one might think she was a lesbian, but she liked guys. She was in her twenties and I was in my thirties, but I *never* thought of her as very attractive. She appealed to Woody because she had that look that he had been programmed to like. I thought he was a better-looking man than Sailee was a woman."

Beauty, however, is in the eye of the beholder, and Spielvogel takes credit for being the first to say, "Robert, I'd like you to meet Sailee, she'll be working with us—and that changed the whole course of his life." Spielvogel thought she was a knockout, and was attracted to her. But he knew he didn't stand a chance against his wealthy partner. "She made Christie Brinkley and Farrah Fawcett look like they were ugly. Anybody who thought differently had to be blind assholes."

Besides questioning Sale's physical attributes, or lack thereof, Tobin couldn't figure out Woody's appeal, either, other than his immense trust fund.

"I don't know how any woman could have gone for him back then. He was awkward socially, and was not a very aggressive kind of guy. He was so laid-back you'd almost have to stick a mirror under his nose to see if he was breathing."

Initially, Sale thought he was somewhat nerdy, but cute. "He definitely was not stylin','" she says looking back many years later, long after they were divorced. "He wore a cashmere blazer missing a button with the right-hand pocket ripped and the lining showed. When we first moved to New York he wore the same outfit until he eventually started having his suits made in London." What initially attracted her to him, she maintains, was that he seemed "responsible and stable and he had a goofy kind of humor that I thought was really funny."

His wealth, she claims, "didn't really register."

Tobin saw Woody as troubled, and "was really out there without a compass. He had no one to tell him what to do, or to give him direction. He had no experience. All he had was a bunch of money."

Sale stepped in and became Woody's "PalmPilot"—a determined young woman who could help him organize his life at a time when he was floundering around professionally and personally.

"Woody had a lot of shit going on in his life," says Tobin. "Sale was anal, organized. She could help Woody get his act together. He found her to be a comfort zone. And she had met a guy who was rich and who could offer her a ticket to ride. When she got with Woody, she shot right to the top and never looked back."

$ $ $

As Woody became more confident in the business world—"he absorbed like a sponge what I was teaching him," asserts Spielvogel—their partnership went from warm to cold seemingly overnight. Woody began bringing in new people who were loyal to him, such as the accountant Joel Latman—"another Jewish guy [who had done work for the Johnson family]," notes Spielvogel.

Woody also began taking advice from a new set of lawyers who, like others, didn't take to Spielvogel and wanted him out of the picture.

"They had a lot of meetings among themselves," he recalls. "They could sense it was time to get rid of me, that Bob didn't need to give twenty-five percent of all future business dealings to me. I believe they were telling him, you got your education in business, you don't need to pay for it the rest of your life."

Spielvogel suddenly was being treated more like an employee and a gofer than a twenty-five percent non-voting partner. After Woody's brother Billy died, for instance, Spielvogel was ordered to go to Hollywood to see what kind of assets and business he had. Spievogel refused, contending it had nothing to do with their deal and Woodric Enterprises.

When the insurance company that had the policy on Keith Johnson balked about paying, Spievogel, who was experienced in the insurance business, told Woody the company was acting within its rights. Woody felt he was siding with the enemy, and being disloyal to the Johnson family. "They were really bitterly mad at me. They felt I was interfering in something that I wasn't supposed to interfere in. They made it seem I was against the family."

Spielvogel, who had a hand in running things at the partnership's Holiday Inn, was soon replaced by an efficiency expert, which resulted in an angry confrontation. When Spielvogel refused to leave the hotel one afternoon, the police were called, he was handcuffed, and escorted off the premises. "I was just there in the hotel. I owned twenty-five percent of the fucking place. They said I didn't know what I was doing, that I was a detriment. We were bucking heads."

Without Spielvogel as a player, new partnerships were formed. One of them, headquartered in Pompano Beach, Florida, was incorporated as Pompano Systems, which was believed to have encompassed Woody's inherited cable TV business, and listed Woody as the director and president; Neil J. Burmeister, the late Keith Johnson's financial advisor, as secretary; and Joel Latman, who handled accounting. Like Latman, Burmeister remained as a principal in Woody's future investment and business enterprises under the umbrella of the Johnson Company, which he formed after he left Florida in the 1980s and moved to New York.

Woody had reportedly invested five hundred thousand dollars of his own money in the cable franchise. When it was sold for some ten million dollars, he was said to have walked away with an enormous but unknown profit.

Spielvogel was seeing a different Woody Johnson than the seemingly naïve guy who had come to his office virtually hat in hand several years earlier asking him to teach him "bidness" in return for a very nice slice of the pie.

"He became standoffish, icy, aloof."

Spielvogel filed a lawsuit, but says that in their final settlement he never saw one red cent of the percentage Woody had promised him and that was part of their formal partnership agreement. In the end, when the dust had settled, he agreed to fifty-five thousand dollars; one of the partnership's business cars, a Chevrolet Impala station wagon; and some office furniture.

In all, the partnership spent a total of eleven million dollars on investments, and Spielvogel claims Woody "made millions more" from those deals.

"I decided to settle because I had a house and a mortgage and suddenly I had no income. It all stopped. I was struggling really badly and at that point you'll take anything to pay your bills. I became a twenty-five percent nobody. But I don't blame Bob. I hold no grudges toward him."

After the partnership ended badly, Spielvogel had his ups and downs in business. But he and Woody would share one mutual tragedy. Like Woody, who lost his daughter, Casey, to drugs in 2010, Spielvogel's daughter, Debra, was murdered in 1998, and Spielvogel fell apart. Also like Woody, he had a second marriage with a younger woman and they had a child.

A year after Woody purchased the New York Jets in 2000, having long ago put his first business partner out of mind, Spielvogel got into some very serious trouble. In the late 1990s, he had gone back to school and earned a law degree, and had become a business consultant and an advisor to an African-American physician, Dr. James Scott Pendergraft, who owned five late-term abortion clinics in Florida.

Christian conservative anti-abortion elements in Marion County, who wanted to keep a Pendergraft clinic from opening there, came up with a list of allegations. In a complex case that pro-choice advocates have asserted was a way of using the judicial system to harass abortion providers, the black doctor was convicted of extortion, conspiracy, and mail fraud, as was his Jewish consultant Spielvogel, who also was accused of lying to the FBI, filing a false statement, and conspiracy.

The jury consisted of eight elderly women and four men, all but one of them white, and the two key government witnesses were members of a local Baptist church whose membership were pro-life advocates. Woody's former business partner didn't stand a chance, and served eight months behind bars before he was released after all but two of the charges against him were dropped on appeal, and he was hoping for a pardon on the remaining ones involving the FBI.

Spielvogel had had quite a tumultuous roller-coaster life since that day that Woody had come to see him. Looking back, he feels that the Band-Aid heir "got exactly what he bargained for—and more—from our partnership. He made millions of dollars, he learned how to spell 'bidness,' and he got a wife out of it."

As for Sale, he jokingly wonders, always the hustler: "Since I introduced them, maybe she should give me a commission for the megamillions she won meeting and marrying and divorcing Bob Johnson."

44

When Nancy Sale Frey was a freshman at the University of Miami she aggressively elected herself captain of the then-lowly women's tennis team, soon had a short-lived, tumultuous relationship with South African Patrick Cramer, one of the star players on the men's championship tennis team, and was named "Princess Sailee" in the Miss Ibis competition for the university's 1968 *Ibis* yearbook. Despite what others may have felt about her looks, she always had confidence that she was gorgeous.

She was one of five girls chosen from a group of about two dozen who had applied for the Miss Ibis pageant out of the entire school. The yearbook carried Alice in Wonderland–like photos of her. One had her looking pensive with a blue ribbon in her long, bleached blond hair, a string of pearls around her neck, gloss on her lips, and wearing a demure white top with a black design. The other had her posed against an exotic Banyon tree, offering the camera a Pepsodent smile, and wearing a black top, tight slacks imprinted with a black and white design, flat sandals, and with her blond tresses flowing down over each of her breasts. Her right leg was bent seductively, her sandaled foot against the tree trunk, her right hand resting suggestively on her thigh.

The panel of "celebrity" judges who had chosen her and the other four included a Miami Dolphins placekicker; a local radio disk jockey; a *Miami Herald* beauty editor; the vice mayor of Coral Gables, where the campus was located; and Sammy Spear, who was the leader of Jackie Gleason's TV show orchestra.

While the *Ibis* yearbook portrayed the event as important, it really wasn't. "It was open to anyone and everyone," recalls one of the other princesses, pretty, blond Irene Bangstrup, who had been the school's 1967 homecoming queen. "There weren't hundreds of women vying to be a princess, believe me. It was a one-shot deal."

But Sale Frey's selection may have gone to her head because later in life, after she became Mrs. Woody Johnson and a New York socialite, she often showed up in published reports described as a model, or former model.

For her tenth reunion in 1977 at University City High School in St. Louis, she submitted a written blurb about herself. In text worthy of a *Playboy* magazine centerfold, she informed her classmates that she was "presently a model and enjoys traveling, diving, and snow skiing," but gave no details about her claimed modeling. Around that time she had been working at the Tobin company where she first met Woody, but the Tobin brothers, who didn't think she was very attractive, say they were unaware of any modeling by their vice president. For her thirtieth high school reunion in 1997, writing in the third person, the Manhattan socialite and mother of three daughters stated that her background included "modeling internationally."

When her high school classmates read her responses their jaws dropped. "I was really surprised and wondered, where's this modeling stuff coming from," says Suzi Matlof, who remembers Nancy Frey as "skinny as skinny can be, like a rail actually, just straight down with no curves, and she was *just* okay looking. We *never* heard about her doing any modeling. She never did that in high school, and usually we would all hear something like that."

But the references to her signifying a big-time modeling career somewhere in the distant past continued.

In an October 2011 *New York Times* profile of her two surviving daughters, Jaime and Daisy, headlined, "Trying to Outrun Wealth and Fame," that image was still perpetuated when, once again, she was described in the second paragraph as "a former model," which may have left *Vogue* catwalk images in readers' minds.

It was nothing on that order.

Nancy Sale Frey Johnson Rashad concedes that her career was minimal at best, and happened just after college. "We're not talking Christy Turlington here," she admits in 2012. "We're not talking New York, high-fashion runway. We're talking about a runway in a Florida department store, and the designer would be brought in to do shows."

She says she also was cast as an extra in a South Florida TV commercial for Chevrolet, but she wasn't the spokesmodel. "The car went through a gas station and I was wearing cut-off jeans and a top and I had long blond hair and I think I roller skated through," she recalls. She also appeared for a time on a billboard on Interstate 95 in the Sunshine State for Costa Rican tourism. "But we're talking forty years ago."

$ $ $

If anyone's face could have graced the cover of a glamour magazine because of her natural beauty, it was actually Nancy Sale Frey's mother, Mary Melisse Nemeth Frey, Woody Johnson's future mother-in-law.

Dr. Ed Saltzman, a longtime friend of the Frey family, "an older big brother" to, and confidant of, Woody and Nancy's before, during, and after their marriage—and the pediatrician of their firstborn daughter, Casey—swears Melisse resembled the stunning Academy Award–winning actress Olivia de Havilland.

"Melisse was absolutely beautiful—I mean *beautiful*."

With her strawberry-blond hair, blue-green eyes, ivory skin, perfect features, and shapely figure, she was a knockout and, according to a close relative, that caused issues between mother and daughter. "Nancy's problem was that she got sick of everybody telling her how gorgeous her mother was. Nancy was perceived as an ugly duckling compared to her mother. She had a very handsome, accomplished older brother and an adorable younger brother and she was the homely child in between. When she was young she would not identify with anything feminine. She only wanted to do athletic things—ride horses, play tennis. She wanted to be a boy."

Years later Sale acknowledges that the domestic life was never her thing, and by marrying into the Johnson dynasty she always had servants at her beck and call. "I didn't want to be a homemaker like my mother. I didn't want to go grocery shopping, or cook. I wanted to be in business, do sports, and Woody never said anything."

Woody's future mother-in-law—who would use her middle name, Melisse, which had a classier ring to it than Mary, just as her daughter used her middle name, Sale—was a first-generation American of blue-collar immigrant Hungarian stock on her father's side and Czech on her mother's side.

Melisse's parents, James and Mary Nemeth, raised chickens in the backyard of the modest multifamily home where they once had lived on the main street that ran through the western New Jersey town of Phillipsburg, across the Delaware River from Pennsylvania.

P'Burg, as it was known, was where a number of college and professional football players had grown up, such as Jim Ringo, a Hall of Fame center who played in the 1950s and '60s for the Green Bay Packers and the Philadelphia Eagles. The town also blossomed some beauties. Along with the Nemeths' daughter, Melisse, who the local boys all chased, P'Burg was hometown to a buxom blond bombshell named Vera Jayne Palmer—better known later as the actress and *Playboy* centerfold Jayne Mansfield.

While the Nemeths always lived no more than an hour from the Princeton estate where their granddaughter Sale's first husband, Woody, was raised, they were always a social and economic world away, and were rarely included in the Johnson's elite circle.

Melisse's father, born April 14, 1890, had arrived in the United States in 1908, and had registered as an alien in 1917, and through his life James Nemeth had held a series of manual labor jobs; he worked in the coal mines of Pennsylvania; he had been an ironworker for the American Horse Shoe Company; he was a teamster and drove a truck; and during World War II, he was employed at the Picatinny Arsenal in North Jersey that turned out bombs and artillery shells.

His wife, Mary Hlavcsek, whom he married when she was nineteen and he was twenty-six, had been born on Christmas Eve in 1896 in Czechoslovakia. She came to the United States in 1913, five years after her husband. Her first child had died in the great flu epidemic of 1918.

The Nemeths had little or no formal schooling, but learned to speak, read, and write rudimentary English; she better than he. They were members of the Jehovah's Witness sect.

James and Mary were the future maternal great-grandparents of the wealthy Johnson & Johnson heiresses and socialites—Woody and Sale's progeny—Casey, Jaime, and Daisy Johnson.

As a family member notes, "James was a very self-sufficient immigrant, a hard-working, simple kind of guy who was handy around the house and even resoled his children's shoes," while his great-granddaughter, Casey, was known to buy dozens of thousand-dollar-a-pair Manolo Bhlaniks in one fell swoop, and usually wore each pair just once.

Many Hungarian immigrants like the Nemeths had settled in New Jersey, and the Johnson & Johnson company had close ties to the Magyar community, and hired many of them to work in the New Brunswick plant; at one point a third of that city's population had Hungarian blood, and 66 percent of Johnson & Johnson's employees had Hungarian roots.

"The Johnsons liked the Hungarians. They were hard-working and honest . . . Before long, the company came to be known as the 'Hungarian University,'" according to Lawrence Foster. Woody's grandfather, Robert Wood Johnson Jr., the General, once boasted that he had "many close friends among the Hungarian people," who invited him to family events such as weddings and christenings. One disgruntled Hungarian employee, however, wasn't so friendly; he tried to extort thousands of dollars from the company, with the threat of blowing up Johnson & Johnson's headquarters. He was arrested before any damage was done.

Melisse, born in 1922, was Mary Nemeth's middle child. A sister, Helen, was two years older, and a brother, Louis, four years younger, died in his late twenties. Helen Nemeth married a veterinarian, Harry Alexander Roney, who served as the chief veterinarian for the New Jersey Civil Defense and Disaster Control Division for two decades beginning right after World War II, and Helen had worked as a bookkeeper for the *New Jersey Herald*. They had a son, Alexander, a teacher, who was one of Sale's cousins.

But it was Helen's sister, the gorgeous, body-beautiful Melisse, who at twenty-three hit the jackpot with her marriage.

In the summer of 1945, when President Truman ordered the atomic bombing of Hiroshima and Nagasaki that forced the surrender of the Japanese,

Melisse, a high school graduate, was working as a beautician at the Richard Hudnut Beauty Salon on Fifth Avenue in Manhattan.

The salon catered to society women, and one of Melisse's duties, with her glowing, radiant skin, was to demonstrate and promote Hudnut's product line called the DuBarry Beauty Ritual Kit, which sold for one dollar and fifty cents and included DuBarry Cleansing Cream, Skin Freshener, and Foundation Lotion for, as the DuBarry advertising declared, "an alluring dawn-to-dusk protective film. Even while you sleep, there's a special rich cream to pamper your pores! Follow your DuBarry Beauty Ritual faithfully, daily. Be the Beauty that makes men ask, 'Who Is She?' "

One of the men who approached Melisse Nemeth as she strolled down Fifth Avenue one afternoon during her lunch break that end-of-the-war summer in 1945 and asked who *she* was, was a tall, handsome navy lieutenant in uniform on his final leave.

His name was Robert David Frey, and he and Melisse had come from two different worlds. He was the son of a prominent Jewish attorney and former circuit judge in St. Louis, Abraham B. Frey, and the former Riette Sale. Nancy Frey would use her paternal grandmother's maiden name throughout her adult life, and it was the name that she would bestow upon her and Woody's firstborn, Sale Trotter Case Johnson, known as Casey. Abe Frey was president of the reform Congregation Shaare Emeth in St. Louis, and Riette Sale Frey was active in the city's Jewish community; she was a leader in the Shaare Emeth Sisterhood, was a member of the Jewish Hospital Auxiliary, and a member of the National Council of Jewish Women.

"My brother Bob, who was still in the navy, but just getting out, and my brother Richard, and their friend Sy Aronson were in New York and saw Melisse walking down the street, and Robert thought she was really attractive, and he stopped to chat with her," recounts Mary Frey Hickman decades later. "Melisse, who was still using the name Mary at the time, and who was a cosmetologist, thought he was *very* attractive, too, and she ended up with Robert, and she married him."

If things had turned out differently two years earlier, Bob Frey might not have made it home in one piece, or at all.

The headline in the *St. Louis Post-Dispatch* dated December 30, 1943, read: "St. Louisan Rides Atop Tank Under Fire to Help Save Bombed Ship."

Frey, then a twenty-six-year-old ensign and an assistant gunnery officer, had taken the borrowed army tank through a "shower of shrapnel," according to the report, "to reach his damaged ship moored to a jetty in Palermo harbor" after German bombers blew up stores of ammunition.

He was serving aboard the destroyer *Mayrant,* and his bunkmate was a naval lieutenant by the name of Franklin D. Roosevelt Jr., the wartime president's twenty-nine-year-old son, who was in command during the fierce attack. Frey was honored with the Legion of Merit, one of the first junior officers in the navy to have been so decorated during the war.

With the war finally over, all those lucky boys like Bob Frey who came home in one piece were getting married to all those pretty girls who had kept the homefront fires glowing as Rosie the Riveters in defense plants or, in Mary Melisse Nemeth's case, had kept the faces of Manhattan's Upper East Side matrons glowing beautifully, or tried to, with DuBarry's Beauty Ritual.

Three days after Thanksgiving 1945, their engagement was announced in *The New York Times,* with a photo of the striking "Miss Mary Melisse Nemeth," and details about the couple, including the fact that Lieutenant Frey was an alumnus of the University of Illinois and the Harvard Graduate School of Business Administration, class of 1940.

Eleven days later, on December 8, the knockout gentile beautician from a poor immigrant family in New Jersey and the handsome Jewish naval officer from a prominent family in St. Louis tied the knot at Manhattan's Commodore Hotel in a ceremony presided over by New York Municipal Court Judge Abraham Goodman. Melisse's sister, Helen, was the maid of honor, and Bob's brother Richard was best man.

Just a month earlier, one of their other brothers—there were four in all—Army First Lieutenant William Howard Frey, had married the first of his three wives, Brena Feldman, the heiress daughter of one of the owners of the Atlanta-headquartered Puritan Chemical Company, whom he met while he was stationed in the south. Bill Frey would rise to president and bring Bob and his brothers into the company.

When Melisse married Bob Frey and moved up in the world, her family in rural New Jersey felt "a little animosity" toward her, according to a family member. "They felt abandoned, and Melisse's sister, Helen, ended up taking care of their parents. But Melisse couldn't wait to get the fuck out of Dodge, and Bob Frey was her ticket out of that small town, provincial life."

$ $ $

Bob Frey took his bride home to the Gateway to the West city where Mary Melisse Nemeth Frey was welcomed warmly by some close friends of the Frey family, and scorned by others mainly because she wasn't Jewish and had come from poor roots.

"Bob came home with this total shiksa, but the darndest thing was she had more Jewish soul than he ever did," asserts family friend Lois Caplan Miller. "If there ever was a trophy bride, it was Melisse. She was blond and beautiful and had a great shape, and a big smile, and big boobs, and we became friends. I think *everybody* loved her because she was warm and outgoing and gracious."

Not everybody.

Others felt Bob Frey had gone off the deep end by marrying her, and rejecting his Jewish, upscale roots.

"Here he was from an aristocratic family, highly educated, highly thought of in the community, very big in the society of giving and philanthropy, and he was bringing home this unknown girl of a different religion who had kind of a low-class background, but was gorgeous, and *everyone* was shocked," observes a Frey family confidant.

Everyone, it seemed, had an opinion about her.

A year after Bob and Melisse got hitched, she gave birth to the first of their three children, a son whom she named James Louis, the boy's middle name in honor of her brother who had died early. Her second, born in 1949, was Nancy Sale, who was given her middle name by Bob in honor of his mother. Melisse's third and last was named Alan and given the middle name Benjamin in homage to Judge Frey.

Nancy's brothers—Woody Johnson's future brothers-in-law—were thought by everyone in the Frey's circle to be handsome, brilliant, and successful.

Jimmy, as he was called, got his medical degree at Duke University and became a neurologist with a specialty in vascular neurology. He would become affiliated with the Barrow Neurological Institute in Phoenix where Woody had been treated after his near-crippling back injury.

Alan B. Frey was a Princeton University Postdoctoral Fellow in molecular biology, and became an associate professor in the department of cell biology at the New York University Langone Medical Center, and lived with his family in Woody's hometown of Princeton, and for a time in Highland Park, where the General years earlier had been the young mayor.

Of the three Frey siblings, though, it was Nancy who would become a boldface name, a New York socialite, and very wealthy beyond anyone's imagination when she became a Johnson dynasty wife.

Bob Frey bought a comfortable late-1920s Tudor-style home with four bedrooms, three baths, and a one-car detached garage that was furnished with some of his mother's hand-me-down antique furniture. The Frey home was at 517 Midvale Avenue in the pleasant University Hills section of University City, a tree-lined neighborhood in St. Louis populated with doctors, dentists, and academics who taught at nearby Washington University.

Despite the Frey family wealth and position in the St. Louis Jewish community—the earlier generation of Frey brothers, including Nancy's father, were delivered to school in a chauffeured limousine and grew up in an eighteen-room mansion on St. Louis's posh Lindell Boulevard—Bob Frey was rather conservative in his own lifestyle. "Bob and Melisse were not living the high life," observes family friend Lois Caplan Miller, who was a columnist for the *St. Louis Jewish Light.* "They lived a kind of ordinary middle-class life."

Woody Johnson's future brother-in-law virtually disappeared for five days a week, returning only on weekends, as the workaholic sales manager who was successfully hawking sanitary maintenance chemicals for the Puritan Company, in Atlanta, of which his brother William had become president.

Unlike his father and grandfather, both highly respected attorneys and judges, Bob was strictly business-minded, a born hustler with a Harvard MBA in economics and a degree in business administration. At Puritan, he went to work in sales, and when the company opened an office in St. Louis he vigorously ran the sales branch, traveling up and down the East Coast.

With Bob constantly traveling, Melisse was left to run things at home, responsible for the early upbringing of her three children.

Possibly overcompensating for the meager surroundings in which she had grown up, Melisse became the epitome of a zealous Stepford housewife. Not only was she gorgeous like the robotic wives in the film, she also was a meticulous Stepford housekeeper who obsessively set the breakfast table perfectly the night before, and even made sure the front lawn was green year-round by having it spray-painted in the winter.

Melisse also embraced her husband's Judaism with a vengeance, converted, and became very active in the Frey family's temple, Shaare Emeth, and at one point was head of the Sisterhood, and celebrated every Jewish holiday. But her daughter, Sale, who converted to Episcopalian before she married Woody, recalls that her mother "listened to church music when my father was away."

As a doting and driven mom, Melisse became the leader of Nancy's Girl Scout troop, ran it with a firm hand—and woe to any of the girls who got out of hand. One of the projects she asked the troop to perform was to make cushions, Martha Stewart–like, for when they sat on dirt around the campfire. One of the scouts, whose parents had run summer camps, had questioned the project, asking, "Why don't we just sit on the ground?" Melisse went ballistic, took it as an affront to her authority, and called the girl's parents and told them, "Debby's not right for the Girl Scouts. She talks back too much."

At the same time, Melisse had little control over her own daughter, who was rebelling against her, and generally against authority, in typical teenage fashion.

While still in high school, she had worked part time at a popular young woman's clothing store called the Honeybee in nearby Clayton, Missouri, that was considered *the* place to shop for preppy apparel such as Villager and Lady Bug things, which was Nancy's style—crewneck sweaters, oxford shirts, kilts, Peter Pan collars, short plaid skirts, kneesocks.

A close Frey relative claims that Nancy's father discovered that his daughter had "sticky fingers" when she worked there.

"Bob came home one day and he walked into Nancy's room and happened to open her closet and there were just piles and piles of these gorgeous things, just piled up, and he asked her where it all came from because she didn't have the money to buy it, and he and her mother didn't give her the money to buy it," claims the Frey relative. "Bob told me she didn't pay for the things, that she took them. When he asked her about it, Nancy thought what she had done was cute, that she was able to sneak things out of the store."

Years later, in 2012, Nancy Sale Frey Johnson Rashad adamantly denies ever shoplifting, and declares, "I spent *every* penny I ever earned there, and all of my allowance of fifteen dollars a month or whatever it was, so I could buy things, and I got a thirty percent discount, and I don't think my father *ever* went into my closet."

45

If Nancy Sale Frey didn't exactly inherit her mother's dazzling looks, she most definitely was her father's daughter in every way. Her aunt, Mary Frey Hickman, for one, says, "Robert was certainly bright, and he was opportunistic. Nancy learned at her daddy's knee."

After seeing her in action working with Woody Johnson, Herb Tobin says he knew immediately whom she took after. "She looked like her father and she acted like her father. Sailee and Bob were similar—they both had the attitude of 'go get 'em!'"

When the Atlanta-headquartered family chemical company for which Bob Frey was working was sold in the early 1970s, he went into the stockbroker-training program in his early fifties at A. G. Edwards & Sons, in St. Louis, and quickly rose to the position of senior vice president of investment management. He made millions of dollars for his clients because of his obsessive stock research. Even more, he became an expert in designing portfolios that permitted his clients to shelter their money to avoid paying high taxes.

"Bob Frey was a guy who oftentimes had money in the things he was telling you to buy," emphasizes Tobin, "and that's what made him unusual—he had skin in the game. Every time you talked to him, he was trying to sell you something. You couldn't say, 'Well, I'll think about it.' He'd hound you."

Tobin and his entire family had become Bob Frey's clients based on a recommendation from his daughter. Even Rabbi Jeffrey Stiffman, of

Congregation Shaare Emeth, of which Frey was president, put his money with him to invest. "He studied voraciously, and was dedicated to his clients," said the clergyman, who would give a eulogy at a memorial service for Frey, who died in early August 2010 at the age of ninety-two. "He was one of the most driven people I've ever known."

However, one very important person in his life who didn't give him his business was surely the wealthiest of his clients—his future son-in-law, Woody Johnson, and that, along with some other issues he had with his daughter's first husband, would provoke resentment on Frey's part for years.

$ $ $

Melisse Frey had wanted Nancy to go to a better college than the hard-partying University of Miami, but she was out-voted because her daughter was able to convince her doting father into allowing her to go there because she could play tennis as much as she wanted. He rarely said no to his little girl.

No one dreamed that while she was living in the Sunshine State she would meet and marry one of the wealthiest eligible bachelors in America.

Before Nancy Sale Frey arrived to begin her freshman year in September 1967, her mother called close Frey family friend Dr. Ed Saltzman, a prominent pediatrician in South Florida's Gold Coast—also a client of Bob Frey's—and asked him to keep a watch on her daughter "in case she had any problems, sort of be a big brother to her," he says.

"When Nancy got here she was a very simple little girl, an unassuming Missouri hayseed, but in her own inner self she was very strong and that soon became quite apparent," Saltzman observes. "With me, she was very sweet and soft and clingy at times, but she had a very tough personality. She was aloof and driven like her father. She got a dollar and ten cents' value out of a dollar. She could be an unlikable person."

Nevertheless, Saltzman, at least two decades her senior, would become a close confidant of Nancy's, which is the name he knew her by until after she married Woody. One day she told him, 'I'm now Sale, so call me Sale.' " He also played the role of a sometime surrogate father to Woody. And he was the pediatrician who cared for their first child, Casey. Through the years he would hear from Sale and even Woody about their own marital relationship issues, from their courtship in the mid-1970s, to which he was an eyewitness, to their breakup and divorce in the early 2000s. When he could, he offered fatherly advice and sage counsel.

Not long after Nancy arrived in Miami, she called Saltzman with a medical problem. Even though she seemed to play tennis around the clock, she had found herself walking with a slight limp, and suffered serious leg pains. Her friends on the men's tennis team at the University of Miami had noticed her gait and assumed one of her legs was shorter than the other, or that she was slightly pigeon-toed. But it was a bit more serious. However, the orthopedists who examined her could find nothing wrong, told her it was all in her head, and advised her to see a psychiatrist.

"I said to her, 'You're *not* crazy,' and I recommended a specialist I knew for her to see," says Saltzman. "The doctor called me, believed her symptoms, and asked for my okay to do exploratory surgery because this was in the days before the CAT scan. He found a neroma, a nerve tumor that was benign, and removed it, and she was then okay. After that Nancy thought I was magical. She thought I invented the anatomy book."

Besides seeking medical opinions, she brought by a few young men she was dating to get her favorite doctor's opinion and approval on whether they were acceptable, thus making Dr. Saltzman kind of a Dr. Drew on her love life.

One of her serious boyfriends was the son of a department store executive, whom she fell for a few weeks into her sophomore year. He was so good-looking, she says, "that he couldn't pass a plate window without checking his profile. We'd go to a party and people would look at *him*. It wasn't good for my confidence, and I had [bleached] blond hair down to my waist, and wore short skirts the length of tennis skirts, and platform shoes that made me six feet tall."

Despite the narcissistic competition for attention, they dated steadily through college. After they graduated, her boyfriend became a contractor with associates who Sale says had shady ties. The two lived together in a one-bedroom condo in a complex that he and his partners had built and in which Bob Frey had made an investment. With the profit he bought his daughter one of the units. At the same time Sale had enrolled at the Allstate Construction College, which advertised in the classified sections of South Florida newspapers, offering courses leading to state-mandated contractor licenses.

Like her boyfriend, she wanted to be a builder and cash in on the Sunshine State's construction boom.

While her relationship with her boyfriend had started going down-hill—he could be violent, she claims—she had bonded with one of his business partners, "who was like my protector."

The grandfatherly-looking partner, according to Sale, was "mob-related, and had been in San Quentin and Leavenworth for many years over a period of time, but he was the world's nicest guy. He hadn't killed anybody. He was like an extortionist kind of person." Another associate in the company, she says, was a Sicilian who "loved to play up that role—not like the I-am-going-to-kill-you role, just the Sicilian role."

Her boyfriend wanted to marry Sale, but one night "he picked up my steel construction manual, which weighed about ten pounds, and threw it so hard while he was screaming at me that it stuck in the drywall in my apartment. So that night I decided, okay, that's it, we're breaking up."

But her friendship with the elderly partner continued, even after he was sent up again and was an inmate at the federal penitentiary in Atlanta. "I visited him constantly," she says. "I'd drive up in my little Mercedes convertible with my schnauzer and spend the night with my aunt and uncle, and I would go see him even when his kids wouldn't visit him. I showed up one time in a very fitted blue jean jumpsuit and a cowboy hat and boots," she vividly recalls, "and he wrote me a letter saying, 'Well, you were a big hit. You give all the guys kind of a thrill every time you come.'" She sent him photos of herself with which he festooned his cell. Years later she observes, "I did a lot of stuff as a young person I can't believe I did. I had this confidence that I could do pretty much whatever I wanted."

The next VIP in her life was far more white bread, and far wealthier. Saltzman immediately liked Woody and found him both "*mensch*-like but at the same time very furtive and secretive. He needed me because I added a certain maturity to his life. He had business advisors, but he needed guidance in personal areas. He had *no* idea of social structure at all. He wasn't sophisticated. What did he ever see in life? He saw nothing. His mother, I gather, was cold and involved with her life. She ran the dynasty and felt everybody was after her money, and she taught Woody that everybody was out to get *his* money. So he was always very careful."

One evening Woody and Sale were having a potluck dinner at Eddie and Joni Saltzman's home. Around eight o'clock, the telephone rang. It was the mother of one of the pediatrician's patients, a famous mother—1971's Miss America, Phyllis George, who was then part of the cast of the popular CBS Sports program *The NFL Today*. One of her two children was sick and she wanted Dr. Saltzman to come over and see what the problem was.

"So I went over and played doctor and I got home about ten o'clock and I was surprised to see that Woody's car was still there. They had waited because, like teenagers, they wanted to know everything there was to know about Phyllis George—what was she like? Was she really as pretty in person? What was the house like? That kind of stuff. I was stunned, and it said something about their interests in celebrity."

Some years later, when they were married and were living the high life in New York, the Johnson dynasty couple would finally become part of their own fawning celebrity and society set. But in Florida before their marriage, and during the early years of it, Woody and Sale had few friends. Woody, who was introverted, mostly palled around with Michael Spielvogel, until he was axed, and hung out with his longtime friend from childhood, the gay boutique owner and interior decorator Guy Vicino.

He also stayed in close touch with his one trusted bosom buddy and fraternity brother at the University of Arizona, Gary Johnson, with whom, back in their hard-partying college days, they were known as the Dupree Brothers. Gary had married Woody's ex-college girlfriend, Diane Vonderahe, who had been with "BJ," as she called him, the inebriated night when he broke his back and was left nearly paralyzed, while on the way to a party in Phoenix at Gary Johnson's parents' home. Woody was subsequently the best man at Gary and Diane's wedding, and had gone on a treacherous white-water rafting trip on the Colorado River with them right after his back had sufficiently healed, risking further injury if an accident had happened. Gary and Diane, who had a daughter, had gotten divorced after eight years of marriage just around the time Woody and Sale were a serious item, and the couples, although living on different coasts, tried to get together as often as possible.

"The first time I met Sale was when Gary and I went down to BJ's place in Florida," Vonderahe says years later. "We went to Super Bowls together, and we went on a cruise with them to the Caribbean. That's when I told Sale that I kind of knew they were going to get married because I could tell she was just a *very* in-charge person, and BJ was really fascinated with her in the sense that she really took control of things, and he definitely needed someone like that because he never really changed from when I knew him in college." Sale, she says, was never a favorite of Gary's, and he told that to Woody because "she was not an easy person to like."

(Woody remained lifelong friends with Gary Johnson, a one-time Phoenix corporate meetings planner, whose claim to fame was as the creator of Topless Golf, featured on the cover of *Playboy*'s March 2001 issue, a year after Woody had bought the Jets and was divorcing Sale. Inside was a titillating layout of buxom girls—dubbed the "All American Topless Golf Team"—who were photographed in living color exposing their ample breasts and fondling phallic woods and irons on a golf course. Woody's pal was quoted as saying, "[W]hy not hire beautiful women to be your golfing buddies . . . ? Better yet, why not hire topless beautiful women?")

While Woody had Gary Johnson as a chum, Sale had no close girlfriends to speak of, Saltzman had observed, and thought it was strange. He later came to realize that "women didn't like her because of her toughness," which had manifested itself at times on the golf course. "The other women *hated* her because she was not friendly. She wouldn't make small talk, or be social. She just wanted to win, and she did."

Saltzman wasn't the only Jewish fatherly-type who Woody had bonded with during that time. Another was Irving Shepard, who also was a good friend of Sale's parents and a client of her father's, and who lived in South Florida. Some three decades Woody's senior, Shepard was a charming, well-to-do businessman who in his younger days had been an airplane company's chief test pilot, and as he aged he was a tanned, happy-go-lucky chap originally from St. Louis who was living large under the Florida sun when Sale introduced him to Woody, and Shepard introduced "the goyish millionaire" to a delicacy Woody never knew existed.

"We had been playing golf and afterwards Woody was hungry so I took him to a Jewish deli—he'd never been in one before—and he ordered paté of all things. The old Jewish waiter didn't know what he was talking about, so I said, 'Give him chopped liver.' He thought it tasted great and he said, 'Why have *you people* been hiding this all this time?' He thought the Jewish people were hiding good food like chopped liver from the gentiles."

At the time, Woody was a member of the very exclusive Coral Ridge Country Club, in Fort Lauderdale, whose golfers over the years included President Dwight D. Eisenhower, golf Hall of Fame's Julius Boros, "Buffalo" Bob Smith of TV's *Howdy Doody* program, along with such VIP guests as Bing Crosby, Bob Hope, Johnny Carson, and the Jets superstar Joe Namath. Also members were Woody's mother, her brother, Dr. Keith Wold and his wife, Elaine, the Johnson & Johnson heiress who was one of J. Seward Johnson Sr.'s daughters.

Shepard had played with Woody at Coral Ridge a number of times, had become enamored of the club's luxe, "and after a while I said to Woody that maybe I should join. He looked at me kind of surprised and said, 'Irving, you wouldn't like it.' Now I'd been around long enough, and I'd been Jewish long enough, to know what that meant—restricted. It turned out that of the several hundred members there were probably two or three Jews, so the club could say they had Jewish members.

"I never did join."

46

D r. Ed Saltzman, who was frequently in Woody and Sale's company when they lived in Fort Lauderdale, saw that she wore the pants in their re- lationship. "She's the one who would say, 'Woody, we can't do this, or Woody, we can't do that, or Woody, it doesn't make sense, or Woody, we don't want to do that, or Woody, I don't care what *they* tell you, I'm not going to do that with you, and you're *not* going to do it!' "

In Sale's own words, written in her 1997 high school reunion update, she stated that she and Woody had dated for a very long "five years" before they were married. She didn't give the reasons for their lengthy courtship, but they mainly had to do with alleged problems Woody was having.

"Woody had habits that weren't necessarily approved by society," asserts Saltzman, who firmly believed that the Johnson heir had an addictive person- ality. "I know he did a lot of partying, and Sale put a stop to all of that. She was in *total* control. She just was *so* strong. She used to say to me, 'Either Woody stops, or I'm gone!' And he stopped the drinking—and I'm talking about *heavy* drinking—and he became a solid citizen because of her. Sale had a *lot* to do with Woody growing up."

But Sale, looking back almost four decades later, didn't believe she forced Woody to do anything. "He turned himself around. I just said to him, 'I don't see myself spending a lifetime with somebody who drinks, or who smokes.' But I was not saying he had to do this, or do that. He just went cold turkey."

At one point during their courtship, Sale broke it off for a number of months, and dated two others, including an award-winning advertising art director connected to the Tobin company who tragically died from cancer during their relationship. "Whether her breakup with Woody had to do with his substance abuse or not, whether she just wanted his personality to be different, she just wanted to cool it," says a close family member. "Maybe she was afraid of committing to him and she wanted to test the waters."

Fearing he might lose her, Woody made a trip to St. Louis in his private plane to try to convince her father to get her to marry him.

Just as Woody would hire shrewd, tough business advisers and lawyers to do his bidding, just as he would have an aggressive, boastful coach like Rex Ryan for his Jets, he needed a woman with an iron fist in a not so velvet glove, and Nancy Sale Frey fit the profile.

By mid-1977, Sale felt Woody was sufficiently under her control, and in control, to finally accept his proposal of marriage.

Besides being able to organize Woody's life and help get his act together, she believes that he wanted to marry her because "he was looking for a woman who was similar to his mother," observes Sale, who felt she met the profile. "Betty Johnson was from the Midwest and was a very solid person, and I was from the Midwest and I was a very solid person."

As preparations for the wedding were under way, there were embarrassing goings-on facing both the Johnsons and the Freys. The New York City murder-for-hire plot involving Mary Lea Johnson Ryan D'Arc was still in the tabloid headlines, as well as her sexual exploits, and in St. Louis, Sale's father out of the blue was separating from her mother and, after some three decades of marriage, they were heading for an unpleasant divorce. The once beautiful Melisse Frey had lost her looks in her fifties due to a serious hyperactive thyroid condition that made her eyes bulge and caused her to lose her figure, which only got worse because of mistreatment of her condition. Later, in her sixties, she began to show the early signs of Alzheimer's, the same disease that had claimed her mother relatively early in life and Melisse's sister, Helen.

Bob Frey met a younger and more glamorous woman, Dolores Plattner Wool, called Dodie, a Jewish divorcee with two children, who became the second Mrs. Robert Frey in 1981.

"Bob and Melisse just kind of grew apart, and he just sort of fell out of love with her," says a Frey family confidant. "Melisse was blindsided and didn't understand why he would leave her. When Bob got together with Dodie, Melisse harassed them with phone calls, called her a whore. It was terrible."

Sale came to despise her father's new wife, irrationally so, say those who knew both, which caused tension and fights between Bob and his daughter for years. "We never considered her part of our family," Sale says after her father's death. "This lady was very Jewish and very controlling."

Because of those dark clouds, Woody and Sale waited a bit longer before tying the knot.

While Melisse was devastated about the breakup of her own marriage, she was overjoyed with their daughter's impending nuptials "because it was going to be a different life for Nancy with stables of horses and homes all over the world and servants and *huge* money," recalls close family friend Francis Brownstein. "I saw them in Florida when they were engaged and Nancy was beaming with happiness and joy because she had snagged this guy." The *St. Louis Jewish Light* columnist Lois Caplan Miller had learned about the engagement from Melisse and Bob, "and what I heard was, 'My Nancy's going to marry *the* richest man in the world!'"

But Bob Frey actually had qualms about Woody. His fortune notwithstanding, Bob didn't think the Band-Aid heir was strong, or bright, or accomplished enough for Nancy, and felt that his daughter needed someone more interesting in her life.

Still, everything seemed to be going according to plan wedding-wise when suddenly Woody's attorney and trustee, Seymour Klein, demanded that Sale sign a prenuptial agreement. That should not have come as a surprise, though it did. Over the years members of the Johnson family had had too many experiences with gold diggers—female *and* male—so the prenup had become part and parcel of entry into the Band-Aid dynasty.

"Bob was disgusted that she had to sign the prenup," recalls Steve Tobin, a client, friend, and confidant. "He felt that this was a young marriage, that they were going to have kids, and that they were going to spend their lives together. Bob was the father of the bride, and he was just very unhappy about it."

Sale acknowledges that her father was upset, "but we didn't go to a lawyer. My father and I just looked at it and said, fine, whatever. We never really paid any attention to it until years later when Woody and I went to get a divorce."

In June 1978, twenty-nine-year-old Nancy Sale Frey became the wife of thirty-one-year-old Robert Wood Johnson IV in a very private wedding ceremony on the grounds of the Princeton estate where he grew up.

Neither the couple's engagement nor their ceremony was publicized, as one would have expected, in the society wedding pages of *The New York Times,* and the Frey's hometown newspaper, the *St. Louis Post-Dispatch.* Betty Johnson had demanded absolute secrecy, and years later Sale curiously claims, "I wasn't anybody that was interested in being in the society pages having an announcement that I was getting married. I didn't want the world to know."

Bob Frey gave away his daughter, who wore her maternal grandmother Riette Sale Frey's wedding dress. Sale's mother, Melisse, kissed and hugged the groom. One Frey relative who had received an invitation from Sale, but who was ordered by her father to stay away, was his only sister, Mary Frey Hickman. At the time, her husband, David Hickman—one of her three husbands—though academically very bright, was an obese oddball who held menial jobs such as delivering packages, and was from a poor farm family.

"Because my brother didn't think that socially speaking it would be a good thing for the Johnson family to discover what an ordinary-type guy I was married to, he called me and told me not to attend. Bob wanted to make sure that I didn't embarrass him and his daughter in front of the Johnsons."

Some years later, when Sale and Woody had three daughters, and Mary Hickman had two girls and two sons, she would regularly send holiday greeting cards to their uncle and aunt, to Woody and Sale, and to their cousins, Casey, Jaime, and Daisy Johnson. But she never received an acknowledgment, not a card, not a call, not a thank you.

"My brother Bob was very blunt about it," she states. "He told me, 'Don't bother. Nancy won't answer, and Woody doesn't care,' so I quit sending."

47

During much of their courtship, Woody Johnson and Nancy Sale Frey had been living in the condominium penthouse apartment in Fort Lauderdale that he had bought during his volatile business partnership with Michael Spielvogel—the unit where he had been sued for reportedly ignoring paying the condo fees. But now that they were married, and planning to start a family, he bought his parents' nearby Bay Colony estate from his mother, and they settled in.

Just before Christmas 1978, six months after their wedding, Sale became pregnant, a time that was an emotional mix of both joy and trepidation for her, according to Dr. Ed Saltzman. "When she was pregnant, she was seeing a psychiatrist in Miami, and it had to do with becoming a mother for the first time, and whether Woody could be a good father," he says. "She researched everything. She didn't leave any stone unturned."

On September 24, 1979, at Hollywood Memorial Hospital, in Hollywood, Florida, Sale gave birth to a girl with a wisp of brownish-blond hair who they named Sale Trotter Case Johnson, and nicknamed Casey. Her first name, Sale, was in honor of her Jewish paternal grandmother, and Trotter was said to be for a long-lost Johnson forebear, or related to the baby's mother's interest in horses; Sale was on the verge of becoming a champion equestrian with priceless breeds in her stable.

Saltzman, Casey's pediatrician, was in the delivery room with the obstetrician who brought her into the world during a normal delivery with a slap on her pink and plump bottom, eliciting her first, but far from her last, loud cry for attention.

Years later, looking back, it seemed ironic that Casey, who had been born in a town named after the Hollywood of movie stars, would die four months after her thirtieth birthday in the real Hollywood, where she hoped to become a star—as a sad, diabetic, emotionally disturbed tabloid train wreck who had been living a very public, scandalous life.

But that's not how her life began.

"Casey was an adorable, sweet, cuddly baby, and she was adorable and sweet as a child," says the octogenarian Saltzman. "But when she got into her teens, when she was sixteen, seventeen, eighteen, she'd tell me, 'I bought a so-and-so pocketbook for five thousand dollars,' and in every color, and so she then was *not* so sweet. She was just a lost child."

Woody had always hoped for a son to carry on the Johnson dynasty name, but he would father two more daughters with Sale—Jaime and Daisy. He would have to wait almost a quarter century until after their divorce to finally have two sons with a much younger woman. She would become his second wife when he was in his late fifties and one of their sons would be his namesake.

Still, Woody loved Casey as much as Sale coddled her, with the help of as many as three nannies, one for each of her daughters as they came along, plus maids, drivers, housekeepers, and personal chefs who also acted as child-keepers when needed. Sale's wish to never be a homemaker had come true.

Among the help were Milly, Casey's half-Jamaican, half-Chinese nanny who was with the family for a quarter century before her death, and Jamaican Marita, who mostly looked after Jaime and Daisy, and was still working for the family in 2012. Another woman, Mozelle, had worked cleaning house and running errands for Sale after she left college and "morphed into full time at Bay Colony," Sale says.

Milly and Marita wielded Dr. Spock–like authority. "They had their own notions to a greater or lesser extent, on how child-rearing was supposed to work, and whether a parenting idea from Sale or Woody was good, or bad, and how closely they would respond to it," observes a family confidant.

Saltzman says that despite all of the help, "Sale was very attentive to her kids. She may have had nannies, but she was always around, and I got plenty of phone calls from her about the health of her kids. She'd call me at 3 A.M. and I'd be at their door."

When Casey turned three in 1982—the same year her sister Jaime was born—Sale began planning for her firstborn's future education. At the same time, Woody had decided it was time for them to leave Florida and set up his business operations and develop a social circle in New York City.

He and Sale had started house-hunting on Manhattan's Upper East Side, and she began looking into fashionable private schools. Attending one had always been a dream of hers. She had gone to public school in St. Louis, but was envious of girls she knew who had attended the exclusive John Burroughs School in the suburb of Ladue. But her father hadn't seen a need to spend the money to send her there.

Sale had applied to one of Manhattan's best schools for Casey and she asked Saltzman to write a letter of recommendation explaining what a wonderful child she was and what a prominent and respected family she came from. As it turned out, Saltzman's sister was the school's psychologist. "Sale and Woody couldn't believe that she was going to make the decision. Casey got in, but they eventually had to change schools because she wasn't much of a student." It wasn't the first or last time that she would be in and out of an elite New York private school—because of disciplinary issues, or lack of interest in her studies, or unsatisfactory grades, or health problems, or a combination of all these.

Despite the fact that Woody was heir to an immense family fortune, his own family's branch of the Johnson & Johnson dynasty was never an integral part of New York's upper echelon of society, and knew few people, if anyone, in the social register. So when Woody and Sale decided to make the big move to the Big Apple they needed someone with taste, style, and entree to lead the way. They chose Guy Vicino, who "was a real social butterfly and very connected to the high social life in New York City," notes his brother Neil. "Guy opened the right doors."

Guy's brother John maintains that Woody needed someone like Guy in his life to show him how to dress, what to wear, where to go. "Woody wasn't the sharpest tack in the box, but where the genius of Woody comes in is that he *knew* his limitations, and he made sure he surrounded himself with people like Guy who could help him. Guy knew the right society people, and he knew all the right properties."

The right property for Woody and Sale was a bargain-priced three-million-dollar, five-bedroom, six-thousand-square-foot duplex with servants' quarters that needed renovation, said to have once been owned by a sheik, at 834 Fifth Avenue, one of the most prestigious cooperative apartment buildings in Manhattan. It once was described as "the most pedigreed building on the snobbiest street in the country's most real-estate-obsessed city."

Woody had joined a gold standard of other heirs and heiresses to great corporate American fortunes who had resided there—Standard Oil, Woolworth, Hearst, Rockefeller, and Ford were among those represented, and now Johnson & Johnson. "Their apartment wasn't just an apartment, it was a palatial mansion," says an awestruck relative who visited often. "It was just *magnificent*. The furnishings cost a fortune alone, and the rooms were *splendorous*."

The pièce de résistance for arriving guests was the grand staircase leading to the second level from the immense foyer with its elaborate console holding an enormous vase whose fresh-cut flowers were changed daily. The staircase reminded visitors of the sumptuously curved one in the opening scene of *Bonfire of the Vanities,* a movie that was marketed as a "story of greed, lust, and vanity."

But the Johnsons' place was the real deal, not some set designer's fantasy.

To some observers, the Johnson palace, steps from the Central Park Zoo, was, well, something like a zoo itself in terms of pets and their messes.

"When they renovated the apartment," a relative says, "they even had a stainless steel shower/toilet for their five dogs because the dogs wouldn't always be taken outside to crap, so they'd crap in this room and the floor would flush it away. If you went into the kitchen, you'd throw up because the dogs peed on little pieces of paper. Sale had Schnauzer puppies who walked around in diapers in the apartment."

On one family vacation, Woody had rented a yacht and the Johnsons' canines did their duty not on paper, not above on the deck, but below on the beautiful rugs in the living quarters. It cost him a pretty penny to have the mess cleaned up. Like her mother, Casey loved dogs, considered them "my babies," but they would make incredible and costly messes, including even in her twelve-thousand-dollar Hermès Birkin bag, where she carried a teacup pooch everywhere. She was in her midtwenties and staying in a luxurious suite at the famed Plaza Athenee in Manhattan, when her Chihuahua, Tukus, had the runs, and defecated everywhere. Woody was forced to foot the clean-up bill, as much as twenty thousand dollars, a mere bag of shells for a man with his kind of money. It was still an embarrassment, a messy one.

Besides their palace on Fifth Avenue, the Johnsons also bought a spectacular spread for weekend relaxation and entertainment in the chic countryside of Bedminster Township, New Jersey, whose other notable residents included *Forbes* magazine CEO Steve Forbes and automobile mogul John DeLorean.

The property, called simply "The Farm," had an octagon-shaped home, a swimming pool with pool house, a helicopter pad, a golf course, and stables. Sale had installed stainless steel sinks for her growing collection of Arabian horses, and the necessary paddocks for riding. At the entrance to Woody's wonderland were lifelike bronze sculptures of each of the Johnson children at play, done by J. Seward Johnson Jr. using a photograph of the girls as a model from which to work since he and Woody and Sale weren't close and he rarely got to see the kids in person.

Having sold the Bay Colony home, the Johnsons bought another mansion in South Florida, in the exclusive Palm Beach Polo & Country Club, in Wellington—Florida's equestrian country where Sale became a well-known horsewoman. The Johnsons often flew down in their private plane on winter weekends.

To outsiders looking in, Woody and Sale appeared to be a golden couple living life to the fullest in a royal manner, but within the first five years there already was trouble in the marriage: Woody was finding Sale difficult to live with, or at least that's what his controlling mother, Betty, had confided to a relative.

"Betty heard Woody complain about Sale and she called me up about five years after they were married and said, 'I need to talk to you about Woody. He's *very* unhappy,' and she asked me what she should do about it," recalls the relative. "Her words, and I've never forgot them, were, 'What is it that makes Sale think she can run everyone's life, and do it totally without grace? She controls my son and he can't take it anymore.' I said, 'Well, I guess she's just a bossy person.' And that was the end of it.

"I didn't want to get involved in a mother-in-law and daughter-in-law catfight."

$ ` $ ` $

By the time Casey turned eight, she already was quite a handful—bratty, demanding, and obnoxious.

As her mother would later describe her behavior, she "was acting up a lot at the dinner table, often to the point where we'd have to ask her to leave the table and go to her room, because we didn't think it was fair that she was rude and disruptive to the rest of the family."

During the Easter-Passover school break in 1988, the Johnsons vacationed at their home in Florida. It turned into a horrible getaway because all three of the girls came down with chicken pox. Sale hustled them off to be looked at by Dr. Ed Saltzman, the pediatrician, who ran them through a battery of routine tests—urine, blood, the usual—and prescribed nothing; they were as healthy as any children could be with chicken pox.

Back in New York, the girls needed another physical for a school requirement. Again, they passed with flying colors—except for Casey; there was some question about her urine. She was called back for a second test, just to make sure there was no mistake. There wasn't. At first her mother thought it might have been some sort of bladder infection. Others educated in medicine, like her brothers, thought it was some sort of kidney infection. The other possibility was diabetes. It was then that Sale remembered how thirsty Casey had been, and how often she ran to the bathroom to urinate.

Casey's New York pediatrician said it was urgent that she be examined more thoroughly.

Woody and Sale took Casey to Mt. Sinai Hospital, which had a highly respected diabetes center staffed by endocrinologists, headed by Dr. Fredda Ginsberg-Fellner, who made the formal diagnosis of Type 1 diabetes, and became Casey's personal doctor. For Casey and her family, it became a life-changer, requiring daily insulin injections, a carefully monitored diet, and other health regimens. Her lifetime with this disease would be marked by difficult physical and emotional consequences.

Before Casey even left the hospital, Woody and Sale began practicing injecting each other with saline, and giving one another blood tests, so they could deal with it when they got her home. Sale later recalled, "It took me a couple of days just to get the nerve up to prick my own finger . . . waiting for the courage to stick myself."

Jaime, too, would become the victim of a serious health issue. As a teenager, she was diagnosed with the autoimmune disease lupus, which, in her case, was considered genetic; a sister of Woody's mother, Mary Wold Strong, a mother of five like Betty, had died from it. But no one in either the Johnson or Frey family was known to have had diabetes.

"Sale was very on top of Casey's condition," says Saltzman. "But Woody would call me and say, 'Tell me what to do. I have to get rid of her diabetes. I have to correct it. Whatever it takes to make the diabetes end, I'll do it, whatever money.' He couldn't grasp the concept that it had nothing to do with his wherewithal, his money."

When Casey was diagnosed, doctors and nurses were brought in to instruct everyone on signs to look for, and what to do in case something happened to Casey, and how to administer insulin if they needed to in an emergency, according to a Johnson staff member at the time. "Everybody was informed because if Casey's sugar level was off, she could black out and go into a coma, and that did happen to her on occasions. We had to know what to do and not just stand there and panic."

The summer after Casey was diagnosed the Johnsons had gone to Africa for a vacation. One afternoon while her parents were out with friends, Casey had gone off on her own and fallen ill, arriving back at their lodging in near diabetic shock. Marita, the nanny, had to track down Sale and Woody using a walkie-talkie so she could be given emergency instructions on what to do.

When Casey was thirteen, Woody and Sale got together with a writer-researcher of how-to books and women's magazine articles, Susan Kleinman, and produced a 224-page volume entitled *Managing Your Child's Diabetes*, published in 1992 by a small, later defunct New York house, MasterMedia Limited. The forward was attributed to one of America's best-known celebrity diabetics, Mary Tyler Moore, diagnosed in 1964. "In these pages," she stated, "a fourteen-year-old and her parents share their experiences with diabetes and their conviction that a cure for the disease will be found . . . The Johnsons' optimism is not just inspiring, it's contagious."

At the time the book was written, Casey was a student at the prestigious Marymount School, a Catholic day school for girls and part of the Sacred Heart of Mary system. Later she attended the Dwight School, whose acronym was "Dumb White Kids Getting High Together," and whose classmates and chums for the rest of her life would be the hard-partying "celebutante" sisters Paris and Nicky Hilton of the Hilton Hotel dynasty.

In the book, the Johnsons noted that after Casey was diagnosed "anger" had set in for them. "We kept asking ourselves: Why is this happening to Casey? Why is this happening to us?" They said, "This anger, in turn, may provoke guilt . . . it's irrational to be angry at your child, but somehow you can't help it . . . We went through enough of that same guilt ourselves."

Casey's diabetes had put enormous pressures on a marriage that already was shaky at times. Woody and Sale acknowledged, "There's no question that Casey's diabetes has affected our family in a very profound way . . . the daily stress of worrying about our daughter's health . . . affected each of us—and the way we relate to one another . . . [marriage partners] have to work doubly hard to keep themselves and their relationship strong . . . we have grappled with all of these issues."

In the back of *Managing Your Child's Diabetes* there was a note to readers stating that Woody and Sale were available for "keynotes and seminars," but that never happened, according to Tony Colao, who handled the publishing house's speaker's bureau. "Publicity was not even a consideration—that they would go out and do speaking," he recalls. "I couldn't see Woody Johnson getting on planes to go around and do groups of two hundred. He was pretty private."

But Casey's diabetes had given Woody an issue to dig into, and he became the poster boy for diabetes research and funding. "He went around the country and would meet people and say, 'I want you to donate twenty-five thousand dollars to diabetes research, and I'll match it,'" says Saltzman.

On his own, Woody wrote a check for $10 million as part of a $100 million-diabetes campaign, and he cofounded the Juvenile Diabetes Research Foundation. Still later, in a lobbying effort, he convinced the U.S. Congress to approve a guaranteed fund for diabetes research.

However, despite all of that money and research and effort by her father, Casey, who had everything money could buy, subsequently ignored all the rules about her disease. "She thought she was invincible," observes a friend. "Casey had always done whatever she wanted to do. She wound up in the hospital a few times, but the diabetes never killed her and I guess she thought she could do whatever she wanted to do—until the diabetes and her lifestyle did kill her."

The former Johnson staff person who had worked for the family on and off for almost a decade and was an eyewitness to the family drama and dynamics had developed a bond of sorts with Woody and was aware of how distressed he was about Casey's illness. "He'd gone through a lot of hell his whole life dealing with the death of family members, and he was still feeling anguish over that when Casey was diagnosed. His comment to me toward all of that tragedy was, 'All my trust fund wealth aside, I'd give it all back if it meant getting all those family members back.'"

48

At virtually the same time that Casey Johnson's diabetes struck the family like a lightning bolt out of the blue, her father, Woody, was slammed with another tragic situation involving someone else he dearly loved. His life-long friend Guy Vicino, who had been living a promiscuous gay life, had contracted what in the mid-1980s was called "the gay plague."

He had AIDS.

Woody, haunted by the onslaught with Casey, was determined to use every means at his disposal to help keep Guy alive, and if he couldn't, to make his last days as comfortable and peaceful as possible. He owed him much.

With his sense of style, Guy early on had become Woody's de-facto *GQ*-like advisor, and Woody, who usually sported shorts, T-shirts, and flip-flops when he could get away with it, required expert sartorial advice. "When Guy and Woody would get together, it was Guy who would say, 'Wear this, don't wear that, it's the same thing you wore last night,' and Woody would do it," notes John Vicino.

Guy was comfortable being gay, but coming out was very difficult for him, and at one point he had contemplated committing suicide. But his emergence from the closet in the mid-1970s was met with shrugs all around by the people who were most important to him, including his closest friend, Woody.

His brother Neil says, "Guy was a bit flamboyant, but he didn't speak with a lisp. He played sports, he rode horses, and, if anybody went in that direction [accusing him of being queer], they were going to be in dangerous territory. Guy was very quick, and very smart, and could tear you apart with his tongue."

Woody had always gotten a kick out of Guy, looked up to him and thought he was smart and funny and sophisticated, and used to recount stories about him to others. Looking back, Neil didn't believe that Woody and Guy ever had anything more than a close friendship. "Knowing Guy and being close to Woody, and Woody being who Woody was—a macho, party kind of guy— Guy never would have said anything to Woody, or done anything to Woody, or made a pass at Woody, because Woody always struck me as the kind of person who probably might have ended the friendship. But Woody was very accepting when Guy came out."

In 1984, thirty-seven-year-old Guy suddenly looked like he was at death's door. A physician who specialized in infectious diseases and who was a friend of John Vicino's had noticed the extreme change in Guy and warned John to keep an eye on his brother. "I went over one day and Guy was terribly emaciated and I was shocked at how sick he was," recalls John of that horrific time. "I said, 'We're going to the hospital.'"

Guy was diagnosed at Broward General with PCP—pneumocystis carinii pneumonia, an early sign of AIDS, a disease that was still something of a medical mystery back then. "The doctors were still telling him he may or may not have AIDS," says John. "I slept on the floor in his hospital room for three nights because the nurses were afraid to come in. They had to wear a gown and a mask and I remember Guy saying that nobody had come in to help him go to the bathroom. They were all too afraid."

Guy Vicino was among the early victims in the worldwide gay community to be struck down. That same year screen idol Rock Hudson, the most famous AIDS victim at the time, was diagnosed and secretly treated in Paris, but it was too late—he died a year later in October 1985. Guy Vicino would live several more years.

While Hudson had hidden his disease from his closest friends and lovers until the news media found out and he was outed, Guy felt Woody should be among the first to know that he had been infected. "We telephoned Woody and my brother told him he had it," says John. "Guy said, 'I'm sorry, Woody, I'm really sorry,' but Woody said, 'There's nothing to be sorry about. You were in the wrong place at the wrong time.' The next day, I heard a knock on Guy's hospital room door and there's Woody. Guy looked at me like—we want to be alone—and Woody stayed there while Guy went through the first crisis period."

The first time John Vicino met Sale Johnson was when she came to Florida to visit Guy and strongly suggested that he be placed in a protective "medical bubble" like David Vetter, the so-called "boy in the bubble" at the Texas Medical Center, who lived inside sterile plastic bubbles to avoid infection because of a fatal immune disease. "She said, 'We want to put you in a bubble. We'll find a clinic until they find a cure for this disease.' But Guy said, 'I don't want to be that guy. I can't do that.'"

Guy had heard that Rock Hudson had received experimental treatments in Paris, and he thought of going to France.

That's when Woody came to the rescue.

"He said he would check to find the best treatment program," says John Vicino. "Nothing happened for about a month. I remember my mother said, 'Woody's not going to come through,' but Guy told her, 'No, you're wrong. Woody's going to come through,' and he did."

Because of Woody and his Johnson & Johnson family influence, Guy got into an exclusive AIDS program at the University of Miami where he was treated with an expensive experimental new drug called AZT, which was then believed to slow the disease. Because Guy had gone through a family inheritance, Woody also picked up all the huge medical bills, and arranged for AIDS expert Dr. Anthony S. Fauci and his assistants to become involved in Guy's case.

Despite the experimental treatments, Guy was slowly dying. Several times he nearly died when he again developed PCP and the tumors known as Kaposi's sarcoma.

In the last months of his life, Guy opened up to his brother Neil about some of his sexual adventures. He told him he had a lover in New York from whom he had contracted the disease, and who had left him. From what he gleaned, Neil always suspected that the carrier was blond, tanned, mustachioed Gaetan Dugas, an Air Canada flight attendant, who died in 1984. Dugas had been labeled AIDS "Patient Zero" because he had been linked by medical investigators to the U.S.'s first reported cases.

If Neil Vicino's suspicions were correct, it meant that Woody Johnson's lifelong friend was one of some twenty-five hundred sex partners that the thirty-one-year-old Dugas claimed he had before he died of AIDS-related kidney failure.

In Guy's last year of life, he and Neil, who had been appointed the executor of his brother's estate, made a pilgrimage from Fort Lauderdale back to their hometown of Princeton. "We went to the Jersey shore and had a photo taken of me and Guy sitting in front of the house that we rented that was next to the Johnsons' beach house." The Johnson and Vicino boys had spent many summers there playing together.

In the late winter of 1988, all of the very special medical care Guy Vicino had been receiving at Woody Johnson's behest had finally failed, time had run out, and he knew that he was about to die.

"As Guy got sicker, he made me promise two things." John Vicino has never forgotten, his voice filled with emotion decades later. "He said, 'I know Woody will try to come down from New York, and I don't want him in the room to see how I look. I don't want him to remember me like this.'"

On Friday, March 11, Guy, who was dying at home, called John, who was living in a small condo apartment, and told him he was signing over his home to him, and when he was gone he wanted his brother to move in.

"I said, 'No, Guy, we'll do that on Monday.' And then on Sunday his temperature spiked and he went into the hospital.

"The last thing he said to me was, 'Don't let Woody in here.' Woody called and he was on the phone with Guy, who was in and out of consciousness and bleeding out of every orifice. Woody was talking to him and Guy was trying to answer him back, but he was having problems forming words," says John, who was at his brother's bedside at North Ridge Medical Center in Oakland Park, Florida.

"I got on the phone and Sale was a wreck. She said, 'There's got to be something we can do. We'll bring him up here to New York.' Woody called again and said, 'I'm coming down,' and I said to him, 'Don't come tonight. Guy's going to get some rest.' All of it was a lie. I told Woody we'd call him on Monday.

"Guy then got on the phone and the last thing I heard him say was, 'I love you, too, Woody.'"

Guy Vicino died on Tuesday, March 15, 1988. He was forty-one years old. Funeral services were held the following Friday at All Saints Episcopal Church in Fort Lauderdale. The Johnson family—Woody, Betty, Libet, and Christopher—flew down in their private jet. Woody took charge and gave an upbeat and loving eulogy about the Johnson and Vicino boys' innocent childhood in Princeton, and how all of them had been so close, and had had such good times.

"Woody was *so* dedicated to Guy, and the Robert Wood Johnson Foundation was the biggest single private contributor to AIDS research in this country," declares Neil Vicino. "I could never help but believe that that was because of my brother and Woody's closeness. I've always felt that Guy left somewhat of a legacy through Woody."

49

Ten-year-old girls fantasized about fashion with their Ken and Barbie dolls, but when Casey Johnson was that age she did real dress-up with her first, but not her last, Chanel bag; a year later at eleven, she donned a pair of snakeskin pumps, and even though she didn't have a driver's license, she was given the keys to her own car at sixteen. At eighteen, she got breast implants.

"I got whatever I wanted," she once boasted.

"Woody *overindulged* Casey and her sisters," a family member asserts. "That was Woody's way—just give them anything they wanted. He was raised with the idea that money can do everything, and that's what worked for him."

Because of all the money, Casey had had an odd childhood. By the time she had reached her early teens, she had never actually been inside a grocery store. Servants did all the shopping for the Johnson table. A relative once took Casey to a supermarket—the first time she'd ever been in one—and she wandered around like an alien creature with wide-eyed amazement, looking at all the products on the shelves.

"The store was holding a cooking class for young children that day," recalls her escort. "Casey sat at the counter with about ten other kids and the two instructors gave them recipes and ingredients and told them what to do. Casey was in absolute shock, but she went through the process. 'Oh, I love this. It's so much fun,' she said, and then gleefully told me, 'I'm going to give all of these recipes to our cook.' I said, 'Casey, let's take a recipe and select the food here in the store for dinner,' and she was elated. She never had an experience like that with her parents. She was *starved* for attention."

The same person once took her to a blue-collar discount store much like Walmart to see how she would react, since she had never been in such a place, either, and to let her see how the other half lived and shopped.

"I said, 'Casey, there are stores like this for people who can't afford Bergdorf Goodman, or Saks Fifth Avenue,' and I gave her fifty dollars and told her to walk around and buy something. She came back to me later with the same fifty-dollar bill and said, 'It's all so ugh!' She did not live in the real world."

When Casey received a present neither she nor her mother rarely sent a thank-you card. When someone asked Sale about it, her response was, "Oh, Casey gets so much stuff, she doesn't have time to write thank-you notes." One giver of gifts to Casey maintains, "She didn't have to do anything to conform to the social values of other people because of the way she was taught—or not taught—at home."

Sale, in her position as a Johnson wife and New York socialite, received lots of gifts, too, but had earned a reputation among some in her circle as one who re-gifted. She even had a room said to have been brimming with stuff that she had received and then sent on to others, sometimes with the original tags and cards intact.

"Sale wasn't penurious and not tight, but she was very careful with her money," asserts her longtime confidante Dr. Ed Saltzman. "You would get gifts from her that she had received three years before. I received lots of stuff—a book, or a shirt, or a sweater—that was three years old. But she also once sent me a new computer."

Another person, less diplomatic, says of Sale, "How about miserly? How about cheap? Sale was *the* queen of recycled gifts. We'd turn around and throw them in the trash, or give them to Goodwill. Some of them still even had cards on them that were addressed to Sale from so-and-so."

Added a relative: "She'll go over telephone bills line by line, but she doesn't think anything about spending one hundred thousand dollars to rent a summer house. She's complicated."

$ $ $

Getting her high school diploma had been quite an achievement for Casey Johnson because she hated school, wouldn't study, refused to complete assignments, and thumbed her nose at all authority.

As a relative says, "Casey rebelled completely. She was really angry at her family because she had diabetes and blamed them. Her attitude was—'I'll show you!'"

Those close to Woody and Sale, knowing Casey's lack of interest in academia and general failure as a student, were astonished when they heard that she had actually been admitted to Brown University, the prestigious Ivy League school with tough admission standards.

"I called the house and I wanted to know how the kids were doing and I spoke to the maid and she told me Casey was going to Brown, and was in Providence arranging for a room," recalls Dr. Ed Saltzman, who intimately knew all about Casey's severe health, academic, and behavioral problems. "I said, '*Brown*! What do you mean she's going to Brown? She *can't* be going to Brown.' I was so dumbfounded I figured the maid didn't know, so I asked, 'You mean Brown *University*, the one in Rhode Island? *The* Brown?' And she said yes. I didn't get it. There was no way that kid could get into Brown.

"So I called Sale a couple of days later and I said, 'Sale, Casey's at Brown?' And she said, 'Well, Woody's on the board,' or something like that. I realized very quickly that obviously that's how she got into Brown—because of Woody's influence."

As it happened, one such connection that the family had was Brown University president Vartan Gregorian, the former president of the New York Public Library, who later served as president of the Carnegie Corporation of New York. Woody and Gregorian also served together as board members of the World Trade Center Memorial Foundation.

Casey had been admitted to Brown as "a provisional, part-time, nonmatriculating student—a provision made for her because of Woody's connections at the university," claims a person with knowledge of the situation. "Woody would never say, 'I got her in,' because he was always proud of her having gone there—even transiently."

While Sale Johnson acknowledges their friendship with Gregorian, she doesn't think there was any blatant influence used, any sort of quid pro quo to get Casey admitted. "I don't think that money was donated. Woody didn't have a new swimming pool built, or put in a new science building. But Casey *wasn't* a good student. She said she didn't want to stay there because they wouldn't let her bring her dog. That was her excuse publicly, and even to us. But she knew she couldn't cut it there. If I were Brown, I wouldn't have accepted her as a student."

Unlike Casey, her sisters Jaime and Daisy did graduate from Brown. "They got in on their own merit," says a relative. "Academically, they were much better than Casey. Jaime had good grades and scores, and Daisy was a nationally ranked equestrian, so both of them had other qualifications. But it didn't hurt that they were children of Woody Johnson."

$ $ $

One of Casey's earliest crushes was on a distant cousin, cute Cameron Morrell Douglas, the son of Michael and Diandra Douglas, the actor's first wife. Diandra was also Casey Johnson's godmother, and Casey had a relatively close relationship with her, especially when Casey was on the outs with her own parents, which was often.

Cameron was the grandson of Kirk Douglas and his first wife, Diana Dill, the sister of Ruth Dill Johnson, the first wife of Casey's great-uncle, J. Seward Johnson Sr. Diana, a onetime actress, had dedicated her 1999 memoir to Cameron. Her son, Michael Douglas, and his second wife, Catherine Zeta-Jones, had also bought the Dill family's aristocratic Ariel Sands hotel, a forty-seven-room cottage colony in Bermuda. The bonds were, indeed, tight between the Johnsons and the Douglases.

Nine months Casey's senior, Cameron was equally as wild and misbehaved. The two had first met in late adolescence when Michael and Diandra were frequent houseguests at Woody and Sale's farm in New Jersey, and the two couples had jet-setted around together to places like the Douglases' home in Majorca.

"Casey had a terrible crush on Cameron and that boy was *bad* news," states a relative. "I know for a fact he was not a good influence on her. He had a very troubled childhood and he began using drugs and he probably acquainted Casey with some of that stuff."

Sale, who was aware of her daughter's close relationship with the young junkie, acknowledges, "It's certainly possible" that he turned Casey on to drugs. "Casey was enamored of Cameron." And she says she knew about his drug use and that he had been in rehab "multiple times." She says that part of Casey's "thought process" was that "Cameron shouldn't be doing things, and she would try to talk him out of it, but then part of her would be mesmerized because Cameron was a club person and she liked him a lot.

"Casey said to me that she did coke on occasion, or she smoked pot because it made her feel good, and she felt she was in pain so much of the time—mental pain, and drugs was the one thing that made her happy. But she wasn't a drug addict."

In April 2010, high school dropout, disk jockey, and heroin addict Cameron Douglas was sentenced to five years in federal prison after he was arrested in the summer of 2009 for dealing the drug crystal meth—at eighty dollars a gram—out of a room in the trendy Gansevoort Hotel in Manhattan's Meatpacking District. He pleaded guilty to charges of drug trafficking.

Like Casey, who always blamed her problems on her parents, Douglas did the same. His lawyers asserted that his "serious heroin addiction" was "not due to any acts of his own but by dint of birth and a difficult upbringing" in a home with a rich, powerful father. He was driven to drugs, they contended, because of "dysfunctional upbringing." At a hearing, a psychiatrist testified on Cameron's behalf, stating that his problems, "car accidents, motorcycle accidents"—it sounded much like a description of Keith and Billy Johnson—". . . had a lot to do with who his parents are."

Michael Douglas had handwritten a five-page letter to the judge pleading for lenience for his son, and noting that Cameron was among other Douglas relatives who had battled addictions. Douglas's half brother, forty-six-year-old sometime actor and aspiring standup comedian Eric—Kirk's son from another marriage—had died of a drug overdose in a New York apartment in 2004. And Michael Douglas himself had once admitted to, and had been treated for, "sex addiction." His wife, Catherine Zeta-Jones, who starred in Marty Richards's *Chicago,* was hospitalized and treated for bipolar II disorder a year after her stepson, Cameron, was sentenced to prison.

The Johnsons and the Douglases had much in common.

The sentencing judge in Cameron's case told the court that the time he had already spent in the minimum security federal prison in Lewisburg, Pennsylvania, was the longest he had been off of drugs since the age of thirteen, which was when Casey and Cameron had their initial flirtation.

A few days before Christmas 2011, Cameron was sentenced to an additional four and a half years behind bars—including eleven months of solitary confinement for violating prison rules—after he was caught again with drugs. A few days later his mother, Diandra, complained to the *New York Post* that what the judge had done was cruel and harsh, and she declared: "Cameron is fighting an addiction which is a disease that runs in the family," and she added, clearly thinking of her late goddaughter, Casey, "Would you put a diabetic in solitary confinement?"

PART VIII

FAMILY MATTERS

50

The end of the 1990s and the beginning of the new millennium was a time of major change for Woody Johnson, his wife, Sale, and their first-born, the increasingly troubled Casey.

Long hidden in the shadows, Woody had spent half of the 1980s and most of the '90s involved in forming and running the very privately held Johnson Company, which was established after he and his family moved from Florida to New York.

The key role of the firm, headquartered in Rockefeller Center, initially was to confidentially manage his Johnson & Johnson fortune—the untold hundreds of millions from his trust funds, from his inheritances, from his immense block of Johnson & Johnson stock, and from enormous profits made from outside investment ventures—plus looking after the wealth of some other members of the dynasty, and acting as a philanthropy.

He had a small, capable crew of accountants, lawyers, and advisors—some of whom had been with him since his late twenties when he was building those condominiums in South Florida with his first partner, Michael Spiel-vogel. His team included Neil Burmeister, who became president of the Johnson Company—he was with Woody for some three decades before he retired—and was the seer who had advised Keith Johnson to invest in a lucrative early cable TV franchise in Florida, which Woody inherited after Keith's overdose, and made a bundle when he sold it.

Along with Burmeister, Woody brought with him from Florida accountant Joel Latman, who became the company's treasurer. Also on board was his trusted longtime administrative assistant, Mary Anne Adams.

Woody, who was brought up to be suspicious of people who might want to take advantage of him and his fortune, thoroughly trusted his small group. Observes Sale Johnson Rashad, "Woody had such quality people around him, people who *never* took advantage of him in any way." She says if she suspected anyone, "I'd be the first person to say to Woody, 'Hey, they are users.'"

Though they would be divorced, Sale years later has great respect for Woody's accomplishments, since he could have just lived large as a playboy. "When he was at the University of Arizona with all those beautiful coeds, it took him seven years to graduate because he was in the hospital during some of that time. But he wasn't in any hurry to leave because he was a party animal," she says. "He was out-of-control wild in *many* ways. But he's done a pretty amazing job in life. He didn't have to do a damn thing. He could have been a total ne'er-do-well, sailing around on a boat and smoking pot, and he didn't."

Woody and his fortune were not in the public eye until the late 1990s when he surfaced as a bidder for the New York Jets. In 1999, he established a business entity called New York Jets LLC, with his mother, Betty, sister Libet, and brother Christopher as minority shareholders.

Chasing the Jets ownership instantly put him in the media spotlight, as he vied for the team against another billionaire who didn't mind all the attention, Charles F. Dolan, the Cablevision and Home Box Office founder, and owner of Madison Square Garden.

With the relatively unknown Johnson heir in the race for the team as the sales deadline neared, *The Times* observed days before Christmas 1999: "If public renown were a prerequisite to owning a sports team, Robert Wood Johnson IV would be excluded."

Though his marriage to Sale was slowly crumbling, they were still together during the bidding process. "We were sitting on the beach using my cell phone because his had run out of juice and he was making his final offer," recalls Sale. "And he said, 'I don't know what to do. I don't know what to bid, it's already so high.' So my suggestion was, bid as high as you feel you can afford and if you get it, you get it, and if you don't, you move on."

The Band-Aid heir upped his bid by ten million dollars as if he was dropping a quarter in a vending machine slot after quickly conferring with his attorney, Ira Akselrad, who later asserted, "There was a lot of deliberation about what was appropriate."

In early January 2000, Woody, at fifty-two, was the victor. The estate of the previous Jets owner—the oilman and New Jersey native Leon Hess, who had died in May 1999 after owning the team for fifteen years—took his check for a whopping $635 million. Early bets were that the team would sell for about $500 million in the deal being brokered by Goldman Sachs, and some analysts even felt the usually losing Jets were only worth $250 million at best.

As it turned out, Woody's final and winning number was the most ever paid at the time for a professional New York sports team, and the payout was considered "remarkable for a team with a downtrodden history, and which finished with a 1–15 record as recently as 1996," observed *The Times,* which also noted that Woody paid for the Jets "with his personal wealth."

George Vecsey, in a *Sports of The Times* piece headlined, "Playing Billionaire Roulette," compared the low-key Woody to the media and sports mogul, Dolan.

He observed:

Normally, we lumpen proles are not inclined to root for any billionaire with an IV after his name, since it implies continuity and power, big bucks begetting big bucks. But in the struggle for control of the Jets, good old Woody came off as a man of the people, an outsider, a lone wolf, with no looming Vaderian [*Star Wars,* Darth Vader] menace. Woody does not own other sports teams [like Dolan]. Woody does not control what is piped into our television sets [like Dolan]. Woody does not raise our cable rates [like Dolan]. He just sells bandages [erroneous]. Good old Woody . . . In the meantime, let's have some fanfare for the common man [tongue in cheek], good old Woody.

For Woody, owning a team in the Big Apple, the biggest sports market in the United States at the time, meant major prestige. He was happy to pay a high price but with it came the loss of his cherished privacy. Stories about him began appearing more frequently in the press, and they often dredged up Johnson dynasty scandals, from the past to the present. When his eldest, Casey, became a tabloid figure in the late 2000s because of her debauched Hollywood lifestyle, it was embarrassing gossip column fodder.

As it turned out, Woody had made a good bet on the Jets; within a decade the team would be worth twice what he had paid, although by the end of the 2011 and 2012 seasons they were still considered "the same old" losing Jets with lots of personal and professional issues, as dysfunctional in many ways as the Johnson dynasty itself through the generations.

Dr. Ed Saltzman, Woody and Sale's longtime friend and confidant, says he "never imagined" Woody ever becoming a professional sports mogul because he didn't think he was that savvy as a businessman, but that soon changed. "I asked him why he bought the Jets and not a professional baseball team that plays 162 games in a season, and he told me that the finances in baseball were terrible. He said, 'The union runs baseball. At least there's a salary cap in the NFL. There's no salary cap in baseball. In football if you don't play, your contract's gone.'"

Within days of Woody's purchase, the Jets' prized coach, Bill Parcells, who Woody desperately hoped to keep, quit, as did his designated successor, Bill Belichick, who would later go on to coach the Jets' biggest rival, the New England Patriots, and embarrass Woody's team, it seemed, game after game, season after season.

In their last face-off in the 2011 season, for instance, the Patriots buried the Jets by a score of 37–16. Leaving the field, the furious Jets coach Rex Ryan was confronted by a fan who shouted, "Belichick is better than you."

The loudmouth Ryan responded, "Shut the fuck up!"

Ryan apologized for his outburst the next day, but the National Football League fined him seventy-five thousand dollars, one of the heftiest ever levied on a head coach, but it was not Ryan's first: In 2010, during Super Bowl week in Miami, he was fined fifty thousand dollars by his own team, a decision sanctioned by Woody, for flipping the bird to a fan, an act that was photographed by someone's cell phone camera and posted online, eventually going viral.

Despite it all, the Johnson scion finally had his own identity as an owner in the NFL, something he had craved since the mid-1970s when, in his twenties, he lost in his serious bid for the new Tampa Bay Buccaneers expansion franchise.

Woody would later be described as "the fat checkbook behind the New York Jets."

$ $ $

While Sale Johnson thought Woody's acquisition of a professional football team was sexy and she loved the celebrity wow factor, she was shocked by his next life-changing proposition.

He wanted a divorce, the latest in a long history of marital splits in the Johnson dynasty.

The timing made it seem as if he was trading in his spouse for tight ends and fullbacks.

But Sale, who had been with the new owner of the Jets for some three decades, and was the mother of his three daughters, was going to want a lot in exchange for giving him his freedom.

"Sale was stunned when he told her it was over," observes Dr. Ed Saltzman. "Early in the marriage he needed Sale to bring his life under control. Later, I think she depended on him more than he depended on her. I never saw a lot of touchy-feely with them. When the marriage was in trouble I flew up to New York to talk to them both, to counsel them in some way so that they handled the children properly."

A relative who watched the marriage disintegrate maintains: "For a long time they were not friendly. They were seldom together, and they each had their own lives. I never walked into a room and saw them sitting and talking—*never*. I never saw anything that one would expect in an intimate, loving relationship. Finally, Woody said to her, 'I just don't want to live this way anymore. I'm very unhappy.' Sale was just floored."

Looking back a decade after their split, Sale has a different take. She says, "It's just not true" that she was taken by surprise. In fact, she asserts, "*I* brought up divorce first, then we talked about it, and then I thought, no, we should discuss this further, maybe try to get some counseling. But we really were living parallel lives. I was off with Daisy with the horses. I was back and forth with Casey [and her problems]. But Woody and I never raised our voices, never cursed. That's why it was such a surprise that we were actually getting a divorce. Long before people knew, we had already made that decision."

Sale had kept a game face. In the early fall of 2000, a few months after Woody bought the Jets and was beginning divorce settlement talks, his soon-to-be ex-wife threw a theme party at their 834 Fifth Avenue palace for Michael Douglas and five other captains of Hollywood and the celebrities who loved them—Barbara Walters; Catherine Zeta-Jones; Universal Studios president Ron Meyer; chairman Scott Greenstein of USA Films; and another equestrian like Sale who was tragically injured during a horse event, Christopher Reeve. What the guests all had in common was that they were born on the same day, the twenty-fifth, in the month of September, but in different years. Sale used the occasion as the kickoff for a Christopher Reeve Paralysis Foundation fundraiser.

Neither the guests, nor *The Times,* which mentioned the party in its "Public Lives" gossip column, had any idea that the Johnsons' marriage was going south in front of their eyes.

But their very quiet split didn't come as any big surprise to those who knew them well. It was as if they already had an open marriage of sorts. Aside from their separate interests, there were whispers about lovers on both sides. Someone claimed to have seen Sale kissing a man on the beach in Southhampton, or letting another male friend of hers drive one of Woody's exotic cars. She heard he was seeing other women. But nothing ever was proven, at least publicly.

$ $ $

While Sale was off riding her prized horses, Woody was off on macho motorcycle jaunts with a small circle of wealthy pals.

The biker events had started in the early 1990s with other masters of the universe who got together, among them the gay media baron Jann Wenner, whose empire included *Rolling Stone* and *Mens' Journal.* Like Woody's marriage, which was getting increasingly rocky, Wenner's had actually fallen apart in 1995 when he left his wife, Jane, for a former Calvin Klein male model. (After a sixteen-year separation, they went for a divorce in 2011.)

While Woody had experienced tragedy years before when his brother Billy was killed on a motorcycle, he still got a thrill out of the speed and danger on a Harley. When he was offered the opportunity to ride with Wenner and his coterie, he jumped on board. And it was quite a jaunt—from the Tavern on the Green in Manhattan's Central Park, cross-country to San Francisco and the Golden Gate Bridge.

Under a cap, the balding Woody wore a wig so he resembled a long-haired biker.

Wenner was fond of Woody, whom he perceived as "slightly vulnerable . . . Like he was searching for who he was," he later observed. Initially thinking of him as kind of a milquetoast figure, Wenner changed his mind after they stopped at a health club in Nevada to work out and he watched in awe as the Band-Aid heir did dozens of chin-ups, and discovered that Woody was "a real ironman type underneath."

Woody's emphasis on keeping his body fit had all to do with his overweight, hard-drinking father's death from cancer at the age of fifty. "He was so afraid he was going to get cancer and die at a young age, so he ate responsibly, worked out constantly, and stopped drinking," says his ex-wife, Sale. "He's in better shape than anyone I know, including professional athletes."

Healthwise, he was more like his weight-conscious grandfather, the General, who so despised the corpulent that he even left his first wife when she grew fat for a thinner model. Among those in Woody's close circle were also men of weight, both power and heft, among them New Jersey governor Chris Christie and the Jets' head coach Rex Ryan, who once topped three hundred pounds. Woody helped Ryan lose more than one hundred pounds through lap-band surgery, and he advised the tough-talking Christie, a big supporter with Woody of the 2012 presidential candidate Mitt Romney, to get a trainer.

So it was no surprise that Wenner was impressed when he saw Woody work out during their motorcycle jaunt across America.

Eric Ryan, a biker himself back in the day, got a kick out of Woody's cross-country adventure, because, he says, they weren't really slumming. While he remembered Woody owning a powerful Norton at the University of Arizona, he didn't view Woody and his rich gang in leathers as Hell's Angels types when they roared to California. "They had a truck follow them around with their luggage and spare bikes—*and* mechanics," he says. "They had an infrastructure. This was not Dennis Hopper and Peter Fonda reliving *Easy Rider*. This was Black American Express card motorcycle touring."

While Woody was cruising on his Harley, Sale was usually riding and showing her champion Arabian horses, one of whom she named "The General," after Woody's grandfather, Robert Wood Johnson Jr. It won a gold medal for the United States in the Olympics.

Horses had virtually become her life. She had riders and trainers and trailers, and state-of-the-art stables with stainless steel water stalls. She was said to have had about three dozen horses, each worth an estimated five hundred thousand dollars to a million dollars, and she lovingly treated them like humans.

At one point, she was running an international breeding operation with two Olympic stallions, selling their sperm to other breeders, which was an opportunity to recoup some of her investment.

She also bred dogs when the opportunity arose, and it was during one of the births of twelve golden retrievers at the Johnsons' New Jersey farm that Sale, a staunch Republican like Woody, disappointed the first family at the time, the liberal Democratic Clintons.

Bill and Hillary had been hunting for a dog for daughter Chelsea after losing a bid for a golden during a benefit auction at the first daughter's school in Washington. They bid thirty-five hundred dollars and lost it by three hundred dollars. Through the wife of Vernon Jordan, chairman of Clinton's transition group, the Clintons heard that Sale Johnson had just the kind of well-bred golden puppy they wanted.

But Sale wasn't about to give the commander in chief of the free world any VIP treatment. "I said, 'Great, but they will have to leave it up to me whether they get a male or female, because other people are ahead of them on the list,'" she told *The Times* at the time.

When Sale heard that the Clintons wanted a dog held for them because Chelsea was suffering from allergies, she gave a resounding no. The last two Johnson puppies in the litter went to a couple of other GOP billionaires— the philanthropist and venture capitalist Laurance Rockefeller, and the five-times-married business magnate Ronald O. Perelman, whose pup "left by helicopter, of course," Sale later boasted.

Woody's decision to acquire the Jets and divest himself of Sale were two of his more popular decisions among a number of members of the Johnson dynasty who never could stomach her aggressive manner.

"Everything one needs to know about Sale Johnson, I can relate in one anecdote," Eric Ryan maintains, calling her "a piece of work. She and Woody stopped by my mom [Mary Lea Johnson Ryan D'Arc Richards] and Marty's [Richards] house on Gin Lane in Southampton one holiday season and they brought two one-kilo cans of Beluga caviar, and they all gorged on champagne and caviar. When the time came for Sale and Woody to leave, she popped by the kitchen and picked up the remaining can and took it with her. That's Sale."

$ $ $

When it came to arriving at a financial settlement with Woody, Sale claims that she just wanted enough money to live comfortably. But the billionaire Jets owner battled to hold on to as much money as he could.

In 2012, Sale says, "I only wanted to just be comfortable."

She says she wasn't aware of any battle over the financial settlement—but only because she never attended any of the negotiations. Instead, she sat outside the talks in another room. "I didn't want anything to ruin my feelings towards Woody in case there was anything negative going on in there," she contends.

At the time the settlement was being hammered out, Woody was still living at home, but he soon moved out and began his newfound bachelorhood in a plush Manhattan apartment at his friend Donald Trump's International Hotel & Tower, where Woody's sister, Libet, had thousands of square feet of luxe accommadations.

The prenuptial agreement that Sale had signed before they got married was worthless by the time of the divorce talks "and wouldn't even hold up in court," Sale maintains.

In one of her more extraordinary assertions, Sale—long considered

Woody's PalmPilot—claims that in all the years she was married to the Johnson & Johnson heir she never knew how wealthy he really was, and it came as a shock to her.

"Woody is very private about anything to do with money, including with me—that's why I *never* knew how much money he had," Sale insists. "I never asked and I never really cared because that's not why I married him. We were together for over thirty years, and I wasn't involved in any of the financial end of anything. We were divorced before I realized the extent of what Woody had, of all of his money. I knew we lived the kind of life where I could buy whatever I wanted, but I was a conservative buyer. I still had my St. Louis mentality. When we got divorced I realized, wow, people [like Woody] actually had a billion dollars besides someone like Adnan Khashoggi [the Saudi Arabian reputed arms dealer]."

When the Johnson divorce was finalized in November 2001, Sale did not get the family's palatial apartment at 834 Fifth Avenue, but she was permitted by Woody to reside there for a year while house-hunting. Woody kept 834 to hold social events.

For ten million dollars in 2002, Sale bought a 5,500-square-foot triplex maisonette with five guest bedrooms and five and a half bathrooms at 817 Fifth Avenue—with a private entrance on Fifth Avenue—just a block south of the family home. Her neighbors included the Las Vegas hotel and casino owner Steve Wynn. Richard Gere also lived there for a time. (In late 2010, while residing mostly in Florida, she listed the apartment during the Great Recession for $21 million, more than twice what she had paid.)

Sale also did not get their spectacular farm property in Bedminster, New Jersey. However, Woody permitted her to use the stables and some of the land, mainly because of their daughter Daisy's equestrian activities.

"The farm was where Daisy's horses were kept and where Daisy would ride," says Eric Ryan. "After the divorce, Sale was allowed to stay on and have access to some of the property and, I guess, have use of the guesthouse to accommodate Daisy's needs."

Woody's land, along with surrounding privately owned property, was often used by a Gladstone, New Jersey, organization called the Essex Fox Hounds, founded in 1912, for elegant foxhunts.

"But post-divorce, Sale shut that down," claims Ryan, a lawyer. "She wouldn't give the foxhunt access there anymore. She didn't have the legal standing to do that because she just had tenancy on the guest property, but nobody wanted to deal with her, and they said, okay, what the fuck, we'll stay off the land. Sale's not a pleasant person."

Sale was later "forbidden" by Woody to use the property, and Daisy moved her horses to the WGHR Farm, also in Bedminister. Moreover, Ed Saltzman understood that the Johnson dynasty essentially "disowned Sale completely" after the divorce, and that "they don't even know she's alive."

But Sale disputes any such estrangement and boasts that more than a decade after the divorce, she has remained especially close to her ex-mother-in-law, Betty Johnson, whom she calls "Granny Princess," a nickname bestowed upon the matriarch by her granddaughter Casey. "Betty and I got along great, and we still get along," maintains Sale. "She hangs up the phone and she goes, 'I love you.' At one point she sent me a letter thanking me for being married to her son and taking such good care of him and her grandkids."

When Sale's financial settlement with Woody was finally worked out, she received a whopping $100 million, or at least that's what her father joyfully boasted to several confidants.

Sale says that figure is "wrong," but refuses to elaborate.

"In hindsight," she declares, "I should have gotten *way more money* than I got."

51

Casey Johnson's childhood diabetes, diagnosed when she was eight and a half years old, was revealed by her parents in their 1990s self-help book. But what they weren't aware of at the time was that her increasingly turbulent behavior was attributable to a form of mental illness. She was subsequently diagnosed with borderline personality disorder (BPD), her mother reveals for the first time in 2012, two years after her daughter's death.

As defined by the National Institute of Mental Health (NIMH), BPD is "a serious mental illness marked by unstable moods, behavior, and relationships," the symptoms that Casey always possessed and that grew increasingly severe in the last years of her life. BPD was first listed as a diagnosable illness in 1980 when Casey was one year old, but little was known about it then. But some reported studies have suggested that early symptoms may occur during childhood. In Casey's case, the studies were accurate, based on her erratic behavior, which also was initially linked to her negative physical, emotional, and social reaction to being diabetic.

"Borderline personality disorder ruled Casey's life," declares her mother. "It stole her teenage years and her young adulthood life away from her. It's a mental health disease that confounds, scares, hurts the victim, her family, her friends, and her doctors. They don't want to treat it because it has the highest suicide rate, and no cure, and [someone like Casey] is a twenty-four/seven patient."

In January 2009, *Time*, in a story headlined "The Mystery of Borderline Personality Disorder," quoted noted BPD expert Marsha Linehan, a psychologist at the University of Washington, as stating: "Borderline individuals are the psychological equivalent of third-degree-burn patients. They simply have, so to speak, no emotional skin. Even the slightest touch or movement can create immense suffering."

Beginning when Casey was about nine years old, her mother began taking her to see the first of a number of psychiatrists to try to get her life in order.

Sale, too, went into therapy to help her deal with Casey. But, she claims, the psychiatrist was more interested in what was happening in her active life as a New York socialite, "not in solving any of my issues. After two years of going to him for, like, twice a week, I realized he wasn't helping me."

Plus, she says, her psychiatrist "wanted to charge me for some revisits when I wasn't there," which the wealthy Johnson dynasty wife, who kept a close watch on whether people were trying to cheat the family, couldn't abide.

In any case, it was that doctor who recommended the first psychiatrist that Casey saw.

She was board certified in pediatric and adolescent psychiatry, and had a practice on the Upper East Side, not far from the Johnsons' Fifth Avenue mansion in the sky.

"I would take Casey there every week," relates Sale, "and Casey didn't really want to go because the psychiatrist had not a sense of humor anywhere in her body, and so everything was very serious, and so Casey didn't want to talk to her."

Sale would sit in the waiting room during Casey's sessions, but when the child came out she refused to talk to her mother about what had been discussed. "I would say to her, 'Was everything okay? Did you talk to her? Was she able to help?' You know, talking to a nine-year-old, and Casey would say, 'I didn't talk to her. I don't like her.'"

After a number of sessions, the psychiatrist suggested that Sale go for coffee and return when Casey's session was finished. "It turned out that Casey would wait for ten minutes until after I left and then she'd say she had to go to the bathroom, and she'd lock herself in and wouldn't come out until I came back to pick her up. The psychiatrist *never* told me that—she just kept *taking* the money."

The next to see Casey was another esteemed New York City child psychiatrist who would remain involved with her case for the rest of her life.

"His initial diagnosis was just that she had some depressive issues somewhat related to her diabetes, but then he realized that it was more than that," says Sale, looking back. "Even though Casey was a minor, she told him she didn't want him to talk to her family, and so as a result he didn't include us like he should have." She adds, "He was aware of more intense problems than he told us."

From the beginning of treatment, Sale claims, the psychiatrist began playing the role of "father figure" to Casey "because Woody was not a warm, cuddly kind of person. With Casey, Woody was so uncomfortable because he didn't know what to do with her, or how to react to her situation because she was not easy to deal with. She was very complicated, and it was overwhelming in a large part for Woody despite his best efforts."

Casey's behavior was consistent with BPD, agrees a relative who was aware of the psychiatric efforts to treat her.

"She really reserved the worst of her personality behavior towards people who were closest to her," states this person. "She was the meanest to those who loved her the most, and it was something she had no control over."

It wasn't until 2008 that Sale Johnson says she first confronted the psychiatrist about his treatment and initial diagnosis. It happened on the day Casey was being hospitalized for the fourth time for the same reason: to detoxify her body of the "cocktail of drugs" she had been prescribed to help with her moods and behavior.

"[He] diagnosed Casey as bipolar, but he didn't discuss any of that with us," claims Sale. "I said to him, 'You've never treated Casey as if she had borderline personality disorder, but you do know that that's what she has, don't you?' And he said, 'Yes, I do.' He admitted it."

She also claims he had "a relationship with Casey that was beyond professional" because he sometimes met with her at his apartment if it was at night and his office was closed and she needed to talk. "I don't think that was professional, but Casey worshiped him because he was there for her at her most serious moments. He was her father figure in many ways, and all Casey wanted was her father's approval. She lived for that, and she was broken down because she didn't get it."

In the last couple of years of her life, "Casey sent love letters to her father. She FedExed love letters. She called and left voice mails, and Woody chose not to respond," her mother adds.

$ $ $

After Casey Johnson finally got her high school diploma with much effort, and following her very brief matriculation at Brown, and after her debutante ball in 1998 at the Waldorf Astoria in New York, she took a couple of glamorous jobs in New York to keep herself occupied.

None of them lasted for very long.

One of the disturbed Johnson heiress's jobs, the kind that had required the Johnson dynasty name and influence to acquire, was at a slick lifestyle magazine called *Manhattan File* that covered the upscale and hip. Its founder, editor in chief, and publisher was a young, attractive Cornell University alumnus by the name of Cristina Greeven, who had married former New York governor Mario Cuomo's son, the ABC news personality Christopher "Chris" Cuomo. His brother, Andrew Cuomo, also was elected governor of the Empire State, and had been married to a Kennedy.

In short, Casey's workplace was full of high-powered connections, a veritable cornucopia of iconic dynasties. The Johnson name added even more pizzazz and influence.

Like Casey, Greeven herself was a socialite from a venerable family; her great-grandfather had once served as the German Minister of State, and was renowned for reportedly founding the legendary Orient Express rail line in the early twentieth century. Greeven, who had a home in tony Southampton near the Johnsons, adored Casey. Because the two had something in common—a girly love of anything involving beauty care—she appointed her as the magazine's beauty editor, Casey's lack of any journalistic training notwithstanding.

"She's definitely way ahead of her time. She's not limited by having grown up in the Johnson and Johnson family, in a sheltered environment. She acts as a bridge between everybody," Greeven was quoted as saying in one of the first articles about Casey Johnson in an October 2000 issue of the weekly *New York Observer* newspaper that was headlined, "How to Be the 'It' Girl."

"Cristina really liked Casey and really was a mentor and an older sister figure to Casey," says Casey's friend the trendy journalist Peter Davis, who was the style editor at *Manhattan File*. "Cristina met Casey and saw potential, and realized this was someone from her world and gave her a shot."

Davis, from a wealthy family himself, had first gotten to know Casey, five years his junior, as a fellow member of the upscale Manhattan young social scene—a world that was right out of the TV soap opera *Gossip Girl*.

At *Manhattan File*, with the Johnson name, Casey easily had entre to the beauty products world, so with that imprimatur she was an asset to the magazine. The job was well suited to her. "She was definitely a beauty products junkie," observes Davis. "She told me she wanted to start her own beauty line, an upscale line of products."

While many of the young people in Casey's circle were still living in their parents' Fifth Avenue and Park Avenue homes—like the Hilton sisters—or were in college and finishing schools, Casey had gotten her own duplex, one-bedroom apartment on the Upper East Side. It was starkly contemporary, painted all white, and filled with photos of her idols, Marilyn Monroe and Madonna. One picture, a semi-pornographic shot, was of the almost nude "Material Girl," practically making love to a bottle of Evian water. It was hung in a prominent position over the baby oil heiress's sofa.

"Her apartment was very girly," says Davis. "There was lots of expensive jewelry, and she played Madonna's 'Vogue' over and over and over."

The first time he was at Casey's was with a mutual friend, Juliet Hartford, the daughter from a third marriage of A&P supermarket heir Huntington Hartford II. Casey and Juliet had become bosom buddies and had similar personalities. As Davis puts it, "Both were shy, but always wanted the spotlight, and craved publicity at any costs. I went over there and they were getting ready to go out and gobbing on tons of really thick makeup."

Casey's bathroom was a sight to behold, recalls Davis.

"It had those mirrors with bright bulbs over them, and it looked like a dressing room for a Broadway actress," says Davis, who has never forgotten it. "There were cartons and cartons of makeup and creams. Girls love to collect makeup and beauty products, but this was *overload*."

If Casey emulated and resembled anyone, it was not her mother, or any other female member of the Johnson dynasty. It was her maternal grandmother, the blond and beautiful Mary Melisse Frey, who, in her early twenties, had lived in New York as a cosmetologist. Like her future granddaughter, she had been preoccupied with beauty products. "Casey was the spitting image of my mother," boasts Sale Johnson Rashad. "There are pictures of Casey at ten and my mother at ten and they looked like the same person. They had a great bond. When my mother visited, Casey would dress her up and put makeup on her, and my mom would let Casey dye her hair. They'd go to the drugstore to shop for cosmetics."

Peers thought of Casey as "fun and spunky," "social and precocious," "like a little butterfly, there's a light inside of her," "she has that old guard charm." But few if any knew about the demons that possessed her. Sometimes Casey herself seemed unaware of them.

Peter Davis, who felt he knew her well, considered her "socially withdrawn. She tagged along with girls that were a lot more aggressive and wild and more motivated to get some spotlight. Casey wasn't someone who went to the front of the line and said, 'I'm Casey Johnson. Let me in.' We went to a party and there were these photographers taking pictures and she almost seemed shocked at that point, shocked that people were taking her picture," continues Davis. "She didn't really know how to handle it. She said to me, 'They think I'm a bitch because I don't smile, but I really don't know how to deal with this.' At the same time she craved it, so it was a double-edged sword."

Casey worked at *Manhattan File* no more than eighteen months, but while she was there she took her job seriously. People considered her mature for her age, and she felt she was, too. "When you're diagnosed with a disease at an early age, you're forced to grow up," she once said.

Her New York nights were spent partying. The hot club of the moment at the time was called Moomba, where Leonardo DiCaprio was a regular, and where Casey Johnson grabbed the microphone to mouth Madonna's lyrics on karaoke night. Or, on a weekend, she'd be at the Conscience Point Inn, the "In" nightspot in the trendy Hamptons, dancing with her so-called "celebutante" pals, Paris and Nicky Hilton, and where another flashy and wealthy acquaintance, Elizabeth "Lizzie" Grubman, the daughter of a powerful entertainment lawyer, hung out.

After Casey decided to leave her job at *Manhattan File,* she went to work for Grubman's New York public relations firm, which handled such clients as Britney Spears. "She made an appointment for an interview," Grubman, eight years Casey's senior, later claimed, as if Casey was like any other job applicant. She described her work as "phenomenal." Peter Davis, who also knew Grubman, asserts that Casey and Grubman "knew each other socially. They hire the people they know."

Wild like Casey, the blond, fit, and always tanned Grubman became a tabloid sensation herself when she was arrested at the Conscience Point in Southampton on charges she ran down a crowd of people in her father's black Mercedes SUV, driving in reverse, and injuring at least sixteen. When a security guard asked her to move her vehicle, he claimed she yelled at him, "Fuck you, white trash." She was sentenced to at least sixty days, and it became known in the tabloids as the "Lizzie Grubman Affair."

Casey worked at Grubman's firm several days a week, and was expected to use her Johnson name, influence, and sources in her jam-packed Louis Vuitton Filofax to get the right kind of people to attend parties and events being promoted by the firm. "If it's for Puff Daddy," she once told a reporter, "I'm not going to call my grandmother and say, 'Hey, granny, come to Puffy.' If it's appropriate, I'll call my mother."

Casey celebrated her twenty-first birthday around the time her father was buying the Jets and her parents were negotiating their divorce settlement. The party was thrown at the famed Manhattan nightclub "21." About two dozen people had shown up to watch the heiress blow out the candles, among them Nicky Hilton, Marty Richards, and Casey's godmother, Diandra Douglas, who considered Casey the daughter she never had, and who would continue to play a key role in Casey's life.

$ $ $

Around 2001, Casey Johnson fled New York for Los Angeles—La-La Land.

Initially, she had a fantasy that she might become an actress or a singer (she'd taken singing lessons since she was twelve), but mainly she just wanted to get away from her family. That was underscored by a story she once told about attending a Hollywood party where she overheard one girl telling another, "'Oh, that's the Johnson and Johnson girl,' and my heart just sank because I don't want to be identified like that. I'm Casey Johnson. I'm not the Johnson and Johnson girl. It really hurt."

In Hollywood, her life would become a nightmare, her already distant relationship with her father and mother would be damaged, and it would all end horrifically.

But, in the beginning, the Baby Powder heiress with the baby face had high hopes, even though she initially knew no one in the City of Angels. It took her almost four years to get adjusted to the L.A. scene.

Like so many members of the Johnson dynasty before her, she was wary of people, and felt some took advantage of her because she was a Johnson. "You really have to get to know why someone wants to be your friend," she firmly believed, "and I've learned that the hard way. I've found a lot of people use me . . . I just let things happen, and then I find out, 'Oh, my God, they're totally taking advantage of me.'"

That's what she would claim to friends after the *Vanity Fair* imbroglio in 2006.

It had all started when Richard Johnson (no relation), then the editor of the *New York Post*'s Page Six gossip column, telephoned Casey, and read to her an exchange of leaked e-mails between a man who had been her boyfriend, John Dee, and her aunt, Casey's father's sister, Elizabeth Ross "Libet" Johnson, strongly suggesting a romance had occurred between the two behind Casey's back.

Rather than offering a "no comment" and hanging up, Casey went ballistic. She blasted Libet in a column that appeared in the *Post* on March 29, 2006, charging that her eccentric, five-times-married, fifty-six-year-old socialite cougar aunt had seduced and stolen her thirty-eight-year-old boyfriend. Casey was quoted as saying Libet "needs help . . . I feel sorry for her. She's single. She's been divorced umpteen times. She's afraid to go out in public . . . She was sleeping with my boyfriend who I was in love with. An old woman with a lot of money is a very powerful aphrodisiac."

It was such a blockbuster of a story, where all the principals were named and/or quoted, that the Rupert Murdoch–owned *Post*, which thrives on scandal, prominently featured the story, as if World War III had been declared.

To the ultra-secret and private Woody Johnson and the Johnson dynasty as a whole, Casey was now considered a tabloid terrorist, and her act of vengeance their own personal 9/11.

Woody, who had mostly washed his hands of Casey because of how troublesome she was, cut off all ties with his daughter. He tied up her trust fund millions, including the interest, which had financed Casey's high-style life in New York and then in Los Angeles ever since she had received her first big check at twenty-one.

Having seen the damage her words had caused within the family, one would have thought she'd go underground and keep her plump, injected lips zipped.

But Casey didn't stop with the *Post*.

When *Vanity Fair* contacted her and said they wanted to write a profile, Casey was in heaven.

Her mother wasn't.

"She talked to me about it and I said, 'Casey, you absolutely should not do this. They don't write nice articles. They write articles that sell magazines,'" recalls Sale, who didn't like or trust journalists. "I told her, 'They are not filled with real facts that make you look good, and you're not going to look good.' She said, 'No, Mom, it's a puff piece. They said they are going to say really nice things and they are going to show beautiful pictures.'"

As usual, Casey didn't take her mother's advice.

She dolled herself up, draped herself in diamonds, and cooperated, meeting with a female writer in a New York restaurant, and then inviting her for more interviewing at her Spanish-style mansion in Bel Air, shoveling more dirt about her aunt in what became a lengthy cover story aptly titled "Heiress vs. Heiress," which ran in September 2006.

When it hit the stands, any hope for a rapprochement with her father, aunt, and paternal grandmother was buried for good.

Beyond Casey's destructive quotes was the shocking photograph for which she agreed to pose: appearing baby-fat chunky at five-foot-two, arrogantly exhaling a haze of cigarette smoke through bloated lips, her blond hair done up like Monroe, she was practically nude, except for a towel covering her surgically enhanced breasts, and her private parts.

"Casey wanted attention, and this was her first big stab at getting it," observes Peter Davis. "And I think what she did with the *Post* and the magazine was kind of a public cry for help. A lot of her behavior was rebellion to piss off her parents."

Casey had certainly succeeded.

"She was not very savvy in the ways of the press," says a Casey confidant in Los Angeles. "Casey told me *Vanity Fair* told her that they were going to write the story anyway without her, and Casey thought if she cooperated the story would be less brutal on her than if she didn't cooperate. She told me, 'If I cooperate with them, they'll write a nice fluff piece. If I don't cooperate with them and they do it without me, God knows what they'll write.' They threw her under the bus, and over the coals. Her reaction to the story was immediate horror," he says. "But she still didn't realize how far-reaching the damage was until it caused her whole family to unravel."

Poor little rich girl Casey, as it turned out, had become the most recent in a series of Johnson dynasty heirs and heiresses who had heaped embarrassment and shame on the family.

"There's been lots of things going on in the Johnson family that have been embarrassing," declares Sale Johnson. "It's not like they were not *used* to that. I mean, Woody's sister has been divorced five times. Between that and his brothers' deaths, and his father and his grandfather [the General], it's been a complicated family. But *Vanity Fair* took complete advantage of Casey. They twisted everything she said, and they said things that weren't true. They inflamed the [family] situation that was only mild and that now became scathing."

Beyond that she asserts that because of Casey's borderline personality disorder she wasn't thinking straight agreeing to cooperate with the magazine because "BPD controlled every aspect of her life. She was unstable."

52

Whatever Casey Johnson's emotional and physical state, her very public and harmful tell-all about her aunt, Libet Johnson, had the instant effect of alienating virtually everyone—on both sides. The Johnson dynasty disowned her, and Libet's own circle was mortified.

Without having any say in the matter, the very private, much older Johnson heiress who had lived with her hundreds of millions of trust fund dollars under the radar for most of her life was suddenly, embarrassingly, caught in the tabloid spotlight.

Still, little was publicly known about Bobby and Betty Johnson's third child, who was born in 1950—the middle child and only girl of a rambunctious brood of boys—after Woody and Keith, and before Billy and Christopher.

Libet's best friend growing up on Edgerstoune Road in Princeton, who remained her lifelong confidante and defender, was pretty, bright Lucinda Ziesing, whose mother, Faith Whitney Ziesing, had served as the president of the New York Junior League and was a founder of the Women's National Republican Club. Her father, Faith's second husband, was Hibben Ziesing, a chemical consultant.

The Ziesings were the Johnsons' next-door neighbors, and because Lucinda's two sisters were a decade older, she immediately bonded with Libet, who back then was skinny, shy, and, like her brothers, had fair skin and was blond like their mother.

"Libet was my gang," says Ziesing many years later. "I would run over there for fun. Libet and I have been friends forever."

Ziesing also adored Libet's mom.

"Very rarely," she says, "do you get a woman who hasn't come from money to be trained to know what to do and how to behave. But Betty stepped into the role after Bob died."

The two bosom buddies, Libet and Lucinda, went to the exclusive Miss Fine's School, founded in the late nineteenth century by May Margaret Fine, offering college preparation classes long before many young women considered going to college.

By the time Libet was matriculating there, however, Miss Fine's had become part of the then all-boys Princeton Country Day, where her brothers Woody and Keith attended. Ziesing would date Jeff Delano, Keith's friend at PCD who was part of the group with Keith that went on to Millbrook School and had to repeat ninth grade. And when Woody broke his back, Ziesing, who was living on an Indian reservation out west during her hippie period, went to visit him in Arizona to cheer him up. (She later made millions as one of the founders of the Celestial Seasonings tea company.)

Ziesing was a class ahead of Libet at Miss Fine's when Betty Johnson transferred her thirteen-year-old daughter, who had become a bit of a wild child like her brothers, to the stricter, Catholic all-girls Stuart Country Day School of the Sacred Heart, in Princeton, when it first opened in 1963, according to Ziesing. The school had been named for Mother Janet Erskine Stuart, a Roman Catholic nun and educator from Britain. One of her books was *The Education of Catholic Girls*, another *Highways and Byways in the Spiritual Life*.

It didn't appear, though, that any of Mother Janet Stuart's stern Catholic teachings had any impact on the wealthy Johnson heiress, who would be married and divorced five times, and have a slew of boyfriends over the years, even including one stolen from her niece, if the published stories were to be believed.

One of the first very young men in Libet's romantic life was the teenager Neil Vicino, her brother Keith's best friend, who wasn't completely swept away by her. Looking back many years later after his own marriage and divorce, he recalls, "Libet was quite quiet and demure and almost introverted, and she certainly didn't seem to have that party thing going on that Woody had. There were times when we would go into Bob and Betty's bedroom and watch TV," he continues, "and when I had a school dance, I invited Libet, and there were a couple of other dates along the way."

After Stuart, Libet was able to get into Sarah Lawrence College with the possible assistance of Lucinda Ziesing's mother, who had been a trustee at the college and was one of the first Sarah Lawrence alumna appointed to the college faculty. Libet spent a year there, says Lucinda.

Like her troubled niece Casey, Libet Johnson apparently wasn't much interested in academia.

Libet did her generations's sex, drugs, and rock 'n' roll thing, too, for a while, to the chagrin of her very conservative mother, Betty, around the time her father, Bobby Johnson, died in 1970.

"She bought a Ford Econoline van and had a carpenter outfit the interior like a camper and spent a summer traveling around to music festivals with another girlfriend," recalls her cousin Eric Ryan. "Her family was *totally* horrified that Libet had developed this burning-incense-and-writing-poetry-by-candlelight kind of persona for a brief period, and maybe even walked around without a brassiere on."

Her first husband was an executive at Columbia Records in New York, by the name of Christopher Wright. Considered "the straightest guy in the world" by the likes of Eric Ryan, Wright also was a talented landscape painter who worked in the style of Andrew Wyeth. When Libet and Chris were dating they had spent a romantic weekend in the town of Blue Hill, in Maine, and had stayed at the Blue Hill Inn, an intimate bed-and-breakfast built in 1835 and near the headwaters of Blue Hill Bay.

They had a big, albeit private, wedding and reception at the Johnson home in Princeton, and had planned to have their honeymoon at the Blue Hill. But Libet's groom was stuck at the record company because of a financial scandal there, and he felt a responsibility to his employer to do damage control, according to Ryan.

"As a result," he says, "Libet was left waiting up in Maine, like, 'Well, where's my new husband? This is *no* fun.'"

After they got married, they were so entranced with the Blue Hill, they actually bought the inn, "thinking they could live a simple life where she would be the innkeeper, and he could use the empty rooms in the inn to paint because the place only did business in the summer," says Ryan.

That first summer, circa 1977, Libet hired Ryan to help run the place at a time when his troubled mother, Mary Lea Johnson, was then in the daily tabloid headlines because of the hit man and kinky sex scandal involving her then husband, Vincent D'Arc. Ryan also brought along his girlfriend of the moment, Rebecca, as his assistant chief cook and bottle washer.

"The inn was doing okay business-wise, and Libet's accountants had told her to run the place as if it was a real business. As a result of that admonition, she paid Rebecca and myself the princely sum of $62.50 a week to work like what turned out to be fourteen hours a day, and Rebecca and I shared a little room in the attic that I actually built in the attic with plywood because, again, Libet's accountants wanted all the real rooms in the inn to generate revenue. Meanwhile, Libet would spend all of her time shopping for antiques."

Libet's first celebrity guest, and possibly her last, was a bodybuilder from Austria by the name of Arnold Schwarzenegger, who at the time had just become known as the star of a documentary called *Pumping Iron*. Libet and Chris happened to be friends with George Butler, the film's director, and invited him and his muscle-bound main attraction to visit the Blue Hill.

"Butler introduced Arnold to Libet and she took a big shine to him," observes Ryan, who broke bread at dinner with them, and saw the sparks fly.

Ryan doesn't know for certain whether anything of a romantic nature happened between his cousin Libet and the future *Terminator* star and governor of California. But Schwarzenegger certainly had a reputation as a womanizer, and later in life fathered a love child with a household staffer during his marriage to the Kennedy clan's Maria Shriver.

"It's hard to say if anything happened between Libet and Arnold, but there was certainly a flirtation between them," notes Ryan. "Chris and Libet ended up getting divorced shortly thereafter. She got bored with the inn, sold it, and they moved to Concord, Massachusetts. Their marriage only lasted about fourteen months, from inception to end."

$ $ $

As with the bed-and-breakfast, Libet also would eventually become bored with another business enterprise that she had jumped headfirst into in the late seventies—an art gallery in Manhattan's trendy SoHo district, inspired by her intense and growing interest in esoteric folk art, which the heiress was collecting in huge and costly quantities.

Some say she was following in the footsteps of Seward Johnson Jr.'s ex-wife, Barbara, who was running the troubled Folk Art Museum in New York, and who herself had built a world-class folk art and whaling collection. Another dynasty member considered an inspiration for Libet's interest was Mary Lea Johnson, who had had an art gallery in Manhattan.

In 1979, a Madison Avenue folk art dealer by the name of Jimmy Cronin, whose best customer was Libet Johnson, introduced her to a new dealer in the business, Roger Ricco. At the time, Ricco and his wife were living in a Chelsea loft that was about to go co-op and he had just three days to come up with the forty-thousand-dollar deposit, which he didn't have. Enter Libet Johnson. She came in to his pop-up gallery on a Wednesday, the first day of Ricco's three-day deadline, and immediately purchased eighty thousand dollars' worth of collectible folk art, the biggest piece costing about ten thousand dollars. Ricco had to split the sale with his business partner, but he now magically had the forty thousand dollars in hand to buy the loft.

"It's this mystical destiny stuff in which I live my life," says Ricco decades later of Libet's appearance and purchase.

A few days later he rode up the service elevator to Libet's penthouse to deliver her latest acquisitions, which he remembers as a "jaw-dropping" moment. "I've met a lot of wealthy people, but this was really *up* there even at that time. I was let in by one of her help, and her apartment was *huge*, and I was standing in the grand living room that was about forty or fifty feet across, and was just amazed at it all."

Two other things amazed him about that second encounter with the Band-Aid millionaires. "She had a problem with alcohol, and even on that first visit to her apartment I realized that she was kind of loose, let's say," recalls Ricco. "I could see that. It doesn't take much to pick it up. What also struck me during that first encounter was that she was extraordinarily lonely. Here was a young woman with unlimited wealth, able to do anything she wanted. But the salient word that just hangs with me is a sense of loneliness. I saw it that day I walked into her apartment and I saw this huge place with this young, beautiful woman wandering on the polished floors. It was in the middle of a sunny New York day and I could tell that she had been drinking, so that made me feel sad."

The other thing that amazed him—and relieved him in that moment of sadness—was that Libet out of the blue asked him if he wanted to go into business with her in a gallery specializing in folk art, and he immediately, joyfully said yes to his wealthy new client and partner, and they shook on it. At the time he had an art restoration business, Whole Art. But with Libet's offer, he immediately sold it to his help for one dollar.

Libet had turned his life upside down and opened up a fantasy-like new world. "I come from the Midwest, from a blue-collar family, and I was thrown into a world in which what she might spend in a day on throw rugs for the bathroom would be close to my yearly salary at that time."

Despite Libet's loneliness and whatever other problem Ricco perceived his new partner had, he says that early on in their relationship, "I just loved her, thought she was terrific, adventurous, had absolute enthusiasm, and everything else."

She put up about three hundred thousand dollars, and the partners immediately began looking for a space in SoHo and found it on Broome Street, and Libet retained an architect to design the place.

"We were buying a lot of inventory—objects that people were selling. But her warning words to me were, 'I'm not going to be a shopkeeper!' But I didn't expect her to be because she was Libet Johnson, a society lady."

With the business running, the two socialized. Along the way, he met her brother Woody a couple of times, and their mother, Betty, who "was kind of proud that Libet had started a gallery."

On one incredible occasion Libet invited Ricco and his wife on a cruise through the Adriatic aboard the *Sea Prince,* the spectacular yacht that had been owned by her late brother, Keith, who had died of a cocaine overdose, and about whom she never spoke. He remembers being aboard the boat with so much beauty and the sea around them, but everyone else aboard seemed "blasé," including a woman guest who spent all of her time knitting, instead of enjoying the setting.

Libet invited him to her estate in Millbrook, where she wanted him to participate in a foxhunt with her and her rich friends and their hounds. "I was very much involved in Buddhism and not in killing anything, and the fun of that day was to do a hounds after the foxes. I didn't lecture her, but I said, 'Can you imagine watching this hunt from a glider and here you all are chasing this little fox for fun. It looks absurd to me.' I wasn't being judgmental, but I realized I couldn't live that life."

One evening in September 1982, he accompanied her to the opera, but Libet was in a state of devastation. She had just heard that a woman she idolized from afar, the actress and Princess of Monaco, Grace Kelly, had been killed in an automobile accident after suffering a stroke at the wheel. "Libet was so upset about the loss of Grace because she admired her so much."

By the third year of their business partnership, Ricco began to feel a chill from Libet, who was less involved and interested in their gallery. "I would attribute it to a certain amount of fickleness on her part, meaning she'd get really interested in something, and then have to move on."

Like her brother Woody's first business partner who got axed, Ricco's days as Libet's associate were numbered.

Finally, around 1983–1984, "Her financial people called me up and asked me to come up to her apartment, and I kind of expected it. She had become less of a participant." At the same time, Ricco says, a new form of folk art made by unknowns was coming into vogue—many of the artists were poor blacks from the South, some others were mental patients. "But Libet didn't get on board with the new stuff. She didn't have or gain quick enough interest. She didn't get the future and she called her people at that point and probably said, What is this guy doing? Fortunately, they got rid of me."

He says he never heard from her again.

"She had supported me out of nowhere, and I felt I had gotten something good out of the situation. I'd later hear things about her, that she was marrying this guy, or that guy. I came to think anything's possible—particularly in that family."

Looking back years later, he says it was sad that they hadn't stayed in touch "because I had a lot to offer her as a friend, not as a commodity."

$ $ $

After her first divorce, Libet had a couple of boyfriends "including country western singers with outlaw reputations," according to Eric Ryan, before she married husband number two, another in the record industry, Arma Andon.

"It was a pretty wild ride," recalls Andon of their relationship. "It was exciting."

It also was tragic and turbulent.

The half-Armenian Andon, a charming and outgoing Fordham University graduate, had first gotten to know Libet when she was married to Chris Wright, who was a colleague of Andon's at Columbia Records, where Andon was then "a young marketing guy" in his midtwenties.

After the Libet-Wright divorce, "Somehow Libet and I just bumped into each other somewhere," he says years later. The two began dating and "eventually moved in with each other." At the time, Libet was living in a sumptuous ground-floor apartment in an Upper East Side brownstone.

"She was the love of my life," notes Andon. "Libet can have a big impact on you. She was also beautiful on top of everything."

Not long after they began cohabitating, they were married in a civil ceremony by a New York City judge. "It was just us, Woody, and the judge—and Woody gave her away," he says. Another who Andon recalls might have been in attendance for the simple nuptials was the couple's pal Jimmy Pullis, who owned JP's, a small Upper East Side bar that was a hangout for the music and druggie crowd.

After Libet and Andon said their vows, they checked into the Eloise Suite at the Plaza Hotel and celebrated with some twenty friends.

It was, he says, "low key."

Later, the young marrieds—along with Pullis—vacationed together for two weeks in the Mexican resort city of Puerto Vallarta. "It was great fun," recalls Andon.

At the time, Pullis and his club had a reputation for always having a supply of cocaine available for friends and customers, according to Libet's cousin Eric Ryan, who frequented JP's. Pullis's involvement with cocaine also was documented by Bob Woodward in *Wired*, his biography of John Belushi, who died of a drug overdose, and was also a chum of Pullis.

JP's had a very private gathering spot downstairs—"a kind of a secret room," according to Ryan. "There was a fair amount of cocaine ingested in the place. Arma was there quite a bit, and Libet probably. On any given night you might run into Belushi, or people from the rock 'n' roll world. I'd go in around closing time and play backgammon and drink brandy and snort coke with the bartender—all the bartenders were in the Social Register—until the sun came up. It was that kind of place."

Because of Andon's career and lifestyle, he was considered by Libet's brothers and cousins to be the coolest of who would be her five husbands. "That's because Arma had a fun life," observes Sale Johnson Rashad. "I loved Arma and he was great for Libet. He became the youngest vice president in charge of artists at Columbia. He had a great job and he was *really* good at his job.'"

Libet was pregnant, or about to become pregnant when her brother Keith died of his cocaine overdose, and their brother Billy died in a motorcycle accident less than two months later. "There were people dropping like flies from overdoses," Andon notes.

Not long after those Johnson tragedies, another occurred, likely as a result of the first two.

"We lost a child," reveals Andon. "Libet had a miscarriage. It was really awful. There was a lot of stress. I was with her when she got both phone calls, that Keith, who I had never even met, and Billy had died. It was devastating—*devastating*. I don't know how that family held up, especially Woody, because he had to become kind of the patriarch of the whole operation, and he still is. He made his own way. He was born into wealth, but he did pretty well on his own."

All told, Libet and Andon were together for "maybe three years—not the marriage, I mean the whole thing. Just because I married a rich girl, I continued to work. She did her thing and I did my thing." He believes it ended because they were "too young" or "not a proper" match. He later rose to head of marketing at Columbia Records, and was instrumental in the careers of the likes of Aerosmith and Bruce Springsteen.

"My marriage to Libet was," he states years later after remarrying and having a family, "a time that was fraught with drama and with tragedy, and there were times of just complete total fun and excitement. It was kind of a mixed bag."

$ $ $

Next on Libet's Hit Parade of husbands—number three—was far different from Andon.

Waspy, tall, and with the look of the Marlboro Man, but with a Jay Leno chin, James "Jamie" Whitall had an MBA, had worked on Wall Street, was in the real estate and communications fields, and was later a mortgage broker. Libet, who was one of five children, had always wanted a big family herself. With Whitall, she had the first of what eventually would be four children, two girls and two boys with three of her five husbands.

Their daughter, born around 1981, was Libet's namesake—Elizabeth Ross Johnson Whitall—but was known as Lily, the great-great-granddaughter, like Casey Johnson, of Johnson & Johnson cofounder Robert Wood Johnson. Lily graduated from the New School and owned a swimwear company. In 2008, at twenty-seven, she married an animation artist in a ceremony officiated by a female interfaith minister at her mother's sprawling estate in Millbrook, New York, the town where the uncle she never knew, Keith Johnson, had first tripped on LSD at Timothy Leary's estate.

By the time Libet's marriage to Whitall ended, most members of the Johnson dynasty had lost track of who was fourth and who was fifth, they seemed to change so often.

One of her next husbands was Christopher James Kennan, one of the four children of the diplomat and Pulitzer Prize–winning historian George F. Kennan, who developed America's Cold War foreign policy. The senior Kennan, who died at 101 in 2005 at his home in Princeton, was considered an "elitist" who wrote an unpublished book asserting that blacks, women, and immigrants should be disenfranchised, according to a book by Walter Isaacson and Evan Thomas that was mentioned in Kennan's *Washington Post* obituary.

Chris Kennan, a Yale graduate, had been the personal assistant to David Rockefeller, and worked as a legislative liaison in the administration of New Jersey governor Brendan Byrne. With him, Libet had a son, Oliver, who became a musician. In October 1994, the tabloid *New York Post* reported in its Page Six gossip column—the same one that would break the news about Libet snagging Casey's boyfriend—that "It's splitsville" for Libet and Kennan. "Libet, sister of Woody Johnson IV, is said to have broken the news with a

'Dear John' letter to her spouse, explaining that the flame had gone out . . . Libet is keeping the apartment in River House and the estate in Millbrook."

Libet was said to have been living at the exclusive River House at the same time that Mary Lea Johnson and Marty Richards were in residence.

After Libet and Kennan were divorced, he remarried, but says many years later he's still "very fond of my former wife, and of her brothers."

Another husband was Jonathan Teal, with whom Libet had two children, Annabel Johnson Teal and John Lansing-Johnson Teal.

All of Libet's husbands were said to have signed prenuptial agreements, just as Sale Johnson had done when she married Libet's brother Woody, and as other men and women had done who had married into the Johnson dynasty over the years. Based on his cousin's marital success rate batting average—0 for 5—Eric Ryan wryly asserts, "Libet should have had a whole stack of pre-nups in her bedside table because she could not stay married. She has the inability to find happiness. The matrimonial bar lost a great client when Libet stopped marrying and divorcing."

He recalls attending a Christmas party with his then wife at Libet's in the early 2000s and Libet, "sort of giggling, said, 'I don't know how the two of you do it—still together after all this time,' and that was basically her greeting to us, being totally shocked that we were still together." In early 2011, however, Ryan and his wife—they had a young adult daughter—were in the process of getting a divorce, which was later finalized.

One of Libet's problems was that she attempted to turn each of her husbands into some ideal of what the perfect husband should be.

"She would find these men and then change them—re-dress them, redirect them, and then she controlled them," a family member asserts. "But then they weren't what she wanted anymore because in the end she didn't really want to be controlling her husband, so then she was unhappy. It was a combination of being spoiled and domineering and controlling. She *loves* her kids, but she never really found what she wanted in a man."

Former sister-in-law Sale Johnson liked and respected Libet and thought she was "a very cool person. She's smart. She's clever. She has a great sense of style and exquisite taste. But she did like to party—and she had a lot of issues."

Those issues resulted in Libet going into rehab, or as Ryan notes, "She has had a couple of runs through Betty Ford. But Libet was never as publicly a train wreck as Casey," he adds. "It was more things like forgetting expensive jewelry in taxi cabs."

When Libet was pregnant and married to John Teal he was said to have told her that if she didn't go into rehab he would divorce her and take their child, so she checked into the Betty Ford Center.

"While Libet was in rehab John, Woody, his wife Sale, and Libet's mother and I think her husband, Doug, flew out there," recounts a relative. "They met with Libet's counselor and they all were asked how they felt about being there. I was told that when they got to Sale she said she never drank and never took drugs, and that now she was in a room full of alcoholics and drug addicts, and didn't like being there. Libet was furious. She said she was embarrassed that she needed the treatment, and that she was especially embarrassed that her sister-in-law Sale was there to hear about her problems because she felt Sale lived on a pedestal and everything she touched turned to gold."

Years later, Sale Johnson says she never realized that her sister-in-law "had any *real* problems because she didn't ever do much with us. We got together mainly for family things, but she did things with *her* friends, and I think she didn't really want Woody to know about her social life."

$ $ $

After her last divorce, the petite, blond Libet Johnson, a jet-setter with a flamboyant lifestyle, had a number of boyfriends—brief romances that put her and them in boldface in the gossip pages. Among them were the singer Michael Bolton; the actor Michael Nouri; the hairdresser to the stars in New York, Frederic Fekkai (who Casey gleefully told *Vanity Fair* dumped her aunt and "she was devastated"). Libet reportedly also became involved with a dashing Frenchman, Jerome Jeandin, who was her chauffeur when she stayed at the chicest hotel in Paris, the Ritz, where Princess Diana was in residence before she was killed. It was reported that when Libet dropped Jeandin, she sent him off with a gift—a fire engine red Ferrari valued at a couple of hundred thousand dollars.

But it was Libet's relationship with a weight-loss doctor from Trinidad by the name of Lionel Bissoon that sparked an embarrassing story in *New York* magazine just eighteen months after Casey's very embarrassing tell-all about Libet in *Vanity Fair*.

The story, entitled "Libet in Love," included among the photographs one of a 1998 oil painting commissioned by the Johnson heiress of herself, tastefully, but seductively reclining on a chaise wearing, as the magazine pointed out, "a stunning Valentino dress of chiffon, silk, and diamonds . . . hiked toward her knees, ruffles cascading carelessly to the leopard-skin rug on the floor . . . It's the portrait of a seductress."

The making of the portrait of Libet Johnson became more of a two-year, sometimes infuriating saga than a series of routine sittings, the society portraitist James Childs recalls in late 2012, fourteen years after he completed his final brush stroke of her in bewitching repose.

"I don't know what she is—a pearl in an oyster, or whatever it is"—is how the artist, looking back at the project, curiously characterizes his difficult model-client as she is depicted on canvas.

Childs wasn't the first painter of the rich and famous whom Libet had sought out to mythologize her in oils. If First Lady Jacqueline Kennedy could choose Aaron Shikler—once described as the "Gilbert Stuart of the jet set"—to immortalize her in a renowned official portrait that prominently hangs in the Vermeil Room of the White House along with those he did of Nancy Reagan and Hillary Clinton, well, he was certainly good enough for Libet, who saw herself as one of the glamorous first ladies of the Johnson dynasty. Shikler's portrait, however, was rather odd, to Childs's classicist artist eyes. "The painting was *huge* and Libet's barefoot in a long black dress, peeking around a doorway. I don't love it, and I think it was really a silly idea. The bare feet—and she has very small feet—was a ridiculous conceit for a woman like her."

Along with Libet commissioning Childs to paint her, she also had him do a portrait of one of her four children, teenager Lily, around the same time, in the mid-1990s. It was a huge, life-size rendition—"it's very beautiful," he boasts—with the child standing on a faux granite stand, made by her mother's people. As Childs describes the "simple and straightforward" portrait, for which Libet had paid a cool fifty thousand dollars (plus more for preliminary sketches), "Lily's a princess on a pedestal," he says, chuckling.

The Childs-Johnson relationship, which would end badly, had started on a high note when she telephoned him "out of the blue," circa 1996, saying, "I've seen your work. I *love* artists, I *love* working with artists." Still, he had no idea who she was because "she stays a little bit below the radar as much as she can." Since he knew a lot of the people she knew—he'd previously done a portrait of her wealthy socialite chum, Carolyne Roehm, who was the second wife of billionaire Wall Street titan Henry Kravitz, and one of another of Libet's acquaintances, the super-rich media mogul Christopher "Kip" Forbes, Malcolm's son—he made a few calls.

"I said this woman called me, who is that? And they said, oh, gosh, she's one of *the* richest people, she's a powerful woman."

Childs's contract with the heiress required that she pose six times "in person" at his studio for three hours at a time, eighteen hours in all—"they have to pose for me no matter who they think they are." But the project would drag on and on, take months and months to complete, because of her demanding ways.

Libet, it appeared, tended to seek out as friends people who worked for her, or with her, and James Childs was no exception.

Immediately, she "tried to pull" him into her social circle. She invited him to dinner parties with guests that included her interior decorator to the socially wealthy Greg Jordan—once described as having a "well-mannered approach and a knack for befriending the right people"—with whom Libet often travelled and had as a walker, and who, Childs says, "she was crazy about" until his death at forty-eight. Another was former National Academy of Design director John Dobkin, who was married to a Habsburg princess, and for whom Childs once worked. Others in the circle included the actor Matthew Modine and his wife, plus a bevy of Manhattan socialites.

Childs was a guest for one of Libet's glitzy, very discreet soirees—with a dee-jay, dancing, dinner, and a sail around Manhattan island—aboard the *Sea Prince*, the beautiful sailing vessel that she had taken over after the drug death of her brother, Keith, many years earlier. The artist also escorted her, and some of her four children, to movies such as *The Birdcage*, a comedy about a drag queen and a gay cabaret owner.

Despite all of her wealth, her relatively large brood of four from her five marriages, her many acquaintances, her constant entertaining, there was something sad about her, Childs felt. Like Roger Ricco, her art gallery partner back in the '70s, the artist thought Libet Johnson "was like a tiny, little lonely person. One of the things that made me feel that she might be kind of a lonely woman was the fact that she always had children with everybody. It made me feel like there was a void somewhere in her life. A lot of women like her who are very conscious of their looks would never have all those children."

She once asked Childs to take her to lunch at the trendy downtown Manhattan restaurant Balthazar, and they were chauffeured there in her gleaming Bentley. "She kept saying she was *starving*, but then she ate hardly anything. I had a glass of wine with lunch and I said, 'Would you like something to drink?' She said, 'I'd love to have a glass of wine, but not today.' And then I remembered that she had alluded to the fact that there was a [drinking] problem before.

"She was very straightforward. She told me about all that, the cocaine and alcohol, and mentioned rehab. She just said she had straightened herself out. She was open about when she was sort of involved with substances. I think she wanted me to know that she had lived, and had overcome."

Through it all he learned much about the very private, very rich Band-Aid heiress, and how she perceived herself, that helped him in the painting of her, dubbed "Lady X," in the tradition of *Madame X,* the artist John Singer Sargent's late-nineteenth-century portrait of a notorious and beautiful young socialite, on display in the Metropolitan Museum of Art, in New York City.

"Having spent time with Libet, I began to see that she thought of herself as a very sensual, very seductive woman," he asserts. "I learned from being around her kind of how she perceived herself, and how she tried to act around men. I don't know how attractive she *thinks* she is, but I know that she does feel like she wants men in her life." But Childs himself didn't find her to be sexy as other men had. "She's a plain woman, really. She looks good when she's put together, but she has a rather average face. She keeps her figure, and she's careful about all those things."

When he began the painting process he noted that she had a very large bosom courtesy, he believed, of breast implants, but that soon changed. "She took them out during the process. I don't know if it was because of a boyfriend, or it was just her own mood at the time. She had the implants and was busty, but in the end she had about half of that [measurement]."

At the time, in her mid-forties, she was romantically involved with a twenty-five-year-old boy from Argentina who was working in finance, but that affair soon ended, according to Childs. "He was an intern or something in a bank, or in Wall Street, and was a well-brought-up boy from a wealthy family, and she went to Argentina to meet his family and I guess they gave her the cold shoulder," recalls Childs. "I don't know if they put the kibosh on it, but they weren't happy to see her, and it ended. It was one of those things that wasn't going to go anywhere."

While the Johnson heiress professed an avid interest in art, she seemed to have little knowledge of it and a rather questionable level of taste, Childs discovered. What she did have, though, was an endless checkbook to buy whatever suited her at the moment, whether or not it was worthy.

"I don't think she was *finished,* as they used to say at the turn of the century when a woman was schooled a certain way and had a drawing master and a dancing master. I think she picked up things as she went along, and she probably found out about [gracious] things from her interior decorator. The Vanderbilt girls, for instance, were very educated. It was taken seriously to prepare these women. It didn't seem that Libet had any of that. She wasn't really a refined woman in those ways.

"She'd have a Sotheby's catalogue and she'd say to me, 'What about these paintings?' that she intended to buy. But she didn't particularly seem to know much about painting, and some of them were not very good."

For her portrait, Libet had a number of demands, things Childs had never before experienced as portraitist of the wealthy. For one, she wanted an entire set built in his studio to accommodate the look she was hoping for, and certain possessions that she had. The leopard skin rug in the painting had come from a jungle cat she said her father claimed he had bagged on a safari, part of that collection he had in his study in Florida. The skin as it turned out was too small for the proportions of the painting—"she looked like she was on a magic carpet, and it just looked stupid"—so he had to spend six weeks to turn it into a bigger rug, just to draw and execute it.

The silk, brown in color, her favorite, that was hung in the background of the portrait came from Fortuny, purveyor of the most expensive fabric money can buy, hand-made in Venice, which arrived at the studio at a cost of about six thousand dollars. The Valentino dress she wore, which also cost thousands, had been selected by Childs from Libet's "incredible" closet of clothes. The mahogany wainscoting on the wall was built by her carpenters, and another of her paid minions did the faux finish.

In order to give the portrait something of the look of a famous painting done in 1800 and housed in the Louvre, that of glamorous French socialite Jeanne-Françoise Julie Adélaïde Récamier, who posed reclining on a chaise, Libet ordered two from high-end Manhattan antiques purveyor Kentshire, sent over to Childs's studio for his selection. The one she posed on was Napoleonic, and "must have cost her a fortune," states Childs.

"She had all this stuff sent to my studio and after I'd arranged it and edited it, I said to her, 'Well, how do you envision the painting?' And she said, 'Oh, life size.' I said, 'No, Libet,' and she just looked at me like—*how dare you!* She's not used to being contradicted."

He explained to her that the picture would have so much detail and precious things in it—jewels and satins—that it had to be painted like a Dutch master, like a Vermeer, which is how it ended up, in Childs's estimation. Even though she had brought in her makeup artist, her photographer, and her hairdresser to make her look glamorous—and she did—they battled over some aspects of her look as he was painting, such as her nose, which she claimed resembled that of a prizefighter. "That wasn't a good day," he recalls. "She's tough and demanding, but I will change anything that doesn't affect the artistic quality." She got the nose she wanted.

But not the negligée that she wanted to pose in, according to Childs. "She actually talked about that at one point." Childs refused to permit it.

Another time, Libet appeared at the studio with three or four very expensive antique frames from Lowy, the fanciest in New York, which she wanted for the portrait. She asked him to choose one. "I said for what, and she said, 'Well, for the painting.' And I said that I didn't believe in putting modern paintings—even if they are classical—in an antique frame. She said, 'Well, you *have* to choose one of them, and I can have it cut down in any way you want.' "

Childs was shocked.

"I wouldn't have destroyed a seventeenth-century Italian masterpiece of a frame in order to change the size of it, but she was willing to."

Instead, he chose one that was the proper size. He learned that it had cost Libet sixty thousand dollars—the same fee that she had paid Childs for his two years of work.

"That was kind of sobering," he says, reflecting back to that time. "It shows what I was worth to her. I was no better than a frame. I was just another supernumerary in her life. It was a slap in the face."

The portrait of Elizabeth Ross "Libet" Johnson was finally completed in 1998, but almost a decade and a half later Childs had no idea where, or if, she had hung it.

"The painting was picked up and that was it," he says. "I never heard another word from her. She never thanked me. She never said she liked it. Nothing. I knocked myself out over that painting, and it wasn't just because it was her, because that doesn't matter so much to me. It's really because I had the opportunity to paint a certain kind of picture that I had never done before, and I was determined to render everything as beautiful as possible and *say* something. The point of view is like a six-foot man looking at her who's entered the room and she's in all her beauty. It's a masterpiece, a *fabulous* painting. I consider it my best work, and I know it's how she sees herself."

Footnote: In the summer of 2003, the *New York Times* critic John Leland contacted James Childs for a lengthy, complimentary profile in the Sunday Arts and Leisure section. *The Times* wanted to illustrate the story with some of Childs's work, and the first piece to cross his mind was his portrait of Libet Johnson.

"As a gentleman," he says, he called her, knowing her propensity for privacy, but also noting that he holds the copyright to the painting and has the right to have it reproduced in positive ways, and because he thought it was so wonderful. "I said, 'Libet, I'd really like to use your picture in the *Times*,' and she didn't even reply to me in person. She had her secretary say no, and gave no reason, except that she's very private and didn't want the painting reproduced in the newspaper.

He calls her response, or lack thereof, "high-handed" and "unreasonable."

However, when *New York* magazine approached him to use a photo of the portrait in its "Libet in Love" story, he gave permission, along with charging a licensing fee of $650.

He heard nothing from Libet. "I think she knew by then that I was irritated with her."

The story in *New York* itself focused on Libet and Lionel Bissoon's curious romantic and passionate, at least at first, relationship. It also detailed the heiress's adoption of a six-month-old orphan in Cambodia, where she had generously and compassionately established an orphanage, Sovann Komar, in the suburbs of Pnohm Penh. And the piece described the couple's bitter custody battle. Bissoon thought the boy would be his, or shared with Libet; she thought otherwise, took control of him, and even established a one-hundred-thousand-dollar trust fund for the boy, whom she named William.

Unlike Casey, who cooperated with *Vanity Fair,* Libet, as was her style, refused to talk with *New York*'s writer, Steve Fishman—at least on the record. Most if not all of the story that was pitched to the magazine by Bissoon's publicist had come from his side, such as the romantic e-mails between the two that were leaked. Those from Libet were signed "DG," for the nickname she had given herself—Dancing Girl.

Anything telling Libet's side of the story came from a short list of names of her trusted friends that Libet herself had supplied to Fishman, among them her best pal from childhood, Lucinda Ziesing. She was quoted as saying, "Cambodia had become her life's work. It's given her meaning, direction." One of Libet's daughters, Annabel, told the magazine that Bissoon "talked about how he wanted to do this thing with his guru where they bury you up to your neck and you go through these spiritual trials. I'm sorry, that is entertaining stuff." The story said that Annabel had come to "hate Lionel."

Several years later, Ziesing calls the *New York* piece "terrible" and says that Libet was "very unhappy" with it. "I mean she got herself in trouble and got with Bissoon."

While Libet didn't go on the record with *New York,* a year later she did cooperate with *The Wall Street Journal* in a story headlined: "An American Heiress Aims to Rescue Cambodia by Giving Orphans a Family." She was quoted as saying, "I've been very, very fortunate in my life and I always wanted to do something larger with the gifts I have been given—and I don't mean financial. I mean my own personal internal resources. I thought there was a way for me to be useful here . . . I am not a trained social worker, but I felt that we should give these children loving parents, a safe environment, lots of opportunities, lots of ideas and an amazing education."

Fishman says he came away from the assignment feeling that, "Libet, who had five husbands and a whole bunch of boyfriends, was clearly very sexual and loves exotic guys . . . but she's not sexy, she's not provocative . . . She falls for guys and she falls fairly hard. Clearly, she fell for Bissoon in a big way. She's a lost girl . . . She found Cambodia and found a purpose, something like a benefactor doing some good there, and that was laudable."

In 2010, the New York Court of Appeals ruled that Bissoon had legitimately adopted William in June 2004. Press reports quoted court documents stating that in 2006, Libet had tried to adopt the boy through the courts without telling Bissoon, and that she had failed to disclose her time in rehab. The ruling stated that Libet "should not have been allowed to adopt [William] without notice to the person who was [William's] father under Cambodian law." But the court's decision permitted the boy to continue living with his heiress mother. Bissoon, the ruling stated, "Has no intention of removing the child from the only home he had ever known."

$ $ $

Besides collecting men, Libet Johnson, one of the wealthiest women in New York, and a minority stockholder in her brother Woody's football team, collected multimillion-dollar properties as routinely as if she was playing Monopoly.

In 2005, she had purchased Meryl Streep's $2 million Greenwich Village town house for $9.1 million as an investment, never moved in—Libet was not a Village person—and in early 2007 had put it on the market for close to $16 million. She sold it later in 2007 for $12.8 million. While Libet owned the twenty-five-foot-wide home with what was described as "wonderful details, excellent sunlight, and magnificent space," according to her agents, she had loaned the house to Michael Douglas's ex-wife and Casey Johnson's godmother, Diandra, who had since married a guitar maker by the name of Michael Klein.

Earlier in 2007, Libet had sold off a more than five-thousand-square-foot penthouse, 51-B, the largest apartment at the Trump International Hotel and Tower on Central Park West, for $18.5 million, which she was said to have bought for $20 million; the buyer reportedly sold it a few hours later for a profit of $2,750,000. As the venerable *New York Post* gossip columnist Cindy Adams often signs off, "Only in New York, kids, only in New York." Libet had previously sold off other pieces of her twenty-thousand-square-foot triplex palace there, which was valued in around 2000 at more than $62 million. At one point she had a total of six apartments on the forty-ninth, fiftieth, and fifty-first floors in the ultra-luxurious building. Her reputed lover at the time, the hair stylist Fekkai, with whom she was reportedly living, was said to have told her to keep just one.

She also owned a spectacular and immense home in Vail, along with her estate in Millbrook.

Her splashiest acquisition occurred in 2011 during the height of the national recession and disastrous housing market when she paid close to fifty million dollars for the Vanderbilt Mansion at 16 East Sixty-Ninth Street, near Central Park on Manhattan's Upper East Side. The late-nineteenth-century palace was once owned by Alice Gwynne Vanderbilt, widow of Cornelius Vanderbilt II, who headed the New York Central Railroad.

As the *New York Post* once noted, Woody Johnson's sister "has a voracious appetite for handsome husbands and big-time real estate."

However, by the summer of 2012, Libet, known for her capriciousness, had already grown tired of her Vanderbilt acquisition and wanted it sold. It wasn't the only high-end property she, or members of her family, were trying to unload under the cover of an entity called Falconer LLC. That other property, according to the *New York Observer*, was a chic Greenwich Village town house, on the market for almost $10 million.

While there was nothing extraordinary about Libet buying and selling big-ticket abodes, the agent overseeing the sale of the Greenwich Village property seemed a curious choice since her surname had some notoriety within the Johnson dynasty. The agent was related to the late psychiatrist Vincent D'Arc, Mary Lea Johnson's second husband, whom she had publicly accused of putting out a murder contract on her, resulting in a front-page scandal that had rocked the dynasty back in the mid-1970s.

53

In 2006, the same year that troubled Casey Johnson attacked her aunt Libet in print, she fell in love with the idea of adopting a baby—an idea that came to her after visiting Libet's Cambodian orphanage. Firmly believing that Casey was incapable of caring for a child, the older Johnson heiress made it clear to the younger Johnson heiress that there was no way she'd permit her to take one of her orphans.

Casey's father's sister appeared to be the only one in the family who had voiced any such objection. "When she was talking about wanting to adopt everybody of sound mind remained stone quiet, or asked very polite questions about the level of commitment required because Casey couldn't even keep a houseplant alive," asserts a family member. "Her parents certainly didn't draw a line in the sand. They were trying to be supportive. Maybe there was an eye-roll."

Casey's mother, Sale, claims otherwise.

"I told her I was totally against the adoption," she emphatically maintains. "I said, 'You don't have your own life together, how are you going to keep track of somebody else's life? This is not a puppy that if it doesn't work out, you can give it to a friend.'"

Casey had never planned to have a child of her own, her mother says, because she was aware, when lucid, of her mental instability from borderline personality disorder and poor health as a result of her diabetes.

At the same time Casey became serious about adoption she had another major item on her to-do list: marriage. She had become quietly engaged to the heir to an Atlanta gasoline station and vending machine fortune, and their wedding was in the planning stages. Casey was even talking about the style of mansion she wanted them to buy, and how she wouldn't let her child watch TV.

"He was crazy about her," her mother states. "I said, 'Casey, you're engaged, don't you think you should have the luxury of enjoying your engagement, your first years of marriage, before you have [adopt] a child? I'm sure that he would love to have kids, but maybe not yet.'"

Casey didn't listen, and she and her fiancé split up.

"I think pretty much the adoption became an issue," says her mother. "Casey became adamant about it, and told him, 'If you don't want the baby, then I don't want you.'"

The only person vociferously cheerleading Casey's decision to adopt was her godmother, Diandra Douglas, mother of heroin addict and drug dealer Cameron Douglas, with whom Casey had a close relationship. Douglas herself had adopted an orphan from Kazakhstan and had started guiding Casey through the process.

Diandra was among several older women, close to Sale and Woody, whom the heiress had informally adopted as surrogate mothers during her twenties. "Diandra and Casey had a relatively close relationship during the many times when Casey was on the outs with her own parents," says the family member. "When it came time for Casey to make that fateful decision to adopt, Diandra was all on-board and encouraging, but she wasn't doing jack-shit in terms of giving *good* advice. Sale was not very happy about it."

In 2007, with the support and guidance of Douglas, and against her divorced parents' wishes, Casey adopted a Kazakh baby girl who had been born premature at twenty-six weeks in 2006, and weighed just two pounds. Casey named her Ava-Monroe, in honor of her idol Marilyn Monroe. She would require special diets and close care through her early years.

The same year Ava-Monroe came into the world, Casey welcomed a new family member. He was named Robert Wood Johnson V and was born to pretty, blond Suzanne Ircha, Casey's father's girlfriend and future second wife. Woody finally had a namesake to carry on the Johnson dynasty line.

In 2008, an emotionally charged and hurtful family confrontation was ignited involving Casey, her father, and Ircha, at the New York Jets owner's Easthampton estate. During one of her up periods, Casey had come east from California with hopes of introducing her father to Ava-Monroe, and ending their long estrangement. She had also been thinking seriously about moving back to New York so she would have the emotional support of her mother and sisters and help with her child, and had even done some apartment shopping, but couldn't find an appropriate place at the right price and in the proper neighborhood.

By the time Casey showed up on her father's fashionable Hamptons doorstep with two-year-old Ava in tow, Woody had been incommunicado for several years. The turning point for him had been her refusal once again to get treatment for her serious emotional and physical issues.

Three years earlier, in 2005, Sale had convinced Woody to accompany her, Jaime, and Daisy to California, so they could surprise Casey and do an intervention, and get her to go to a clinic that her mother had arranged. It didn't work out and caused more problems. "We got there," reveals Sale, "and Casey just blew us off. She said, 'I don't need any help. I'm sorry you wasted a trip.' After that, Woody basically washed his hands of Casey." Moreover, her public bashing of Libet a year later was the final straw for her billionaire father.

"It's a *horrible* saga," declares Sale.

When Casey arrived at her father's mansion in Easthampton to introduce Ava, Woody wasn't home, but Ircha was. It was actually Casey who had first introduced her father to Ircha. Several years earlier, Casey, then still on relatively good terms with her father, had flown to Miami to see the Jets play the Dolphins. A girlfriend who had accompanied her brought along her pal, Ircha. A few days later Woody called Casey and asked for Ircha's number, and they began dating.

Ircha, however, later claimed that she and Woody were introduced by a publicist. "My friend said, 'You know Woody Johnson is single, you should meet him . . . Two days later he called.'" Afterward, she taught him how to use his new BlackBerry and "from then it was history."

Whichever way they met, there was no friendliness the afternoon Casey arrived at her father's home. Casey's nanny was waiting in the car with Ava along with a couple of Casey's friends. Ircha, Casey let everyone know, was far from hospitable.

"What are *you* doing here?" Ircha fumed, Casey later told her mother.

When Casey explained that she had come to see her father, Ircha, was said to have replied, "This is *my* house, so leave." But Casey stood her ground. "This is my father's house and I'm staying here until he gets here because I want him to meet my daughter."

Ircha then warned, "If you don't get out of my house, I'm going to call the police."

Casey told her, "I'm not going anywhere."

Ircha dialed 911.

About the same time that the police arrived and told Casey she had to leave because she was trespassing, Woody pulled up. Backing the new love of his life, he also demanded that his daughter get off of his property, stay off, and never come back.

"Woody doesn't like confrontation. He doesn't like negative publicity. He doesn't like anything like that," maintains Sale Johnson Rashad of the incident.

The confrontation at the mansion would be one of the last times Woody would ever see his daughter alive. The clock was ticking. She had just months left to live.

A close relative recalls a conversation with Casey not long after the Hamptons fireworks.

"I said, 'Well, how are things,' and she said, 'My fondest wish, my dearest wish, is that I can someday be on good terms and talk with my father again.' I was *shocked*. I said, 'Casey, what are you telling me?' And she says, 'He won't have anything to do with me. If I go to his house he tells me to get off his property.' It was really heart-wrenching."

In October 2008, Ircha had Woody's second son, about eight months before the couple finally tied the knot. As she was giving birth at a New York hospital—the bouncing baby boy was named John and weighed seven pounds, three ounces—Woody's girlfriend prior to Ircha, Erika Mariani, received a bizarre ten-minute voice mail left from his cell phone, according to a report in the *New York Post* headlined, "Oh, Baby, Listen to This." Mariani said she was "shocked" when she heard the infant crying and Woody talking to hospital staff, even discussing his newborn's weight. "It was pretty surreal," said

Mariani. "I felt like I was in the room. I'm just glad I wasn't the one giving birth."

The question remained—why did Woody Johnson still have a former girlfriend's number in his phone book?

There may have been more.

Ircha and Mariani were among a number of attractive, bright, well-educated career women with whom Woody had become involved after he and Sale had split. One of the first, who he was said to have met at his gym, was a model-thin, buxom thirty-year-old investment banker and heartbreaker by the name of Holly Newman. She was from an upscale Jewish family in Buffalo, New York, where her father was a prominent lawyer, and her mother a retired librarian. She and Woody first caught the attention of gossip writers in early 2003 when she was spotted at his side at Jets games and at the fancy restaurant in the Trump building where Woody had established his bachelor pad.

Before Woody, Newman had been involved with a rich hedge-fund manager. The *New York Observer* quoted someone who knew her as saying, "Holly gets what Holly wants . . . a girl with a mission," and the weekly newspaper described her as the Jets owner's "discreet main squeeze . . . who plays sports [and] knows about football."

In many ways she was a lot like Sale—a driven, ambitious Jewish jock.

Like his relationships with other women, Woody's with Holly didn't last long. In early 2004, the New York Social Diary, a Web site that covers New York society, reported that the romance between Woody and Newman, who had been living with the billionaire, had "gone kaput." She later got married.

It was Suzanne Ircha who won the Johnson heir's big diamond ring.

The sixty-two-year-old Woody and the forty-two-year-old Ircha had a June 4 wedding in 2009 at the fashionable Brick Presbyterian Church, founded in 1767, on Manhattan's Upper East Side.

"Woody Weds," declared the headline in the *Post,* reporting that "the stars were out to toast" the Jets owner "who tied the knot with longtime squeeze" Ircha at an early-evening ceremony. Among the guests were the usual suspects—Donald Trump and the Douglases, Michael and Catherine Zeta-Jones. "The party of about one hundred and fifty then shot down Park to the Four Seasons Hotel, where revelers were treated to an intimate reception."

For a brief time in the mid-1990s, the second Mrs. Woody Johnson reportedly did some minor acting, garnering small roles as a go-go girl, as a waitress, and her image even made an appearance in a video game.

When 9/11 happened she was working as a trader for the investment firm Sandler O'Neill & Partners, which had offices on the 104th floor of World Trade Center's tower two. Sixty-six of Ircha's one hundred and forty-eight coworkers were killed.

On the tenth anniversary of 9/11, Woody had his Jets play, calling it "a great honor," and saying it brought back memories of Ircha's experience when the attack occurred. "My wife, who wasn't my wife at that time, just happened to be late [for work] because she was out with clients the night before and didn't go in . . . Everybody has a story from that day."

Suzanne Ircha was brassy with a penchant for glittery high heels, and a reputation for being tough, according to people who knew her. She also was said to have had a lot in common with his first wife. As a Johnson family friend notes, "Suzanne's like Sale—very assertive and high energy."

Not long after Woody and Suzanne tied the knot, wife number two followed in the Louboutin footsteps of wife number one and reinvented herself as a Manhattan socialite, boasting of the boldface names in her new platinum circle. And, enjoying her husband's very public business, the Jets, she became a spokeswoman for the women's apparel line that was promoted by the National Football League. She saw Woody's "thing" as football and her "thing" as fashion. She claimed Woody once told her, "Go ahead, you've had babies, so go out there and be your own person again."

Because the new parents required close-by help with the little ones, Woody reportedly bought an almost $3 million apartment to house nannies in the Trump International Hotel and Tower, where Woody and his bride were ensconced in a $10 million penthouse.

Besides Casey, Ircha also was said to have had conflicts and run-ins with Woody's other two daughters, Jaime, and especially Daisy, the youngest, who was her mother's favorite because of their close bond as champion equestrians. Twenty-five-year-old Daisy (with her favorite horse, a Hanoverian named Atlanta 447) was among a group of equestrian heiresses featured in a *Town & Country* cover story in August 2012 called "RISKY RICH

GIRLS: Why They're Obsessed with Competing in the Most Dangerous Olympic Game."

"Daisy's like Sale," says a friend. "She has a million trophies and medals from riding." When someone would ask the baby powder heiress Daisy how long she'd been on horseback, her glib response was, "Since I was a fetus," because, "I was riding when I was pregnant with her," boasts her mother.

$ $ $

On Sunday, June 21, 2009—Father's Day—all hell broke loose between the increasingly emotionally disturbed Casey Johnson and her mother, who was desperate to get her into treatment for her borderline personality disorder.

While Casey was scheduled to be hospitalized that day at the exclusive and luxurious Cliffside Malibu clinic overlooking the Pacific, a stay expected to last anywhere from several weeks to several months, Sale Johnson Rashad planned to take Casey's adored three-year-old, Ava-Monroe, back to New York, and care for her while Casey was in treatment, but she had promised to bring her back for visits.

None of it happened the way Sale had envisioned.

Before the day had ended, Casey had ordered her mother from her rented Beverly Hills home—literally threw her out into the street, luggage and all—called the police claiming that her mother was trespassing and attempting to take her baby, and had her trained attack dog, a fierce German shepherd by the name of Ollie who Casey had gotten because of a previous claimed stalker, on hand to guard her premises.

"Casey knew in her heart that she couldn't take care of Ava, but she couldn't ego-wise and illness-wise say *I know I can't take care of her like she needs to be cared for, you should keep her while I get help,*" says Sale, recalling that horrific day and the terrible events that would soon follow.

Sale had asked the nanny, Katrina, who helped Casey care for Ava "and loved her very much" to pack a bag for the toddler because "she's going to come with me. Ava was sitting on my lap and Casey got upset and got jealous that Ava was with me and *screamed,* 'Get out of my house. If you don't get out of my house, I'm calling the police and have you arrested for trespassing.' Casey did call the police, put my bag outside, and locked me out."

The confrontation occurred just seventeen days after her estranged father married Suzanne Ircha, who had become Casey's nemesis.

Evicted and stranded in the street with her luggage, furious but also concerned about Casey and Ava's welfare, Sale Johnson used her iPhone to also call the police, telling the dispatcher: "My daughter may have called you for you to come to this address and I just want you to know that you should send two officers, not just one, because she's not stable, and I just don't want there to be any big problems."

When the officers arrived, Sale advised them, "She's on medication, she has a dog in there that's an attack dog, so do not just walk in the house, and she had a couple of drinks."

Earlier that same day, mother and daughter and one of Casey's friends had had lunch together. At that point in time, Casey was all set to enter the clinic; they were even going to let her bring one of her dogs—but while Sale was on the phone around the corner from the outdoor café wishing her own ninety-two-year-old father in Northern California happy Father's Day, Casey had downed at least two Bellinis, "which was not a great plan," says Sale. Angry because her mother had taken too much time on the phone, light-headed because the alcohol was now working on top of whatever medications were in her system, Casey had become belligerent.

"And once she gets mad"—Sale Johnson can never forget—"all hell breaks loose, and when we got home she was screaming and yelling. I said I would take Ava back to New York, and bring her back and forth whenever the clinic said she could have visitors, and she said, 'Well, I'm *not* going to the clinic.'"

And the standoff began.

At first Casey refused to admit the police officers, demanding to see a search warrant.

"She was even angrier now," recalls Sale, "because she saw through the window that I had talked to the police first, so now they were *my* police, not *her* police, so she didn't want to open the door."

The police finally convinced her to put the guard dog away and come outside. When they asked her if she was on medication, she told them it was none of their business, and they had to pry her full name out of her. Finally, she let them inside, but nothing was amiss: Ava was running around happily playing with her nanny.

The officers finished their inspection, came back outside, and told Casey's mother that there was nothing they could do. At that moment, the nanny, who knew better, sent a text to Sale's iPhone, telling her that she had unlocked the door "and will you please come and take Ava." Sale showed the message to the sergeant in charge, who warned, " 'She will have you arrested for kidnapping.' I was distraught at this point."

Sale checked into a hotel in Marina Del Rey.

"I sat in a chair in the window, looked out at the boats, and made a million phone calls and sent a million e-mails trying to figure out what to do, and finally decided on the second day that I was going to organize an intervention."

It all was on Sale's shoulders because Woody was completely out of the picture in terms of helping, or caring, in her view.

"He didn't want to have anything to do with Casey," she says. "It was too much trouble. But fathers are supposed to take a bullet for their kids, and he went the other way. I can't defend his behavior for that because I thought it was *appalling*. But that's who he is. He doesn't have the emotional makeup to deal with it. It's like, *I'll be an ostrich and put my head in the sand, and when I pull it out, everything will be good.*"

$ $ $

Casey's mother began to put together a list of those whom she wanted to participate in her planned intervention.

The group included a doctor from the clinic that Casey had been booked into. It included a former assistant of Casey's who still cared for her and had remained a friend. Sale had hoped to have Casey's best friend—Ava's godmother, Nicky Hilton—involved, but Paris Hilton's sister said she was flying to New York and couldn't attend, but told Sale to call her on the phone and she'd talk to Casey long-distance during the intervention. Sale called Barry Peale, a Beverly Hills real estate agent and photographer who had helped Casey buy and sell homes, had become a confidant of hers, and had been named Ava-Monroe's godfather. Sale also invited a British girl who was a friend of Casey's, "who had some sort of title but did nothing in her life."

The last person she added to the list was Kathy Hilton, Nicky and Paris Hilton's mother. Like the middle-class Nancy Sale Frey from St. Louis who had married into the Johnson dynasty and had reinvented herself as a socialite, the former Kathy Richards, born in middle-class Long Island and raised in the L.A. suburbs, had done the same. She had married Richard Howard "Rick" Hilton, a grandson of the founder of the Hilton hotel chain. The Hiltons married about a year after the Johnsons. "If I hadn't married Rick, Mom would have taken me down the aisle with a gun in my back," Kathy later told her sister, the actress Kim Richards.

When the Hiltons moved to New York from Los Angeles, it was Sale Johnson who introduced Kathy around to the right people—"I've known her since her kids were babies and we've been friends for many years"—and Casey and the Hilton girls became bosom buddies and party girls together, dubbed "celebutantes" by an intrigued media, especially when the talentless Paris earned her star by turning an amateur sex tape into a multimillion-dollar career of sorts.

Like Diandra Douglas, Kathy Hilton was another one of those older women whom Casey had considered a surrogate mother, so when Sale asked Kathy to participate in Casey's intervention, she naturally agreed. "I knew Kathy had dealt with an intervention before because she had somebody in her family, her sister, Kim, who'd already been through this," says Sale. "Kathy told me, 'I'm an expert.' "

Casey's intervention was scheduled for the third day after her confrontation with her mother, and Sale arranged for everyone to meet in a park near Casey's home. Sale laid out the strategy. "I told them that the only way this is going to work is if we all go in and tell Casey how much we all love her, but that we are there to help her, and that we hope she's going to accept our help. We can't make her think that she is okay the way she is."

After the huddle, Sale, still upbeat about getting her desperately needed treatment, hustled everyone over to her daughter's home.

Casey opened the door. She was practically naked, and with her was a longtime girlfriend, Courtenay Semel, the daughter of Terry Semel, former chairman of Yahoo! Inc. and Warner Bros.

When Semel saw Sale and the others walking into the house, she darted into a bedroom and locked the door.

By the time everyone was in the house, Casey was furious. She started cursing at her mother, and demanded, "What the fuck are they all doing here? Get out of here." To the clinic doctor she hollered, "You are *not* welcome."

Sale explained as calmly as she could that they just wanted to talk to her, and asked her to sit down, but Casey didn't want to hear from any of them. One of the interventionists said, "Casey, we know your dad cut you off, and you don't have any money." Sale says it was actually she who had suggested to Woody that he cut off the flow of money.

The issue with her father further infuriated Casey, who screamed. "My mother doesn't know anything," she yelled. "I spoke to my father yesterday and I'm not cut off at all." Sale responded, "Casey, you know that's not true."

Everyone else remained silent.

"I called Nicky Hilton," says Sale, "and she tried to talk to Casey, but Casey didn't want to hear it."

Glaring at the doctor from the clinic, Casey ordered her out of the house.

Then Kathy Hilton spoke up, telling Casey, "You just seem to be really stressed. Why don't you let *me* take Ava, and you take a little break."

Casey instantly agreed.

Sale couldn't believe what she was hearing.

"It was not like Casey needed a vacation, and if anybody took Ava, it should *not* have been Kathy Hilton. She should have been saying, why don't you let your mom take care of Ava."

That was it.

Everyone else at the failed intervention left.

Sale, hurt and upset, watched as Casey placed a car seat for Ava in Kathy Hilton's car.

At that point, Sale confronted Hilton.

" 'Kathy, what are you doing?' She said, 'Well, Casey said *I* should take Ava.' I said, 'No, you suggested that you take Ava, but I'm Ava's grandmother, and I'm supposed to be taking Ava,' and she goes, 'Well, Casey's giving her to *me*.' So they put Ava in Kathy Hilton's car and she drove off with *my* granddaughter."

At that point Sale, stressed and anxious about Ava and Casey, decided to return home to regroup and confer with her second husband, former professional football player and NBC sportscaster Bobby Earl Moore, known professionally as Ahmad Rashad. A convert to Islam in the early 1970s, his new name meant "Admirable One Led to Truth."

54

Sale Johnson was Ahmad Rashad's fourth wife. One of his previous three was the popular actress Phylicia Ayers-Allen Rashad, who had played Bill Cosby's wife on TV's *The Cosby Show*. Rashad's best man at that wedding was O. J. Simpson. From all of Rashad's marriages he had quite a brood when he married Woody's ex: three daughters, two sons, and one stepson. With Sale, he added three stepdaughters.

In 2005, Sale, single since her divorce in 2001, was playing golf with a male friend at Donald Trump's National Golf Club in Briarcliff Manor, New York, a Manhattan suburb. The only other party on the course that day—the club still wasn't finished—was one that included the real estate mogul and reality TV star Trump, the professional basketball great Michael Jordan, and Rashad.

"We all happened to stop at the little shack to get a sandwich, and Donald introduced me to Ahmad that day," says Sale. "When Ahmad got back on the course he asked Donald about me, and Donald told him that I knew *everybody*, that I was involved in a lot of things, and then Ahmad had his assistant try to find me."

They eventually began a serious relationship, but at first the fact that he was black was a hurdle for her.

"I had a lot of friends that were people of different colors," she says, "but to date, much less marry somebody [who was black], was like a real departure.

But Ahmad didn't have a color. He was his own person, and his friends didn't really have a color, and I didn't think about [race] when I was with him."

They were married on his fifty-eighth birthday on November 19, 2007, in a small ceremony at the Manhattan restaurant La Grenouille. Among the guests was Trump, along with National Basketball Association commissioner David Stern. Also in attendance was the groom's buddy Derek Jeter, and Princess Yasmin Aga Khan.

Casey was not among the celebrants.

Shortly after they were wed, Sale purchased an almost five-million-dollar French Palladian-style mansion with a guesthouse and forty-five-foot-long swimming pool on two acres overlooking the eleventh green of the Jack Nicklaus–designed Bears Club golf course in Jupiter, Florida—nirvana for the two because they both were golf nuts.

Sale says her friends, for the most part, were happy for her, but some, like Casey's first pediatrician, Dr. Ed Saltzman, reacted with surprise that she had married a black man.

"I was stunned," he says. "I'm not a bigot, but to me it [interracial marriage] adds a lot of problems to a person's life. After they were married Sale complained to me that Ahmad was very demanding. I didn't get the impression it was a great life."

$ $ $

Nancy Sale Frey Johnson Rashad desperately tried to contact Kathy Hilton in California to find out how and where Ava-Monroe was. Finally, she tracked her down at the Bel Air Hotel where the Hiltons were staying with the baby.

Sale gave them a list of necessities for Ava such as the vitamins and special milk that she required, and then called each day to make certain the Hiltons were following her instructions.

At the end of that week, Sale made her daily check and learned from Rick Hilton that the Hiltons were flying off to Dubai for a week to see Paris, where she was shooting a reality show called *Paris Hilton's Dubai BFF,* and that they were turning over the child to a trusted friend.

When the Hiltons returned from Dubai, the woman gave Ava back to them, apparently no worse for their absence.

Rick Hilton then called Sale and told her that Kathy was going to hire her niece to take care of Ava "and they wanted me to pay for her hotel room at the Bel Air and all of her wages and expenses. I said, 'Rick, you've got to be kidding! The idea is to make Casey take responsibility for her child and realize that she can't, and then ask for help, not bail her out. You're just enabling her behavior.'"

At that point, Casey was in the midst of an even more serious emotional downward spiral, and finally checked herself in to rehab at Cliffside Malibu, and turned Ava over to Kathy's sister Kim (of *The Real Housewives of Beverly Hills* reality TV program), who had her own long history of alcohol addiction. Back in the 1970s, pushed by her aggressive stage mother, she had appeared in a number of films and TV series such as *Nanny and the Professor,* and had two marriages, one to Gregg Davis, the son of billionaire oilman and Hollywood mogul Marvin Davis, with whom she had two children.

At first, Sale accepted the situation because "Kim had been sober for ten years and at that point she was fine." What soon infuriated Casey was that the child had started calling Kim "Mommy."

Casey "went ballistic and said to Kim, 'Give me my kid back! What do you mean she's calling you mommy. *I'm* her mommy." And Casey, going from the frying pan into the fire, called her chum Jasmine Lennard, who then watched Ava for a number of days.

Lennard was another controversial young woman in Casey's orbit—skinny with low-slung breast implants (which she reportedly later had removed), she once was described by the snarky media Web site Gawker as a "transatlantic fameball," and "a hypersexual British socialite" who was part of the Hollywood celebutante train-wreck crowd.

Back in the Malibu clinic, Casey claimed that while she was taking a shower someone, presumably a man, had walked into her room and stood watching her and wouldn't leave. As a result Casey left the clinic for the last time.

"He wasn't molesting her," says her mother, noting that, "Casey can be sensationalistic, so you never knew whether to believe something like that, but that was her excuse for leaving the second time."

$ $ $

The last time Casey saw her daughter was on August 27, 2009, when her step-father, Ahmad Rashad, accompanied by Casey's sister Daisy, arrived in Los Angeles to rescue the three-year-old from her emotionally drowning adoptive mother, who once again had been hospitalized for her diabetes while her child was being passed around from one friend to another.

"Nobody went and *took* Casey's baby," declares her mother. "Casey asked Daisy to come and get Ava after conversations with me. Casey had said this before and I said to Daisy, 'I don't want you to waste a trip flying to California and she's going to change her mind.'"

A single-page document was prepared, stating that Daisy was coming to take Ava for as long as deemed necessary, and without any legal repercussions. "They certainly would not have taken Ava without Casey's agreement," emphasizes her mother. "But everyone was saying that I swooped in and kidnapped Ava. I didn't do any of that. I wasn't there."

When Casey was released from the hospital, she moved back into her rented Beverly Hills home with Jasmine Lennard, but by the fall of 2009, the Johnsons had stopped paying Casey's rent, and Jasmine had no money. With her millions cut off by her estranged, divorced parents, who were playing tough love, Casey was getting deeper into debt. Her Porsche was repossessed, a former landlord sued her for back rent and property damage, and other bills for her extravagences had piled up.

Casey's uncle, Christopher Johnson—Woody's youngest brother and a stockholder in the Jets—was one of the trustees of her fortune, and was often left in shock by his niece's crazy spending. "He did his best to impart a sense of values in Casey by putting a lid on her acquisitions," maintains Eric Ryan. "Chris was in the position of having certain legal and fiduciary responsibilities regarding Casey and also had a great deal of affection for her. But it was a cantankerous relationship on Casey's part, and a couple of times she threatened to sue. Chris would say to her—no money for a house, but I'll pay for your rehab, and Casey would be like, 'How dare you withhold my funds. It's *my* money.'"

Facing eviction, Casey moved out, and found new lodging—what would be her next to final stop—in the luxurious, gated, and private two-bedroom

West Hollywood guesthouse at 910 North Orlando Avenue, owned by Nancy Stoddart, a longtime acquaintance of Casey's mother.

A decorator, Stoddart was another one of those older women whom Casey had adopted as a sort of surrogate mother, like Diandra Douglas, Kathy Hilton, and New York socialite Susan Gutfreund, a former stewardess who also married into money, and who lived in the Johnsons' Park Avenue building.

Casey's rent at Stoddart's house was paid for by a sympathetic male former tenant, according to Sale.

Sale had first met Stoddart when she and Woody moved to New York. She had seen a portrait of someone's dogs and thought it was exquisite, and was told that Nancy Stoddart was the artist. Sale invited Stoddart to the Johnsons' Fifth Avenue apartment, gave her photographs of her four schnauzers, and Nancy later returned with a lovely portrait. Subsequently, Sale had her paint the son of her first golden retriever.

Like Casey, Stoddart moved to Los Angeles—where she started an interior design company.

"Casey was out and about out there and somehow Nancy met Casey and she told Casey that we were good friends," says Sale, "and so Casey *thought* that she was being friends with my friend. At one point I said to Casey that she should be spending time with people her own age. I just thought it wasn't normal, but Nancy, I guess, was nice to her. Nancy came to Ava's first birthday party, which I gave at my house in Southampton."

Stoddart saw herself as a writer and was said to have been working on a memoir, dealing in part with all the famous people she knew, so it was natural that she was intrigued with the Johnson & Johnson heiress. Stoddart clearly liked to dish about the celebrities she knew, such as Oprah Winfrey. She was quoted by Oprah's biographer Kitty Kelley as saying, "When we went skiing together, Oprah was so fat she had to buy her ski clothes in the men's department."

$ $ $

December 2009 was a bizarre month in Casey's increasingly bizarre life. Jasmine Lennard, for one, charged that Casey had broken into her Hollywood apartment and had stolen shoes, jewelry, pages from a legal document, and underwear. The *New York Post*, in a story headlined "Heiress in Theft Scandal," reported, "The thief also left a bizarre calling card—a used vibrator was found in her bed and a wet towel was on the floor. Lennard suspected Johnson, whom she said had 'been like a little sister to me.' Then she got a text message from Johnson's off-again, on-again girlfriend, Courtenay Semel. 'There's a problem, Jaz, Casey just got into bed with me and she is wearing your underwear. You need to call the police . . .' "

As a result, the emotionally disturbed heiress was arrested and was held for twenty thousand dollars bail. The skeletal-looking Lennard—who craved media attention and thrived on controversy that got her picture in the celebrity media and name in boldface—took credit for being Casey's savior, while at the same time accusing her of the break-in.

She was quoted in the *Post* as saying, "Since the day I met Casey, I have only been a good force in her life. I tried to get her off drugs and alcohol. I tried to get her in a twelve-step program. I tried to take care of her daughter. I've given her money. I am the only person who helped this girl . . ."

After Casey was released from jail facing charges of grand theft, she adamantly denied Lennard's accusations. By then she had retained the prominent Los Angeles attorney Robert Shapiro, who had been part of the successful O. J. Simpson defense team.

Around the same time, Casey got into what was reported to be a "vicious catfight" with Semel who allegedly "beat the crap out of her, and then she lit her hair on fire. Casey had to be hospitalized," according to press reports. Semel would later boast to *People* magazine that Casey was "the love of my life."

It only got more crazy.

In the last weeks of December 2009, in one of her more outlandish, publicity-generating episodes, Casey had gone public with the bisexual reality TV personality and exhibitionist Tila Tequila, who boasted—with the two posing together for the paparazzi, and even kissing—that they were going to get married, and that Casey had given her a rock of an engagement ring. She called Casey her "Wifey."

Back east her father and other members of the Johnson dynasty cringed. With all of the past Johnson dynastic scandals through the generations, this was one of the most publicly shameful and humiliating because of the worldwide media and 24/7 Internet coverage.

A number of media outlets reported that Casey was gay because of her very public relationships with Tequila and Courtenay Semel. The New York *Daily News* had once described Casey as a "beautiful blond lesbian," but her mother adamantly denies that her daughter was gay, and scoffs that she might even have been bisexual "by any means." Her interpretation is that Casey "was very needy and couldn't be alone and at that point in her life it was very difficult to keep it together so that a nice man was going to want to be with her."

A relative concurs.

"The whole lesbian thing was something that she fell in with, with other of her acquaintances in California who were bisexual in that fast-partying crowd. Casey *never* expressed any interest in gay relationships up until that point. It was sort of an affectation she found to be attractive for its shock value because she liked to stick it to her family."

$ $ $

As the 2009 Christmas and New Year's holidays approached, Tila Tequila left Los Angeles to spend time with her family. Left alone in her rented guesthouse, Casey's very fragile emotional and physical state was fast deteriorating. She had all but stopped taking her insulin, she was eating junk food, and swigging Nyquil in order to sleep. She also had started communicating via Twitter and Facebook with her friends and those in the outside world who were following her increasingly sordid real-life soap opera that was being played out in the tabloids and online.

On Christmas Day she wrote, "I was *very* lucky this year." Three days later, she declared, "I'm in heaven . . . Happy as a clam xo." And her final one said, "sweet dream everyone . . . I'm getting a new car . . . Any ideas? Cant b a two seater cause we have a daughter . . . sedan, sports car, suv??."

From what was known, she spent New Year's Eve, when she usually was out partying, alone in bed.

Around eleven thirty on the morning of January 4, 2010, when Casey didn't respond to knocks on her door, someone entered and found her unconscious. For Woody, who got the terrible news later in the day, it was like reliving the discovery of his brother Keith, dead of a drug overdose, more than three decades earlier.

Shortly before noon, Pacific time, a 911 call was placed by an unidentified female from Casey's residence on Nancy Stoddart's estate once known as "Grumblenot."

"She's ice-cold and her hands are turning blue," stated the caller. "I have two other people here with me and we all think she's dead. I don't know if it's suicide. Very often her medication gets all screwed up, so it's probably that."

Paramedics arrived shortly thereafter.

At the age of thirty, the Johnson & Johnson heiress whose life had been both a Cinderella fantasy and a living hell was pronounced dead on the scene.

It was around three o'clock on the East Coast when Sale Johnson's iPhone rang and the caller ID displayed Nancy Stoddart's L.A. number. Casey's friend and landlord was personally relaying the tragic news that she was dead.

"The fire-rescue people were still there and I talked to them, too," says Sale, recalling that horrific day.

Sale then called Woody, who had kept his distance from Casey for at least five years, but was naturally devastated when her end came. He later termed her death, "the worst day of my life" in a lifetime of many tragic days.

A month before Casey died, Dr. Ed Saltzman had had dinner with Sale and Ahmad Rashad in Florida. From what Sale had confided to him, he says, "Casey's death was imminent. It was a foregone conclusion."

When word of Casey's death reached the outside world, the media jumped on the story. There were unsubstantiated reports that Casey had died of a drug overdose, or had committed suicide, and that she had been living in filth.

But Sale Johnson, wanting to set the record straight, declares, "My daughter did not die in squalor, not with rats, not with trash."

One of London's Fleet Street newspapers had reported that Casey had "no water, electricity or gas" and that "dirty dishes were piled in the kitchen and the pool was a rat-infested swamp." The *New York Post* filled the front page with an eerie photo of Casey Johnson in a virginal white gown holding the leash of one of her dogs with the giant headline "Poor Little Rich Girl. Casey's Tragic Fall into Squalor," and inside was another headline that declared: "Heiress Lived Amid Rats and Trash." Another blared: "WOODY'S ANGUISH AS LOST GIRL DIED ALONE."

But there were no words from her father who had abandoned her.

The *Post*'s lead story, similar in content to front-page accounts around the world, began: "Tragic baby-shampoo heiress Casey Johnson spent the last months of her life in a suicidal drug haze, living in squalor, surrounded by hangers-on and cut off from the family fortune . . ."

Almost three years after Casey's death, her mother was still angry at how the media portrayed her daughter's last days.

"Casey's painful death and the absurdity of the so-called medical experts and the Emmy-winning talk show hosts and award-winning journalists all had not one clue as to the real workings of Casey's life," declares Sale Johnson Rashad. "Not one of them knew she had no drugs in her body. Not one of them knew she had a mental health issue [borderline personality disorder] that ruled her life and her behavior, and that because of that illness her behavior was erratic and could easily have been misconstrued.

"The press that followed her passing was out of control. Not one journalist, or self-claimed expert on Casey's life, ever tried to reach me. Woody's extensive and powerful PR machine put out their statements, [but] they never mentioned a word about her illness [BPD]. That was a huge mistake. It was all so painful, and so untrue."

All kinds of people who were part of the Johnson circle were quoted as saying what a tragedy her death was, and what a sad figure the poor little rich girl had been throughout her life. Michael Douglas, whose son Cameron might have turned Casey on to drugs, and whose ex-wife, Diandra, had helped Casey with her ill-fated adoption, curiously described himself as "a distant relative," but a "dear, dear friend" of Woody. He told reporters Casey's death was "a terrible, terrible tragedy. . . . It's the worst thing that could happen to anyone, losing a child. They're grieving, as one would expect."

Arrangements were immediately made to have her body flown east for a private funeral. Her family issued a statement, through Woody Johnson's public relations firm, asking "for a measure of privacy over the next several days as they mourn their loss."

The very private funeral, with about forty in attendance, was held in Princeton, and family members and other invited mourners were instructed to first meet at Woody Johnson's mother's house.

"We really didn't know how to behave because it wasn't scripted, or formulated," says a family member. "Betty, who's pretty stoic, pretty tough, was kind of in charge, and she just orchestrated it, having had a lot of experience with death in the family."

It was Betty May Wold Johnson Gillespie Bushnell, the family member said, who made the decision (with Woody and Sale's consent) that Casey should be buried in the same small plot in Princeton where the Johnson dynasty matriarch's sons, Keith and Billy, had been interred some thirty-five years earlier.

"I'm very close to Betty," asserts Sale Johnson Rashad, "and I think that's where Casey would have wanted to be. That was her family."

Sale had arrived with her husband, Ahmad, and she had invited Casey's beloved Jamaican nanny, Milly, along with Ava's godmother, Nicky Hilton, and another close friend of Casey's, the sometimes model and actress Bijou Phillips, a hard-partying high school dropout who was the daughter of John Phillips of the sixties group The Mamas & the Papas. In Casey's last days, Hilton and Phillips had rescued two of Casey's dogs, her furs, and some other personal belongings after a brief confrontation with Tila Tequila.

"The whole day was a blur," recalls a family member. "Betty tried to keep people on their good behavior" because there was some animosity among those in attendance. Casey's father, Woody, for instance, had arrived with his second wife, Suzanne, "against the begging and pleading" of Casey's sisters, Jaime and Daisy, who disliked her.

Casey's service—her body was in a closed casket—was held at the cemetery and presided over by a minister who, it was believed, hadn't actually known the Johnson family, or for very long.

"This guy was a stranger as best as I could tell," says one of the mourners. "He gave the eulogy—and it was freaking bitter cold at the gravesite—and he was there being supportive and helping out with the family, who was distraught, and sort of confused, and saddened about this terrible tragedy."

It took a grieving Woody Johnson almost three weeks before he said something publicly about losing his daughter. "There's no way to bring her back. I wish I could change it, but I can't. I think of [Casey's death] all the time. It's been a seesaw in terms of [grieving and] the business of the team."

Five days after his firstborn died, he had gone to Cincinnati for the Jets wildcard playoff game against the Bengals. "I thought, 'Geez, it would be kind of weird if I had asked the players to come to play a game after they had trag-edy in their family and I don't come,' so I had to do it."

After the Jets won, Coach Rex Ryan gave his boss the game ball and "that was just too many things hitting me at once," said Woody. While the Jets never won the playoffs, he gave the ball to his namesake from his second mar-riage. "He loves it. He's only three and a half but he thinks it's pretty good."

It took a month for the Los Angeles County coroner's office to issue its final report on "Coroner Case Number 2010-00090—JOHNSON, Sale Trot-ter Case." It ruled that her "natural death" was the result of "diabetic ketoaci-dosis," which was a complication of her diabetes and inadequate insulin. Neither cocaine nor alcohol were detected.

"The decedent had seen a psychiatrist in the past," the report noted, "but that physician has been out of town. On the Thursday before her death she had been evaluated by another psychiatrist and he had concluded that she was not suicidal. The family's attorney had requested that the decedent be evalu-ated by the psychiatrist as part of the process in reuniting the decedent with her family."

Some two months after Casey died, Woody Johnson told a reporter who covered the Jets for *The New York Times* that his long-estranged daughter had been "trying to find her own identity. She was rebellious. She made some judgment errors. Been there, done that. She had to take responsibility. And it couldn't be me pushing. Or her mother. Or her doctor. She would ultimately have to do it herself."

EPILOGUE

For Sale Johnson, who continued to use her famous dynastic last name, and her second husband, Ahmad Rashad, life for some of the second decade of the 2000s was all about travel, golf tournaments, her adult daughter Daisy's equestrian activities, and most of all raising her adoptive granddaughter, Ava-Monroe—who turned six years old in 2012—in their gated estate in South Florida.

"Ava's the most beguiling creature on this planet," declares a joyous Sale. "She's just a freak of nature. She's just happy and smart, and so up for anything. Life is an adventure. Ahmad loves her. The biggest smile I ever see on his face—which used to be when he saw *me*—is when he sees Ava and she comes running when he walks into the house. She squeals, Daddy, and runs and jumps on him. How can you not love that?"

Since both Sale and Ahmad were in their sixties, they planned to raise the child "day by day," says Sale. "My plan was that she would live with Jaime, but Jaime wasn't ready to raise a child."

While cute Ava Monroe was a joy to bring up, all was not copacetic in the house of Johnson-Rashad. There had been serious relationship issues between Woody Johnson's ex-wife and her ex–football star second husband for some time, and by the winter of 2013 their six-year marriage appeared to be seriously in trouble, according to family members and confidants.

The primary issue of contention was money—wealth earned and

unearned—the usual reason for problems among Johnson dynasty members. In the Sale Johnson–Ahmad Rashad matter, it was mostly about her millions that were far, far greater than any money he might have had.

"Even before they were married, there was concern that Ahmad was marrying somebody who was significantly wealthier than he, and that maybe he wouldn't have done so had she not been so wealthy as a result of her divorce settlement with Woody," maintains a close family member. "Sale expressed that concern herself. But she sort of swept it under the rug during the excitement of the courtship and engagement and wedding."

After they were married, Sale herself complained to her long-time confidant, Dr. Ed Saltzman, that "Ahmad was very demanding, and that she had to buy this, she had to buy that," he clearly recalls. "She told me that he wanted a certain watch when they were in Europe and that it cost about ten thousand dollars, and she bought it for it for him, and she was pissed off about it. I asked her why she bought it, why she just didn't say no, and she said, 'Eddie, oh, you know . . .'" But never gave him a direct reason.

However, close observers of Sale's second marriage had no reason to believe that Rashad was, in any way, a gold digger, which was always a concern within the Johnson dynasty about future wives and husbands, and sometimes rightfully so.

As one close source notes: "Ahmad didn't approach his relationship and marriage with Sale with malice aforethought, intending to enrich himself. He wasn't planning on stealing her fortune and putting his family or hangers-on in villas in Monaco. He probably just wanted to spend and live a fast life without being fiscally responsible, which is very in contrast to Sale's sort of core values. She's very frugal, in spite of the fact that she lives in an insane sort of manner with her money."

That person recalls that when Sale was married to the billionaire Jets owner and Band-Aid heir, "Woody used to joke with me about her frugality. He said she would go over the telephone bill for the household. Woody would say, 'It's just nickels and dimes.' But Sale never grasped that. So money has bothered her all along regarding Ahmad. Sale got really sort of fed up and bent out of shape."

In mid-January of 2013, the *New York Post* published a gossip column item under the headline "Jets Ex-wife's Marriage Woe." The story stated that there was "trouble in paradise" for the couple, that their union was "on the rocks," and that she was worried about "the influence of his friends, described as "known adulterers" Tiger Woods and Michael Jordan.

But people close to Sale and Ahmad scoffed at some of the report.

As one of them asserted, "Ahmad likes to maintain the aura that his star hasn't dimmed and so he hobnobs with Tiger Woods and Michael Jordan."

There was, however, no evidence of any womanizing as the gossip item seemed to imply.

"Sale never mentioned any other woman in Ahmad's life," maintains the family source. "She did talk about him traveling a lot. And when he does, he likes to hang around babes and party. But Sale complained that she wasn't included in any of those adventures, which are sometimes work-related, or celebrity golf-related."

With the relationship deteriorating, Rashad moved out of their shared homes that Sale owned in Manhattan and Florida in the early winter of 2012, and she began letting family members and close friends know in e-mails and telephone calls what had happened between them.

Among those she contacted was her former mother-in-law, Betty Johnson, letting her and the others know that she was "very unhappy, stressed, and anxious, and wanted to reconcile with Ahmad and re-adopt the sort of loving relationship they had when they first got together. Sale talked for two hours in some detail that was way too much information for Betty," one of those family members says.

But still, another divorce seemed in the future for the Johnson dynasty.

Surprisingly, Woody's mother continued to communicate with her ex-daughter-in-law, mainly because she felt a kinship with her granddaughters—Jaime, who suffers from lupus, and Daisy, who had been taking medication for a blood clotting disorder that began in her late teens when she suffered a deep vein thrombosis after a long plane trip to South America to visit a polo player she had been dating. Moreover, Betty had completely embraced emotionally disturbed and diabetic Casey's adopted healthy daughter, Ava-Monroe.

When there was a party in the summer of 2012 for a gaggle of grandchildren—the next generation of the Johnson dynasty—Ava was included, and it's believed that the de facto matriarch attended.

The event had been thrown by her youngest son, Christopher, at his home in Easthampton.

But, notes a family member who attended, "Woody wasn't there, and it's pretty clear he has no interest in recognizing Ava, or acknowledging her—that she's just another thorn in his side concerning Casey."

$ $ $

In the spring and summer of 2012, Woody's life was wrapped up with the future of the presumptive Republican presidential candidate, Mitt Romney, for whom Woody had raised millions of campaign dollars, and the upcoming Jets season.

A few weeks before his sixty-fifth birthday, he was in Palm Beach for the annual meeting of NFL owners, and he was gloating. He had just authorized his team's acquisition of the controversial Christian pigskin wunderkind Tim Tebow, the Bible-thumping quarterback who boasted that he had "a relationship with Jesus Christ."

"TebowMania," the media had called it, and it had swept the Western world, with supporters imitating what became the good-looking twenty-four-year-old's prayer-like signature bow of victory on one knee.

Woody, the businessman, and his team executives, felt it was absolute brilliance to have acquired him. As they saw it, Tebow would sell everything from tickets to T-shirts to lucrative TV advertising, and the Jets would be closely watched from coast to coast.

But whether Tebow would help the team win games and finally get Gang Green to the Super Bowl was another story that didn't even seem relevant.

To blunt criticism, Woody declared, "Our main line of business is winning games. It's a good decision [acquiring Tebow]. I will take full accountability for that."

But sportswriters and pundits saw Tebow as a polarizing force who had had a lucky streak during the Denver Broncos 8–8 2011 season—the same sad win-loss record as those same old Jets—and they were using the same description often used about the Johnson dynasty itself to characterize the Band-Aid heir's team:

"The Jets are a dysfunctional team, bringing the circus to town," declared the outspoken veteran New York sports radio commentator Mike Francesa.

The *New York Post*'s banner headline about the Jets and Tebow's acquisition aptly declared: "Dysfunction Junction."

But Woody's sense was: "You can never have too much Tebow."

Like Tebow and the Jets, Mitt Romney was a sure winner, a confident Woody was boasting. In the Hamptons during the Independence Day holiday of 2012—just four months before the November presidential election—Woody joined with several other conservative Republican billionaires—among them Revlon chairman Ronald O. Perelman and industrialist David H. Koch—to host fancy fundraisers that brought in at least three million dollars to Romney's already bulging coffers of an estimated $100 million.

Woody was likely hoping that if his man won the Oval Office away from President Obama he would receive some sort of honorary position in the administration as a reward for all of his hard work bringing in stacks of campaign money. It had happened in the past. For his fundraising work for President George W. Bush, Woody got to serve on the President's Export Council. An honorary position, its members advise on international trade, an area in which Woody probably had little interest, or knowledge. And he had been a member of the Council on Foreign Relations, a group that consists of some 4,500 members. But both positions looked good next to his name in press clippings, and a new one with a Romney-Ryan administration would further add to his political power broker prestige.

While Woody could raise big money for Romney, there were entities in the media such as the snarky sports site Deadspin that questioned his political IQ. One such criticism surfaced in the wake of the 2012, 5–4 U.S. Supreme Court decision upholding Obamacare, with the surprising positive vote being made by the conservative Chief Justice John Roberts. Right after the decision Woody was the host for yet another Romney fundraiser. In introducing the candidate, the billionaire Republican asserted that Roberts gave Romney a rallying call.

"I think Judge Roberts did this intentionally," declared Woody. "He's really revved up our base from what we're able to gather. He's really revved us up."

Deadspin made note of Woody's words under a headline that proclaimed "Jets Owner Woody Johnson Is an Expert on Constitutional Law, in His

Mind," and went on to derisively call him "a complete moron" and "a complete dolt, or else he's a demented would-be propagandist, who thinks his crackpot version of events will inspire his fellow big-money donors to donate even bigger money . . . Woody Johnson has checked out of reality."

Woody and Romney made a good team and shared a billionaire's personality trait: both were intensely secretive, especially about their finances, which was underscored when Romney sparked a campaign controversy by declining to disclose all of his tax returns and other details about his wealth. One area of dispute was Romney's secret holdings in the Cayman Islands, similar to what had gotten Woody in a bind in the past because of his involvement with a tax haven in the Isle of Man that resulted in him having to ante up seventeen million dollars to the IRS. *The New York Times* chastised Woody's candidate in a strong editorial headlined, "Mr. Romney's Financial Black Hole." Under pressure, he eventually offered up details about his 2011 return.

A curious thing happened during Romney's 2012 run for the White House job that surely must have rubbed his big money man, Woody, the wrong way. The same day that Obama publicly stated that he supported gay marriage, *The Washington Post* revealed that during Romney's prep school days in the mid-1960s, he had attacked an effeminate classmate with a pair of scissors and cut off his recently bleached blond hair, an act that years later in the era of gay rights probably would be considered a hate crime.

Romney's reported prank echoed the humiliation Woody's late brother Keith had suffered from a few bullies in the mid-1960s at Millbrook School, the Johnson siblings' prep school, when he was called names and made fun of because of his effeminate mannerisms. Moreover, Woody's best friend, Guy Vicino, had been a flamboyant gay man who had died of AIDS, which had been devastating for Woody.

Unless Woody was completely insensitive to the past, Romney's reported prank must have had him questioning the character of the man he hoped would be the next commander in chief, especially after Romney apologized for the detestable act, but also claimed, incredibly, that he didn't remember it. But with Woody, a father who had cut himself off from a very troubled daughter, anything seemed possible.

As 2012 neared an end, it was mostly a professional washout for Woody. Despite his efforts as a GOP power broker, his vaunted candidate, Romney, for whom he had worked so hard, was soundly defeated by Obama, just as Woody's previous Republican choice, Senator John McCain, had been tromped by the president four years earlier.

Woody must have been devastated by the victory of Obama, whom he detested, and it must have caught him by surprise, so confident was he and the Republican party as a whole of a Romney win.

In Woody's eyes, Romney was a lot different than the way many people perceived, which was mainly as a straightlaced, rich, vanilla type of guy. "He's very, very funny. He's a riot. Mitt loves to tell a joke," he claimed to a reporter during the failed campaign. Plus, he added, Romney "believes in the principles of the country"—despite the fact that in a private talk to fat-cat supporters, Romney had essentially written off as losers 47 percent of the country's populace, much of the same group that would help to reelect Obama.

Moreover, Woody felt a Romney victory was more important than seeing his Jets have a winning season, which shocked sportswriters, and infuriated rabid Jets fans. He had offered his feelings about Romney versus the Jets to Bloomberg TV just a day after "Gang Green" was trounced by the San Francisco 49ers 34–0 in late September.

By mid-season, the Jets had won only three of nine games; the *Sporting News* in early November released a poll that rated Woody's beloved coach, Rex Ryan, as the "most overrated coach in the NFL"; *The New York Times* soon followed with a major story, blaming Woody in part for the team's "talent drain," and calling his support of Tim Tebow a "publicity stunt" to counter the Jets' "own miserable 2011 season."

The *Times* headline declared, "In Analyzing Jets' Failings, Start at the Top."

Adding insult to injury, the *Daily News* ignited a firestorm in mid-November—with less than half the season still to go—when it quoted unnamed Jets players saying that Tebow was "terrible" and "nothing more than a gimmick." The *New York Post* followed by calling Ryan "delusional" and describing the team as being in "a full-blown crisis," and noted that Woody "adores Ryan and the attention he draws to the franchise, and had no interest in firing him" over the locker room catfights and mounting Jets losses.

Woody had been so involved with the Romney campaign that since late August he hadn't met with the wolf pack of aggressive reporters who covered the Jets and who had become hypercritical of the team's management and its embarrassing record. But with another explosive round of negative stories he spoke out for the first time a week before Thanksgiving, meeting with the press on the sidelines at his MetLife stadium.

He emphatically denied assertions that Tebow was hired for publicity value—and to sell tickets and "hot dogs."

Criticizing the media, he called it a "phony story," and claimed, "My job, one, two, and three, is to win games. That's why I got into football. . . . That's what my passion is. That's what I want to do. It's not to sell PSLs [personal seat licenses] or hot dogs."

And, with a slap at the team, he declared: "I didn't sign up for a 3–6 season. I'm not happy about it. Yet I am optimistic." More losses were to come.

For Woody, the "same old Jets" refrain was surely ringing in his ears, and, worse, he had to face yet another four years of the same old Obama.

The disastrous, laughable, circus-like 2012 season—with the team failing to make the playoffs for the second year running, which is what the game's all about next to the Super Bowl—must have been a nightmare for Woody Johnson.

He, who was so enamored and proud of being an NFL owner; he, who had turned a $635 million investment a dozen years earlier into a gold mine, earning him respect, identity, and social gravitas, was, at sixty-five, being laughed at and scorned behind his back by other football brain trusts, and publicly by a powerful, out-for-blood sports media.

The Jets' rabid fans were quickly abandoning ship, underscored by a devoted cheerleader, a character known as "Fireman Ed," who stalked out of MetLife Stadium with a promise never to return after many seasons of stoking the rabble.

Legendary sports announcer Marv Albert described one of the Jets' final games of 2012 as "lots of empty seats." This, however, probably put only a very slight dent in Woody's billions.

Still, as the owner of the Jets, Woody had received more public criticism for his executive and leadership abilities than had any other member of the Johnson dynasty regarding their business interests.

The buck clearly stopped with Woody—not with his egotistical head coach of four years, Rex Ryan, or with his general manager and close associate of fifteen years, Mike Tannenbaum, who helped build the losing team with Woody's money, but with no depth; nor with his failed offensive coordinator, Tony "The Wildcat" Sparano, who resembled a gum-chewing Yassar Arafat, or Woody's bumbling, fumbling, interception-prone, benched-for-one-game, multimillion-dollar franchise quarterback Mark Sanchez; nor with his much publicized, but rarely played, backup, the God-fearing Tim Tebow, who had been hyped as the team's Messiah. As Woody had stated, hiring Tebow was "a good decision."

But was the bizarre refusal to let Tebow actually play with any frequency some sort of payback to embarrass him? In a franchise in which anything seemed to be acceptable, it was quite possible. Some conspiratorial types thought Tebow was mostly stuck on the sidelines, a clipboard holder, because he had helped kick the Jets out of the playoffs at the close of the team's terrible 2011 season when he ran a twenty-yard touchdown for a Denver win. The Jets' loss of that crucial game reportedly was so shocking to the divaesque Ryan that he thought he was having a heart attack when it was only a bad case of indigestion.

It was clear by the end of the 2012 season that the frustrated Tebow wanted a real football life for himself, far away from the Jets.

"They took a year out of his life," declared the popular New York sports radio talk show host Steve Somers, clearly upset. "I will believe he was misled and lied to [about how he would be used]. Instead of us talking about how awful the season was . . . we're talking about Tebow."

The Jets management, he asserted, "did the Pinocchio with Tebow."

At year's end, *The New York Times* called the Tebow situation "a public relations fiasco perhaps unequaled in N.F.L. history . . . the combination of on-field fizzle and off-field frenzy has made the Tebow story an unmitigated disaster for the Jets."

In the nation's capital, where Woody Johnson's political nemesis, President Obama, had to battle the GOP leadership to stave off the so-called fiscal cliff of 2012, the Redskins had a genuine winning rookie quarterback, Robert Griffin III (called RG3), who led them into the post-season. *The Washington Post* quoted an ESPN writer as declaring, "Clearly, the Jets are afraid of Tebow, afraid that he'd succeed. That, of course, would fuel a chorus of second-guessers, fans, and media types screaming that Tebow should've [been allowed to play more]. The Jets want no part of that cauldron."

It all came down to Woody as the owner, the moneyman, the ultimate decision maker, who claimed he lived and loved football ever since his Tebow-like, bench-warming prep school days.

There were unrealistic calls from some in the sports media for Woody to put his losing team on the block. As Somers colleague, Evan Roberts, declared on popular WFAN radio: "The Jets need a new owner. . . . This franchise needs a cleansing. . . . Something's rotten in Denmark."

Woody's Gang Green had become irrelevant, a laughing stock, They were, it seemed, like the Three Stooges, Laurel and Hardy, Abbott and Costello, the Marx Brothers, and Borat all morphed into one Barnum & Bailey sideshow.

At a press conference near the end of 2012, a defeated Rex Ryan was asked whether the season was the most bizarre he had ever lived through. His response, for once, was reasonably articulate, and to the point: "I would say that's pretty accurate . . . and we've had some strange ones."

Emotional, and appearing to tear up, he subsequently denied news reports that he wanted out unless "Mr. Johnson" anted up more of his fortune to build a better, winning team.

A day after the Jets mercifully finished 2012 with an embarrassing 6–10 record—Woody was conspicuously absent from the visiting owner's box when the Buffalo Bills won—the owner began taking action; he started by firing Tannenbaum, but keeping Ryan on, at least for 2013, and more heads were expected to roll.

"Our 2012 season was a disappointment to all of us," Woody said on the morning of New Year's Eve, not meeting reporters face-to-face but rather by issuing a prepared statement. "My goal every year as owner is to build a team that wins consistently. This year we failed to achieve that goal. . . . Like all Jets fans, I am disappointed with this year's results."

He predicted "greater success going forward."

The *New York Post* declared, "Shame on Johnson" for "cowering behind a lame, prepared statement." As for saving head coach Ryan, the tabloid's headline blared: "STAY OF REXECUTION."

The consensus in the sports media was that sacking Sanchez and Ryan would be too costly for Woody, about $15 million. But for a billionaire whose divorce settlement with his first wife was an astronomical $100 million (if her father's boast was to be believed), the cost of splitting from his quarterback and head coach would be a mere bag of shells for the Band-Aid heir.

As the boss, Woody had every right to sack Ryan for overseeing two miserable seasons. But on an emotional level, perhaps he couldn't bring himself to pull the trigger because when he was in his teens he had witnessed his father being unceremoniously fired as president of Johnson & Johnson by Woody's grandfather. Besides recalling how hurtful it was, Woody personally had much affection for Ryan, whose earthy personality and physical type reminded him of his late father.

Nine days into the new year, Woody, joined by Ryan, faced the sports media a few hours after it was announced that Tony Sparano had been canned, the second sacrificial lamb sacked and blamed for the team's dysfunction since the firing of Tannenbaum.

Surprisingly, after two terrible losing seasons, Ryan was his same old blustery self, bragging that the Jets "are going to be a dangerous football team. You're not going to want to play the New York Jets."

And Woody fondly showed his appreciation for Ryan, declaring, "I have ultimate confidence in Rex as a head coach, as a leader, as a motivator, as a play caller."

The whole curious scene came under intense criticism again by the media, and more Jets circus acts were expected in 2013.

Nearing his seventieth year, Robert Wood "Woody" Johnson IV surely knew he would have to revamp his team if he ever wanted to win his first Super Bowl, which, no doubt, would be the crowning glory of his Johnson dynasty legacy.

And on April 29, 2013, Tebow's time was up. He was booted in favor of a draft pick.

$ $ $

Back in 1943, when Woody's grandfather, General Johnson, penned "Our Credo," the Johnson & Johnson anthem and mission statement, the company, which was booming and about to go public, was already one of the world's most respected in the health-care products business.

It would one day be described as the "gold standard" for American corporations.

The credo had hung on the wall of Woody Johnson's office for sentimental reasons many decades after his grandfather had written it, and many years after his father, as president, had become the last of the Johnson dynasty to help run the family business.

Among the eloquent and sincere credo's words were these:

"We believe our first responsibility is to . . . mothers and fathers and all others who use our products . . . everything we do must be of high quality . . ."

But, by the start of the second decade of the twenty-first century, the company, begun by Woody's great-grandfather and his two brothers in the late nineteenth century, found itself under a dark cloud.

Behemoth Johnson & Johnson, which had made Woody and other members of the dynasty all so wealthy through trust funds, bequeaths, and platinum Johnson & Johnson stock holdings, found itself dealing with scandals related to a number of its products, and the way it did some of its business.

Virtually overnight, the company's long-held promise "of high quality" was being seriously questioned by consumer groups, government agencies, and retail customers.

In April 2012, for example, the company and a subsidiary, Janssen Pharmaceuticals, was fined a whopping $1.2 billion—the biggest ever in a state fraud case—after an Arkansas jury decided that it had hidden or trivialized the dangers of the antischizophrenia drug Risperdal. Similar cases involving the drug had earlier been settled for hundreds of millions of dollars in Texas, South Carolina, and Louisiana.

As *The New York Times* noted in the wake of the Arkansas case, "Consumer confidence in Johnson & Johnson, once one of the most trusted brands, has dropped in recent years as the company recalled dozens of products, including millions of bottles of children's Tylenol and other medications, as well as artificial hips and other products."

One of those in question was an artificial hip device called the Articular Surface Replacement (ARS), which was being marketed by a Johnson & Johnson division at a time when the company allegedly knew that it had a 40 percent failure rate. As a result, some ten thousand lawsuits were filed by people who had had the device implanted. In early 2013, the first trial in the case was set to begin in a California court, and the outcome was expected to have a major impact on the company.

The General, who had had such obsessive hands-on control when he ran the company and penned the credo, must have been spinning in his grave.

There hadn't been product scandals within Johnson & Johnson of such headline-making magnitude since 1983 when a homicidal maniac laced Tylenol Extra-Strength Capsules with the poison cyanide. Seven people who had bought eight bottles of the over-the-counter medication in the Chicago area had died. At the time, it was considered Johnson & Johnson's "darkest hour . . . someone was using our brand as a vehicle for murder," stated Lawrence Foster, who was then the corporate PR vice president who helped manage the company's emergency response.

Following the General's credo to safeguard its customers, Johnson & Johnson immediately took the capsules off of the market and replaced them with another, safe tablet called a "caplet" that made tampering impossible. The killer, however, was never found, only an extortionist, an out-of-work accountant, was arrested for demanding one million dollars to "stop the killing."

But the tragic Tylenol case had nothing to do with the manner in which Johnson & Johnson did business or manufactured products in the 2000s.

When a new chief executive by the name of Alex Gorsky was promoted in 2012—he was a former pharmaceutical sales representative and company insider—he pledged to rebuild consumer confidence following the slew of government investigations, recalls of various products, and serious manufacturing glitches.

Looking to the future he declared:

"The events over the last couple of years have had a negative impact, but we've been, I think, encouraged by how resilient our brands and our company reputation have been . . .

"I think we're going to need to be bold, disciplined and decisive," the fifty-one-year-old Gorsky intoned.

That was just the way Woody's grandfather Robert Wood Johnson Jr., the General, had run the company almost seven decades earlier—he was very bold, he was very disciplined, and he was very decisive. But his "Our Credo" seemed to have been all but forgotten in the early years of the twenty-first century, even though—engraved in limestone, it was prominently displayed in the lobby of the New Brunswick headquarters—and appeared as engravings on desktops, and on walls throughout the massive building.

As Stephen A. Greyser, a marketing professor at Harvard Business School told a reporter for the *Asbury Park* (N.J.) *Press* newspaper in a 2011 story that was picked up by *USA Today*'s Web site under the headline "Woes for Johnson & Johnson":

". . . one has to conclude that the corporate culture wasn't—and maybe isn't—as strongly embracing of the principles of the credo as used to be the case."

At the 2012 Johnson & Johnson shareholders meeting, Johnson family members who held a ton of company stock, but had no more involvement in running the 125-year-old worldwide business, made their displeasure known regarding the ills of the health-care company founded by their forebears. They did so with their purse strings.

"The family got together and voted against the executive compensation package that management was trying to put forward," says Eric Ryan who, like Woody Johnson, was of the fourth generation. "The family was expressing that a lot of shareholders—and a lot of family shareholders—were not particularly happy with the direction the company has gone in."

Whatever happens at Johnson & Johnson, future generations of the Johnson dynasty will continue benefiting from rich trusts and stock holdings. Whether all that unearned wealth will be handled functionally and without scandal was in question.

But Ryan, heading a committee working to preserve the legacy of his octogenarian sculptor uncle J. Seward Johnson Jr., and to "celebrate the accomplishments of the family," saw a different future for the dynasty.

"There's a desire to leave a positive mark on the planet rather than the private airplane, the bigger yacht, the collection of bimbos," he asserts. "There's less grandiosity.

"I look around at some of my contemporaries and a lot of them are really viewing social consciousness as not being directly related to wealth acquisition. It's like, well, we have enough, how are we going to leave this place better? The future looks more realistic in terms of the Johnsons being part of the world than in the past."

ACKNOWLEDGMENTS

Early in my research I sent an e-mail to Robert Wood (Woody) Johnson IV describing the parameters of my book, and requesting an interview. About a month later I received an e-mail response from the Johnson dynasty's de facto patriarch's public relations person, Jesse Derris, vice president of "crisis communications" at Sunshine, Sachs & Associates.

We arranged to chat by phone, and it quickly became apparent that to Mr. Derris I *was* a crisis waiting to happen to his billionaire client. Derris ended what began as congenial, introductory small talk by demanding, "who else in the [Johnson] family have you spoken to?"

When I naturally refused to name names, his immediate response was: "To be absolutely clear, there won't be any interview until I know who you've spoken to in the family, and I have a better idea of the other things you've gathered, because I'm not going to let him sit down and just field questions from you out of nowhere. That *won't* happen."

Even though I realized from a lifetime of journalism experience with his type that he was just doing what PR people do to earn their keep, I expressed genuine surprise because the New York Jets owner, when he's around, routinely fields questions from sports reporters with no apparent ground rules.

But Derris pointed out that my request was "a different situation."

In what way, I asked?

"Because Mr. Johnson, with his interviews, and depending on who else you've spoken to from the family—you are going to sell a lot more books, so it's different . . . There's a distinct [monetary] value for you having Mr. Johnson in your book."

His reasoning was mind-boggling.

I pointed out that my one and only reason for interviewing Mr. Johnson was to be fair, objective, and accurate based on things I had been told about him, and that the idea of making money off his name was, as I stated to Derris, "off the wall." But it was like trying to prevail on one of those football dummies, the kind players slam into during training camp. Unless I named names, it was clear I was persona non grata in Woody Johnson's well-guarded camp.

"I know for a fact [an interview with Woody Johnson] won't happen," Derris repeated. "I want to know who you spoke to . . . I want to have a better idea of the types of things you want to talk to him about."

When I asked Derris to reiterate his requests in an e-mail so I could further consider them, as I still had months of research ahead of me, he responded: "Come on, you think I'm born yesterday? I'm not going to put in writing everything I want to see . . ."

So that's where it ended with Woody Johnson's flack. He was as unbeatable as the New England Patriots were to the Jets.

While no member of the Johnson dynasty had had an active management role in the company since the deaths of Wood Johnson's grandfather, the General, in 1968, and his father, Bobby, in 1970, the Jets owner and a number of other Johnsons—all big stockholders—wielded considerable influence in the company's upper echelon in the second decade of the twenty-first century.

That fact was underscored when I requested several historic photos from the Johnson & Johnson archive—of the original three founders and the first company headquarters—and was immediately turned down by Bill Price, vice president of corporate media relations, who told me, "If you're writing about the family, we won't give you the photos." Anything about the dynasty was considered verboten.

Later, as my reporting continued, I discovered that Woody Johnson was telling certain people I had contacted not to talk to me. When I asked Derris in an e-mail about this stonewalling, he denied knowing anything about it.

But it soon became apparent to me that the heir to the Johnson & Johnson fortune had every reason to try to silence some sources. He had many secrets that he wanted to remain hidden about himself and his family. Few, however, abided by his plea.

In the end, I interviewed scores of people, including a number of Johnson dynasty members, to paint as definitive and accurate a portrait as possible of the generations that became immensely wealthy from the sale of many Band-Aids and cans of baby powder.

For the uninitiated, literary acknowledgments are monotonous, like those endless titles that scroll after a Hollywood epic ends. The only people who actually ever read them, I'm convinced after writing this, my eleventh biography, are the sources who were interviewed, mainly to make sure their names are correctly spelled, and often to see who else in their circle had also cooperated.

The other people who finely comb acknowledgments are those who had asked to remain anonymous, who want to make certain that the author kept the inviolable pledge not to blow their Deep Throat cover. Those very few who asked to remain anonymous in this book did so in order to not injure fragile dynastic relationships, some held together only by a Band-Aid after years of feuding and litigation.

The former, those who spoke on the record, far outnumber the latter. But all gave me their time and energy through hours of interviewing, supplied photos and documentation, and graciously opened doors. I'm indebted to both groups for their honesty, integrity, insight, and candidness.

In alphabetical order by first name, my thanks and gratitude goes out to:

Alan Steinberg, Alex Michelini, Andrea Pernick, Anita Tiburzi Johnson, Arma Andon, Rev. Arthur Rudman, Aubrey Huston, Austin Wand, Barbara Hudson, Barry Peele, Bernard Peyton Watson, Betty Niemeyer Whitley, BettyRay Epstein, Bonnie Tiburzi Faulkner, Brian Sisselman, Charlene Cherry Monahan, Chuck Doubet, Chuck Irwin, Claudia Forman Pleasants, Creighton Hooker, Dale Ryan, Dan Fick, Darby Bannard, David Margolick, Debby Sceli Peacock, Diana Roney, Diane Vonderahe, Don Sico, Dr. Ed Saltzman, Dr. Michael Shepard, Edward Bermingham, Edward Mead Johnson III, Eleanora Walker Tevis, Eric Ryan, Francis Browenstein, Fred Lowell, Garry Randall, Gene Beckwith, Geoffrey Geary, George Cowan, George

Rush, Georgeann Gillespie Fox, Gerald Sherrill, Gladys Hudson, Griffin Oakie, Harvey Kitchell, Hendrik Hertzberg, Henry Gardiner, Herb Tobin, Herrick Stickney, Ida Gayden, Irene Bangstrup Theakston, Irving Shepard, Isabella Hutchison, J. Seward Johnson Jr., Joyce Cecilia Johnson, James Childs, James Field Delano, Jaime Fillol, Judge Janet Moschetta, Jasmine Lennard, Jean and Arthur Anshel, John Bigelow Taylor, John Stewart Mills, Neil Vicino, Karen D'arc, Karl Williams, Kathleen Keenan Snow, Kent Muccilli, Laura Freeman Mills, Lawrence Foster, Leslie Caplan, Lew Blatte, Linda Lanceaux Teillon, Linda Vaughn Potter, Lloyd Williams, Lois Caplan Miller, Louis Meader, Lucinda Ziesing, Margaret Oppliger Boyd, Margie Lazarus, Marianne Strong, Marilyn Raiffe Leach, Mark Smith, Martin Muncy, Mary Frey Hickman, Mary Miller, Michael Richard Spielvogel, Mike Cooper, Miles B. Neustein, Nancy Brownstein, Nancy Frank Hauserman, Nancy Sale Frey Johnson Rashad, Nancy White, Neil Vicino, Nicholas Gouverneur Rutgers IV, Pat Lynch, Patricia Johnson, Patricia Potter, Patrick McCarthy, Paul Tobin, Peter Gillespie, Peter Holbrook, Peter Lambert, Phil Calihan, Philip Hagenah, Philip Lanier Ross, Quaint Doelger, Quentin Ryan, Racey Cohen, Ralph Hart, Rebecca Himeles Smith, Rhody Eisenstein, Rich Randall, Richard Q. Praeger Jr., Rod Mandelstam, Roger Ricco, Ron Artinian, Sadja (Johnson) Greenwood, Sarah Strong Drake, Sherwin Harris, Sofia Pappatheodorou, Sonya Maria Noel Stokowsky Thorbeck, Stan Shanbron, Stanley Engle, Stephen Cutler Gidley, Steve Fishman, Steve Kroll, Steve Rempe, Steve Tobin, Sue Ellen Firestone Sherman, Sue Goodman, Suellen Epstein, Susan Matlof Harris, Suzie Goldstein Epstein, Sven Ginman, Thomas Doelger, Tila Tequila, Tom Proctor, Tom Wilson, Walter Lovejoy, William Culver White, William Jessup. There are others whose names and appreciation you know.

AUTHOR'S NOTE ON
SOURCES

While the business news media reports extensively on the financial affairs, consumer issues and personnel changes involving Johnson & Johnson, the family behind the popular brands—from the founders in the later nineteenth century to the contemporary family members of the twenty-first century— have received far less attention, except when some are involved in court cases and scandals that ignite headlines.

As a result, my goal to research and write as thorough and complete an independent biography as possible of the Johnson dynasty involved tracking down credible and knowledgeable relatives, friends, and close associates.

Of aid in my early research—along with hundreds of newspaper clippings and magazine articles—were three books, the first published in the late 1980s, the second in the early 1990s, and the third in the late 1990s. The first two— *Johnson v. Johnson* by Barbara Goldsmith and *Undue Influence* by David Margolick—focused on a highly publicized court battle over an immense fortune that underscored some Johnson family members' litigiousness and desire for more unearned wealth. A fascinating, previously unreported side-light to that case—the battle involving those two books—is detailed in this volume.

The third book that was of immense help was a self-published biography, *Robert Wood Johnson, The Gentleman Rebel*, written by Lawrence G. Foster, who had retired as Johnson & Johnson's corporate vice president of public relations. While focusing mainly on the life and leadership of "the General," Foster's book also offered an extensive history of the company's founders based on his insider corporate access, along with interviews he had conducted years ago with a number of now deceased family members and associates.

Accessing some of his reportage, which I credit where due in these pages, and with my own independent interviews, a number of which were conducted with sprightly octogenarian members of the Johnson dynasty who had direct knowledge of the early days, I was able to paint a portrait of the Johnson forebears and early corporate history as part of the wider story I tell.

Much of my account of the Johnson dynasty, however, deals with more contemporary members, such as Robert Wood "Woody" Johnson IV. With that in mind I would like to point out that all source quotes—people interviewed by me—are usually written in the present tense ("he says," "she observes.") Material quotes gathered from published accounts are usually written in the past tense ("he said," "she observed.") As much as possible without interfering with the flow of the narrative, I identified the source for those quotes, or accounts (for example, *The New York Times*), and the date, or time frame, and/or author. Refer to my acknowledgments for those interviewed by me, and see my selected bibliography for books used in my research, or from which I quoted. I also quote from correspondence shared with me that is attributed where mentioned.

Included among the publications referred to as part of my research and mostly attributed in these pages include, but are not limited to: *The New York Times*, New York *Daily News, New York Post, New York Observer, The Washington Post, The Wall Street Journal, Los Angeles Times, The Princeton Packet, Princeton Town Topics, South Florida Sun-Sentinel, The Palm Beach Post, Time, Fortune, People, Newsweek, Reuters, Associated Press, New York* magazine, *Town & Country*, and a number of Web sites that are identified in the referenced material of this volume.

SELECTED BIBLIOGRAPHY

Allen, Michael Patrick. *The Founding Fortunes.* New York: E.P. Dutton, 1987.

Bainbridge, John. *Garbo.* New York: Holt, Rinehart and Winston, 1955.

Chasins, Abram. *Leopold Stokowski.* New York: Hawthorn Books, 1979.

Daniel, Oliver. *Stokowski, A Counterpoint of View.* New York: Dodd, Mead, 1982.

Darrid, Diana Douglas. *In the Wings.* New York: Barricade Books, 1999.

Douglas, Kirk. *The Ragman's Son.* New York: Pocket Books, 1989.

Foster, Laurence G. *A Company That Cares, One-Hundred-Year Illustrated History of Johnson & Johnson.* New Brunswick, NJ, 1986.

Foster, Laurence G. *Robert Wood Johnson, The Gentleman Rebel.* State College, PA: Lillian Press, 1999.

Goldsmith, Barbara. *Johnson v. Johnson.* New York: Alfred A. Knopf, 1987.

Greenfield, Robert. *Timothy Leary.* New York: Harcourt, 2006.

Hoffman, Philip B. *General Johnson Said.* North Brunswick, NJ: Leury, Marks & Strasser, 1971.

Johnson, Robert Wood IV, Sale Johnson, Casey Johnson, and Susan Kleinman. *Managing Your Child's Diabetes.* New York: MasterMedia Limited, 1992, 1994.

Kelley, Kitty. *Oprah, A Biography.* New York: Crown, 2010.

Kolva, Jeanne, and Joanne Pisciotta, for the Highland Park Historical Society. *Highland Park, Borough of Homes.* Charleston, SC: Arcadia Publishing, 2005.

Margolick, David. *Undue Influence, The Epic Battle for the Johnson & Johnson Fortune.* New York: William Morrow, 1993.

Miller, Mary E. *Baroness of Hobcaw, The Life of Belle W. Baruch.* Columbia, SC: University of South Carolina Press, 2006.

Nielsen, Waldemar A. *The Big Foundations.* New York: Columbia University Press, The Twentieth Century Fund, 1972.

Nielsen, Waldemar A. *The Golden Donors, A New Anatomy of the Great Foundations.* New York: E.P. Dutton, 1985.

Paris, Barry. *Garbo.* New York: Alfred A. Knopf, 1995.

Ryan, Rex with Don Yaeger. *Play Like You Mean It, Passion, Laughs, and Leadership in the World's Most Beautiful Game.* New York: Doubleday, 2011.

Schleicher, William A., and Susan J. Winter. *In the Somerset Hills, the Landed Gentry.* Charleston, SC: Arcadia Publishing, 1997.

Shilts, Randy. *And the Band Played On.* New York: St. Martin's Press, 1987.

Tequila, Tila. *Hooking Up with Tila Tequila, A Guide to Love, Fame, Happiness, Success, and Being the Life of the Party.* New York: Scribner, 2008.

Tiburzi, Bonnie, and Valerie Moolman. *Takeoff! The Story of America's First Woman Pilot for a Major Airline.* New York: Crown, 1973.

Vanderbilt, Gloria. *Gloria Vanderbilt, It Seemed Important at the Time.* New York: Simon & Schuster, 2004.

Wedeking, Susan, editor. *A Century of Caring, Celebrating the First 100 Years of Mead Johnson & Company.* Mead Johnson & Company, 2005.

INDEX

Note: RWJ stands for Robert Wood Johnson (I, II, III, IV, and V). J&J means Johnson & Johnson company. Women are usually listed under their maiden names, with cross-references from married names.

CPSIA information can be obtained
at www.ICGtesting.com
Printed in the USA
LVHW041244050123
736482LV00006B/65